The Broadview Reader

The
Broadview Reader

edited by

Herbert Rosengarten and Jane Flick

broadview press

Canadian Cataloguing in Publication Data

Main entry under title:

The Broadview Reader

ISBN 0-921149-10-7

1. English prose literature.   2. College readers.
3. English language – Rhetoric.   I. Rosengarten,
Herbert.   II. Flick, Jane, 1944-

PE1417.B76   1987   818'.08   C87-093477-5

broadview press
P.O. Box 1243
Peterborough, Canada, K9J 7H5

Printed and bound in Canada by
Gagné Ltd.

Cover design by Falcom Design & Communications

Preface

Like many anthologies, *The Broadview Reader* was born out of a conviction that most other collections of this kind failed in one way or another to meet students' needs, and that it would not be difficult to improve on the efforts of our predecessors. In the event, the experience proved to be a humbling one. What began as an almost casual enterprise, to be completed in a short time, turned into a year-long search through books, magazines, newspapers, indexes, and catalogues. The process of selection became more and more complicated as we proceeded; many of the essays we had first chosen were edged out by later discoveries; categories formed and reformed with bewildering frequency; firm favorites suddenly lost their appeal and found their way into an ever-growing discard file. But for the exigencies of publishers' deadlines, *The Broadview Reader* might still be gestating in a hundred dog-eared yellow folders.

In making our final choices, we were guided by three considerations: would the essay be interesting to a variety of readers? would it lend itself to discussion and analysis? would it demonstrate some of the techniques and strategies of effective writing? We have not sought to present a history of the prose essay; though a few of our examples have been drawn from earlier periods, the emphasis is very much on twentieth-century writing. Nor have we attempted to assemble a "manual of styles" of the kind sometimes offered to students as models for their own writing. Our hope is rather that student writers will be stimulated by the ideas and issues presented in the essays, and be encouraged to search for ways of articulating their own ideas effectively.

The essays are grouped by subject to facilitate a thematic focus and a comparison of writers, attitudes, and approaches. Each essay is followed by a list of questions intended to help the reader identify the main lines of thought, and recognize some of the writer's strategies of language and organization. The questions are not comprehensive, or chosen with some particular rhetorical prescription in mind; rather, their function is to prepare the reader for more detailed discussion and analysis in the classroom, and to suggest writing exercises that might form a natural culmination of the critical process.

To help the reader focus on salient aspects of technique, we have also provided a "Guide to Rhetorical Patterns and Devices," and a glossary of terms commonly used in the critical analysis of prose discourse.

HJR
JMF

Table of Contents

Guide to Rhetorical Patterns and Devices

Essays which employ analogy

Frye	The Motive for Metaphor
Hoban	Thoughts on a Shirtless Cyclist, Robin Hood and One or Two Other Things
Lubow	A Space 'Iliad': The *Star Wars* War: I
Swift	A Modest Proposal
Trefil	Unexpected Vistas
Woolf	How Should One Read a Book?

Essays which employ analysis

Arkin	At the Movies
Bettelheim	The Art of Moving Pictures
Dryden	The Game
Fox	Star Drek: The *Star Wars* War: II
Lurie	Women's Clothes – Towards Emancipation
Orwell	Politics and the English Language
Richler	An Unquiet Awakening
Rosenbaum	The Solitary Pleasures of *Star Wars*
Rybczynski	Nostalgia
Steinem	Marilyn Monroe: The Woman Who Died Too Soon

Essays which employ argumentation and persuasion

Atwood	The Writer's Responsibility
Bronowski	The Real Responsibilities of the Scientist
Carson	The Obligation to Endure
Dryden	The Game
Gould	Let's Ban Applause!
Haldane	Some Enemies of Mankind
Hoggart	The Case Against Advertising
Kennedy	Who Killed King Kong?
Muggeridge	My True Love Hath My Heart
Sillitoe	Sport and Nationalism
Suzuki	A Planet for the Taking
Swift	A Modest Proposal
Thomas	Humanities and Science
Woodcock	The Tyranny of the Clock

Essays which employ cause and effect

Addison	On Party-lying
Bronowski	The Real Responsibilities of the Scientist
Carson	The Obligation to Endure
Davies	The Purpose of Pornography
Forster	My Wood
Gould, S.J.	Posture Maketh the Man
Kennedy	Who Killed King Kong?
MacLennan	The Shadow of Captain Bligh
Orwell	Politics and the English Language
Richler	An Unquiet Awakening
Rybczynski	Nostalgia
Sillitoe	Sport and Nationalism
Suzuki	A Planet for the Taking
Vanderhaeghe	Influences
Woodcock	The Tyranny of the Clock

Essays which employ classification

Addison	On Party-lying
Avis	Canadian Spoken Here
Bacon	Of Studies
Lurie	Women's Clothing — Towards Emancipation
Orwell	Politics and the English Language
Woolf	How Should One Read a Book?

Essays which employ comparison and contrast

Bacon	Of Marriage and Single Life
Brody	A Hearing
Eiseley	The Bird and the Machine
Flanner	Murder Among the Lovebirds
Fox	Star Drek: The *Star Wars* War: II
Frye	The Motive for Metaphor
Fulford	The Grand Illusion
Lubow	A Space 'Iliad': The *Star Wars* War: I
MacLennan	The Shadow of Captain Bligh
Plumb	De Mortuis
Rosenbaum	The Solitary Pleasures of *Star Wars*
Thurber	Courtship Through the Ages
Twain	A River Pilot Looks at the Mississippi
Vanderhaeghe	Influences

Essays which employ definition

Allen	Slang Origins
Avis	Canadian Spoken Here

Essays which employ narration

Essays which employ humour and satire

Chronological Table of Contents

Acknowledgements

Woody Allen, 'Slang Origins,' from *Without Feathers* © 1969 Random House Inc. Reprinted by permission.

William Arkin, 'At the Movies,' reprinted by permission of the *Bulletin of Atomic Scientists,* a magazine of science and world affairs. Copyright © 1986 by the Educational Foundation for Nuclear Science, Chicago, IL 60637.

Margaret Atwood, 'The Writer's Responsibility,' published as 'Amnesty International: An Address' in *Second Words: Selected Critical Prose* (Toronto: House of Anansi Press, 1982).

Walter Avis, 'Canadian Spoken Here,' from *Looking at Language,* M.H. Scargill and P.G. Penner (eds.). Copyright © W.J. Gage Limited 1966. Reprinted by permission of Gage Educational Publishing Company.

Russell Baker, 'Little Red Riding Hood Revisited,' Jan. 13, 1980, Copyright © by The New York Times Company. Reprinted by permission.

Bruno Bettelheim, 'The Art of Moving Pictures,' reprinted by permission of the author and his agents. This article originally appeared in *Harper's Magazine.* Copyright © 1981 by Bruno Bettelheim.

Hugh Brody, 'A Hearing,' from *Maps and Dreams* by Hugh Brody. Copyright © 1981 Douglas & McIntyre Ltd. Reprinted by permission.

Jacob Bronowski, 'The Real Responsibilities of the Scientist,' reprinted by permission of the *Bulletin of Atomic Scientists,* a magazine of science and world affairs. Copyright © 1956 by the Educational Foundation for Nuclear Sciences, Chicago, IL 60637.

Rachel Carson, 'The Obligation to Endure,' from *Silent Spring* by Rachel Carson. Copyright © 1962 by Rachel L. Carson. Reprinted by permission of Houghton Mifflin Company.

Language and Communication

Slang Origins
by Woody Allen

How many of you have ever wondered where certain slang expressions 1
come from? Like "She's the cat's pajamas," or to "take it on the lam."
Neither have I. And yet for those who are interested in this sort of thing
I have provided a brief guide to a few of the more interesting origins.

Unfortunately, time did not permit consulting any of the established 2
works on the subject, and I was forced to either obtain the information
from friends or fill in certain gaps by using my own common sense.

Take, for instance, the expression "to eat humble pie." During the 3
reign of Louis the Fat, the culinary arts flourished in France to a degree
unequaled anywhere. So obese was the French monarch that he had
to be lowered onto the throne with a winch and packed into the seat
itself with a large spatula. A typical dinner (according to DeRochet)
consisted of a thin crêpe appetizer, some parsley, an ox, and custard.
Food became the court obsession, and no other subject could be discussed
under penalty of death. Members of a decadent aristocracy consumed
incredible meals and even dressed as foods. DeRochet tells us that M.
Monsant showed up at the coronation as a weiner, and Étienne Tisserant
received papal dispensation to wed his favorite codfish. Desserts grew
more and more elaborate and pies grew larger and larger until the
minister of justice suffocated trying to eat a seven-foot "Jumbo pie."
Jumbo pie soon became *jumble* pie and "to eat a jumble pie" referred
to any kind of humiliating act. When the Spanish seamen heard the word
jumble, they pronounced it "humble," although many preferred to say
nothing and simply grin.

Now, while "humble pie" goes back to the French, "take it on the 4 lam" is English in origin. Years ago, in England, "lamming" was a game played with dice and a large tube of ointment. Each player in turn threw dice and then skipped around the room until he hemorrhaged. If a person threw seven or under he would say the word "quintz" and proceed to twirl in a frenzy. If he threw over seven, he was forced to give every player a portion of his feathers and was given a good "lamming." Three "lammings" and a player was "kwirled" or declared a moral bankrupt. Gradually any game with feathers was called "lamming" and feathers became "lams." To "take it on the lam" meant to put on feathers and later, to escape, although the transition is unclear.

5   Incidentally, if two of the players disagreed on the rules, we might say they "got into a beef." This term goes back to the Renaissance when a man would court a woman by stroking the side of her head with a slab of meat. If she pulled away, it meant she was spoken for. If, however, she assisted by clamping the meat to her face and pushing it all over her head, it meant she would marry him. The meat was kept by the bride's parents and worn as a hat on special occasions. If, however, the husband took another lover, the wife could dissolve the marriage by running with the meat to the town square and yelling, "With thine own beef, I do reject thee. Aroo! Aroo!" If a couple "took to the beef" or "had a beef" it meant they were quarreling.

6   Another marital custom gives us that eloquent and colorful expression of disdain, "to look down one's nose." In Persia it was considered a mark of great beauty for a woman to have a long nose. In fact, the longer the nose, the more desirable the female, up to a certain point. Then it became funny. When a man proposed to a beautiful woman he awaited her decision on bended knee as she "looked down her nose at him." If her nostrils twitched, he was accepted, but if she sharpened her nose with pumice and began pecking him on the neck and shoulders, it meant she loved another.

7   Now, we all know when someone is very dressed up, we say he looks "spiffy." The term owes its origin to Sir Oswald Spiffy, perhaps the most renowned fop of Victorian England. Heir to treacle millions, Spiffy squandered his money on clothes. It was said that at one time he owned enough handkerchiefs for all the men, women and children in Asia to blow their noses for seven years without stopping. Spiffy's sartorial innovations were legend, and he was the first man ever to wear gloves on his head. Because of extra-sensitive skin, Spiffy's underwear had to be made of the finest Nova Scotia salmon, carefully sliced by one particular tailor. His libertine attitudes involved him in several notorious

scandals, and he eventually sued the government over the right to wear earmuffs while fondling a dwarf. In the end, Spiffy died a broken man in Chichester, his total wardrobe reduced to kneepads and a sombrero.

Looking "spiffy," then, is quite a compliment, and one who does is 8 liable to be dressed "to beat the band," a turn-of-the-century expression that originated from the custom of attacking with clubs any symphony orchestra whose conductor smiled during Berlioz. "Beating the band" soon became a popular evening out, and people dressed up in their finest clothes, carrying with them sticks and rocks. The practice was finally abandoned during a performance of the *Symphonie Fantastique* in New York when the entire string section suddenly stopped playing and exchanged gun-fire with the first ten rows. Police ended the melee but not before a relative of J.P. Morgan's was wounded in the soft palate. After that, for a while at least, nobody dressed "to beat the band."

If you think some of the above derivations questionable, you might 9 throw up your hands and say, "Fiddlesticks." This marvelous expression originated in Austria many years ago. Whenever a man in the banking profession announced his marriage to a circus pinhead, it was the custom for friends to present him with a bellows and a three-year supply of wax fruit. Legend has it that when Leo Rothschild made known his betrothal, a box of cello bows was delivered to him by mistake. When it was opened and found not to contain the traditional gift, he exclaimed, "What are these? Where are my bellows and fruit? Eh? All I rate is fiddlesticks!" The term "fiddlesticks" became a joke overnight in the taverns amongst the lower classes, who hated Leo Rothschild for never removing the comb from his hair after combing it. Eventually "fiddlesticks" meant any foolishness.

Well, I hope you've enjoyed some of these slang origins and that they 10 stimulate you to investigate some on your own. And in case you were wondering about the term used to open this study, "the cat's pajamas," it goes back to an old burlesque routine of Chase and Rowe's, the two nutsy German professors. Dressed in oversized tails, Bill Rowe stole some poor victim's pajamas. Dave Chase, who got great mileage out of his "hard of hearing" specialty, would ask him:

Chase: Ach, Herr Professor. Vot is dot bulge under your pocket?
Rowe: Dot? Dot's de chap's pajamas.
Chase: The cat's pajamas? Ut mein Gott?

Audiences were convulsed by this sort of repartee and only a premature 11 death of the team by strangulation kept them from stardom.

(1975)

The Writer's Subject

1. Allen's essay is an example of literary burlesque. What form of writing is Allen burlesquing in this essay?

2. The essay depends for its effect upon inventing incredible etymologies for well-known phrases such as "to eat humble pie" or "to look down one's nose." With the help of a dictionary of etymology, choose any of the words or phrases that Allen pretends to explain, and trace its real origin.

The Writer's Style and Strategy

1. What assumptions does Allen make about his audience in paragraph 1?

2. What methods associated with sociology does Allen pretend to employ in his study of word origins?

3. Allen uses a variety of techniques to achieve his humorous effects, such as inflating the trivial, reversing the reader's expectations, juxtaposing sense and nonsense, mixing real names (Morgan, Rothschild) with invented ones (Sir Oswald Spiffy), or combining objects or ideas in unexpected ways. Take one of Allen's explanations (e.g., "to eat humble pie" in para. 3), and try to pinpoint the means by which he creates humour.

4. Allen imposes an apparent order on his material by means of transitions. Examine some of these transitions and comment on their logic.

Suggested Topics for Writing and Discussion

1. Allen pokes fun at odd customs, as well as at essays on the curiosities of language. For example, the "custom" he describes in paragraph 5 concerning the use of a slab of meat in courtship and marriage during the Renaissance is not significantly more ridiculous than such real customs as a girl's putting a slice of wedding cake under her pillow, or having baby shoes coated in bronze. Discuss one or two odd or peculiar customs you are familiar with, and trace their origins as far as you can.

2. Choose one of the following slang expressions, and make up your own derivation in the style of Allen's essay: off his rocker; round the bend; dressed fit to kill.

3. Give a description of a group of slang terms which you or your friends currently use. Write explanations of these terms for a member of the older generation.

Canadian Spoken Here

by Walter S. Avis

Fifteen years ago a writer in a Canadian magazine complained that the   1
word *snye* was not defined in any dictionary in spite of the fact that
the Canadian Board on Geographical Names had certified it as "a lawful
and proper generic term." A few years later another writer, in another
journal, complained that none of his dictionaries included the word
mukluk. Nor have these been the only voices raised in frustration because
so many terms met with in Canada were ignored by dictionaries. Until
quite recently, however, all were voices crying in the wilderness; for
few Canadians were interested enough in their speech to undertake the
gigantic task of finding out about it. Consequently, there were no Canadian dictionaries worthy of the name; and our imported dictionaries virtually ignored Canadian usage. After all, British dictionaries are primarily intended for Britons and American dictionaries for Americans; no
reputable editor claims anything more.

To say that British and American dictionaries do not reflect Cana-   2
dian usage is to say that Canadian English is neither British nor
American, that the English spoken in Canada is distinct in many ways
from that spoken in the United Kingdom and from that spoken in the
United States. It should be observed that this distinctive variety of speech
is referred to as "Canadian English" and not as the "Canadian language,"
for Canadians share one language with Britons, Americans, and a host of
other people both inside the Commonwealth and beyond it. To claim
that there is a Canadian language, or, as many Americans do, an
American language, is to distort the meaning of the word *language* for
nationalistic purposes. On the other hand, it is a form of blindness to

insist, as many do, that "English is English" and that it is folly to dignify the "slang and dialect" of Canada by discussing it as if it merited serious attention.

3   Any Canadian who has spent some time in both the United Kingdom and the United States knows that his English is recognized as non-British by Britons and (perhaps less often) as non-American by Americans. While it is true that the uninformed in Britain may identify us with Americans and the uninformed in the United States may identify us with Englishmen, people in both countries who are familiar with Canadians recognize speech habits that are unlike their own. An American, for example, may point to our way of using *blind* where he would use *shade*, *tap* where he would use *faucet*, *serviette* where he would use *napkin*, *braces* where he would use *suspenders*, and *porridge* where he would use *oatmeal*; or he might point to our way of pronouncing *been* to rhyme with "bean" instead of "bin," *ration* to rhyme with "fashion" instead of "nation," *lever* to rhyme with "beaver" instead of "never," and Z to rhyme with "bed" instead of "knee." He will certainly notice that most of us pronounce *lout* with a different sounding vowel from that of *loud*. He will, in fact, wrongly insist that we pronounce *out* to rhyme with "shoot," just as speakers of Scots dialect do.

4   The Britisher, on the other hand, will observe that we pronounce *aunt*, *glass, path, clerk, war,* and *tomato* in a way quite different from his; he may also note that most of us make no distinction between the vowel of *caught* and that of *cot*, whereas for him the vowels are very different indeed. He observes, too, that many of the words he uses every day in England are simply not understood by his Canadian friends. Suppose he gets into a conversation about cars. Says he, "I think a car should have a roomy boot." Communication will come to a halt until someone rescues him by pointing out that Canadians call a *boot* a "trunk." Before this chat is over, he will learn that Canadians use *hood* for his *bonnet, muffler* for *silencer, bumper* for *fender,* and (egad, sir!) *fender* for *wing.* These few examples illustrate the point that Canadian patterns of speech are neither British nor American, though they are in some degree a blend of both.

5   Canadian English, then, is a dialect which resembles American English in some respects and British English in others and includes, at the same time, a great deal that is significantly Canadian. The explanation of this mixed character lies in the settlement history of the country. As the eastern regions of British North America were opened for settlement, before, during, and after the Revolutionary War, Americans were promi-

nent among the settlers. New Englanders began moving into Nova Scotia several decades before the Revolution and the Loyalist influx of 1790 brought thousands more. Today, as in the days of Judge Haliburton's *Sam Slick, the Clockmaker,* the New England origin of large numbers of Bluenoses is evident in the speech and customs of the province. Both New Brunswick and the Eastern Townships of Quebec were first colonized by American Loyalists and, in both areas, post-Loyalist settlers added to the preponderance of American stock.

In Upper Canada the early influx of American settlers was especially significant, for Ontario was to become the populous heart of English-speaking Canada. By 1795 there were some 10,000 Loyalists settled around Kingston and Niagara, at opposite ends of Lake Ontario. When the War of 1812 began, the population of Upper Canada had grown to some 50,000, almost entirely made up of former Americans, both Loyalist and post-Loyalist, none of whom were any less American in language and manners than their former compatriots to the south. This American preponderance is evident from the composition of the legislative assembly in 1828, there being four members born in Ireland, six in Scotland, seven in England, three in other British colonies, thirteen in Canada, and fifteen in the United States. **6**

In Ontario, there is no doubt, American speech habits have been entrenched from the beginning. The settlers from south of the line introduced their system of education along with their system of municipal government. The public elementary school was always the normal thing in Upper Canada, many of the textbooks being imported from the United States or adapted from American models. This state of affairs did not pass unnoticed, as is made clear in the following observations made by a British doctor travelling through the province in 1832: **7**

It is really melancholy to traverse the province and go into many of the common schools; you find a herd of children instructed by some anti-British adventurer, instilling into the young and tender mind sentiments hostile to the parent state [that is, American geography and history with a republican bias]; and American spelling books, dictionaries and grammars, teaching them anti-British dialect and idiom.

Later in the century the conditions which so irritated the doctor were somewhat moderated by the mildly pro-British reforms of Egerton Ryerson, a second-generation Loyalist from New York, who was superintendent of education in Ontario from 1844 to 1876. One of the reforms **8**

is alluded to in the following quotation from a contemporary issue of
The Voice of the Fugitive (Oct. 23, 1851) published in Sandwich, Canada
West:

> We are also in great need of reading books, slates, and some 6
> or 7 dozen of Webster's spelling book (only American spelling book
> allowed in Government schools) for the use of poor scholars.

Ryerson's success in eliminating American influence from the schools
was far from complete; yet his efforts and those of others with similar
views have doubtless had a significant effect on the English of Canadians, for the practice of "teaching British" has a long history in this
country. It must be remembered that the prestige of British English has
always exerted a strong influence on Canadian patterns of speech,
especially among the educated. Nevertheless, it seems clear that the
American idiom was already implanted deep in Upper Canada when
the great stream of British immigrants began to flow into the country
during the later stages of settlement.

9   Population movements between the United States and Canada have
never ceased to be an important factor in the settlement of the Dominion
of the North. When hard times struck Upper Canada in the 1830's, many
Canadians joined the American settlers, who, freed from the Indian
menace in Illinois and Indiana, were moving into the Middle West. The
exodus of Canadians to the States during this period brought about the
opening up of the old Northwest. The transcontinental railway was undertaken by the Canadian government and attractive land grants were made
available to prospective homesteaders. The forty-ninth parallel during
this period was little more than a geographical abstraction; the tax collector was, as one historian has said, the only important indication that
a boundary existed.

10   In the 1870's and the 1880's many farmers in Upper Canada contracted
"Manitoba fever" and hastened to take advantage of the opportunities
Manitoba had to offer. These settlers, many of them of Loyalist
background, reached their new homes by way of the United States, being
joined en route by many landhungry Americans. Immigrants from the
Old Country were very much in the minority and generally settled in
their own communities, as did the Red River Scots of Lord Selkirk.

11   Twenty years later, Saskatchewan and Alberta were opened up, at
a time when the American Northwest had been largely settled. The
C.P.R., completed in 1885, carried great numbers of Eastern Canadians and some Britishers to the new territories. But the greatest number

of settlers came from the south, where the frontier was fast disappearing, almost a million Americans entering southern Alberta and Saskatchewan from 1900 to 1915. Thus, the North American character of the English spoken on the Prairies was entrenched through the domination of Canadians (mostly Ontarians but a substantial number of Maritimers) and Americans among the English-speaking settlers. The thousands of non-English-speaking Scandinavians and Central Europeans who immigrated to the Prairie Provinces learned the kind of English spoken by their neighbors, most of whom, as we have seen, spoke the North American variety. Latter-day American arrivals, particularly in oil-rich Alberta, have reinforced this North American pattern.

Fewer Americans were drawn to British Columbia, largely because **12** the type of farming land was not to their liking. As a result, the Pacific-coast province was settled, in large measure, by emigrants from the British Isles, although Canadians from both Ontario and the Maritimes were well represented. This British predominance has had a noticeable but as yet undefined effect on the nature of British Columbia English, especially in certain areas — as the Okanagan Valley and southern Vancouver Island — and among people at the higher social levels, who traditionally send their children to private schools conducted more or less on the British pattern. On the other hand, British Columbia has strong lines of north-south communication with the United States, lines which have in many ways been more active than those running eastward through the Rockies. This close bond with the United States has also had its effect on the English of British Columbia, perhaps most noticeably in Vancouver and its areas of influence.

This summary of population movements, oversimplified as it obviously **13** is, should serve to emphasize the significance of the American element in Canadian settlement history. Influence from the United States has been constant and strong from the beginning. Canadians are often taught from American textbooks; they listen to American radio programs, watch American television and movies, read American novels; in large numbers they are constantly moving back and forth across the border, as immigrants, as tourists, as students, and as bargain hunters. Finally, as a North American country, Canada quite naturally shares a large vocabulary with the United States, a vocabulary made up of words designating all manner of things indigenous to this continent. One need only leaf through the *Dictionary of Canadianisms* or the *Dictionary of Americanisms* to appreciate this fact. There is nothing very surprising about the closeness of Canadian and American English.

14   It must be understood that the United Kingdom has also made an enormous contribution to the settlement of English-speaking Canada. For more than a century an almost continuous stream of Britishers, speaking various dialects, have emigrated to Canada. In most communities, especially those along the Canada-United States border (where Canada's population is still concentrated), these newcomers came into contact with already established Canadians and, as might be expected, their children adopted the speech habits of the communities they settled in. Only in certain areas, where relatively homogeneous Old Country groups established themselves, did markedly British dialectal features survive through several generations. Such communities can be found in Newfoundland, northern Nova Scotia, the Ottawa Valley, the Red River region, and the parts of British Columbia already mentioned. It might be added that the English-speaking natives of Montreal and Quebec have an English and Scots heritage going back nearly two centuries, a fact that is often evident in their speech, which is, nevertheless, obviously Canadian. British immigrants have unquestionably made substantial contributions to every department of the language, none perhaps in greater degree than the Scots and Scots-Irish, who have from earliest times been prominent in Canada's affairs, the Scots schoolteacher, or dominie, being a part of the community scene in so many areas in colonial times. To a great extent, what is not American about Canadian English has been brought directly from the Old Country, such features often competing with American variants already current in Canada, and even gradually displacing them. Just such a process seems to be taking place at present with respect to the pronunciation of *schedule:* the British (shej ül), though apparently used by a minority, might well be displacing the characteristically American (skej ül), very probably influenced by the practice of CBC announcers.

15   With the passing years, the speech habits of educated Canadians have become remarkably homogeneous, though by no means free of regional variety. Taken as a whole, the language of this country is neither British nor American; it is distinctively Canadian. This distinctiveness is most easily demonstrated with reference to the vocabulary, for there are hundreds of words which are native to Canada or which have meaning peculiar to this country. All of these words, which may be called Canadianisms, and many more, are defined in Canadian dictionaries already available or soon to be published; many, indeed, will be found in Canadian editions of foreign dictionaries, especially of the larger size, for foreign dictionary-makers are at last aware that Canadians, who form

an important part of their market, are nowadays expecting dictionaries to give information about Canadian words, pronunciations, and spellings.

There is a surprisingly large number of Canadianisms, some of national **16** currency, others largely regional; still others are confined mainly to special fields of activity, such as logging, fishing, or athletics. Most are terms coined in this country from English-language resources, or words borrowed here from the several other-language groups encountered by English-speaking Canadians. Others are native English words which have taken on specialized or transferred meanings here in Canada.

Prominent among Canadianisms are proper nouns, such as names of **17** regions: *French Shore, Cariboo;* of natives of certain regions: *Herring Chokers, Spud Islanders;* of things associated with persons or places: *Calgary redeye, Digby chicken.* Needless to say, many terms referring to things political are peculiarly Canadian: *Grit, Socred, reeve, rural municipality, police village.* Moreover, various institutions of a social character have Canadian names, most of them being Canadian institutions: *collegiate institute, separate school.* A great many words are loanwords from other languages: French, *aboideau, shanty;* Eskimo, *komatik, oomiak;* Amerindian languages, *chipmunk, pemmican.* Sometimes the origin of such loanwords is obscured in the process of adoption: *chowder, shanty, mush, shivaree, snye,* for example, are all borrowings from Canadian French, the original forms being *chaudière, chantier, marche, charivari,* and *chenail.*

Many Canadianisms seem more or less limited to certain regions: **18** to Newfoundland, *jinkers, glitter;* Maritimes, *gaspereau, Cape Island Boat;* Ontario, *fire-reels, Aurora trout;* Prairies, *pothole trout, grid road;* British Columbia, *salt chuck, kokanee;* Northland, *cat-swing, cheechako.*

The field of sports has made its contributions as well, for hockey and **19** lacrosse, and probably broomball, were born and developed here, while a native variety of rugby, that is, football, has developed among us. Furthermore, curling, introduced from Scotland, has flourished so remarkably in Canada that many of the terms our curlers use came into being in this country. From hockey and lacrosse we get *blueline, rover, spearing, crosse;* from rugby-football, *rouge, flying-wing;* from curling, *spieler, knockout game.* And in the area of sport, needless to say, numerous slang terms have made their appearance: *import, homebrew, rink rat, deke.* In other areas, too, slang has been born: *suitcase farmer, screech, Spam medal, pogey,* although most slang heard in Canada is imported from south of the border.

20   Sometimes names for a commonly encountered thing will be numerous
indeed. The perky little Canada jay, familiar to all who frequent the
Canadian bush, has been called many names over the years and across
the country; here are a number (28) that have been met with by readers
for the *Dictionary of Canadianisms* (not all, of course, are in current
use; some are highly regional; and a few may well have been used in
error by early travellers unfamiliar with the country and its creatures):
*blue pie, butcher bird, camp bird, camp robber, Canada jay, Cana-
dian jay, Canadian wood jay, caribou bird, carrion bird, cinerous crow,
grease bird, gray jay, Hudson Bay bird, Johnnie, Labrador jay, lumber-
jack, meat bird, meat hawk, meatjay, moose bird, moose jay, Oregon
jay, Rocky Mountain jay, Rupert's bird, venison bird, whisky-jack,
whisky-jay, whisky-john.*

21   The proliferation of names for the Canada jay is, obviously, an exceptional case; it is much more usual for a word to become popular
and take on a wide range of meanings over a period of time, often in
a relatively limited geographical region. Take for example, the word
Siwash, which came into English from the Chinook Jargon, a once widely
used trade-language on the Pacific Coast. In Chinook Jargon the word
meant "Indian" and was derived from French *sauvage,* as Indians were
called by the coureurs de bois and voyageurs in the days of exploration. Our earliest evidence of the word in a normal English context is
in a trader's journal dated 1851 at Kamloops Fort. It may be that the
word originally referred to the Salish Indians of Southwestern British
Columbia and adjacent parts of Washington, but in due course it came
to mean any Indian. The term spread into the Yukon and the Northwest
Territories during the late nineteenth century, probably by way of the
fur traders and later by way of the sourdoughs, many of whom had
worked in the Cariboo gold diggings before moving on to the Klon-
dike. As the years passed, *Siwash* took on additional meanings, one
of them being "any Indian language" and still another "the Chinook
Jargon." Some persons appear to have used the word to mean "male
Indian" only, using *klooch* or *kloochman* for "woman" or "wife"; still
others used the word to refer to a person camping on the trail Indian-
style, that is with no shelter other than that provided by nature. For
the word had by now taken on verbal meanings, one of these being "to
travel light, establishing *Siwash camps*" (an Indian-style camp using
natural resources for protection from the elements). Another verbal
meaning, this one at the slang level, is "prohibit from obtaining liquor;
place on the Indian list," a meaning developing out of the fact that it

was illegal in British Columbia and the Northwest (as in other provinces) to sell liquor or beer to Indians.

Although the word had no apparent derogatory connotations in the 22 beginning, it certainly developed them in the nineteenth century, at least in the senses having to do with people. It first came to be used of Indians in a derogatory way, and later of any person as a term of contempt. It was a "fighting word," so to speak, and as such fell out of decent use. Indeed, such names as *Siwash sweater,* a long-established term for the warm pullover of gray, unbleached wool made by the native Indians of southern Vancouver Island, became unusable, being displaced in recent years by *Indian sweater* or *Cowichan sweater.* Thus when a word loses prestige in one area of its use, the unfavorable connotations invariably spread to other areas, causing an avoidance of the term by sensitive persons and creating a need for new words having favorable or neutral connotations.

This word *Siwash* has been especially prolific in compounds over the 23 past century; in addition to *Siwash camp* and *Siwash sweater,* already mentioned, the *Dictionary of Canadianisms* lists *Siwash berry* (the saskatoon), *Siwash blanket* (a low cloud ceiling), *Siwash dog* (a hybrid sled dog in the Northwest), *Siwash goose* (the western grebe), *Siwash house* (the Indian hall at a trading post), *Siwash logger* (a no-account beachcomber), *Siwash pudding* (a pudding made with saskatoon berries), *Siwash rhubarb* (a kind of plant; Indian rhubarb), *Siwash slipper* (a mocassin), *Siwash sock* (a puttee-like duffel sock worn inside mocassins), *Siwash tongue* (the Chinook Jargon), *Siwash wapatoo* (an edible tuber; Indian potato), *Siwash wind* (a brisk wind). When to this impressive list we add such derivatives as *Siwashing, Siwashdom, Siwash fashion,* and *Siwash style,* it can be seen that this term has been uncommonly productive.

Another word of great interest is *snye,* which comes into Canadian 24 English from Canadian French, the source being the dialectal *chenail* (as opposed to Mod.F *chenal* channel). We encounter this word first in the 1820's during the building of the Rideau Canal between Ottawa (then Bytown) and Kingston. As among the voyageurs, it referred to a side-channel, especially one which by-passed a rapids or falls, creating a kind of island. Such snyes, often shallow and sometimes dry, were deepened and widened to serve as channels for the Ottawa lumbermen to run their timber rafts through in by-passing obstructions in the river. During the height of the lumbering period in this neck of the woods, *snye* was a widely used word, occurring in such compounds as *dry snye,*

snye dam, and *timber snye,* and in numerous place names, as *Gloucester Snye* and *Mississippi Snye.* It is as a place name that the word is best known today in the Ottawa Valley.

25   Later in the century the word *snye* makes its appearance in the Northwest. Here too it was taken into English from the French of the voyageur, but here it has continued to flourish. In the Northwest *snye* refers primarily to a narrow, meandering, sluggish side-channel of a river, usually shallow and often coming to a dead end (also called a *blind snye* or *blind slough).* It does, however, seem to have developed some secondary meanings in recent years: (a) a stream connecting two rivers some distance away from their confluence, thus creating an island (a meaning apparently developing out of the familiarity many persons had with "the Snigh," a water-course of just this description at Fort McMurray on the Mackenzie River); (b) a channel, or other adequate stretch of water, utilized as a landing place for bush planes (also called a *landing snye);* and (c) any small tributary stream. Over the years this borrowing from Canadian French has had many spellings, including *schny, she-ny, shnay, snie,* and *snigh,* several of them revealing early stages in the process of anglicization, *sh* representing the pronunciation of French *ch.* The currently accepted pronunciation is (sni), although older (shni) is said to be heard in places still; the usual spelling is *snye,* the older *sny* also being met occasionally. The plural, it seems, may be either *snyes* or *snies.*

26   This process of borrowing and the continuing development of meanings within the language is one of the most intriguing aspects of English, or any other language, for that matter. Canadian English provides numerous examples of just such proliferation, as in the case of *bateau, cariole, cache, shanty,* and many more. Often words which are not themselves of Canadian origin develop meanings or become elements in compounds which are, and here we might cite such words as *beaver, bush, Indian, lumber, slough, timber,* and *wood.* Of course, many of the words which we call Canadian are now to be classed as "historical" or "obsolete." But the meanings of such no-longer-used words are important to people who read earlier writings for whatever reason and, of course, to those who read historical novels about the early days of life in Canada. For this reason as well as for their intrinsic interest, such terms as *York boat, Red River cart, Montreal canoe, buffalo runner, home-guard Indian, pork-eater, Eastmain, Rupert's Land, New Caledonia,* and a host of others have their claim to the attention of the student of Canadian English.

Of course, the field of Canadian English involves much more than 27
the searching out and defining of words and expressions. One must be
concerned with the study of regional speech, called "dialect geography,"
a thoroughly fascinating area of study; one must also be concerned with
pronunciation patterns, not only from a regional point of view but from
a social point of view as well. And, finally, although this is a rather
special area of language that is purely visual, one must be concerned
with practices of spelling, for here perhaps more than anywhere else
inadequately informed critics of language focus their attention. Such
problems can be understood only after an extensive and thorough examination of the language as it is spoken in Canada and after an intelligent assessment of the practices of educated Candians in these
matters. The worker in the vineyard is sometimes frustrated by the very
complexity of the evidence, but the irritations are more than balanced
by the utterly thrilling discoveries one makes and by the pleasure that
comes with deepening one's knowledge of man's most precious possession − his language.

(1966)

The Writer's Subject

1. What distinctions does the writer draw between the phrases "Canadian
   English" and "the American language"? (para. 2)

2. What, according to Avis, are the principal elements that make up Canadian English? (paras. 3-5)

3. Explain the importance of patterns of immigration to Canada in the development of Canadian English. (paras. 6-13)

4. What reasons does Avis give for the greater influence of British English
   in British Columbia than in other areas of Canada? (para. 12)

5. What, according to Avis, constitutes a Canadianism? (para. 15)

6. What are the chief categories which Avis identifies in his account of the
   development of Canadianisms?

7. In what ways has the development of Canadian English been influenced
   by other languages?

8. Using an example provided by Avis, show how a word can change in meaning over a period of time.

The Writer's Style and Strategy

1. This essay is primarily expository in nature, its main function being to define and illustrate Canadian English. What methods does Avis use to make an otherwise dry subject interesting?

2. Avis presents a variety of materials in this essay. How does he organize these materials?

3. In what way does the title throw light on Avis's purposes in writing this essay?

Suggested Topics for Writing and Discussion

1. Avis points to spelling differences between Canadian and British English, and between Canadian and American English. Using your college library, consult three or four handbooks of English designed for use by Canadian students. Show the points upon which these agree and the points upon which they differ with regard to spelling.

2. Avis mentions dialect geography in his closing paragraph. Using your college library, find out what you can about dialect geography and discuss striking features of the English dialect of a particular area of North America (e.g., Newfoundland, Texas, Cape Breton Island, North Carolina).

3. Do you think that those who speak the dialect of a particular region should be encouraged to preserve that dialect or to adopt the standard forms and pronunciation of "received" English?

4. Examine your own "dialect." Explain, for a speaker of English from another region or another country, the features of your dialect which make it distinctive.

Little Red Riding Hood Revisited

by Russell Baker

In an effort to make the classics accessible to contemporary readers, 1
I am translating them into the modern American language. Here is the
translation of *Little Red Riding Hood:*

Once upon a point in time, a small person named Little Red Riding 2
Hood initiated plans for the preparation, delivery and transportation of
foodstuffs to her grandmother, a senior citizen residing at a place of
residence in a wooded area of indeterminate dimension.

In the process of implementing this program, her incursion into the 3
area was in mid-transportation process when it attained interface with
an alleged perpetrator. This individual, a wolf, made inquiry as to the
whereabouts of Little Red Riding Hood's goal, as well as inferring that
he was desirous of ascertaining the contents of Little Red Riding Hood's
foodstuffs basket, and all that.

"It would be inappropriate to lie to me," the wolf said, displaying 4
his huge jaw capability. Sensing that he was a mass of repressed hostility
intertwined with acute alienation, she indicated.

"I see you indicating," the wolf said, "but what I don't see is whatever 5
it is you're indicating at, you dig?"

Little Red Riding Hood indicated more fully, making one thing perfect- 6
ly clear — to wit, that it was to her grandmother's residence and with
a consignment of foodstuffs that her mission consisted of taking her
to and with.

At this point in time the wolf moderated his rhetoric and proceeded 7
to grandmother's residence. The elderly person was then subjected to

the disadvantages of total consumption and transferred to residence in the perpetrator's stomach.

8   "That will raise the old woman's consciousness," the wolf said to himself. He was not a bad wolf, but only a victim of an oppressive society, a society that not only denied wolves' rights, but actually boasted of its capacity for keeping the wolf from the door. An interior malaise made itself manifest inside the wolf.

9   "Is that the national malaise I sense within my digestive tract?" wondered the wolf. "Or is it the old person seeking to retaliate for her consumption by telling wolf jokes to my duodenum?" It was time to make a judgment. The time was now, the hour had struck, the body lupine cried out for decision. The wolf was up to the challenge. He took two stomach powders right away and got into bed.

10   The wolf had adopted the abdominal distress recovery posture when Little Red Riding Hood achieved his presence.

11   "Grandmother," she said, "your ocular implements are of an extraordinary order of magnitude."

12   "The purpose of this enlarged viewing capability," said the wolf, "is to enable your image to register a more precise impression upon my sight systems."

13   "In reference to your ears," said Little Red Riding Hood, "it is noted with the deepest respect that far from being underprivileged, their elongation and enlargement appear to qualify you for unparalleled distinction."

14   "I hear you loud and clear, kid," said the wolf, "but what about these new choppers?"

15   "If it is not inappropriate," said Little Red Riding Hood, "it might be observed that with your new miracle masticating products you may even be able to chew taffy again."

16   This observation was followed by the adoption of an aggressive posture on the part of the wolf and the assertion that it was also possible for him, due to the high efficiency ratio of his jaw, to consume little persons, plus, as he stated, his firm determination to do so at once without delay and with all due process and propriety, notwithstanding the fact that the ingestion of one entire grandmother had already provided twice his daily recommended cholesterol intake.

17   There ensued flight by Little Red Riding Hood accompanied by pursuit in respect to the wolf and a subsequent intervention on the part of a third party, heretofore unnoted in the record.

18   Due to the firmness of the intervention, the wolf's stomach underwent ax-assisted aperture with the result that Little Red Riding Hood's

grandmother was enabled to be removed with only minor discomfort.

The wolf's indigestion was immediately alleviated with such effec-   19
tiveness that he signed a contract with the intervening third party to
perform with grandmother in a television commercial demonstrating
the swiftness of this dramatic relief for stomach discontent.

"I'm going to be on television," cried grandmother.   20

And they all joined her happily in crying, "What a phenomena!"   21

(1979)

The Writer's Subject

1. Baker takes the traditional folktale of "Little Red Riding Hood" and
   "translates" it into an inflated jargon-ridden English. What is his purpose
   in doing this?

2. What are the objects of Baker's satire in his opening sentence?

3. In the original story, the wolf was clearly the villain, but in Baker's version he is described as "a victim of an oppressive society" (para. 8). What
   is Baker making fun of through this change?

4. The traditional story ends with the death of the wolf at the hands of a
   woodsman. What is the point Baker makes through the changed ending?

5. What comment on modern American values is Baker making in this essay?

The Writer's Style and Strategy

1. Why does Russell Baker use the phrase "the modern American Language"
   in paragraph 1? (In this connection, see Avis's "Canadian Spoken Here,"
   paragraph 2.)

2. The inflated language of this essay draws attention to the abuse of English
   by writers who use jargon, euphemism, and needlessly elaborate diction.
   Pick out examples of each of these abuses as they are mimicked by Baker,
   and suggest what areas they might be drawn from (e.g., politics, law,
   psychology, advertising).

3. At what kind of audience is Baker aiming his essay?

4. What effect is created by the sudden injection of slang in paragraphs 5
   and 14?

5. Comment on Baker's use of clichés in this essay.

6. "Translate" one of the paragraphs of the essay (e.g., paras. 2,3,7,16) into plain English, and compare the number of words you require with the number in the original.

7. Baker uses many passive constructions (e.g., "it is noted that . . ."; "it might be observed that . . ."; "this observation was followed by . . ."). What is Baker's purpose?

8. Comment on the closing sentence of the essay.

Suggested Topics for Writing and Discussion

1. Choose a well known folktale or fairy tale, and "translate it for a modern reader" in the way that Baker has done with "Little Red Riding Hood."

2. Discuss the ways in which Baker's essay is similar to Orwell's "Politics and the English Language" or Malcolm Cowley's "Sociological Habit Patterns in Linguistic Transmogrification" in its attitude to the uses and abuses of language.

3. Choose a well known folktale or fairy tale and write a satirical modern ending of the kind which Baker has provided in "Little Red Riding Hood Revisited." Explain why you have changed the ending.

4. Baker's treatment of "Little Red Riding Hood" suggests that he does not think such classics need "updating." One area in which "updating" is taking place is in literature for children. What is your view of the current trend to update classic children's stories, notably to remove elements now thought to be sexist or violent? Consult your local library for information on this movement.

Sociological Habit Patterns in Linguistic Transmogrification

by Malcolm Cowley

I have a friend who started as a poet and then decided to take a 1
postgraduate degree in sociology. For his doctoral dissertation he combined his two interests by writing on the social psychology of poets.
He had visited poets by the dozen, asking each of them a graded series
of questions, and his conclusions from the interviews were modest and
useful, though reported in what seemed to me a barbarous jargon. After
reading the dissertation I wrote and scolded him. "You have such a fine
sense of the poet's craft," I said, "that you shouldn't have allowed the
sociologists to seduce you into writing their professional slang — or
at least that's my judgmental response to your role selection."

My friend didn't write to defend himself; he waited until we met again. 2
Then dropping his voice, he said: "I knew my dissertation was badly
written, but I had to get my degree. If I had written it in English, professor Blank" — he mentioned a rather distinguished name — "would
have rejected it. He would have said it was merely belletristic."

From that time I began to study the verbal folkways of the sociologists. 3
I read what they call "the literature." A few sociologists write the best
English they are capable of writing, and I suspect that they are the best
men in the field. There is no mystery about them. If they go wrong,
their mistakes can be seen and corrected. Others, however — and a
vast majority — write in a language that has to be learned almost like
Esperanto. It has a private vocabulary which, in addition to strictly
sociological terms, includes new words for the commonest actions, feelings, and circumstances. It has the beginnings of a new grammar and

syntax, much inferior to English grammar in force and precision. So far as it has an effect on standard English, the effect is largely pernicious.

4   Sometimes it misleads the sociologists themselves, by making them think they are profoundly scientific at points where they are merely being verbose. I can illustrate by trying a simple exercise in translation, that is, by expressing an idea first in English and then seeing what it looks like in the language of sociology.

5   An example that comes to hand is the central idea of an article by Norman E. Green, printed in the February, 1956, issue of the *American Sociological Review*. In English his argument might read as follows:

6   "Rich people live in big houses set farther apart than those of poor people. By looking at an aerial photograph of any American city, we can distinguish the richer from the poorer neighborhoods."

7   I won't have to labor over a sociological expression of the same idea, because Mr. Green has saved me the trouble. Here is part of his contribution to comparative linguistics. "In effect, it was hypothesized," he says — a sociologist must never say "I assumed," much less "I guessed" — "that certain physical data categories including housing types and densities, land use characteristics, and ecological location" — not just "location" mind you, but "ecological location," which is almost equivalent to locational location — "constitute a scalable content area. This could be called a continuum of residential desirability. Likewise, it was hypothesized that several social data categories, describing the same census tracts, and referring generally to the social stratification system of the city, would also be scalable. This scale could be called a continuum of socio-economic status. Thirdly, it was hypothesized that there would be a high positive correlation between the scale types on each continuum."

8   Here, after ninety-four words, Mr. Green is stating, or concealing, an assumption with which most laymen would have started, that rich people live in good neighborhoods. He is now almost ready for his deduction, or snapper:

9   "This relationship would define certain linkages between the social and physical structure of the city. It would also provide a precise definition of the commonalities among several spatial distributions. By the same token, the correlation between the residential desirability scale and the continuum of socio-economic status would provide an estimate of the predictive value of aerial photographic data relative to the social ecology of the city."

Mr. Green has used 160 words — counting "socio-economic" as only 10
one — to express an idea that a layman would have stated in thirty-
three. As a matter of fact, he has used many more than 160 words,
since the whole article is an elaboration of this one thesis. Whatever
may be the virtues of the sociological style — or Soc-speak, as George
Orwell might have called it — it is not specifically designed to save
ink and paper. Let us briefly examine some of its other characteristics.

Fuzzing Up the Obvious

A layman's first impression of sociological prose, as compared with 11
English prose, is that it contains a very large proportion of abstract
words, most of them built on Greek or Latin roots. Often — as in the
example just quoted — they are used to inflate or transmogrify a meaning that could be clearly expressed in shorter words surviving from King
Alfred's time.

These Old English or Anglo-Saxon words are in number less than 12
one-tenth of the entries in the largest dictionaries. But they are the names
of everyday objects, attributes, and actions, and they are also the pronouns, the auxiliary verbs, and most of the prepositions and conjunctions, so that they form the grammatical structure of the language. The
result is that most novelists use six Anglo-Saxon words for every one
derived from French, Latin, or Greek, and that is probably close to
the percentage that would be found in spoken English.

For comparison or contrast, I counted derivations in the passage quoted 13
from the *American Sociological Review,* which is a typical example of
"the literature." No less than forty-nine per cent of Mr. Green's prose
consists of words from foreign or classical languages. By this standard
of measurement, his article is more abstruse than most textbooks of
advanced chemistry and higher mathematics, which are said to contain
only forty per cent of such words.

In addition to being abstruse, the language of the sociologists is also 14
rich in neologisms. Apparently they like nothing better than inventing
a word, deforming a word, or using a technical word in a strange context. Among their favorite nouns are "ambit," "extensity" (for "extent"),
"scapegoating," "socializee," "ethnicity," "directionality," "cathexis," "affect" (for "feeling"), "maturation" (for both "maturing" and "maturity"),
and "commonalities" (for "points in common"). Among their favorite
adjectives are "processual," "prestigeful," and "insightful" — which last
is insightful to murder — and perhaps their favorite adverb is "minimal-

ly," which seems to mean "in some measure." Their maximal pleasure seems to lie in making new combinations of nouns and adjectives and nouns used as adjectives, until the reader feels that he is picking his way through a field of huge boulders, lost among "universalistic-specific achievement patterns" and "complementary role-expectation-sanction systems," as he struggles vainly toward "ego-integrative action orientation," guided only by "orientation to improvement of the gratification deprivation balance of the actor" — which last is Professor Talcott Parsons's rather involved way of saying "the pleasure principle."

15   But Professor Parsons, head of the Sociology Department at Harvard, is not the only delinquent recidivist, convicted time and again of corrupting the language. Among sociologists in general there is a criminal fondness for using complicated terms when there are simple ones available. A child says "Do it again," a teacher says "Repeat the exercise," but the sociologist says "It was determined to replicate the investigation." Instead of saying two things are alike or similar, as a layman would do, the sociologist describes them as being either isomorphic or homologous. Instead of saying that they are different, he calls them allotropic. Every form of leadership or influence is called a hegemony.

16   A sociologist never cuts anything in half or divides it in two like a layman. Instead he dichotomizes it, bifurcates it, subjects it to a process of binary fission, or restructures it in a dyadic conformation — around polar foci.

The New Grammar

17   So far I have been dealing with the vocabulary of sociologists, but their private language has a grammar too, and one that should be the subject of intensive research by the staff of a very well-endowed foundation. I have space to mention only a few of its more striking features.

18   The first of these is the preponderance of nouns over all the other parts of speech. Nouns are used in hyphenated pairs or dyads, and sometimes in triads, tetrads, and pentads. Nouns are used as adjectives without change of form, and they are often used as verbs, with or without the suffix "ize." The sociological language is gritty with nouns, like sanded sugar.

19   On the other hand, it is poor in pronouns. The singular pronoun of the first person has entirely disappeared, except in case histories, for the sociologist never comes forward as "I." Sometimes he refers to himself as "the author" or "the investigator," or as "many sociologists,"

or even as "the best sociologists," when he is advancing a debatable opinion. On rare occasions he calls himself "we," like Queen Elizabeth speaking from the throne, but he usually avoids any personal form and writes as if he were a force of nature.

The second-personal pronoun has also disappeared, for the sociologist pretends to be speaking not to living persons but merely for the record. Masculine and feminine pronouns of the third person are used with parsimony, and most sociologists prefer to say "the subject," or "X−," or "the interviewee," where a layman would use the simple "he" or "she." As for the neuter pronoun of the third person, it survives chiefly as the impersonal subject of a passive verb. "It was hypothesized," we read, or "It was found to be the case." Found by *whom?*

The neglect and debasement of the verb is another striking feature of "the literature." The sociologist likes to reduce a transitive verb to an intransitive, so that he speaks of people's adapting, adjusting, transferring, relating, and identifying, with no more of a grammatical object than if they were coming or going. He seldom uses transitive verbs of action, like "break," "injure," "help," and "adore." Instead he uses verbs of relation, verbs which imply that one series of nouns and adjectives, used as the compound subject of a sentence, is larger or smaller than, dominant over, subordinate to, causative of, or resultant from another series of nouns and adjectives.

Considering this degradation of the verb, I have wondered how one of Julius Caesar's boasts could be translated into Soc-speak. What Caesar wrote was "*Veni, vidi, vici*" − only three words, all of them verbs. The English translation is in six words: "I came, I saw, I conquered," and three of the words are first personal pronouns, which the sociologist is taught to avoid. I suspect that he would have to write: "Upon the advent of the investigator, his hegemony became minimally coextensive with the areal unit rendered visible by his successive displacements in space."

The whole sad situation leads me to dream of a vast allegorical painting called "The Triumph of the Nouns." It would depict a chariot of victory drawn by the other conquered parts of speech − the adverbs and adjectives still robust, if yoked and harnessed; the prepositions bloated and pale; the conjunctions tortured; the pronouns reduced to sexless skeletons; the verbs dichotomized and feebly tottering − while behind them, arrogant, overfed, roseate, spilling over the triumphal car, would be the company of nouns in Roman togas and Greek chitons, adorned with laurel branches and flowering hegemonies.

(1956)

The Writer's Subject

1. Why did Cowley's friend fear that his dissertation might be rejected if it were well written? (paras. 1-2)

2. What point is Cowley making by his quotation of an excerpt from the article by Norman E. Green? (paras. 4-10)

3. What are the chief characteristics of the sociological style as identified by Cowley?

4. Why, in Cowley's view, does Norman Green's use of words from foreign or classical languages produce an article "more abstruse than most textbooks of advanced chemistry and higher mathematics"? (para. 13)

5. Summarize Cowley's principal criticisms of the vocabulary of sociologists. (paras. 14-16)

6. Why is Cowley so critical of the sociologists' neglect of first and second-person pronouns? (paras. 19-20)

The Writer's Style and Strategy

1. Discuss the appropriateness of Cowley's title.

2. What is the function of the anecdote with which Cowley begins his essay? Where does he first state his thesis?

3. What methods does Cowley use to demonstrate the bad writing of sociologists?

4. How does Cowley convey his attitude to the vocabulary of sociology in paragraph 14?

5. Show how Cowley uses metaphor and simile as means of strengthening his argument in paragraphs 15, 18, and 19.

6. Discuss the effectiveness of the essay's conclusion. How does it sum up the principal elements of Cowley's argument?

7. Compare this essay to Orwell's "Politics and the English Language." What are the differences in their purposes? How are these differences reflected in the tone of each essay?

Suggested Topics for Writing and Discussion

1. Cowley's article is an attack on the language used by sociologists. Choose a book or journal in a different field (e.g., education, economics, political science). Basing your views on a sample passage from your source, indicate whether the writer is guilty of any of the sins with which Cowley charges sociologists.

2. What measures do you think should be taken by colleges and universities to ensure that *all* their graduates, whether in Arts or the Sciences, write good, clear English? What changes or improvements would you make in the writing requirements at your own institution?

3. Cowley takes an article from the February 1956 issue of the *American Sociological Review* to illustrate his criticism of the language of sociology. Choose a recent article from this or a similar journal, or a chapter from a book on the social sciences, and offer your own views on the current state of sociological writing as reflected in your source.

The Case Against Advertising
by Richard Hoggart

1   By turns hurt, defiant, apologetic and self-justifying, advertising men
seem particularly sensitive to criticism just now. Criticism has certainly been heavy in the last few years, perhaps because the number of
reasonably well-informed people is somewhat greater than it used to
be. You need a fairly widespread critical public opinion to get the Consumers' Association, the Advertising Inquiry Council and similar
organizations started. Yet few people in advertising have taken the
measure of this development. Some have seen its superficial aspects
and made their advertising more self-conscious and sophisticated; but
the moderate widening of critical opinion has so far escaped almost all
of them.

2   I will try to sum up as directly as I can the case against advertising.
Even so, I do not expect to have much, if any, effect. None of us likes
our profession to be attacked, and we fight back when it is. But usually
someone somewhere in a profession steps out of line and says that he
does see some justice in the criticisms, that some things in his particular
house do need to be put in order. This can be seen in the quite fierce
arguments about the function and financing of universities today. But
I have not heard any spokesman of the advertising (or public relations)
industry admit to other than minor faults (that claims are sometimes
a bit exaggerated, say, or not strictly truthful); I have not heard any
spokesman of the industry take the full measure of the case against advertising, let alone answer it.

3   Why is this? Is it because a profession which lives by manipulating
reality, by weaving attractive but deceptive verbal links between products and potential consumers, gets taken in by its own sleight-of-hand?

And that, by-and-large, such a trade gets the servants it needs, who fit its demands and are suited by them? For such men, when they find themselves criticized, the temptation to sell themselves a rationalization, like an outfitter clothing himself from stock, must be strong. Still, if the case against advertising is going to be seen (not necessarily accepted, but at least seen), then people in advertising have to make a harder effort than they have made so far. The time for easy rides, especially for the big public spokesman of advertising, is past.

To get a few red herrings out of the way first. There can be some **4** unexceptionable advertising (and it need not be dull). It has not been proved that advertising in its present form (the kind of advertising that is being criticized) is essential to the economy, or reduces costs. It is true that the industry has done some self-policing; but only at an innocuous, true-or-false level. Last, no one in his senses is proposing censorship; anyway, the important problems could not be touched by censorship.

The really serious questions raised by advertising are much wider **5** than advertising itself. If critics spend a lot of time attacking advertising this is not because advertising is a peculiar kind of vice, but because it is a symptom, because it exhibits more plainly and persistently than anything else the issues raised by mass persuasion. At bottom the case against advertising is the same as that against political propaganda, much religious proselytizing and any other form of emotional blackmail.

The case is this: that advertising tries to achieve its ends by emo- **6** tionally abusing its audiences. Recognizing that we all have fears, hopes, anxieties, aspirations, insecurities, advertisers seek not to increase our understanding of these feelings and so perhaps our command of them, but to use their existence to increase the sales of whatever product they happen to have been paid to sell at any particular time. They exploit human inadequacy, and we have the right to say to them what Hamlet said to Guildenstern: "Why look you now, how unworthy a thing you make of me; you would play upon me; you would seem to know my stops; you would pluck out the heart of my mystery; you would sound me from my lowest note, to the top of my compass. . . . Why do you think that I am easier to be played on, than a pipe?"

There is no point in illustrating, since illustrations are all around, **7** nor in elaborating on the occasional exceptions. The basic charge is indisputable, unless you adopt a purely predatory — every man for himself — attitude; in which case there is no basis for argument. But if you accept some responsibility in your conduct towards others then you have problems, in advertising, which verbal manoeuvres can only evade, not solve.

8   Some apologists seek to rebut all this by taking up the Stance of the Licensed Pantaloon. You are too solemn, they argue. No one really believes what we say. The ordinary chap is much more subtle than you give him credit for. He recognizes that we add to the amusement and colour of his life — and that's all there is to it.

9   Coming from anyone who has read the research literature this is disingenuous. The evidence shows, and a reasonably close acquaintance with 'ordinary people' will tell you anyway, that a lot of people do literally believe what they read in the ads. A surprising number, when you think of the effort which goes into training in literacy. Still, that effort has been long delayed and is still small in proportion to the need. Most men in advertising are, of course, more effectively trained, more articulate and mentally quicker than their audiences — which doesn't make the business any pleasanter. What usually passes for sophisticated advertising (e.g. in the Sunday glossies) is at bottom as simple in its appeals as the stuff in the mass circulation papers; its stage-properties and snobberies are different, that's all. Outside that range there is, I suppose, a small core of self-aware intellectuals who do enjoy, or claim to enjoy, advertisements as aesthetic objects, as sources of verbal, sociological or psychological fun. Most talk of this kind strikes me as disingenuous; but men in advertising are grateful for it. It confirms their status as harmless amusers and pays tribute to their verbal inventiveness. Since there is a poet or novelist manqué inside many a copywriter, this is a benison. And an outsider may feel that, though it is a sad little claim they are making, at least it isn't portentous.

10   It is easy to appreciate the excitement, even the glamour, which advertising can have. Playing with words, making them do tricks for you within narrowly prescribed rules (this product, this target audience, this number of words), is obviously fascinating and in some ways similar to working within the rules of a simple literary form. I once passed hours, on a sticky hot journey by troop-train from Italy, inventing copy (with a man who is now a very popular columnist) for 'Critch', a mythical powder which would eliminate the awful persistent itch in our crutches. Still, how long can that sort of fun satisfy a man? A long time, I suppose, if the rewards are good, and if you find something cathartic for your spare time. But it's a shabby business.

11   Which is why the least attractive people in the whole advertising business are the front men with the public relations voices — the men

who cheer up conferences with fighting keynote speeches about the public-service element in advertising and make prepared palliative statements on all other suitable occasions. Their routine is usually predictable. They assert that advertising is the linch-pin or lubricant of a modern progressive economy. They use words like 'creative', 'dedicated' and 'sincere', so much that you remember Hemingway's *A Farewell to Arms*: "I was always embarrassed by the words. There were many words that you could not stand to hear and finally only the names of places had dignity. Abstract words were obscene. . . ." They take a few cheering-up-the-troops swipes at critics (this is a fairly recent development), and offer the services of advertising to promote any good cause the community can name — citizenship, education, religion.

With people like that you are really up against it. They seem to have **12** no sense of the difficulty of truth and of the need to respect other people's effort after it: "There's no limit to the wonderful things advertising can be made to sell . . . religion, social conscience, racial tolerance, education. . . ." How do you explain that if religion is to mean anything it must be founded on personal commitment, arrived at with any help others can disinterestedly give, but in the end arrived at personally and in the fullest possible emotional clarity? Or how do you explain that illicit manoeuvres (associating religion with togetherness or smartness) cannot really convert anyone and only prepare the ground for equally illicit manoeuvres with more questionable ends. As 'professionals', Goebbels' ad men were very efficient indeed.

There is, of course, good persuasion as well as bad persuasion; and **13** advertisers keep the debate murkier than it should be by sliding between the two types. In one sense, any good book is an act of persuasion. But the gap between that and the persuasion of advertisers is so large as to make virtually a difference of kind. Good persuasion, whether in dispassionate argument or in a powerfully moving novel, has two root qualities: respect for the reality of the subject, and respect for the listener's right to judge for himself his attitude to the subject. This definition does not rule out emotional engagement; any important commitment is a mixture of emotion and intellect. But it insists on emotional relevance — that the emotion, in both its nature and its intensity, fit the theme.

Naturally, the line between this and illicit emotional persuasion is **14** a continuous one, and it is difficult to decide just where the watershed comes. But look at each end of the line and you see the distinction at once, and see its importance; and this makes it all the more important not to blur distinctions in the large middle area (which is where most of the battles about persuasion are fought), but to try to make them clearer.

15   It is important for outside critics not to use advertisers as scapegoats for bigger social problems; they reflect more than they affect in society. There are a lot of reasons why a society such as this throws up so much persuasion, and so to many people in advertising theirs seems as respectable a trade as many others.

16   That much can be granted. But it is just as important not to make easy accommodations. The overriding fact is that much of the work of this profession, as it is at present practised, consists of exploiting weakness, through language. Anyone who thinks it is better to try to understand one's weaknesses than to indulge them, anyone who thinks that language (the articulation of our thoughts and feelings in communicable form) can help in that better grasp, anyone with these two premises must regard most modern advertising as, at the best, a waste of good human resources and, at the worst, a misuse of other people.

(1970)

The Writer's Subject

1. Why, in Hoggart's view, have advertisers failed to criticize themselves? (paras. 2-3)

2. How, according to Hoggart, do advertisers emotionally abuse their audiences? (para. 6)

3. What kind of apology for advertising does Hoggart discuss in paragraph 8? How does he regard such an apology?

4. What is Hoggart's view of "sophisticated advertising"? (para. 9)

5. Why, in speaking of the apparently limitless possibilities of advertising, does Hoggart end his paragraph with a reference to Goebbels? (para. 12)

6. How does Hoggart distinguish between good persuasion and bad persuasion in paragraphs 12-14?

The Writer's Style and Strategy

1. What kind of audience is implied in this essay? (See, for example, paragraphs 7 and 16.)

2. A way of dealing with opponents to an argument is to denigrate their views by making them seem trivial, irrelevant, or absurd. Find instances in this essay of Hoggart's use of this strategy.

3. Do you think Hoggart presents his "case" fairly and objectively?

4. Comment on Hoggart's use of the two literary references to works by Shakespeare and Hemingway. (paras. 6, 11)

5. What use does Hoggart make of personal anecdote to support his case against advertising?

Suggested Topics for Writing and Discussion

1. Write an argument in defense of advertising.

2. Hoggart sees advertising as merely one example of the workings of mass persuasion in our society. (para. 5) Discuss another example of mass persuasion (e.g., election campaigns, religious broadcasting), showing how it makes use of the techniques commonly used to sell products.

3. Hoggart says a few individuals "claim to enjoy advertisements as aesthetic objects." Can a serious claim be made for advertising as an art form? Give examples to support your view.

4. Describe an advertisement which has wide currency (i.e., on television, in national magazines) as "a source of verbal, sociological or psychological fun" and discuss the nature of its appeal.

The Abuses of Advertising

by Samuel Johnson

The Idler No. 40 — Saturday, 20 January 1759

1 The practice of appending to the narratives of public transactions, more minute and domestic intelligence, and filling the news-papers with advertisements, has grown up by slow degrees to its present state.

2 Genius is shewn only by invention. The man who first took advantage of the general curiosity that was excited by a siege or battle, to betray the readers of news into the knowledge of the shop where the best puffs and powder were to be sold, was undoubtedly a man of great sagacity, and profound skill in the nature of man. But when he had once shewn the way, it was easy to follow him; and every man now knows a ready method of informing the publick of all that he desires to buy or sell, whether his wares be material or intellectual; whether he makes cloaths, or teaches the mathematics; whether he be a tutor that wants a pupil, or a pupil that wants a tutor.

3 Whatever is common is despised. Advertisements are now so numerous that they are very negligently perused, and it is therefore become necessary to gain attention by magnificence of promises, and by eloquence sometimes sublime and sometimes pathetic.

4 Promise, large promise, is the soul of an advertisement. I remember a "wash-ball" that had a quality truly wonderful, it gave "an exquisite edge to the razor." And there are now to be sold "for ready money only," some "duvets for bed-coverings, of down, beyond comparison superior to what is called otter down," and indeed such, that its "many excellencies cannot be here set forth." With one excellence we are made acquainted, "it is warmer than four or five blankets, and lighter than one."

5 There are some, however, that know the prejudice of mankind in

favour of modest sincerity. The vendor of the "Beautifying Fluid" sells a lotion that repels pimples, washes away freckles, smooths the skin, and plumps the flesh; and yet, with a generous abhorrence of ostentation, confesses, that it will not "restore the bloom of fifteen to a lady of fifty."

The true pathos of advertisements must have sunk deep into the heart **6** of every man that remembers the zeal shewn by the seller of the anodyne necklace, for the ease and safety "of poor toothing infants," and the affection with which he warned every mother, that "she would never forgive herself" if her infant should perish without a necklace.

I cannot but remark to the celebrated author who gave, in his notifica- **7** tions of the camel and dromedary, so many specimens of the genuine sublime, that there is now arrived another subject yet more worthy of his pen. "A famous Mohawk Indian warrior, who took Dieskaw the French general prisoner, dressed in the same manner with the native Indians when they go to war, with his face and body painted, with his scalping knife, tom-ax, and all other implements of war: a sight worthy the curiosity of every true Briton!" This is a very powerful description; but a critic of great refinement would say that it conveys rather "horror" than "terror." An Indian, dressed as he goes to war, may bring company together; but if he carries the scalping knife and tom-ax, there are many true Britons that will never be persuaded to see him but through a grate.

It has been remarked by the severer judges, that the salutary sorrow **8** of tragick scenes is too soon effaced by the merriment of the epilogue; the same inconvenience arises from the improper disposition of advertisements. The noblest objects may be so associated as to be made ridiculous. The camel and dromedary themselves might have lost much of their dignity between "The True Flower of Mustard" and "The Original Daffy's Elixir"; and I could not but feel some indignation when I found this illustrious Indian warrior immediately succeeded by "A Fresh Parcel of Dublin Butter."

The trade of advertising is now so near to perfection, that it is not **9** easy to propose any improvement. But as every art ought to be exercised in due subordination to the publick good, I cannot but propose it as a moral question to these masters of the publick ear, whether they do not sometimes play too wantonly with our passions, as when the register of lottery tickets invites us to his shop by an account of the prize which he sold last year; and whether the advertising controvertists do not indulge asperity of language without any adequate provocation; as in the dispute about "straps for razors," now happily subsided, and in the altercation which at present subsists concerning *Eau de Luce*.

10   In an advertisement it is allowed to every man to speak well of himself, but I know not why he should assume the privilege of censuring his neighbour. He may proclaim his own virtue or skill, but ought not to exclude others from the same pretensions.

11   Every man that advertises his own excellence, should write with some consciousness of a character which dares to call the attention of the publick. He should remember that his name is to stand in the same paper with those of the King of Prussia, and the Emperor of Germany, and endeavour to make himself worthy of such association.

12   Some regard is likewise to be paid to posterity. There are men of diligence and curiosity who treasure up the papers of the day merely because others neglect them, and in time they will be scarce. When these collections shall be read in another century, how will numberless contradictions be reconciled, and how shall fame be possibly distributed among the tailors and boddice-makers of the present age.

13   Surely these things deserve consideration. It is enough for me to have hinted my desire that these abuses may be rectified; but such is the state of nature, that what all have the right of doing, many will attempt without sufficient care or due qualifications.

(1759)

The Writer's Subject

1. What are Johnson's speculations on how advertising began?

2. Explain what Johnson means by "Genius is shewn only by invention." (para. 2)

3. According to Johnson, what means do advertisers employ to attract attention to their products? (paras. 3-7)

4. In paragraphs 5 and 6, what styles or techniques of advertising does Johnson illustrate?

5. In paragraphs 7 and 8 Johnson describes an advertisement for the public exhibition of a Mohawk Indian Warrior. What aspects of advertising does he comment on through reference to this example?

6. In paragraphs 9 and 10, what faults of advertisers does Johnson point to?

7. Why, according to Johnson, should advertisers be concerned about "posterity"? (para. 12)

The Writer's Style and Strategy

1. Find an example of parallel structure in paragraph 2.

2. Johnson, it is often said, is excessively fond of lengthy, complex structures, yet in this essay he makes pointed use of the short simple sentence. Find several short sentences and comment upon their effectiveness.

3. What is the tone of the first sentence of paragraph 9?

4. How does Johnson structure the long sentence that makes up most of paragraph 9?

5. How does Johnson use sentence structure to present opposing views in paragraph 10?

6. What clues in paragraph 12 suggest that Johnson's concerns about posterity may not be entirely serious?

Suggested Topics for Writing and Discussion

1. Johnson complains of the state of advertising in his day — the mid-eighteenth century. In what ways are advertisements of today similar to those which Johnson discusses? Provide specific examples to support your view.

2. Johnson states that "Promise, large promise, is the soul of an advertisement." Choose one or two advertisements in which you feel the "promise" of the advertisement is a false one. Discuss the way in which language either exaggerates, distorts, or misrepresents the product being sold.

3. Johnson talks about the advertisers' unfair appeals to emotion in selling their products. Discuss one or two advertisements that seem to you to indulge in this same reprehensible practice. Identify the nature of these appeals to emotion.

Politics and the English Language
by George Orwell

1   Most people who bother with the matter at all would admit that the
English language is in a bad way, but it is generally assumed that we
cannot by conscious action do anything about it. Our civilization is decadent and our language — so the argument runs — must inevitably share
in the general collapse. It follows that any struggle against the abuse
of language is a sentimental archaism, like preferring candles to electric light or hansom cabs to aeroplanes. Underneath this lies the half-
conscious belief that language is a natural growth and not an instrument which we shape for our own purposes.

2   Now, it is clear that the decline of a language must ultimately have
political and economic causes: it is not due simply to the bad influence
of this or that individual writer. But an effect can become a cause, reinforcing the original cause and producing the same effect in an inten-
sified form, and so on indefinitely. A man may take to drink because
he feels himself to be a failure, and then fail all the more completely
because he drinks. It is rather the same thing that is happening to the
English language. It becomes ugly and inaccurate because our thoughts
are foolish, but the slovenliness of our language makes it easier for us
to have foolish thoughts. The point is that the process is reversible.
Modern English, especially written English, is full of bad habits which
spread by imitation and which can be avoided if one is willing to take
the necessary trouble. If one gets rid of these habits one can think more
clearly, and to think clearly is a necessary first step towards political
regeneration: so that the fight against bad English is not frivolous and
is not the exclusive concern of professional writers. I will come back
to this presently, and I hope that by that time the meaning of what I

have said here will have become clearer. Meanwhile, here are five specimens of the English language as it is now habitually written.

These five passages have not been picked out because they are especial- 3 ly bad — I could have quoted far worse if I had chosen — but because they illustrate various of the mental vices from which we now suffer. They are a little below the average, but are fairly representative samples. I number them so that I can refer back to them when necessary:

"(1) I am not, indeed, sure whether it is not true to say that the Milton who once seemed not unlike a seventeenth-century Shelley had not become, out of an experience ever more bitter in each year, more alien [*sic*] to the founder of that Jesuit sect which nothing could induce him to tolerate."

Professor Harold Laski (Essay in *Freedom of Expression*).

"(2) Above all, we cannot play ducks and drakes with a native battery of idioms which prescribes such egregious collocations of vocables as the Basic *put up with* for *tolerate* or *put at a loss* for *bewilder*."

Professor Lancelot Hogben *(Interglossa)*.

"(3) On the one side we have the free personality: by definition it is not neurotic, for it has neither conflict nor dream. Its desires, such as they are, are transparent, for they are just what institutional approval keeps in the forefront of consciousness; another institutional pattern would alter their number and intensity; there is little in them that is natural, irreducible, or culturally dangerous. But *on the other side,* the social bond itself is nothing but the mutual reflection of these self-secure integrities. Recall the definition of love. Is not this the very picture of a small academic? Where is there a place in this hall of mirrors for either personality or fraternity?"

Essay on psychology in *Politics* (New York).

"(4) All the 'best people' from the gentlemen's clubs, and all the frantic fascist captains, united in common hatred of Socialism and bestial horror of the rising tide of the mass revolutionary movement, have turned to acts of provocation, to foul incendiarism, to medieval legends of poisoned wells, to legalize their own destruction of proletarian organizations, and rouse the agitated petty-bourgeoisie to chauvinistic fervour on behalf of the fight against the revolutionary way out of the crisis."

Communist pamphlet.

"(5) If a new spirit *is* to be infused into this old country, there is one thorny and contentious reform which must be tackled, and that is the humanization and galvanization of the B.B.C. Timidity here will bespeak canker and atrophy of the soul. The heart of Britain may be sound and of strong beat, for instance, but the British lion's roar at present is like that of Bottom in Shakespeare's *Midsummer Night's Dream* — as gentle as any sucking dove. A virile new Britain cannot continue indefinitely to be traduced in the eyes or rather ears, of the world by the effete languors of Langham Place, brazenly masquerading as 'standard English'. When the Voice of Britain is heard at nine o'clock, better far and infinitely less ludicrous to hear aitches honestly dropped than the present priggish, inflated, inhibited, school-ma'amish arch braying of blameless bashful mewing maidens!"

Letter in *Tribune*.

4   Each of these passages has faults of its own, but, quite apart from avoidable ugliness, two qualities are common to all of them. The first is staleness of imagery: the other is lack of precision. The writer either has a meaning and cannot express it, or he inadvertently says something else, or he is almost indifferent as to whether his words mean anything or not. This mixture of vagueness and sheer incompetence is the most marked characteristic of modern English prose, and especially of any kind of political writing. As soon as certain topics are raised, the concrete melts into the abstract and no one seems able to think of turns of speech that are not hackneyed: prose consists less and less of *words* chosen for the sake of their meaning, and more and more of *phrases* tacked together like the sections of a prefabricated hen-house. I list below, with notes and examples, various of the tricks by means of which the work of prose-construction is habitually dodged:

5   *Dying Metaphors.* A newly invented metaphor assists thought by evoking a visual image, while on the other hand a metaphor which is technically "dead" (e.g. *iron resolution*) has in effect reverted to being an ordinary word and can generally be used without loss of vividness. But in between these two classes there is a huge dump of worn-out metaphors which have lost all evocative power and are merely used because they save people the trouble of inventing phrases for themselves. Examples are: *Ring the changes on, take up the cudgels for, toe the line, ride roughshod over, stand shoulder to shoulder with, play into the hands of, no axe to grind, grist to the mill, fishing in troubled waters, on the order of the day, Achilles' heel, swan song, hotbed.* Many of these are used without knowledge of their meaning (what is a "rift", for instance?), and incompatible metaphors are frequently mixed, a sure sign that the writer is not interested in what he is saying. Some metaphors now current have been twisted out of their original meaning without those who

use them even being aware of the fact. For example, *toe the line* is sometimes written *tow the line*. Another example is *the hammer and the anvil*, now always used with the implication that the anvil gets the worst of it. In real life it is always the anvil that breaks the hammer, never the other way about: a writer who stopped to think what he was saying would be aware of this, and would avoid perverting the original phrase.

Operators or *verbal false limbs*. These save the trouble of picking 6 out appropriate verbs and nouns, and at the same time pad each sentence with extra syllables which give it an appearance of symmetry. Characteristic phrases are: *render inoperative, militate against, make contact with, be subjected to, give rise to, give grounds for, have the effect of, play a leading part (role) in, make itself felt, take effect, exhibit a tendency to, serve the purpose of, etc., etc.* The keynote is the elimination of simple verbs. Instead of being a single word, such as *break, stop, spoil, mend, kill,* a verb becomes a *phrase,* made up of a noun or adjective tacked on to some general-purposes verb such as *prove, serve, form, play, render.* In addition, the passive voice is wherever possible used in preference to the active, and noun constructions are used instead of gerunds *(by examination of* instead of *by examining).* The range of verbs is further cut down by means of the *-ize* and *de-* formations, and the banal statements are given an appearance of profundity by means of the *not un-* formation. Simple conjunctions and prepositions are replaced by such phrases as *with respect to, having regard to, the fact that, by dint of, in view of, in the interests of, on the hypothesis that;* and the ends of sentences are saved from anticlimax by such resounding commonplaces as *greatly to be desired, cannot be left out of account, a development to be expected in the near future, deserving of serious consideration, brought to a satisfactory conclusion,* and so on and so forth.

Pretentious diction. Words like *phenomenon, element, individual* (as 7 noun), *objective, categorical, effective, virtual, basic, primary, promote, constitute, exhibit, exploit, utilize, eliminate, liquidate,* are used to dress up simple statements and give an air of scientific impartiality to biased judgments. Adjectives like *epoch-making, epic, historic, unforgettable, triumphant, age-old, inevitable, inexorable, veritable,* are used to dignify the sordid processes of international politics, while writing that aims at glorifying war usually takes on an archaic colour, its characteristic words being: *realm, throne, chariot, mailed fist, trident, sword, shield, buckler, banner, jackboot, clarion.* Foreign words and expressions such as *cul de sac, ancien régime, deus ex machina, mutatis mutan-*

dis, status quo, gleichschaltung, weltanschauung, are used to give an air of culture and elegance. Except for the useful abbreviations *i.e., e.g.,* and *etc.,* there is no real need for any of the hundreds of foreign phrases now current in English. Bad writers, and especially scientific, political and sociological writers, are nearly always haunted by the notion that Latin or Greek words are grander than Saxon ones, and unnecessary words like *expedite, ameliorate, predict, extraneous, deracinated, clandestine, subaqueous* and hundreds of others constantly gain ground from their Anglo-Saxon opposite numbers.[1] The jargon peculiar to Marxist writing (*hyena, hangman, cannibal, petty bourgeois, these gentry, lacquey, flunkey, mad dog, White Guard,* etc.) consists largely of words and phrases translated from Russian, German or French; but the normal way of coining a new word is to use a Latin or Greek root with the appropriate affix and, where necessary, the -ize formation. It is often easier to make up words of this kind (*deregionalize, impermissible, extramarital, non-fragmentatory* and so forth) than to think up the English words that will cover one's meaning. The result, in general, is an increase in slovenliness and vagueness.

8   *Meaningless words.* In certain kinds of writing, particularly in art criticism and literary criticism, it is normal to come across long passages which are almost completely lacking in meaning.[2] Words like *romantic, plastic, values, human, dead, sentimental, natural, vitality,* as used in art criticism, are strictly meaningless, in the sense that they not only do not point to any discoverable object, but are hardly ever expected to do so by the reader. When one critic writes, "The outstanding feature of Mr. X's work is its living quality", while another writes, "The immediately striking thing about Mr. X's work is its peculiar deadness", the reader accepts this as a simple difference of opinion. If words like *black* and *white* were involved, instead of the jargon words *dead* and *living,* he would see at once that language was being used in an improper way. Many political words are similarly abused. The word *Fascism* has now no meaning except in so far as it signifies "something not desirable". The words *democracy, socialism, freedom, patriotic, realistic, justice,* have each of them several different meanings which cannot be reconciled with one another. In the case of a word like *democracy,* not only is there no agreed definition, but the attempt to make one is resisted from all sides. It is almost universally felt that when we call a country democratic we are praising it: consequently the defenders of every kind of régime claim that it is a democracy, and fear that they might have to stop using the word if it were tied down

to any one meaning. Words of this kind are often used in a consciously dishonest way. That is, the person who uses them has his own private definition, but allows his hearer to think he means something quite different. Statements like *Marshal Pétain was a true patriot, The Soviet Press is the freest in the world, The Catholic Church is opposed to persecution,* are almost always made with intent to deceive. Other words used in variable meanings, in most cases more or less dishonestly, are: *class, totalitarian, science, progressive, reactionary, bourgeois, equality.*

Now that I have made this catalogue of swindles and perversions, **9** let me give another example of the kind of writing that they lead to. This time it must of its nature be an imaginary one. I am going to translate a passage of good English into modern English of the worst sort. Here is a well-known verse from *Ecclesiastes:*

"I returned and saw under the sun, that the race is not to the swift, nor the battle to the strong, neither yet bread to the wise, nor yet riches to men of understanding, nor yet favour to men of skill; but time and chance happeneth to them all."

Here it is in modern English: **10**

"Objective consideration of contemporary phenomena compels the conclusion that success or failure in competitive activities exhibits no tendency to be commensurate with innate capacity, but that a considerable element of the unpredictable must invariably be taken into account."

This is a parody, but not a very gross one. Exhibit (3), above, for **11** instance, contains several patches of the same kind of English. It will be seen that I have not made a full translation. The beginning and ending of the sentence follow the original meaning fairly closely, but in the middle the concrete illustrations − race, battle, bread − dissolve into the vague phrase "success or failure in competitive activities". This had to be so, because no modern writer of the kind I am discussing − no one capable of using phrases like "objective consideration of contemporary phenomena" − would ever tabulate his thoughts in that precise and detailed way. The whole tendency of modern prose is away from concreteness. Now analyse these two sentences a little more closely. The first contains forty-nine words but only sixty syllables, and all its words are those of everyday life. The second contains thirty-eight words of ninety syllables: eighteen of its words are from Latin roots, and one from Greek. The first sentence contains six vivid images, and only one phrase ("time and chance") that could be called vague. The second contains not a single fresh, arresting phrase, and in spite of its ninety syllables it gives only a shortened version of the meaning contained in the first.

Yet without a doubt it is the second kind of sentence that is gaining ground in modern English. I do not want to exaggerate. This kind of writing is not yet universal, and outcrops of simplicity will occur here and there in the worst-written page. Still, if you or I were told to write a few lines on the uncertainty of human fortunes, we should probably come much nearer to my imaginary sentence than to the one from *Ecclesiastes*.

12   As I have tried to show, modern writing at its worst does not consist in picking out words for the sake of their meaning and inventing images in order to make the meaning clearer. It consists in gumming together long strips of words which have already been set in order by someone else, and making the results presentable by sheer humbug. The attraction of this way of writing is that it is easy. It is easier — even quicker, once you have the habit — to say *In my opinion it is a not unjustifiable assumption that* than to say *I think.* If you use ready-made phrases, you not only don't have to hunt about for words; you also don't have to bother with the rhythms of your sentences, since these phrases are generally so arranged as to be more or less euphonious. When you are composing in a hurry — when you are dictating to a stenographer, for instance, or making a public speech — it is natural to fall into a pretentious, Latinized style. Tags like *a consideration which we should do well to bear in mind* or *a conclusion to which all of us would readily assent* will save many a sentence from coming down with a bump. By using stale metaphors, similes and idioms, you save much mental effort, at the cost of leaving your meaning vague, not only for your reader but for yourself. This is the significance of mixed metaphors. The sole aim of a metaphor is to call up a visual image. When these images clash — as in *The Fascist octopus has sung its swan song, the jackboot is thrown into the melting pot* — it can be taken as certain that the writer is not seeing a mental image of the objects he is naming; in other words he is not really thinking. Look again at the examples I gave at the beginning of this essay. Professor Laski (1) uses five negatives in fifty-three words. One of these is superfluous, making nonsense of the whole passage, and in addition there is the slip *alien* for akin, making further nonsense, and several avoidable pieces of clumsiness which increase the general vagueness. Professor Hogben (2) plays ducks and drakes with a battery which is able to write prescriptions, and, while disapproving of the everyday phrase *put up with,* is unwilling to look *egregious* up in the dictionary and see what it means. (3), if one takes an uncharitable attitude towards it, is simply meaningless: probably one could

work out its intended meaning by reading the whole of the article in which it occurs. In (4), the writer knows more or less what he wants to say, but an accumulation of stale phrases chokes him like tea leaves blocking a sink. In (5), words and meaning have almost parted company. People who write in this manner usually have a general emotional meaning — they dislike one thing and want to express solidarity with another — but they are not interested in the detail of what they are saying. A scrupulous writer, in every sentence that he writes, will ask himself at least four questions, thus: What am I trying to say? What words will express it? What image or idiom will make it clearer? Is this image fresh enough to have an effect? And he will probably ask himself two more: Could I put it more shortly? Have I said anything that is avoidably ugly? But you are not obliged to go to all this trouble. You can shirk it by simply throwing your mind open and letting the ready-made phrases come crowding in. They will construct your sentences for you — even think your thoughts for you, to a certain extent — and at need they will perform the important service of partially concealing your meaning even from yourself. It is at this point that the special connection between politics and the debasement of language becomes clear.

In our time it is broadly true that political writing is bad writing. Where **13** it is not true, it will generally be found that the writer is some kind of rebel, expressing his private opinions and not a "party line". Orthodoxy, of whatever colour, seems to demand a lifeless, imitative style. The political dialects to be found in pamphlets, leading articles, manifestos, White Papers and the speeches of under-secretaries do, of course, vary from party to party, but they are all alike in that one almost never finds in them a fresh, vivid, home-made turn of speech. When one watches some tired hack on the platform mechanically repeating the familiar phrases — *bestial atrocities, iron heel, bloodstained tyranny, free peoples of the world, stand shoulder to shoulder* — one often has a curious feeling that one is not watching a live human being but some kind of dummy: a feeling which suddenly becomes stronger at moments when the light catches the speaker's spectacles and turns them into blank discs which seem to have no eyes behind them. And this is not altogether fanciful. A speaker who uses that kind of phraseology has gone some distance towards turning himself into a machine. The appropriate noises are coming out of his larynx, but his brain is not involved as it would be if he were choosing his words for himself. If the speech he is making is one that he is accustomed to make over and over again, he may be almost unconscious of what he is saying, as one is when one utters the responses in church. And this reduced state of consciousness, if not indispensable, is at any rate favourable to political conformity.

14   In our time, political speech and writing are largely the defence of the indefensible. Things like the continuance of British rule in India, the Russian purges and deportations, the dropping of the atom bombs on Japan, can indeed be defended, but only by arguments which are too brutal for most people to face, and which do not square with the professed aims of political parties. Thus political language has to consist largely of euphemism, question-begging and sheer cloudy vagueness. Defenceless villages are bombarded from the air, the inhabitants driven out into the countryside, the cattle machine-gunned, the huts set on fire with incendiary bullets: this is called *pacification*. Millions of peasants are robbed of their farms and sent trudging along the roads with no more than they can carry: this is called *transfer of population* or *rectification of frontiers*. People are imprisoned for years without trial, or shot in the back of the neck or sent to die of scurvy in Arctic lumber camps: this is called *elimination of unreliable elements*. Such phraseology is needed if one wants to name things without calling up mental pictures of them. Consider for instance some comfortable English professor defending Russian totalitarianism. He cannot say outright, "I believe in killing off your opponents when you can get good results by doing so". Probably, therefore, he will say something like this:

"While freely conceding that the Soviet régime exhibits certain features which the humanitarian may be inclined to deplore, we must, I think, agree that a certain curtailment of the right to political opposition is an unavoidable concomitant of transitional periods, and that the rigours which the Russian people have been called upon to undergo have been amply justified in the sphere of concrete achievement."

15   The inflated style is itself a kind of euphemism. A mass of Latin words falls upon the facts like soft snow, blurring the outlines and covering up all the details. The great enemy of clear language is insincerity. When there is a gap between one's real and one's declared aims, one turns as it were instinctively to long words and exhausted idioms, like a cuttlefish squirting out ink. In our age there is no such thing as "keeping out of politics". All issues are political issues, and politics itself is a mass of lies, evasions, folly, hatred and schizophrenia. When the general atmosphere is bad, language must suffer. I should expect to find — this is a guess which I have not sufficient knowledge to verify — that the German, Russian and Italian languages have all deteriorated in the last

ten or fifteen years, as a result of dictatorship.

But if thought corrupts language, language can also corrupt thought. **16**
A bad usage can spread by tradition and imitation, even among people
who should and do know better. The debased language that I have been
discussing is in some ways very convenient. Phrases like *a not unjustifiable assumption, leave much to be desired, would serve no good
purpose, a consideration which we should do well to bear in mind,* are
a continuous temptation, a packet of aspirins always at one's elbow.
Look back through this essay, and for certain you will find that I have
again and again committed the very faults I am protesting against. By
this morning's post I have received a pamphlet dealing with conditions
in Germany. The author tells me that he "felt impelled" to write it. I
open it at random, and here is almost the first sentence that I see: "(The
Allies) have an opportunity not only of achieving a radical transformation of Germany's social and political structure in such a way as to avoid
a nationalistic reaction in Germany itself, but at the same time of lay-
ing the foundations of a co-operative and unified Europe." You see,
he "feels impelled" to write — feels, presumably, that he has something
new to say — and yet his words, like cavalry horses answering the bugle,
group themselves automatically into the familiar dreary pattern. This
invasion of one's mind by ready-made phrases *(lay the foundations,
achieve a radical transformation)* can only be prevented if one is constantly on guard against them, and every such phrase anaesthetizes a
portion of one's brain.

I said earlier that the decadence of our language is probably curable. **17**
Those who deny this would argue, if they produced an argument at all,
that language merely reflects existing social conditions, and that we cannot influence its development by any direct tinkering with words and
constructions. So far as the general tone or spirit of a language goes,
this may be true, but it is not true in detail. Silly words and expressions
have often disappeared, not through any evolutionary process but owing to the conscious action of a minority. Two recent examples were
explore every avenue and *leave no stone unturned,* which were killed
by the jeers of a few journalists. There is a long list of flyblown
metaphors which could similarly be got rid of if enough people would
interest themselves in the job; and it should also be possible to laugh
the *not un-* formation out of existence,[3] to reduce the amount of Latin
and Greek in the average sentence, to drive out foreign phrases and
strayed scientific words, and, in general, to make pretentiousness unfashionable. But all these are minor points. The defence of the English

language implies more than this, and perhaps it is best to start by saying what it does *not* imply.

18　　To begin with it has nothing to do with archaism, with the salvaging
of obsolete words and turns of speech, or with the setting up of a "standard English" which must never be departed from. On the contrary,
it is especially concerned with the scrapping of every word or idiom
which has outworn its usefulness. It has nothing to do with correct grammar and syntax, which are of no importance so long as one makes one's
meaning clear, or with the avoidance of Americanisms, or with having
what is called a "good prose style". On the other hand it is not concerned with fake simplicity and the attempt to make written English
colloquial. Nor does it even imply in every case preferring the Saxon
word to the Latin one, though it does imply using the fewest and shortest
words that will cover one's meaning. What is above all needed is to
let the meaning choose the word, and not the other way about. In prose,
the worst thing one can do with words is to surrender to them. When
you think of a concrete object, you think wordlessly, and then, if you
want to describe the thing you have been visualizing you probably hunt
about till you find the exact words that seem to fit it. When you think
of something abstract you are more inclined to use words from the start,
and unless you make a conscious effort to prevent it, the existing dialect
will come rushing in and do the job for you, at the expense of blurring
or even changing your meaning. Probably it is better to put off using
words as long as possible and get one's meaning as clear as one can
through pictures or sensations. Afterwards one can choose — not simply
accept — the phrases that will best cover the meaning, and then switch
round and decide what impression one's words are likely to make on
another person. This last effort of the mind cuts out all stale or mixed
images, all prefabricated phrases, needless repetitions, and humbug and
vagueness generally. But one can often be in doubt about the effect of
a word or a phrase, and one needs rules that one can rely on when instinct fails. I think the following rules will cover most cases:

(i)　Never use a metaphor, simile or other figure of speech which
you are used to seeing in print.

(ii)　Never use a long word where a short one will do.

(iii)　If it is possible to cut a word out, always cut it out.

(iv)　Never use the passive where you can use the active.

(v)　Never use a foreign phrase, a scientific word or a jargon word
if you can think of an everyday English equivalent.

(vi) Break any of these rules sooner than say anything outright
    barbarous.

These rules sound elementary, and so they are, but they demand a deep change of attitude in anyone who has grown used to writing in the style now fashionable. One could keep all of them and still write bad English, but one could not write the kind of stuff that I quoted in those five specimens at the beginning of this article.

I have not here been considering the literary use of language, but **19** merely language as an instrument for expressing and not for concealing or preventing thought. Stuart Chase and others have come near to claiming that all abstract words are meaningless, and have used this as a pretext for advocating a kind of political quietism. Since you don't know what Fascism is, how can you struggle against Fascism? One need not swallow such absurdities as this, but one ought to recognize that the present political chaos is connected with the decay of language, and that one can probably bring about some improvement by starting at the verbal end. If you simplify your English, you are freed from the worst follies of orthodoxy. You cannot speak any of the necessary dialects, and when you make a stupid remark its stupidity will be obvious, even to yourself. Political language — and with variations this is true of all political parties, from Conservatives to Anarchists — is designed to make lies sound truthful and murder respectable, and to give an appearance of solidity to pure wind. One cannot change this all in a moment, but one can at least change one's own habits, and from time to time one can even, if one jeers loudly enough, send some worn-out and useless phrase — some *jackboot, Achilles' heel, hotbed, melting pot, acid test, veritable inferno* or other lump of verbal refuse — into the dustbin where it belongs.

(1946)

1. An interesting illustration of this is the way in which the English flower names which were in use till very recently are being ousted by Greek ones, *snapdragon* becoming *antirrhinum, forget-me-not* becoming *myosotis*, etc. It is hard to see any practical reason for this change of fashion; it is probably due to an instinctive turning-away from the more homely word and a vague feeling that the Greek word is scientific.

2. Example: "Comfort's catholicity of perception and image, strangely Whitmanesque in range, almost the exact opposite in aesthetic compulsion, continues to evoke that trembling atmospheric accumulative hinting at a cruel, an inexorably serene timelessness . . . Wrey Gardiner scores by aiming at simple bull's-eyes with precision. Only they are not so simple, and through this contented sadness runs more than the surface bitter-sweet of resignation." *(Poetry Quarterly)*

3. One can cure oneself of the *not un-* formation by memorizing this sentence: *A not unblack dog was chasing a not unsmall rabbit across a not ungreen field.*

The Writer's Subject

1. What cause and effect relationship does Orwell perceive between language and thought? (paras. 2, 16)

2. What vices of bad writing does Orwell illustrate in citing the five passages given in paragraph 3? (See paras. 4, 12)

3. Why is Orwell so critical of "dying metaphors"? (para. 5)

4. What is Orwell's objection to the use in English writing of foreign words and phrases? (para. 7)

5. Why, according to Orwell, are words like "democracy," "freedom," and "patriotic" used dishonestly? (para. 8)

6. What is Orwell's point in comparing a political speaker with a dummy or a machine? (para. 13)

7. Why, according to Orwell, is it necessary for modern political language to consist largely of "euphemism, question-begging, and sheer cloudy vagueness"? (para. 14)

8. What connection does Orwell see between the decline of language and the rise of modern dictatorships? (para. 15)

9. Why, in Orwell's view, must one be on guard against the ready-made phrases found in political writing? (para. 16)

The Writer's Style and Strategy

1. What purposes are served by the first two paragraphs of the essay?

2. In paragraph 16, Orwell invites the reader to "look back through this essay, and for certain you will find that I have again and again committed the very faults I am protesting against." Why does Orwell make this statement?

3. Orwell constantly emphasizes the need for concrete images in place of vague abstractions or ready-made phrases. Does his own writing exemplify this principle? Find examples of Orwell's attempt to give concrete expression to his ideas.

4. In paragraph 9 and again in paragraph 22 Orwell demonstrates the misuse of language by modern writers. How does he do this?

5. What is the tone of Orwell's essay? Does it change in any way as he moves from a consideration of language to a discussion of politics?

6. How effectively does the final paragraph sum up the main points of Orwell's argument? Why, in the last sentence, does Orwell use the words "verbal refuse" and "dustbin"?

Suggested Topics for Writing and Discussion

1. Find a printed version of a political speech, and analyze it along the lines of Orwell's comments about political writing. Is it guilty of any of the sins he attributes to political speakers or writers, such as stale images, imprecision, ready-made phrases, meaningless words, or euphemisms?

2. Choose an issue that has aroused controversy, such as abortion, capital punishment, or sex education, and write a speech that might be delivered on the subject by a politician hoping to win votes. Then offer an analysis of the speech, showing where you have used the kind of language attacked by Orwell.

3. Read Russell Baker's "Little Red Riding Hood Revisited" in this reader. Write an essay in which you demonstrate how much Baker's "translation" of the traditional tale owes to the bad habits discussed by Orwell.

Literature and Audience

Of Studies

by Francis Bacon

Studies serve for delight, for ornament, and for ability. Their chief use
for delight is in privateness and retiring; for ornament, is in discourse;
and for ability, is in the judgement and disposition of business. For expert men can execute and perhaps judge of particulars, one by one; but
the general counsels and the plots and marshalling of affairs come best
from those that are learned. To spend too much time in studies is sloth;
to use them too much for ornament is affectation; to make judgement
wholly by their rules is the humour of a scholar. They perfect Nature
and are perfected by experience. For natural abilities are like natural
plants, that need pruning by study; and studies themselves do give forth
directions too much at large, except they be bounded in by experience.
Crafty men condemn studies; simple men admire them; and wise men
use them; for they teach not their own use, but that is a wisdom without
them and above them, won by observation. Read not to contradict and
confute, nor to believe and take for granted, nor to find talk and discourse,
but to weigh and consider. Some books are to be tasted, others to be
swallowed, and some few to be chewed and digested: that is, some books
are to be read only in parts; others to be read but not curiously; and
some few to be read wholly and with diligence and attention. Some books
also may be read by deputy, and extracts made of them by others, but
that would be only in the less important arguments and the meaner sort
of books; else distilled books are like common distilled waters, flashy
things. Reading maketh a full man; conference a ready man, and writing
an exact man. And therefore if a man write little, he had need have
a great memory; if he confer little, he had need have a present wit;

and if he read little, he had need have much cunning to seem to know that he doth not. Histories make men wise; poets, witty; the mathematics, subtle; natural philosophy, deep; moral, grave; logic and rhetoric, able to contend. *Abuent studia in mores.*[1] Nay there is no stond or impediment in the wit but may be wrought out by fit studies, like as diseases of the body may have appropriate exercises. Bowling is good for the stone and reins; shooting for the lungs and breast; gentle walking for the stomach; riding for the head; and the like. So if a man's wit be wandering, let him study the mathematics, for in demonstrations, if his wit be called away never so little, he must begin again. If his wit be not apt to distinguish or find differences, let him study the schoolmen, for they are *Cymini sectores.*[2] If he be not apt to beat over matters and to call up one thing to prove and illustrate another, let him study the lawyers' cases. So every defect of the mind may have a special receipt.

(1613)

1. Studies are transformed into behaviour.
2. hair-splitters. "Schoolmen" in this context refers to medieval scholars such as Thomas Aquinas and John Duns Scotus, who spent much time arguing very subtle theological distinctions.

The Writer's Subject

1. What is the difference between a learned man and an expert, according to Bacon?

2. In Bacon's view, what are the possible evils of study?

3. Why do "Crafty men condemn studies, simple men admire them, and wise men use them"?

4. What uses of reading does Bacon warn against?

5. What does Bacon mean when he says "some books may be read by deputy"?

6. What particular virtues does Bacon see in specific types of reading?

7. What "prescriptions" for reading does Bacon provide?

The Writer's Style and Strategy

1. How does Bacon develop his opening assertion?

2. What figure of speech does Bacon employ when he writes, "for natural abilities are like natural plants, that need pruning by study"? How is this figure of speech "explained" by Bacon?

3. How does Bacon develop the analogy between "diseases" of the wit and those of the body?

4. Consider Bacon's sentence style. Find instances of parallel structures and balanced structures. What rhetorical effects are gained by using these sentence strategies?

Suggested Topics for Writing and Discussion

1. In "Of Studies" Bacon says, "Reading maketh a full man." What do you understand by this statement? Use specific details to explain your view.

2. Bacon says, "Some books are to be tasted, others to be swallowed, and some few to be chewed and digested." Write an essay in which you develop Bacon's classification by means of reference to and discussion of particular books.

The Purpose of Pornography
by Robertson Davies

1   Why do readers want pornographic and obscene books, ask the moralists, expecting, as is their wont, that every decent and responsible person will agree that only perverse minds could harbor such a taste. The answer is plain: such books deal with one of the subjects, like war and religion, about which mankind can never hear enough. Taste governs our choice of such books, as it does in all literature; the man who likes *Mademoiselle de Maupin* is not usually the man who delights in *Eskimo Nell*. The public for *Lady Chatterley* is not the same as for Mark Twain's *Domestic Conversation*, though both use the same forbidden words; the one is the novel of a philosopher and the other is unmistakably the diversion of a river pilot. Nor does the outhouse humor of Eugene Field or James Whitcomb Riley appeal to readers whose interest is sexual rather than excremental; no Freudian needs to be told why. These works, of whatever category, supply an element which is lacking in the lives of most men and women. The demanding and inexorable tension of modern life, expecially in North America, and the countless duties which are imposed by getting a living and maintaining the type of domesticity now fashionable, do not bring the satisfaction of some of the heart's deepest desires. These desires are not necessarily reprehensible, but they are at odds with much of our democratic slavery. Our modern way of life has not created the need for erotica, but it has perhaps increased it, and has made possible such a phenomenon as the publication, by a reputable house, of *A Treasury of Ribaldry,* edited by a respected man of letters, Louis Untermeyer, and sold freely in all bookshops. Ribaldry and erotica are safety valves for people who feel the weight of modern

life heavily upon them; those whose ideal of civilized man approximates to the ox or the gelding, toiling to drag the plow, do not approve, and this is not the place to try to persuade them that their attitude is a dangerous one for the future of civilization.

Erotic books feed a part of that fantasy life without which man cannot 2 exist. Contrary to the belief of the fearful, this fantasy life rarely has any manifestation in the outer world; it is a private realm of gratification, where its possessor is supreme and where he enjoys those sweets which real life has denied him — including forbidden sweets. Those who starve the fantasy life in the name of morality do so at their peril: reading has for the past century been the principal ministrant to it, offering, in Carlyle's phrase, "phantasmagoria and dream-grotto" which enlarges life in directions where external and daily living cannot approach. The fantasy life is not an end in itself, but a long road by which we travel toward the deepest truth about ourselves; to close that road is to deny much of the best life has to give.

It is recognition of this need in modern life which has brought so 3 much liberty to the modern novel — liberty which may well be temporary and which, certainly, some writers have abused. The filthier a modern novel is, the better it sells, cry the moralists. This is not quite true; it is only a part of a much wider truth. And why does it never occur to the moralists to ask themselves why there should be such a need today for the kind of book which they call filthy, and which critics untroubled by their preoccupation describe very differently?

Those who complain about erotic books should confine themselves 4 to *Amadis de Gaule*, that old romance whose author, when a man and a woman are left together, writes "And nothing shall be here related; for these and suchlike things which are conformable neither to good conscience nor nature, man ought in reason lightly to pass over, holding them in slight esteem as they deserve." For the majority of readers the touchstone is one of taste; if an author offends you, do not read him. But it will not occur to any true booklover, I think, to take another man's book from him.

(1960)

The Writer's Subject

1. What, according to Davies, accounts for the general interest in pornographic books? (para. 1)

2. What distinction is Davies drawing when he says that *Lady Chatterley's Lover* is "the novel of a philosopher" and *Domestic Conversation* "the diversion of a river pilot"? (para. 1)

3. What features of modern life, in Davies' view, may possibly encourage an interest in books which may loosely be considered pornographic? (para. 1)

4. What connections does Davies make between the reading of erotica and the fantasy life? (para. 2)

5. What part has pornography played in the development of the modern novel, in Davies' view? (para. 3)

6. What is the function of "taste" with regard to pornographic literature? (paras. 1 and 4)

The Writer's Style and Strategy

1. What purpose does Davies' opening question serve?

2. What is Davies' strategy in categorizing some critics of pornography as "the moralists"? (paras. 1-3)

3. Davies describes some critics of pornography as "those whose ideal of civilized man approximates to the ox or gelding, toiling to drive the plow." How does this description, particularly the diction, suit Davies' purpose?

4. In paragraph 1 Davies alludes to *Mademoiselle de Maupin* and *Eskimo Nell*. How do these titles suggest the tastes of two hypothetical readers?

5. Davies uses the terms "pornographic," "obscene," "erotic," and "ribald" without defining them. Why doesn't he define them?

Suggested Topics for Writing and Discussion

1. Do you think that some form of censorship should be exercised over the publication and sale of pornographic literature?

2. Davies makes no distinction between erotica and pornography, a distinction which is frequently made to defend books against the charge of being pornographic. What, in your view, is an erotic book? Is an erotic book also pornographic?

3. Davies refers to *Lady Chatterley's Lover*. Find out what you can about the celebrated "trial" of the book. Have public attitudes towards such novels changed?

4. Using your local or college library, prepare a report on the current state of censorship in Canada.

The Motive for Metaphor
by Northrop Frye

1   For the past twenty-five years I have been teaching and studying English
literature in a university. As in any other job, certain questions stick
in one's mind, not because people keep asking them, but because they're
the questions inspired by the very fact of being in such a place. What
good is the study of literature? Does it help us to think more clearly,
or feel more sensitively, or live a better life than we could without it?
What is the function of the teacher and scholar, or of the person who
calls himself, as I do, a literary critic? What difference does the study
of literature make in our social or political or religious attitude? In my
early days I thought very little about such questions, not because I had
any of the answers, but because I assumed that anybody who asked them
was naïve. I think now that the simplest questions are not only the hardest
to answer, but the most important to ask, so I'm going to raise them
and try to suggest what my present answers are. I say try to suggest,
because there are only more or less inadequate answers to such questions — there aren't any right answers. The kind of problem that literature
raises is not the kind that you ever 'solve'. Whether my answers are
any good or not, they represent a fair amount of thinking about the questions. As I can't see my audience, I have to choose my rhetorical style
in the dark, and I'm taking the classroom style, because an audience
of students is the one I feel easiest with.

2   There are two things in particular that I want to discuss with you.
In school, and in university, there's a subject called 'English' in English-
speaking countries. English means, in the first place, the mother tongue.
As that, it's the most practical subject in the world: you can't under-

stand anything or take any part in your society without it. Wherever illiteracy is a problem, it's as fundamental a problem as getting enough to eat or a place to sleep. The native language takes precedence over every other subject of study: nothing else can compare with it in usefulness. But then you find that every mother tongue, in any developed or civilized society, turns into something called literature. If you keep on studying 'English', you find yourself trying to read Shakespeare and Milton. Literature, we're told, is one of the arts, along with painting and music, and, after you've looked up all the hard words and the Classical allusions and learned what words like imagery and diction are supposed to mean, what you use in understanding it, or so you're told, is your imagination. Here you don't seem to be in quite the same practical and useful area: Shakespeare and Milton, whatever their merits, are not the kind of thing you must know to hold any place in society at all. A person who knows nothing about literature may be an ignoramus, but many people don't mind being that. Every child realizes that literature is taking him in a different direction from the immediately useful, and a good many children complain loudly about this. Two questions I want to deal with, then, are, first: what is the relation of English as the mother tongue to English as a literature? Second: what is the social value of the study of literature, and what is the place of the imagination that literature addresses itself to, in the learning process?

Let's start with the different ways there are of dealing with the world   3
we're living in. Suppose you're shipwrecked on an uninhabited island in the South Seas. The first thing you do is to take a long look at the world around you, a world of sky and sea and earth and stars and trees and hills. You see this world as objective, as something set over against you and not yourself or related to you in any way. And you notice two things about this objective world. In the first place, it doesn't have any conversation. It's full of animals and plants and insects going on with their own business, but there's nothing that responds to you: it has no morals and no intelligence, or at least none that you can grasp. It may have a shape and a meaning, but it doesn't seem to be a human shape or a human meaning. Even if there's enough to eat and no dangerous animals, you feel lonely and frightened and unwanted in such a world.

In the second place, you find that looking at the world, as something   4
set over against you, splits your mind in two. You have an intellect that feels curious about it and wants to study it, and you have feelings or emotions that see it as beautiful or austere or terrible. You know that both these attitudes have some reality, at least for you. If the ship

you were wrecked in was a Western ship, you'd probably feel that your intellect tells you more about what's really there in the outer world, and that your emotions tell you more about what's going on inside you. If your background were Oriental, you'd be more likely to reverse this and say that the beauty or terror was what was really there, and that your instinct to count and classify and measure and pull to pieces was what was inside your mind. But whether your point of view is Western or Eastern, intellect and emotion never get together in your mind as long as you're simply looking at the world. They alternate, and keep you divided between them.

5   The language you use on this level of the mind is the language of consciousness or awareness. It's largely a language of nouns and adjectives. You have to have names for things, and you need qualities like 'wet' or 'green' or 'beautiful' to describe how things seem to you. This is the speculative or contemplative position of the mind, the position in which the arts and sciences begin, although they don't stay there very long. The sciences begin by accepting the facts and the evidence about an outside world without trying to alter them. Science proceeds by accurate measurement and description, and follows the demands of the reason rather than the emotions. What it deals with is there, whether we like it or not. The emotions are unreasonable: for them it's what they like and don't like that comes first. We'd be naturally inclined to think that the arts follow the path of emotion, in contrast to the sciences. Up to a point they do, but there's a complicating factor.

6   That complicating factor is the contrast between 'I like this' and 'I don't like this'. In this Robinson Crusoe life I've assigned you, you may have moods of complete peacefulness and joy, moods when you accept your island and everything around you. You wouldn't have such moods very often, and when you had them, they'd be moods of identification, when you felt that the island was a part of you and you a part of it. That is not the feeling of consciousness or awareness, where you feel split off from everything that's not your perceiving self. Your habitual state of mind is the feeling of separation which goes with being conscious, and the feeling 'this is not a part of me' soon becomes 'this is not what I want'. Notice the word 'want': we'll be coming back to it.

7   So you soon realize that there's a difference between the world you're living in and the world you want to live in. The world you want to live in is a human world, not an objective one: it's not an environment but a home; it's not the world you see but the world you build out of what you see. You go to work to build a shelter or plant a garden, and as

soon as you start to work you've moved into a different level of human life. You're not separating only yourself from nature now, but constructing a human world and separating it from the rest of the world. Your intellect and emotions are now both engaged in the same activity, so there's no longer any real distinction between them. As soon as you plant a garden or a crop, you develop the conception of a 'weed', the plant you don't want in there. But you can't say that 'weed' is either an intellectual or an emotional conception, because it's both at once. Further, you go to work because you feel you have to, and because you want something at the end of the work. That means that the important categories of your life are no longer the subject and the object, the watcher and the things being watched: the important categories are what you have to do and what you want to do — in other words, necessity and freedom.

One person by himself is not a complete human being, so I'll provide **8** you with another shipwrecked refugee of the opposite sex and an eventual family. Now you're a member of a human society. This human society after a while will transform the island into something with a human shape. What that human shape is, is revealed in the shape of the work you do: the buildings, such as they are, the paths through the woods, the planted crops fenced off against whatever animals want to eat them. These things, these rudiments of city, highway, garden and farm, are the human form of nature, or the form of human nature, whichever you like. This is the area of the applied arts and sciences, and it appears in our society as engineering and agriculture and medicine and architecture. In this area we can never say clearly where the art stops and the science begins, or vice versa.

The language you use on this level is the language of practical sense, **9** a language of verbs or words of action and movement. The practical world, however, is a world where actions speak louder than words. In some ways it's a higher level of existence than the speculative level, because it's doing something about the world instead of just looking at it, but in itself it's a much more primitive level. It's the process of adapting to the environment, or rather of transforming the environment in the interests of one species, that goes on among animals and plants as well as human beings. The animals have a good many of our practical skills: some insects make pretty fair architects, and beavers know quite a lot about engineering. In this island, probably, and certainly if you were alone, you'd have about the ranking of a second-rate animal. What makes our practical life really human is a third level of the mind, a level where consciousness and practical skill come together.

10   This third level is a vision or model in your mind of what you want to construct. There's that word 'want' again. The actions of man are prompted by desire, and some of these desires are needs, like food and warmth and shelter. One of these needs is sexual, the desire to reproduce and bring more human beings into existence. But there's also a desire to bring a social human form into existence: the form of cities and gardens and farms that we call civilization. Many animals and insects have this social form too, but man knows that he has it: he can compare what he does with what he can imagine being done. So we begin to see where the imagination belongs in the scheme of human affairs. It's the power of constructing possible models of human experience. In the world of the imagination, anything goes that's imaginatively possible, but nothing really happens. If it did happen, it would move out of the world of imagination into the world of action.

11   We have three levels of the mind now, and a language for each of them, which in English-speaking societies means an English for each of them. There's the level of consciousness and awareness, where the most important thing is the difference between me and everything else. The English of this level is the English of ordinary conversation, which is mostly monologue, as you'll soon realize if you do a bit of eavesdropping, or listening to yourself. We can call it the language of self-expression. Then there's the level of social participation, the working or technological language of teachers and preachers and politicians and advertisers and lawyers and journalists and scientists. We've already called this the language of practical sense. Then there's the level of imagination, which produces the literary language of poems and plays and novels. They're not really different languages, of course, but three different reasons for using words.

12   On this basis, perhaps, we can distinguish the arts from the sciences. Science begins with the world we have to live in, accepting its data and trying to explain its laws. From there, it moves towards the imagination: it becomes a mental construct, a model of a possible way of interpreting experience. The further it goes in this direction, the more it tends to speak the language of mathematics, which is really one of the languages of the imagination, along with literature and music. Art, on the other hand, begins with the world we construct, not with the world we see. It starts with the imagination, and then works towards ordinary experience: that is, it tries to make itself as convincing and recognizable as it can. You can see why we tend to think of the sciences

as intellectual and the arts as emotional: one starts with the world as it is, the other with the world we want to have. Up to a point it is true that science gives an intellectual view of reality, and that the arts try to make the emotions as precise and disciplined as sciences do the intellect. But of course it's nonsense to think of the scientist as a cold unemotional reasoner and the artist as somebody who's in a perpetual emotional tizzy. You can't distinguish the arts from the sciences by the mental processes the people in them use: they both operate on a mixture of hunch and common sense. A highly developed science and a highly developed art are very close together, psychologically and otherwise.

Still, the fact that they start from opposite ends, even if they do meet 13 in the middle, makes for one important difference between them. Science learns more and more about the world as it goes on: it evolves and improves. A physicist today knows more physics than Newton did, even if he's not as great a scientist. But literature begins with the possible model of experience, and what it produces is the literary model we call the classic. Literature doesn't evolve or improve or progress. We may have dramatists in the future who will write plays as good as *King Lear*, though they'll be very different ones, but drama as a whole will never get better than *King Lear*. *King Lear* is it, as far as drama is concerned; so is *Oedipus Rex*, written two thousand years earlier than that, and both will be models of dramatic writing as long as the human race endures. Social conditions may improve: most of us would rather live in nineteenth-century United States than in thirteenth-century Italy, and for most of us Whitman's celebration of democracy makes a lot more sense than Dante's Inferno. But it doesn't follow that Whitman is a better poet than Dante: literature won't line up with that kind of improvement.

So wc find that everything that does improve, including science, leaves 14 the literary artist out in the cold. Writers don't seem to benefit much by the advance of science, although they thrive on superstitions of all kinds. And you certainly wouldn't turn to contemporary poets for guidance or leadership in the twentieth-century world. You'd hardly go to Ezra Pound, with his fascism and social credit and Confucianism and anti-semitism. Or to Yeats, with his spiritualism and fairies and astrology. Or to D.H. Lawrence, who'll tell you that it's a good thing for servants to be flogged because that restores the precious current of blood-reciprocity between servant and master. Or to T.S. Eliot, who'll tell you that to have a flourishing culture we should educate an élite, keep most people living in the same spot, and never disestablish the

Church of England. The novelists seem to be a little closer to the world they're living in, but not much. When Communists talk about the decadence of bourgeois culture, this is the kind of thing they always bring up. Their own writers don't seem to be any better, though; just duller. So the real question is a bigger one. Is it possible that literature, especially poetry, is something that a scientific civilization like ours will eventually outgrow? Man has always wanted to fly, and thousands of years ago he was making sculptures of winged bulls and telling stories about people who flew so high on artificial wings that the sun melted them off. In an Indian play fifteen hundred years ago, *Sakuntala,* there's a god who flies around in a chariot that to a modern reader sounds very much like a private aeroplane. Interesting that the writer had so much imagination, but do we need such stories now that we have private aeroplanes?

15   This is not a new question: it was raised a hundred and fifty years ago by Thomas Love Peacock, who was a poet and novelist himself, and a very brilliant one. He wrote an essay called *Four Ages of Poetry,* with his tongue of course in his cheek, in which he said that poetry was the mental rattle that awakened the imagination of mankind in its infancy, but that now, in an age of science and technology, the poet has outlived his social function. 'A poet in our times,' said Peacock, 'is a semi-barbarian in a civilized community. He lives in the days that are past. His ideas, thoughts, feelings, associations, are all with barbarous manners, obsolete customs, and exploded superstitions. The march of his intellect is like that of a crab, backwards.' Peacock's essay annoyed his friend Shelley, who wrote another essay called *A Defence of Poetry* to refute it. Shelley's essay is a wonderful piece of writing, but it's not likely to convince anyone who needs convincing. I shall be spending a good deal of my time on this question of the relevance of literature in the world of today, and I can only indicate the general lines my answer will take. There are two points I can make now, one simple, the other more difficult.

16   The simple point is that literature belongs to the world man constructs, not to the world he sees; to his home, not his environment. Literature's world is a concrete human world of immediate experience. The poet uses images and objects and sensations much more than he uses abstract ideas; the novelist is concerned with telling stories, not with working out arguments. The world of literature is human in shape, a world where the sun rises in the east and sets in the west over the edge of a flat earth in three dimensions, where the primary realities are not atoms or elec-

trons but bodies, and the primary forces not energy or gravitation but love and death and passion and joy. It's not surprising if writers are often rather simple people, not always what we think of as intellectuals, and certainly not always any freer of silliness or perversity than anyone else. What concerns us is what they produce, not what they are, and poetry, according to Milton, who ought to have known, is 'more simple, sensuous and passionate' than philosophy or science.

The more difficult point takes us back to what we said when we were on that South Sea island. Our emotional reaction to the world varies from 'I like this' to 'I don't like this'. The first, we said, was a state of identity, a feeling that everything around us was part of us, and the second is the ordinary state of consciousness, or separation, where art and science begin. Art begins as soon as 'I don't like this' turns into 'this is not the way I could imagine it'. We notice in passing that the creative and the neurotic minds have a lot in common. They're both dissatisfied with what they see; they both believe that something else ought to be there, and they try to pretend it is there or to make it be there. The differences are more important, but we're not ready for them yet. **17**

At the level of ordinary consciousness the individual man is the centre of everything, surrounded on all sides by what he isn't. At the level of practical sense, or civilization, there's a human circumference, a little cultivated world with a human shape, fenced off from the jungle and inside the sea and the sky. But in the imagination anything goes that can be imagined, and the limit of the imagination is a totally human world. Here we recapture, in full consciousness, that original lost sense of identity with our surroundings, where there is nothing outside the mind of man, or something identical with the mind of man. Religions present us with visions of eternal and infinite heavens or paradises which have the form of the cities and gardens of human civilization, like the Jerusalem and Eden of the Bible, completely separated from the state of frustration and misery that bulks so large in ordinary life. We're not concerned with these visions as religion, but they indicate what the limits of the imagination are. They indicate too that in the human world the imagination has no limits, if you follow me. We said that the desire to fly produced the aeroplane. But people don't get into planes because they want to fly; they get into planes because they want to get somewhere else faster. What's produced the aeroplane is not so much a desire to fly as a rebellion against the tyranny of time and space. And that's a process that can never stop, no matter how high our Titovs and Glenns **18** may go.

19   For each of these six talks I've taken a title from some work of literature, and my title for this one is 'The Motive for Metaphor', from a poem of Wallace Stevens. Here's the poem:

> You like it under the trees in autumn,
> Because everything is half dead.
> The wind moves like a cripple among the leaves
> And repeats words without meaning.
>
> In the same way, you were happy in spring,
> With the half colors of quarter-things,
> The slightly brighter sky, the melting clouds,
> The single bird, the obscure moon —
>
> The obscure moon lighting an obscure world
> Of things that would never be quite expressed,
> Where you yourself were never quite yourself
> And did not want nor have to be,
>
> Desiring the exhilarations of changes:
> The motive for metaphor, shrinking from
> The weight of primary noon,
> The A B C of being,
>
> The ruddy temper, the hammer
> Of red and blue, the hard sound —
> Steel against intimation — the sharp flash,
> The vital, arrogant, fatal, dominant X.

What Stevens calls the weight of primary noon, the A B C of being, and the dominant X is the objective world, the world set over against us. Outside literature, the main motive for writing is to describe this world. But literature itself uses language in a way which associates our minds with it. As soon as you use associative language, you begin using figures of speech. If you say this talk is dry and dull, you're using figures associating it with bread and breadknives. There are two main kinds of association, analogy and identity, two things that are like each other and two things that are each other. You can say with Burns, 'My love's like a red, red rose', or you can say with Shakespeare:

> Thou that art now the world's fresh ornament
> And only herald to the gaudy spring.

One produces the figure of speech called the simile; the other produces the figure called metaphor.

20   In descriptive writing you have to be careful of associative language. You'll find that analogy, or likeness to something else, is very tricky to handle in description, because the differences are as important as the resemblances. As for metaphor, where you're really saying 'this *is* that', you're turning your back on logic and reason completely, because logically two things can never be the same thing and still remain two things. The poet, however, uses these two crude, primitive archaic forms of thought in the most uninhibited way, because his job is not to describe nature, but to show you a world completely absorbed and possessed by the human mind. So he produces what Baudelaire called a "suggestive magic including at the same time object and subject, the world outside the artist and the artist himself". The motive for metaphor, according to Wallace Stevens, is a desire to associate, and finally to identify, the human mind with what goes on outside it, because the only genuine joy you can have is in those rare moments when you feel that although we may know in part, as Paul says, we are also a part of what we know.

The Writer's Subject

1. What does the title of this essay mean?

2. In paragraph 2, Frye distinguishes between English as "the mother tongue, the most practical subject in the world," and "English as a literature." How does he illustrate this distinction in the paragraphs that follow?

3. What is the distinction Frye draws between the intellectual response and the emotional response to the world? (para. 4) How does he think these responses might be shaped by a Western or an Oriental view?

4. Frye uses an extended analogy of life on a desert island as a model to discuss levels of thought and language. What are the stages of human development that Frye identifies through use of this analogy? (paras. 3-11)

5. Frye identifies three levels of the mind and, correspondingly, three levels of language. What are these? (paras. 4-11)

6. According to Frye, how do the sciences deal with the external world differently than do the arts? (para. 5)

7. What turns the external objective world into a human world? What gives the human world its "human shape"? (paras. 7-8)

8. What processes of thought distinguish the artist's approach from the scientist's? (para. 12)

9.   In paragraph 14 Frye asks the question, "Is it possible that literature, especially poetry, is something that a scientific civilization like ours will eventually outgrow?" How does he answer this question in paragraphs 16-18?

10.   Why, according to Frye, does the poet make use of metaphor and simile? (paras. 19-20)

The Writer's Style and Strategy

1.   This essay is the first of six published lectures. How does Frye establish the context for his discussion? Where, in the essay, are you aware that this essay is an introduction to the series?

2.   Frye says, "I'm taking the classroom style." How is the classroom style demonstrated in the tone, structure, and diction of the essay?

3.   Analyze the structure of Frye's essay as a whole. Indicate the major stages of the essay. How does Frye effect the transitions from one part to another?

4.   What is the function of paragraph 11?

5.   What means does Frye use to demonstrate his point that literary artists don't serve as useful social guides? (para. 14)

6.   How does the lengthy reference to Thomas Love Peacock in paragraph 15 contribute to Frye's arguments at this point?

7.   What is Frye's purpose in including the poem by Wallace Stevens?

Suggested Topics for Writing and Discussion

1.   In an age of science and technology, does the poet have a role to play?

2.   Frye talks about the imaginative processes involved in scientific thinking. Do you think that scientific advances depend upon the imagination as much as upon the analytical process of thought? Provide an example to support your point of view.

3. Many students going on to college feel they already "know" enough English to get on in the world without studying more — especially literature. What are your views on the place of literature courses in colleges and universities?

4. Choose an article from a popular magazine (e.g., *Time, Maclean's, Saturday Night, Science Digest*) and analyze the article to determine the extent to which the writer uses metaphorical language.

Paperback Mentors
by Robert Fulford

1   Robert J. Ringer was one of the great American success stories of the
1970s, though his success didn't come easily. In his early years he failed
as a dental student, as a designer and salesman of men's clothes, and as
a manager of discount stores. He made some money selling real estate
in the Midwest, then lost it while trying to create a conglomerate in
California — a conglomerate that attracted the attention of the Securities
and Exchange Commission in Washington. But in 1973 Ringer's career
took a turn that magnificently illustrates an ancient maxim: those who
can't do, teach. He went into the business of telling other people how
to be successful.

2   Ringer wrote a book describing the forceful way he had handled those
real-estate transactions that had turned out well. He emphasized that
what he had learned was universally applicable: "If you don't happen
to be a 'salesman,' that's irrelevant; the general principles — not the
techniques — apply to every phase of life." This didn't seem obvious
to the half-dozen book publishers to whom he submitted his manuscript;
they all rejected it. Ringer published it himself, under the title *Winning
through Intimidation*, and advertised it widely in the newspapers. He
sold 190,000 copies in hard cover and 1.6-million in paperback. He
wrote a sequel, *Looking out for #1*, and a third book, *Restoring the
American Dream*, an expression of his conservative political and
economic views. Each of these was also published by Ringer himself,
and each in turn became a best seller. His three books have sold in all
nearly 5-million copies. Now he's publishing a few books by other
authors, such as Douglas Casey's *Crisis Investing*, and these too are

selling well.

Ringer's career can stand as an emblem of the most interesting recent 3 phenomenon in popular publishing, the rise of self-help books. Sometime during the mid 1970s, self-help literature moved out of the obscure corners of book publishing and became one of the staples of the industry. Ringer's books appeared on the newsstands alongside *Power! How To Get It, How To Use It* and *Success!*, by Michael Korda; *Creative Aggression*, by Dr. George R. Bach and Dr. Herb Goldberg; *How to Get Control of Your Time and Your Life*, by Alan Lakein; and *Your Erroneous Zones* and *Pulling Your Own Strings*, by Dr. Wayne W. Dyer. What was a trickle around 1974 has become a flood. This spring Collier Macmillan's Canadian catalogue, covering the early 1981 lists of only two American publishing houses, contained twenty-five self-help books, from *The Great Money Panic: A Guide for Survival and Action* to *Excuses: How to Spot Them, Deal with Them, and Stop Using Them*.

Most authors of successful self-help books produce sequels, which 4 also become best sellers. This suggests that to some considerable extent the buyers are receiving value. An author with an engaging manner on TV talk shows may fool some book-buyers once, but if they come back for more, or tell others to buy his book, then they have been at least partly satisfied. Clearly, self-help writers have not only identified certain problems, they have persuaded a few million readers that those problems can be partially solved by reading *The Art of Selfishness* or *Pulling Your Own Strings*.

This isn't easy to understand. Most of the books — I've read or looked 5 through about a dozen of them in the past few weeks — offer advice that is either obvious or silly. David Seabury in *The Art Of Selfishness*, for example, tells us we can improve our lives if we "eliminate every day one or two things that cause discontent. Find two or three acts that give you satisfaction. Keep shifting steadily toward an agreeable way of life." *How to Get Control of Your Time and Your Life* advises us to spend with care even the time we are kept waiting — by reading the classics, for instance: "You may not always feel like reading *Don Quixote* as you wait for the bus at the corner of Main and Pine, but isn't it nice to have the option?" Keep the paperback with you, the book suggests. Michael Korda, in *Success!*, notes that bald men may be tempted to wear wigs but should decline to do so if there is any chance they will be found out: "Once you have been caught out as a wig wearer, nobody is likely to trust you about anything else." Mildred Newman and Bernard Berkowitz, in *How To Be Awake and Alive*, tell us right from the start: "Every life needs a direction, a purpose. Without goals, we drift uncomfortably." Sometimes the author has an idea or two – enough, say, for a few thousand words in *New York* magazine – but stretches it over a dozen chapters to make a book. The result is a painful sense of desperate padding. *The Art of Selfishness* contains this sentence: "If there is no immediate solution to a problem, just keep looking for one." That book also shamelessly rewrites the Bible in modern jargon: "There is, in fact, no worse ego satisfaction than to seek riches and lose yourself." Newman and Berkowitz, for their part, throw in a paraphrase of Socrates: "A life that's examined is more worth living."

6   If the ideas are unoriginal, the prose is dispiriting: none of these authors can be accused of getting by on fine writing. Nor do any of them exhibit a sense of humour. You can read a pile of them and never run into wit that approaches the level of, say, Ann Landers' newspaper column. In most of these books the writers present themselves as earnest and simple-minded, in the apparent belief that their readers are the same. Their anecdotes tend to lack both interest and charm, and their comparisons are dull or pointless. Robert Ringer is the master of the inappropriate comparison. When he tries to tell us how tough he found the business world, he writes: "In general, I, like most everyone else, wished that the game of business took place on a nursery-school playground; the reality, however, was that the game of business is played in a vicious jungle." No one who has spent a little time in a nursery-school playground, and thought about it for a minute, would make a remark that dumb.

7   Those words, however, indicate a characteristic of most of these books. Each author, whatever his field, seems to work from the assumption that, until the moment of reading, the reader has been living in a dream-world. Ringer believes that we don't know how cold-blooded business can be and takes it upon himself to introduce us to what he calls "reality". The authors of *Creative Aggression* assume that their readers are all stifling their hostility in the interests of pleasantness. Michael Korda, in *Success!*, assumes we don't know that successful people act differently from unsuccessful people; he tells us that they do and that we can emulate them, to our profit. ("Successful people are fussy about shoes, and you should be too.") Alan Lakein believes that most of us spend our time wastefully, but that with a few simple tricks we can reorganize our lives. ("Take your Lifetime Goals list in hand and spend one minute selecting your top three goals.") In each case the author assumes the existence of an enormous body of extremely

naive readers who are anxious enough for guidancc to pay at least $2.25 for it. And in each case the author's considerable success has proven that the assumption is not entirely wrong.

The history of popular self-help books goes back to the etiquette **8** manuals widely published in the nineteenth century, and perhaps beyond. The immediate ancestor of the current books is Norman Vincent Peale's *The Power of Positive Thinking* (1952), in which 3-million readers were told that prayer would invoke a Higher Power ("constantly available . . . a mighty tide") which would provide them with both material success and tranquillity. But nothing in publishing history resembles the outpouring of titles during the past seven or eight years.

The phenomenon carries several fascinating implications. They touch **9** on the class sytem, the hangover of 1960s mythology, and what has recently been called "the crisis of authority."

Because the English class system is by comparison so rigid, and so **10** well advertised, North Americans tend to assume that they have no class system or that whatever they have is of minor importance. This is a mistake, as much of contemporary sociology indicates. Until very recently, most of us have tended to be heavily influenced by the class from which we sprang, and more often than not to stay roughly within it. But the enormous growth of higher education, beginning about two decades ago, began to change our expectations and our prospects. At the same time, industrial growth opened up opportunities for this newly educated class. It became commonplace rather than atypical for the child of a farmer or a workman to move into the business class — to move, that is, into surroundings to which his background had not accustomed him. Many of the self-help books on the newsstands are directed to people who have found themselves living business lives for which their upbringing left them unprepared. A young man who finds a minor job with an insurance company discovers that he must deal with people of a kind he has never encountered before; so Michael Korda and Robert J. Ringer and the rest step forth helpfully to instruct him. In a sense the self-help books are an acculturation process for newcomers to the business class; they work in much the same way that Emily Post's book on etiquette drew untutored young women into the polite classcs half a century ago by giving instructions on wedding invitations and salad forks.

At the same time, self-help books are a kind of distorted echo of the **11** 1960s, particularly of the human-potential movement. At Esalen and many other places in the 1960s, psychotherapists conducted their students in the general direction of self-realization through various communal and private exercises. Many of those instructors have since disappeared into other lines of work, and today you seldom meet someone whose life has been changed by a weekend of encounter therapy. But that movement's central belief — that within every human being there is enormous potential, lying unexploited — was lodged securely in the popular mind. It haunts the whole society, even the salesman who is hurrying through an airport bookstore. It is one reason why he passes over mystery novels and porn romances and seizes instead a copy of *The Magic of Self Direction*, by David J. Schwartz, PhD, a book whose first chapter ("How You Can Have A Larger Share Of The Better Things In Life") contains this sentence: "Nothing in life is more fascinating than understanding — and then harnessing — the amazing power of your psyche." The politics of the 1960s have also had an influence on the self-help books. Millions of young people, in that period, came to expect that their political efforts — however meagre or thoughtless — would somehow result in a more agreeable world. When this didn't happen they were frustrated politically, but perhaps still optimistic in personal terms. Ambition for social improvement was replaced by ambition for self-improvement, an impulse that is always alive in a democracy but became still more widespread after the 1960s.

12   The self-help books also signal, with more clarity than any sociological essay, the erosion of personal authority as a major factor in our lives. The guidance these books offer is precisely what people in previous generations took from authority figures around them — parents, teachers, and the various mentors encountered at work. Those older people taught, by precept or example, everything from work habits to the way you address a meeting. But social change has happened so fast that for many people traditional authority figures have ceased to be credible — they *can't* know how one should dress, or how to close a business deal, at least not as well as Michael Korda or Robert J. Ringer. The public and private events of the past twenty years have created a gulf of disbelief between those who once handed on the rules of life and those who have to learn them. Self-help books are the feeble effort of the publishing business to fill a vacuum created by the rush of change.

(1981)

The Writer's Subject

1. What are Fulford's main criticisms of self-help books? (paras. 5-6)

2. What kinds of readers, in Fulford's view, are attracted to the self-help books he describes? To what audience is he directing his argument?

3. To what causes does Fulford ascribe the enormous success of self-help books in recent years? (paras. 8-12)

4. What connection does Fulford see between the current popularity of self-help books and the "human potential" movements of the 1960s? (para. 11).

5. Why, according to Fulford, do modern self-help books signal "the erosion of personal authority as a major factor in our lives"? (para. 12)

The Writer's Style and Strategy

1. Why does Fulford begin his essay with the story of Robert J. Ringer? Discuss the effectiveness of this strategy.

2. Fulford includes many quotations from a variety of self-help books. Choose two or three and explain the effect of these references.

3. Trace the progress of Fulford's discussion from the particular to the general, noting the major stages of his argument.

4. Consult a dictionary for the meaning of "mentor." What connotations does this word carry? Comment on Fulford's title, "Paperback Mentors."

Suggested Topics for Writing and Discussion

1. Choose one or two self-help books from your local library or bookstore and examine these in light of Fulford's observations. Do you agree with Fulford's conclusions?

2. Do you agree with Fulford's view that traditional authority figures (such as teachers, parents and the various mentors encountered at work) have ceased to be credible? Is he overstating his case? Use specific examples to explain your view.

3. Is there an authority figure in your life who teaches you by precept or example? Explain what significance this person has for you.

4. Fulford alludes to the etiquette books which became popular half a century ago. Choose a current book on etiquette (e.g., *Miss Manners' Guide
   to Excruciatingly Correct Behavior, Miss Manners' Guide to Rearing
   Perfect Children* by Judith Martin) and compare its treatment of a particular social situation with that in Emily Post's or Amy Vanderbilt's books
   of etiquette. What differences can you observe? To what major social
   changes in society might you attribute these differences?

Let's Ban Applause!
by Glenn Gould

The good citizens of Toronto, my hometown, received last spring their 1
annual visit from the Metropolitan Opera Company. This is an occasion much looked forward to by all of us, and this season was the subject of special attention, since it involved the transfer of that splendid
ensemble from the regal expanse of a hockey arena to the more confined proscenium of a new theatre constructed in our behalf through
the generosity, civic vision, and tax advantage of a local brewing firm.
The Metropolitan, with its accustomed tact and diplomacy, wisely declined to present to us the alcoholic dissipations of Sir John Falstaff
or the aphrodisiac delusions of Master Tristan or, indeed, any other
tableaus which might compromise the corporate image of its host. But,
despite these courtesies, the visit was attended by a most disagreeable
correspondence in the local press. This emanated from the displeasure
which several writers voiced with the relatively restricted capacity of
the new salon and from sympathy with those of our less affluent fellow
citizens who found the consequent raise in admission prohibitive.

It was not these modest, though justified, complaints that arrested 2
my attention, however, but the grave alarms raised by several of our
more worldly-wise columnists (those who have attended concerts as far
afield as Buffalo) that what we had lost with the reduced attendance
at the Metropolitan was not money — a concept which all Torontonians
could readily grasp — but was, rather, that intangible spirit of theatrical
excitement generated by those whose native customs permit the unabashed display of enthusiasm or displeasure. We had, we were told,
callously excluded the services of that indispensable component of grand

opera — the upper-balcony jeer leader. This view, disseminated in the local press, caused much consternation among my fellow citizens, an effect it would surely not have achieved in any other city. This is, of course, because Toronto is one of the last bastions of puritan influence in North America, and, despite the encroachment of science, Henry Miller, and immigration, we have managed to hold firm those convictions upon which the faith of our fathers was founded.

3   We do not regard the theatre as an intrinsically wicked institution; we do consider it in need of careful and constant scrutiny. But once we have satisfied ourselves as to the moral discernment of its productions, we proceed to it with a total humility born of reverence for that which we do not wholly understand. It would never have occurred to us to demand for ourselves the right to proclaim our approbation demonstratively by rudely punctuating a work of musical theatre. Even less would we presume, by forwarding uncomplimentary noises from the stalls, to express our distaste for the message of a composer which we found difficult or the hapless screechings of an ill-advised soprano.

4   This is not to say that we would withhold a measure of encouragement from an artist whose work and whose private life are beyond reproach. I have seen elderly ladies remove their gloves to render their tribute to the symphonies of Mr. Elgar — after all, he was well received at court, wasn't he? — and certainly our pleasure with Dr. Mendelssohn knows no bounds. And I can attest from personal experience that Torontonians are well able to convey their consternation at the beeps and groans of Mr. Anton Webern by a silence as timeless as those within that gentleman's music itself.

5   But now we were being told by this racy contingent of high-living newspapermen that we must surrender our right to the genteel response of our cultural tradition and look for leadership to those whose heritage does not consider musical theatre an adjunct of the church (as ours does) but rather as a comfortably upholstered extension of the Roman Colosseum. This has given me occasion to ponder the relationship of applause to musical culture, and I have come to the conclusion, most seriously, that the most efficacious step which could be taken in our culture today would be the gradual but total elimination of audience response.

6   I am disposed toward this view because I believe that the justification of art is the internal combustion it ignites in the hearts of men and not its shallow, externalized, public manifestations. The purpose of art is not the release of a momentary ejection of adrenaline but is, rather, the gradual, life-long construction of a state of wonder and serenity.

Through the ministrations of radio and the phonograph, we are rapidly and quite properly learning to appreciate the elements of aesthetic narcissism — and I use that word in its best sense — and are awakening to the challenge that each man contemplatively create his own divinity.

The effect of this newly acquired introspection has been salutary upon our culture as a whole. Never before have Ockeghem and Costeley invaded our drawing room in the company of Chopin and Liszt. Never before has Gesualdo competed with Schubert for our attention. Never before has a composer been able to render electronically the exact specifications of his intention without resorting to the self-centered affectations of a performing middleman. If, then, it has been possible to achieve within one generation this degree of conditioned listening, surely the next generation will find it no mighty task to carry this quality of introspection one step further — into the concert hall and theatre themselves.   7

There are those, of course, who counsel that only in the theatre, only with the direct communion of artist to listener, can we experience the high drama of human communication. The answer to this, it seems to me, is that art on its loftiest mission is scarcely human at all.   8

"But surely," some may counter, "applauding after a performance is as natural to a listener as sneezing at the sun on a windy day." I reply that one may listen to a recording of a Beethoven symphony alone or in the company of friends and, though deeply moved at its conclusion, experience no more urgent need than a quick trip to the icebox for a soda water. And if we concede, then, that it is the law of the heard that governs the response of an audience to a performer, can this response be further justified?   9

"Democracy, the rule of Majority," someone argues. "Why should the paying customer be deprived of the right to voice his opinion?" Well, apart from the fact that the other paying customers did not subscribe to hear his opinion, one must take into account the peculiar laws of acoustical psychology, whereby a strategically placed rooter or detractor may, by applying the proper vocal leverage at a judicious moment, enlist the bellowing echo of many hundreds of his fellows.   10

"But what harmful effect can it have?" someone asks. "Everybody knows that artists are incredibly conceited and quite able to survive the taunts of an impolite laity." Ah, are they indeed? I ask. Or are the absurdly competitive extravaganzas of our operatic colleagues not the product of, or maybe the antidote to, the vulgar artistic hostility of those sun-baked societies who have built an operatic tradition in which their   11 primal instinct for gladiatorial combat has found a more gracious but thinly disguised sublimation?

12   "All right," our disputant allows, "granted that a few of the less sturdy vocalists must concede in the fray, but what about the composers? Let's not forget that many of our great composers became famous by having more disorderly premieres than their colleagues were able to muster. Let's not forget Stravinsky and the riots at the *Rite* or Schoenberg and the pummelings at *Pierrot*." True, I retort, they did become famous, and they deserved to become famous, but not because of the riots and not even, I would venture to suggest, because of those particular works. A more just citation, if you will allow me, would be an incident at one of our own Toronto premieres − an incident which deeply shocked all true Torontonians. It happened several years ago, at the first performance of a new concerto by a Canadian composer, a lady of considerable gift, though perhaps of less resilient spirit than a Stravinsky or a Schoenberg. Preceding the performance, an introductory speaker (non-Torontonian) spoke harshly to us on the subject of apathy toward contemporary composition. He urged us, as only a non-Torontonian would, to express our approval of the works we enjoyed, or, if we were so inclined, our disapproval. Now, this adjuration would certainly have gone for naught but for the unlucky chance that in the audience that night there sat another non-Torontonian, a historian by profession and an intelligent chap, but a fellow whose musical sympathies stop somewhere short of Josquin des Prés. Well, as you can imagine, the new concerto did not fall upon receptive ears, and so our friend the historian, having been encouraged to voice his estimation, did so. Regrettably, he was being closely scrutinized at the time by some eager members of his graduate class (non-Torontonians all), who were seated nearby. And so "Hoot," said the professor, and "Hoot, hoot," said the students, while visions of better grades danced in their heads. I wish I could relate that the concerto and its composer became infamous that night, but such was not to be the case, and it has not been rendered since. There is, however, a sequel to the story. The lady composer had another premiere in Toronto quite recently − a new symphony. Our historian was not present, but nonetheless the new work was shown the same intolerance as its elder brother − the only work in our concert season to be so honored. Clearly, the herd is breeding.

13   "Aha," says the disputant in a final effort to demolish my case, "this fellow Gould speaks with a singular passion. Perhaps he, too, has been put to his heels to escape the wrath of an outraged public!" Yes, I ad-

mit candidly, there was such an occasion. It was in Florence, or, as we international men prefer to say, Firenze. I had just concluded a performance of the Schoenberg Suite, Op. 25, which, although it was at the time thirty-five years old, had not yet been admitted to the vocabulary of the Florentines. I arose from the instrument to be greeted by a most disagreeable chant from the upper balcony, which was at once contradicted by feverish encouragements from the lower levels. Although I was new to this experience, I instinctively realized that no harm could come to me so long as I permitted the spectators to vent their fury upon each other. Therefore, I cunningly milked the applause for six curtain calls (an exceptional acclaim for Op. 25), and, thereafter, the exhausted audience sat back in a liverish somnolence to attend the "Goldberg" Variations.

I feel that I have now presented my case with true candor, and so 14 it only remains to suggest ways and means to implement my proposal that the audience of the future should be seen but not heard. To this end, and for the assistance of any concert manager who may care to make use of it, I have drawn up the Gould Plan for the Abolition of Applause and Demonstrations of All Kinds, hereinafter referred to as GPAADAK. Needless to say, GPAADAK in its early stages will require, in addition to an active promotional campaign, a measure of goodwill on the part of artist, audience, and management alike.

The first step in instituting GPAADAK will be the scheduling of ap- 15 plauseless concerts on each Friday, Saturday, and Sunday. These three days, with their inherent liturgical connotations, are best able to evoke a suitably reverent state of mind. Concerts during the balance of the week, Monday to Thursday, could be billed as Family Excursion Events, if I may beg a term from the airlines. Reduced prices would apply, and, of course, applause would be permitted. Children would be encouraged to attend during the week, and the duty to guide them there would provide a convenient excuse for those of the older generation who found the conversion difficult. The performers, naturally, would be strictly second-team. At the prestige weekend concerts, the most serious problem in the early stage of GPAADAK will be the selection of appropriate repertoire — works which will most contribute to the overall solemnity. I would suggest that large-scale oratorios be tried first, followed, perhaps, by a series consisting of music composed by members of royal houses. There is a wide field here, and works such as the Piano Concerto in A by Louis Ferdinand of Prussia or the *Pastorale Cantata for Lady Augusta's Birthday* by Frederick Louis, Prince of Wales (and father, incidentally, of George III), deserve a firm place in our musical life. There might, of course, be certain judicious exclusions. Perhaps a composition by the Maharaja of Porbandar would not be appropriate for a Sunday concert in Karachi.

16   The next area of repertoire to be included in GPAADAK should be the presentation of ninth symphonies — anybody's Ninth Symphony, really, although Shostakovitch's might be a little flip — but, after exploring the Beethoven-Bruckner-Mahler parallel, it would be wise to conclude with Schubert's Ninth, since, being really his Seventh, it would introduce an appropriate note of secularism into the numerical piety of the series. I think that these few suggestions already indicate that the concert managers of the future will be under pressure to display an unaccustomed initiative in programming. Indeed, under the aegis of GPAADAK, many of these gentlemen may well advance from their present status as bookers and become worthy of the old and noble title of impresario.

17   In the early stages of GPAADAK, the performers may feel a moment of unaccustomed tension at the conclusion of their selection, when they must withdraw to the wings unescorted by the homage of their auditors. For orchestral players this should provide no hazard: a platoon of cellists smartly goose-stepping offstage is an inspiring sight. For the solo pianist, however, I would suggest a sort of lazy-Susan device which would transport him and his instrument to the wings without his having to rise. This would encourage performance of those sonatas which end on a note of serene reminiscence, and in which the lazy Susan could be set gently in motion some moments before the conclusion. I foresee a heavy run on Op. 109, which could almost be staged, provided there were a clear understanding between the soloist and the commissionaire backstage.

18   As the founder and chronicler of GPAADAK, I feel that it behooves me to be among the first to put it into practice. Needless to say, I have given this responsibility much consideration. Regrettably, Toronto does not provide the ideal site, since, apart from the fact that it needs GPAADAK less urgently than almost any other center, I personally would be confronted with the age-old civic antagonism for the local boy with a vision. It has occurred to me as a codirector of the Stratford Music Festival that the unique intimacy of our beautiful stage there might be especially appropriate for applauseless concerts, but then, those actors are such a wild, unpredictable bunch. Perhaps my chance will come at Mr. Tom Patterson's recently announced Dawson City Festival of

1962. Here indeed is virgin territory. Here is an audience without pre-judice, without preconception. I wonder how Diamond Lil would react to the Maharaja of Porbandar?

(1962)

The Writer's Subject

1. According to Gould, how did Torontonians receive the visit of the Metropolitan Opera to their new theatre? (para. 1)

2. What was the "grave alarm" sounded in the local press? (para. 2)

3. What attitudes to theatre, especially musical theatre, does Gould attribute to Torontonians? (paras. 3, 5)

4. Why does Gould suggest "total elimination of audience response"? (paras. 5-6)

5. How, according to Gould, has listening to music changed as a consequence of the development of the radio and the phonograph? (para. 7)

6. What objections does Gould anticipate from those who would not share his desire to ban applause? How does he answer these objections? (paras. 8-13)

7. What steps does Gould say are necessary if the "Gould Plan for the Abolition of Applause and Demonstrations of All Kinds" is to be implemented? (paras. 15-16)

8. Gould rejects Toronto as the place for the introduction of his Plan. Why? (para. 18)

9. How serious do you think Gould is in making this proposal?

The Writer's Style and Strategy

1. What is Gould's tone?

2. What features of the essay suggest that it was originally written for a music magazine?

3. How does Gould lead up to the presentation of his "Plan"?

4. What persona does Gould create for himself as the proposer of a plan to ban applause? At several points in the essay he draws attention to himself as a performing musician. What is his purpose in doing so?

5. What use does Gould make of the Toronto audience throughout his essay? How does he create the "character" of this audience?

6. What use does Gould make of relatively unpopular composers (e.g., Webern, Stravinsky, Schoenberg) or little-known early composers (e.g., Ockeghem, Costeley, Gesualdo, Josquin des Prés)? (paras. 4, 7, 12)

7. Choose two or three examples of inflated and ornate diction in this essay. What purposes are served by Gould's choices of words and phrasing?

8. Gould uses parallel structures for a variety of purposes. Choose one or two sentences with parallelism and explain the effects Gould achieves (e.g., "constructed in our behalf through the generosity, civic vision, and tax advantage of a local brewing firm," in paragraph 1; "despite the encroachment of science, Henry Miller, and immigration," in paragraph 2).

9. In what way is Gould's closing strategy like that of the projector in Swift's "A Modest Proposal"?

Suggested Topics for Writing and Discussion

1. Write a proposal (serious or otherwise) to ban some activity or behaviour which you find objectionable (e.g., dogs on public beaches, traffic in a congested area, "ghetto-blasters" in public places).

2. Gould suggests that the pleasure in listening to recorded music is possibly greater than that experienced in listening to music performed live. Do you agree?

3. Gould suggests that certain kinds of music are unlikely to elicit much applause from an audience (e.g., large-scale oratorios, music composed by members of royal houses). Write your own proposal for a programme of music you think would be boring or unlikely to please an audience. (Explain the audience you have in mind and the type of music least likely to please that audience.)

Where the World Began

by Margaret Laurence

A strange place it was, that place where the world began. A place of   1
incredible happenings, splendours and revelations, despairs like
multitudinous pits of isolated hells. A place of shadow-spookiness, inhabited by the unknowable dead. A place of jubilation and of mourn-
ing, horrible and beautiful.

It was, in fact, a small prairie town.   2

Because that settlement and that land were my first and for many years   3
only real knowledge of this planet, in some profound way they remain
my world, my way of viewing. My eyes were formed there. Towns
like ours, set in a sea of land, have been described thousands of times
as dull, bleak, flat, uninteresting. I have had it said to me that the railway
trip across Canada is spectacular, except for the prairies, when it would
be desirable to go to sleep for several days, until the ordeal is over.
I am always unable to argue this point effectively. All I can say is —
well, you really have to live there to know that country. The town of
my childhood could be called bizarre, agonizingly repressive or cruel
at times, and the land in which it grew could be called harsh in the
violence of its seasonal changes. But never merely flat or uninteresting.
Never dull.

In winter, we used to hitch rides on the back of the milk sleigh, our   4
moccasins squeaking and slithering on the hard rutted snow of the roads,
our hands in ice-bubbled mitts hanging onto the box edge of the sleigh
for dear life, while Bert grinned at us through his great frosted moustache
and shouted the horses into speed, daring us to stay put. Those mornings, rising, there would be the perpetual fascination of the frost feathers

on windows, the ferns and flowers and eerie faces traced there during
the night by unseen artists of the wind. Evenings, coming back from
skating, the sky would be black but not dark, for you could see a cold
glitter of stars from one side of the earth's rim to the other. And then
the sometime astonishment when you saw the Nothern Lights flaring
across the sky, like the scrawled signature of God. After a blizzard,
when the snowploughs hadn't yet got through, school would be closed
for the day, the assumption being that the town's young could not possibly
flounder through five feet of snow in the pursuit of education. We would
then gaily don snowshoes and flounder for miles out into the white dazzl-
ing deserts, in pursuit of a different kind of knowing. If you came back
too close to night, through the woods at the foot of the town hill, the
thin black branches of poplar and chokecherry now meringued with frost,
sometimes you heard coyotes. Or maybe the banshee wolf-voices were
really only inside your head.

5   Summers were scorching, and when no rain came and the wheat
became bleached and dried before it headed, the faces of farmers and
townsfolk would not smile much, and you took for granted, because
it never seemed to have been any different, the frequent knocking at
the back door and the young men standing there, mumbling or thrusting
defiantly their request for a drink of water and a sandwich if you could
spare it. They were riding the freights, and you never knew where they
had come from, or where they might end up, if anywhere. The Drought
and Depression were like evil deities which had been there always. You
understood and did not understand.

6   Yet the outside world had its continuing marvels. The poplar bluffs
and the small river were filled and surrounded with a zillion different
grasses, stones, and weed flowers. The meadowlarks sang undaunted
from the twanging telephone wires along the gravel highway. Once we
found an old flat-bottomed scow, and launched her, poling along the
shallow brown waters, mending her with wodges of hastily chewed
Spearmint, grounding her among the tangles of soft yellow marsh
marigolds that grew succulently along the banks of the shrunken river,
while the sun made our skins smell dusty-warm.

7   My best friend lived in an apartment above some stores on Main Street
(its real name was Mountain Avenue, goodness knows why), an elegant
apartment with royal-blue velvet curtains. The back roof, scarcely sloping at all, was corrugated tin, of a furnace-like warmth on a July afternoon, and we would sit there drinking lemonade and looking across
the back lane at the Fire Hall. Sometimes our vigil would be rewarded.

Oh joy! Somebody's house burning down! We had an almost-perfect callousness in some ways. Then the wooden tower's bronze bell would clonk and toll like a thousand speeded funerals in a time of plague, and in a few minutes the team of giant black horses would cannon forth, pulling the fire wagon like some scarlet chariot of the Goths, while the firemen clung with one hand, adjusting their helmets as they went.

The oddities of the place were endless. An elderly lady used to serve, **8** as her afternoon tea offering to other ladies, soda biscuits spread with peanut butter and topped with a whole marshmallow. Some considered this slightly eccentric, when compared with chopped egg sandwiches, and admittedly talked about her behind her back, but no one ever refused these delicacies or indicated to her that they thought she had slipped a cog. Another lady dyed her hair a bright and cheery orange, by strangers often mistaken at twenty paces for a feather hat. My own beloved stepmother wore a silver fox neckpiece, a whole pelt, *with the embalmed (?) head still on*. My Ontario Irish grandfather said, "sparrow grass," a more interesting term than asparagus. The town dump was known as "the nuisance grounds," a phrase fraught with weird connotations, as though the effluvia of our lives was beneath contempt but at the same time was subtly threatening to the determined and sometimes hysterical propriety of our ways.

Some oddities were, as idiom had it, "funny ha ha"; others were "funny **9** peculiar." Some were not so very funny at all. An old man lived, deranged, in a shack in the valley. Perhaps he wasn't even all that old, but to us he seemed a wild Methuselah figure, shambling among the underbrush and the tall couchgrass, muttering indecipherable curses or blessings, a prophet who had forgotten his prophesies. Everyone in town knew him, but no one knew him. He lived among us as though only occasionally and momentarily visible. The kids called him Andy Gump, and feared him. Some sought to prove their bravery by tormenting him. They were the medieval bear baiters, and he the lumbering bewildered bear, half blind, only rarely turning to snarl. Everything is to be found in a town like mine. Belsen, writ small but with the same ink.

All of us cast stones in one shape or another. In grade school, among **10** the vulnerable and violet girls we were, the feared and despised were those few older girls from what was charmingly termed "the wrong side of the tracks." Tough in talk and tougher in muscle, they were said to be whores already. And may have been, that being about the only profession readily available to them.

The dead lived in that place, too. Not only the grandparents who had, **11** in local parlance, "passed on" and who gloomed, bearded or bonneted, from the sepia photographs in old albums, but also the uncles, forever eighteen or nineteen, whose names were carved on the granite family stones in the cemetery, but whose bones lay in France. My own young mother lay in that graveyard, beside other dead of our kin, and when I was ten, my father, too, only forty, left the living town for the dead dwelling on the hill.

12   When I was eighteen, I couldn't wait to get out of that town, away from the prairies. I did not know then that I would carry the land and town all my life within my skull, that they would form the mainspring and source of the writing I was to do, wherever and however far away I might live.

13   This was my territory in the time of my youth, and in a sense my life since then has been an attempt to look at it, to come to terms with it. Stultifying to the mind it certainly could be, and sometimes was, but not to the imagination. It was many things, but it was never dull.

14   The same, I now see, could be said for Canada in general. Why on earth did generations of Canadians pretend to believe this country dull? We knew perfectly well it wasn't. Yet for so long we did not proclaim what we knew. If our upsurge of so-called nationalism seems odd or irrelevant to outsiders, and even to some of our own people *(what's all the fuss about?)*, they might try to understand that for many years we valued ourselves insufficiently, living as we did under the huge shadows of those two dominating figures, Uncle Sam and Britannia. We have only just begun to value ourselves, our land, our abilities. We have only just begun to recognize our legends and to give shape to our myths.

15   There are, God knows, enough aspects to deplore about this coun-try. When I see the killing of our lakes and rivers with industrial wastes, I feel rage and despair. When I see our industries and natural resources increasingly taken over by America, I feel an overwhelming discourage-ment, especially as I cannot simply say "damn Yankees." It should never be forgotten that it is we ourselves who have sold such a large amount of our birthright for a mess of plastic Progress. When I saw the War Measures Act being invoked in 1970, I lost forever the vestigial remains of the naive wish-belief that repression could not happen here, or would not. And yet, of course, I had known all along in the deepest and often hidden caves of the heart that anything can happen anywhere, for the seed of both man's freedom and his captivity are found everywhere, even in the microcosm of a prairie town. But in raging against our in-justices, our stupidities, I do so *as family*, as I did, and still do in writing,

about those aspects of my town which I hated and which are always in some ways aspects of myself.

The land still draws me more than other lands. I have lived in Africa 16 and in England, but splendid as both can be, they do not have the power to move me in the same way as, for example, that part of southern Ontario where I spent four months last summer in a cedar cabin beside a river. "Scratch a Canadian, and you find a phony pioneer," I used to say to myself in warning. But all the same it is true, I think, that we are not yet totally alienated from physical earth, and let us only pray we do not become so. I once thought that my lifelong fear and mistrust of cities made me a kind of old-fashioned freak; now I see it differently.

The cabin has a long window across its front western wall, and sit- 17 ting at the oak table there in the mornings, I used to look out at the river and at the tall trees beyond, green-gold in the early light. The river was bronze; the sun caught it strangely, reflecting upon its surface the near-shore sand ripples underneath. Suddenly, the crescenting of a fish, gone before the eye could clearly give image to it. The old man next door said these leaping fish were carp. Himself, he preferred muskie, for he was a real fisherman and the muskie gave him a fight. The wind most often blew from the south, and the river flowed toward the south, so when the water was wind-riffled, and the current was strong, the river seemed to be flowing both ways. I liked this, and interpreted it as an omen, a natural symbol.

A few years ago, when I was back in Winnipeg, I gave a talk at my 18 old college. It was open to the public, and afterward a very old man came up to me and asked me if my maiden name had been Wemyss. I said yes, thinking he might have known my father or my grandfather. But no. "When I was a young lad," he said, "I once worked for your great-grandfather, Robert Wemyss, when he had the sheep ranch at Raeburn." I think that was a moment when I realized all over again something of great importance to me. My long-ago families came from Scotland and Ireland, but in a sense that no longer mattered so much. My true roots were here.

I am not very patriotic, in the usual meaning of that word. I cannot 19 say "My country right or wrong" in any political, social or literary context. But one thing is inalterable, for better or worse, for life.

This is where my world began. A world which includes the ancestors 20 — both my own and other people's ancestors who became mine. A world which formed me, and continues to do so, even while I fought it in some of its aspects, and continue to do so. A world which gave me

my own lifework to do, because it was here that I learned the sight of
my own particular eyes.

(1971)

The Writer's Subject

1. On what grounds does Laurence reject the stereotypical description of
   the prairie as "dull, bleak, flat, uninteresting"?

2. In referring to the child's response to the Depression, Laurence says, "You
   understood and did not understand" (para. 5). Explain what she means
   by this statement.

3. What is revealed about small-town attitudes in Laurence's description of
   the town dump? (para. 8)

4. Why does Laurence say that she would carry the land and town within
   her all her life? (paras. 12-13)

5. What connections does Laurence perceive between small town prairie
   life and Canadian life on the national scale? (paras. 14-15)

6. Why is Laurence drawn so strongly to "the land"?

7. Suggest possible interpretations of what Laurence calls "a natural symbol,"
   the river's flowing both ways. (para. 17)

8. What does Laurence mean by "patriotic, in the usual meaning of that word"?
   (para. 19)

9. Why is the essay entitled "Where the World Began" (and not "Where My
   World Began," for example)?

The Writer's Style and Strategy

1. Why does Laurence begin her description of a small prairie town with a series of fragments?

2. The second paragraph consists of only one sentence. Why?

3. How does Laurence make the reader see the prairie winter through a child's eyes? (para. 4)

4. How does Laurence recreate the romantic excitement the child felt at the prospect of a fire? Where is the consciousness of the writer as adult apparent? (para. 7)

5. Discuss the shift in tone at the end of paragraph 9. How is this shift achieved? What is its purpose?

6. How does Laurence achieve the transition from a discussion of mistaken perceptions of the prairie town and the land to a discussion of perceptions of Canada?

7. Why does Laurence describe the small prairie town as a microcosm? (para. 15)

8. There are obvious similarities between the opening and concluding paragraphs. What are these similarities? What are the differences?

Suggestions for Writing and Discussion

1. Where did your world begin? Write an essay introducing and explaining what you believe to be the beginnings of your particular world.

2. Margaret Laurence writes about a very personal place that carries special significance for her. Describe a place that has particular significance for you and explain its importance.

3. Laurence suggests that Canada is commonly viewed as dull. Defend Canada — or your region — against this common view.

4. Laurence writes with obvious pleasure of the adventures of childhood in winter and in summer. If you could return to childhood, what season would you choose, and why?

Writing Short Stories
by Flannery O'Connor

1   I have heard people say that the short story was one of the most difficult literary forms, and I've always tried to decide why people feel
this way about what seems to me to be one of the most natural and fundamental ways of human expression. After all, you begin to hear and
tell stories when you're a child, and there doesn't seem to be anything
very complicated about it. I suspect that most of you have been telling
stories all your lives, and yet here you sit — come to find out how to
do it.

2   Then last week, after I had written down some of these serene thoughts
to use here today, my calm was shattered when I was sent seven of
your manuscripts to read.

3   After this experience, I found myself ready to admit, if not that the
short story is one of the most difficult literary forms, at least that it
is more difficult for some than for others.

4   I still suspect that most people start out with some kind of ability to
tell a story but that it gets lost along the way. Of course, the ability
to create life with words is essentially a gift. If you have it in the first
place, you can develop it; if you don't have it, you might as well forget it.

5   But I have found that the people who don't have it are frequently the
ones hell-bent on writing stories. I'm sure anyway that they are the ones
who write the books and the magazine articles on how-to-write-short-
stories. I have a friend who is taking a correspondence course in this
subject, and she has passed a few of the chapter headings on to me -
such as, "The Story Formula for Writers," "How to Create Characters,"
"Let's Plot!" This form of corruption is costing her twenty-seven dollars.

I feel that discussing story-writing in terms of plot, character, and   6
theme is like trying to describe the expression on a face by saying where
the eyes, nose, and mouth are. I've heard students say, "I'm very good
with plot, but I can't do a thing with character," or, "I have this theme
but I don't have a plot for it," and once I heard one say, "I've got the
story but I don't have any technique."

Technique is a word they all trot out. I talked to a writers' club once,   7
and during the question time, one good soul said, "Will you give me
the technique for the frame-within-a-frame short story?" I had to admit
I was so ignorant I didn't even know what that was, but she assured
me there was such a thing because she had entered a contest to write
one and the prize was fifty dollars.

But setting aside the people who have no talent for it, there are others   8
who do have the talent but who flounder around because they don't really
know what a story is.

I suppose that obvious things are the hardest to define. Everybody   9
thinks he knows what a story is. But if you ask a beginning student
to write a story, you're liable to get almost anything — a reminiscence,
an episode, an opinion, an anecdote, anything under the sun but a story.
A story is a complete dramatic action — and in good stories, the
characters are shown through the action and the action is controlled
through the characters, and the result of this is meaning that derives
from the whole presented experience. I myself prefer to say that a story
is a dramatic event that involves a person because he is a person, and
a particular person — that is, because he shares in the general human
condition and in some specific human situation. A story always involves,
in a dramatic way, the mystery of personality. I lent some stories to
a country lady who lives down the road from me, and when she returned them, she said, "Well, them stories just gone and shown you
how some folks *would* do," and I thought to myself that that was right;
when you write stories, you have to be content to start exactly there
— showing how some specific folks *will* do, *will* do in spite of everything.

Now this is a very humble level to have to begin on, and most people   10
who think they want to write stories are not willing to start there. They
want to write about problems, not people; or about abstract issues, not
concrete situations. They have an idea, or a feeling, or an overflowing
ego, or they want to Be A Writer, or they want to give their wisdom
to the world in a simple-enough way for the world to be able to absorb
it. In any case, they don't have a story and they wouldn't be willing
to write it if they did; and in the absence of a story, they set out to

find a theory or a formula or a technique.

11   Now none of this is to say that when you write a story, you are supposed to forget or give up any moral position that you hold. Your beliefs
will be the light by which you see, but they will not be what you see
and they will not be a substitute for seeing. For the writer of fiction,
everything has its testing point in the eye, and the eye is an organ that
eventually involves the whole personality, and as much of the world
as can be got into it. It involves judgment. Judgment is something that
begins in the act of vision, and when it does not, or when it becomes
separated from vision, then a confusion exists in the mind which transfers
itself to the story.

12   Fiction operates through the senses, and I think one reason that people
find it so difficult to write stories is that they forget how much time
and patience is required to convince through the senses. No reader who
doesn't actually experience, who isn't made to feel the story is going
to believe anything the fiction writer merely tells him. The first and
most obvious characteristic of fiction is that it deals with reality through
what can be seen, heard, smelt, tasted, and touched.

13   Now this is something that can't be learned only in the head; it has
to be learned in the habits. It has to become a way that you habitually
look at things. The fiction writer has to realize that he can't create compassion with compassion, or emotion with emotion, or thought with
thought. He has to provide all these things with a body; he has to create
a world with weight and extension.

14   I have found that the stories of beginning writers usually bristle with
emotion, but *whose* emotion is often very hard to determine. Dialogue
frequently proceeds without the assistance of any characters that you
can actually see, and uncontained thought leaks out of every corner of
the story. The reason is usually that the student is wholly interested
in his thoughts and his emotions and not in his dramatic action, and
that he is too lazy or highfalutin to descend to the concrete where fiction operates. He thinks that judgment exists in one place and sense-
impression in another. But for the fiction writer, judgment begins in
the details he sees and how he sees them.

15   Fiction writers who are not concerned with these concrete details are
guilty of what Henry James called "weak specification." The eye will
glide over their words while the attention goes to sleep. Ford Madox
Ford taught that you couldn't have a man appear long enough to sell
a newspaper in a story unless you put him there with enough detail to
make the reader see him.

I have a friend who is taking acting classes in New York from a Rus- **16** sian lady who is supposed to be very good at teaching actors. My friend wrote me that the first month they didn't speak a line, they only learned to see. Now learning to see is the basis for learning all the arts except music. I know a good many fiction writers who paint, not because they're any good at painting, but because it helps their writing. It forces them to look at things. Fiction writing is very seldom a matter of saying things; it is a matter of showing things.

However, to say that fiction proceeds by use of detail does not mean **17** the simple, mechanical piling-up of detail. Detail has to be controlled by some overall purpose, and every detail has to be put to work for you. Art is selective. What is there is essential and creates movement.

Now all this requires time. A good short story should not have less **18** meaning than a novel, nor should its action be less complete. Nothing essential to the main experience can be left out of a short story. All the action has to be satisfactorily accounted for in terms of motivation, and there has to be a beginning, a middle, and an end, though not necessarily in that order. I think many people decide that they want to write short stories because they're short, and by short, they mean short in every way. They think that a short story is an incomplete action in which a very little is shown and a great deal suggested, and they think you suggest something by leaving it out. It's very hard to disabuse a student of this notion, because he thinks that when he leaves something out, he's being subtle; and when you tell him that he has to put something in before anything can be there, he thinks you're an insensitive idiot.

Perhaps the central question to be considered in any discussion of **19** the short story is what do we mean by short. Being short does not mean being slight. A short story should be long in depth and should give us an experience of meaning. I have an aunt who thinks that nothing happens in a story unless somebody gets married or shot at the end of it. I wrote a story about a tramp who marries an old woman's idiot daughter in order to acquire the old woman's automobile. After the marriage, he takes the daughter off on a wedding trip in the automobile and abandons her in an eating place and drives on by himself. Now that is a complete story. There is nothing more relating to the mystery of that man's personality that could be shown through that particular dramatization. But I've never been able to convince my aunt that it's a complete story. She wants to know what happened to the idiot daughter after that.

Not long ago that story was adapted for a television play, and the **20** adapter, knowing his business, had the tramp have a change of heart and go back and pick up the idiot daughter and the two of them ride away, grinning madly. My aunt believes that the story is complete at last, but I have other sentiments about it — which are not suitable for public utterance. When you write a story, you only have to write one story, but there will always be people who will refuse to read the story you have written.

21   And this naturally brings up the awful question of what kind of a reader you are writing for when you write fiction. Perhaps we each think we have a personal solution for this problem. For my own part, I have a very high opinion of the art of fiction and a very low opinion of what is called the "average" reader. I tell myself that I can't escape him, that this is the personality I am supposed to keep awake, but that at the same time, I am also supposed to provide the intelligent reader with the deeper experience that he looks for in fiction. Now actually, both of these readers are just aspects of the writer's own personality, and in the last analysis, the only reader he can know anything about is himself. We all write at our own level of understanding, but it is the peculiar characteristic of fiction that its literal surface can be made to yield entertainment on an obvious physical plane to one sort of reader while the selfsame surface can be made to yield meaning to the person equipped to experience it there.

22   Meaning is what keeps the short story from being short. I prefer to talk about the meaning in a story rather than the theme of a story. People talk about the theme of a story as if the theme were like the string that a sack of chicken feed is tied with. They think that if you can pick out the theme, the way you pick the right thread in the chicken-feed sack, you can rip the story open and feed the chickens. But this is not the way meaning works in fiction.

23   When you can state the theme of a story, when you can separate it from the story itself, then you can be sure the story is not a very good one. The meaning of a story has to be embodied in it, has to be made concrete in it. A story is a way to say something that can't be said any other way, and it takes every word in the story to say what the meaning is. You tell a story because a statement would be inadequate. When anybody asks what a story is about, the only proper thing is to tell him to read the story. The meaning of fiction is not abstract meaning but experienced meaning, and the purpose of making statements about the meaning of a story is only to help you to experience that meaning more fully.

24   Fiction is an art that calls for the strictest attention to the real — whether

the writer is writing a naturalistic story or a fantasy. I mean that we always begin with what is or with what has an eminent possibility of truth about it. Even when one writes a fantasy, reality is the proper basis of it. A thing is fantastic because it is so real, so real that it is fantastic. Graham Greene has said that he can't write, "I stood over a bottomless pit," because that couldn't be true, or "Running down the stairs I jumped into a taxi," because that couldn't be true either. But Elizabeth Bowen can write about one of her characters that "she snatched at her hair as if she heard something in it," because that is eminently possible.

I would even go so far as to say that the person writing a fantasy **25** has to be even more strictly attentive to the concrete detail than someone writing in a naturalistic vein — because the greater the story's strain on the credulity, the more convincing the properties in it have to be.

A good example of this is a story called "The Metamorphosis" by **26** Franz Kafka. This is a story about a man who wakes up one morning to find that he has turned into a cockroach overnight, while not discarding his human nature. The rest of the story concerns his life and feelings and eventual death as an insect with human nature, and this situation is accepted by the reader because the concrete detail of the story is absolutely convincing. The fact is that this story describes the dual nature of man in such a realistic fashion that it is almost unbearable. The truth is not distorted here, but rather, a certain distortion is used to get at the truth. If we admit, as we must, that appearance is not the same thing as reality, then we must give the artist the liberty to make certain rearrangements of nature if these will lead to greater depths of vision. The artist himself always has to remember that what he is rearranging *is* nature, and that he has to know it and be able to describe it accurately in order to have the authority to rearrange it at all.

The peculiar problem of the short-story writer is how to make the **27** action he describes reveal as much of the mystery of existence as possible. He has only a short spacc to do it in and he can't do it by statement. He has to do it by showing, not by saying, and by showing the concrete — so that his problem is really how to make the concrete work double time for him.

In good fiction, certain of the details will tend to accumulate mean- **28** ing from the action of the story itself, and when this happens they become symbolic in the way they work. I once wrote a story called "Good Country People," in which a lady Ph.D. has her wooden leg stolen by a Bible salesman whom she has tried to seduce. Now I'll admit that, paraphrased in this way, the situation is simply a low joke. The average reader is pleased to observe anybody's wooden leg being stolen. But without ceasing to appeal to him and without making any statements of high intention, this story does manage to operate at another level of experience, by letting the wooden leg accumulate meaning. Early in the story, we're presented with the fact that the Ph.D. is spiritually as well as physically crippled. She believes in nothing but her own belief in nothing, and we perceive that there is a wooden part of her soul that corresponds to her wooden leg. Now of course this is never stated. The fiction writer states as little as possible. The reader makes this connection from things he is shown. He may not even know that he makes the connection, but the connection is there nevertheless and it has its effect on him. As the story goes on, the wooden leg continues to accumulate meaning. The reader learns how the girl feels about her leg, how her mother feels about it, and how the country woman on the place feels about it; and finally, by the time the Bible salesman comes along, the leg has accumulated so much meaning that it is, as the saying goes, loaded. And when the Bible salesman steals it, the reader realizes that he has taken away part of the girl's personality and has revealed her deeper affliction to her for the first time.

29   If you want to say that the wooden leg is a symbol, you can say that. But it is a wooden leg first, and as a wooden leg it is absolutely necessary to the story. It has its place on the literal level of the story, but it operates in depth as well as on the surface. It increases the story in every direction, and this is essentially the way a story escapes being short.

30   Now a little might be said about the way in which this happens. I wouldn't want you to think that in that story I sat down and said, "I am now going to write a story about a Ph.D. with a wooden leg, using the wooden leg as a symbol for another kind of affliction." I doubt myself if many writers know what they are going to do when they start out. When I started writing that story, I didn't know there was going to be a Ph.D. with a wooden leg. As the story progressed, I brought in the Bible salesman, but I had no idea what I was going to do with him. I didn't know he was going to steal that wooden leg until ten or twelve lines before he did it, but when I found out that this was what was going to happen, I realized that it was inevitable. This is a story that produces a shock for the reader, and I think one reason for this is that it produced a shock for the writer.

31   Now despite the fact that this story came about in this seemingly mindless fashion, it is a story that almost no rewriting was done on. It

is a story that was under control throughout the writing of it, and it might be asked how this kind of control comes about, since it is not entirely conscious.

I think the answer to this is what Maritain calls "the habit of art." 32 It is a fact that fiction writing is something in which the whole personality takes part — the conscious as well as the unconscious mind. Art is the habit of the artist; and habits have to be rooted deep in the whole personality. They have to be cultivated like any other habit, over a long period of time, by experience; and teaching any kind of writing is largely a matter of helping the student develop the habit of art. I think this is more than just discipline, although it is that; I think it is a way of looking at the created world and of using the senses so as to make them find as much meaning as possible in things.

Now I am not so naive as to suppose that most people come to writers' 33 conferences in order to hear what kind of vision is necessary to write stories that will become a permanent part of our literature. Even if you do wish to hear this, your greatest concerns are immediately practical. You want to know how you can actually write a good story, and further, how you can tell when you've done it; and so want to know what the form of a short story is, as if the form were something that existed outside of each story and could be applied or imposed on the material. Of course, the more you write, the more you will realize that the form is organic, that it is something that grows out of the material, that the form of each story is unique. A story that is any good can't be reduced, it can only be expanded. A story is good when you continue to see more and more in it, and when it continues to escape you. In fiction two and two is always more than four.

The only way, I think, to learn to write short stories is to write them, 34 and then to try to discover what you have done. The time to think of technique is when you've actually got the story in front of you. The teacher can help the student by looking at his individual work and trying to help him decide if he has written a complete story, one in which the action fully illuminates the meaning.

Perhaps the most profitable thing I can do is to tell you about some 35 of the general observations I made about these seven stories I read of yours. All of these observations will not fit any one of the stories exactly, but they are points neverthless that it won't hurt anyone interested in writing to think about.

The first thing that any professional writer is conscious of in reading 36 anything is, naturally, the use of language. Now the use of language in these stories was such that, with one exception, it would be difficult to distinguish one story from another. While I can recall running into several clichés, I can't remember one image or one metaphor from the seven stories. I don't mean there weren't images in them; I just mean that there weren't any that were effective enough to take away with you.

37   In connection with this, I made another observation that startled me considerably. With the exception of one story, there was practically no use made of the local idiom. Now this is a Southern Writers' Conference. All the addresses on these stories were from Georgia or Tennessee, yet there was no distinctive sense of Southern life in them. A few place-names were dropped, Savannah or Atlanta or Jacksonville, but these could just as easily have been changed to Pittsburgh or Passaic without calling for any other alteration in the story. The characters spoke as if they had never heard any kind of language except what came out of a television set. This indicates that something is way out of focus.

38   There are two qualities that make fiction. One is the sense of mystery and the other is the sense of manners. You get manners from the texture of existence that surrounds you. The great advantage of being a Southern writer is that we don't have to go anywhere to look for manners; bad or good, we've got them in abundance. We in the South live in a society that is rich in contradiction, rich in irony, rich in contrast, and particularly rich in its speech. And yet here are six stories by Southerners in which almost no use is made of the gifts of the region.

39   Of course the reason for this may be that you have seen these gifts abused so often that you have become self-conscious about using them. There is nothing worse than the writer who doesn't *use* the gifts of the region, but wallows in them. Everything becomes so Southern that it's sickening, so local that it is unintelligible, so literally reproduced that it conveys nothing. The general gets lost in the particular instead of being shown through it.

40   However, when the life that actually surrounds us is totally ignored, when our patterns of speech are absolutely overlooked, then something is out of kilter. The writer should then ask himself if he is not reaching out for a kind of life that is artificial to him.

41   An idiom characterizes a society, and when you ignore the idiom, you are very likely ignoring the whole social fabric that could make a meaningful character. You can't cut characters off from their society and say much about them as individuals. You can't say anything meaningful about the mystery of a personality unless you put that personality in a believable and significant social context. And the best way to

do this is through the character's own language. When the old lady in one of Andrew Lytle's stories says contemptuously that she has a mule that is older than Birmingham, we get in that one sentence a sense of a society, and its history. A great deal of the Southern writer's work is done for him before he begins, because our history lives in our talk. In one of Eudora Welty's stories a character says, "Where I come from, we use fox for yard dogs and owls for chickens, but we sing true." Now there is a whole book in that one sentence; and when the people of your section can talk like that, and you ignore it, you're just not taking advantage of what's yours. The sound of our talk is too definite to be discarded with impunity, and if the writer tries to get rid of it, he is liable to destroy the better part of his creative power.

Another thing I observed about these stories is that most of them don't 42 go very far inside a character, don't reveal very much of the character. I don't mean that they don't enter the character's mind, but they simply don't show that he has a personality. Again this goes back partly to speech. These characters have no distinctive speech to reveal themselves with; and sometimes you feel in the end that no personality is revealed because no personality is there. In most good stories it is the character's personality that creates the action of the story. In most of these stories, I feel that the writer has thought of some action and then scrounged up a character to perform it. You will usually be more successful if you start the other way around. If you start with a real personality, a real character, then something is bound to happen; and you don't have to know what before you begin. In fact it may be better if you don't know what before you begin. You ought to be able to discover something from your stories. If you don't, probably nobody else will.

(1957)

The Writer's Subject

1. What is O'Connor's view of books or courses on the techniques of writing short stories? (paras. 5-7)

2. What does O'Connor mean by the statement that a story involves "the mystery of personality"? (para. 9) (Note her use of this phrase in paras. 19 and 41.)

3. What does O'Connor mean by saying that the writer must "create a world with weight and extension"? (para. 13) How does she show that this is to be accomplished? (paras. 12-16).

4. In paragraphs 19-20 O'Connor describes one of her stories which was adapted for television. What disturbed her about the adaptation? What did the adapter fail to recognize?

5. What distinction does O'Connor draw between "meaning" and "theme" in the discussion of short stories? (paras. 22-23)

6. Why, according to O'Connor, must the writer pay "the strictest attention to the real" even if the story is a fantasy? How does she illustrate this assertion? (paras. 24-26)

7. Summarize O'Connor's explanation in paragraphs 28 and 29 of the creation and function of symbols in a short story.

8. What does O'Connor mean by the statement, "In fiction two and two is always more than four"? (para. 33)

9. What importance does O'Connor attach to the use of local idioms by fictional characters? How does she illustrate her point by reference to the stories submitted to her? (paras. 36-41)

10. What, finally, are O'Connor's criteria for a good short story?

The Writer's Style and Strategy

1. O'Connor's essay was written to be delivered as an address to a Southern Writers' Conference. Pick out details that reflect O'Connor's awareness of her audience, and show how she adapts her material to the interests of that audience. Pay particular attention to diction, sentence patterns, and the use of personal pronouns.

2. Discuss O'Connor's use of anecdote and personal detail as a means of developing her ideas.

3. A definition may be arrived at through negation. Where does O'Connor use negation as well as positive assertion to explain what constitutes a good short story? Discuss some of the ways in which she offers her definition.

4. Discuss the opening and the closing of this essay. At what point does the writer move from her introduction to the body of her discussion? What is she attempting to do in the introduction? Does the last paragraph form a fitting conclusion to the essay?

Topics for Writing and Discussion

1. Choose a good short story, preferably one discussed in your class, and discuss whether it meets O'Connor's criteria for the successful depiction of character.

2. O'Connor maintains that the writer of fantasy must be "even more attentive to the concrete detail than someone writing in a naturalistic vein — because the greater the story's strain on the credulity, the more convincing the properties in it have to be." (para. 25) Choose a work of science fiction or fantasy, and discuss the writer's use of concrete details.

3. Use your college or local library to find a book intended to teach would-be authors how to write fiction. Discuss the organization and content of the book in light of O'Connor's criticism in paragraphs 5-7.

4. Using O'Connor's suggestions about creating character, write a character sketch of a close friend or a member of your family.

An Unquiet Awakening
by Mordecai Richler

1   Reading was not one of my boyhood passions. Girls, or rather the absence of girls, drove me to it. When I was 13 years old, short for my age, more than somewhat pimply, I was terrified of girls. They made me feel sadly inadequate.

2   Retreating into high seriousness, I acquired a pipe, which I chewed on ostentatiously, and made it my business to be seen everywhere, even at school basketball games, absorbed by books of daunting significance. The two women who ran the lending library, possibly amused by my pretensions, tried to interest me in fiction.

3   "I want fact. I can't be bothered with stories," I protested, waving my pipe at them affronted, "I just haven't got the time for such nonsense."

4   Novels, I knew, were mere romantic make-believe, not as bad as poetry, to be fair, but bad enough.

5   I fell ill with a childhood disease, I no longer remember which, but obviously I meant it as a rebuke to those girls in tight sweaters who continued to ignore me. Never mind, they would mourn at my funeral, burying me with my pipe. Too late, they would say, "Boy, was he ever an intellectual."

6   The women from the lending library, concerned, dropped off books for me at our house. The real stuff. Fact-filled. Providing me with the inside dope on Theodore Herzl's childhood and *Brazil Yesterday, Today, and Tomorrow.*

7   One day they brought me a novel: *All Quiet on the Western Front* by Erich Maria Remarque. The painting on the jacket that was taped to the book showed a soldier wearing what was unmistakably a Ger-

man Army helmet. What was this, I wondered, some sort of bad joke?

Nineteen forty-four that was, and I devoutly wished every German **8** left on the face of the earth an excruciating death. The Allied invasion of France had not yet begun, but I cheered every Russian counterattack, each German city bombed, and — with the help of a map tacked to my bedroom wall — followed the progress of the Canadian troops fighting their way up the Italian boot. Boys from our street had already been among the fallen. Izzy Draper's uncle. Harvey Kegelmass' older brother. The boy who was supposed to marry Gita Holtzman.

All Quiet on the Western Front lay unopened on my bed for two days. **9** Finally, I was driven to picking it up out of boredom. I never expected that a mere novel, a stranger's tale, could actually be dangerous, creating such turbulence in my life, obliging me to question so many received ideas. About Germans. About my own monumental ignorance of the world. About what novels were.

At the age of 13 in 1944, happily as yet untainted by English 104, **10** I couldn't tell you whether Remarque's novel was

a. a slice of life
b. symbolic
c. psychological
d. seminal.

I couldn't even say if it was well or badly written. In fact, as I recall, it didn't seem to be "written" at all. Instead, it just flowed. Now, of course, I understand that writing that doesn't advertise itself is art of a very high order. It doesn't come easily. But at the time I wasn't capable of making such distinctions. I also had no notion of how *All Quiet on the Western Front* rated critically as a war novel. I hadn't read Stendhal or Tolstoy or Crane or Hemingway. I hadn't even heard of them. I didn't know that Thomas Mann, whoever he was, had praised the novel highly. Neither did I know that in 1929 the judges at some outfit called the Book-of-the-Month Club had made it their May selection.

But what I did know is that, hating Germans with a passion, I had **11** read only 20, maybe 30, pages before the author had seduced me into identifying with my enemy, 19-year-old Paul Baumer, thrust into the bloody trenches of the First World War with his schoolmates: Muller, Kemmerich and the reluctant Joseph Behm, one of the first to fall. As if that weren't sufficiently unsettling in itself, the author, having won my love for Paul, my enormous concern for his survival, then betrayed me in the last dreadful paragraphs of his book:

"He fell in October 1918, on a day that was so quiet and still on the **12**

whole front, that the army report confined itself to the single sentence:
All Quiet on the Western Front.

13   "He had fallen forward and lay on the earth as though sleeping. Turning him over one saw that he could not have suffered long; his face
had an expression of calm, as though almost glad the end had come."

14   The movies, I knew from experience, never risked letting you down
like that. No matter how bloody the battle, how long the odds, Errol
Flynn, Robert Taylor, even Humphrey Bogart could be counted on to
survive and come home to Ann Sheridan, Lana Turner or − if they
were sensitive types − Loretta Young. Only character actors, usually
Brooklyn Dodger fans, say George Tobias or William Bendix, were
expendable.

15   Obviously, having waded into the pool of serious fiction by accident,
I was not sure I liked or trusted the water. It was too deep. Anything
could happen.

16   There was something else, a minor incident in *All Quiet on the Western
Front* that would not have troubled an adult reader but, I'm embarrassed
to say, certainly distressed that 13-year-old boy colliding with his first
serious novel:

17   Sent out to guard a village that has been abandoned because it is being
shelled too heavily, Katczinsky, the incomparable scrounger, surfaces
with suckling pigs and potatoes and carrots for his comrades, a group
of eight altogether:

18   "The suckling pigs are slaughtered, Kat sees to them. We want to
make potato cakes to go with the roast. But we cannot find a grater
for the potatoes. However, that difficulty is soon over. With a nail we
punch a lot of holes in a pot lid and there we have a grater. Three fellows
put on thick gloves to protect their fingers against the grater, two others
peel the potatoes, and business gets going."

19   The business, I realized, alarmed − not affronted − was the making
of potato latkes, a favorite of mine as well as Paul Baumer's, a dish
I had always taken to be Jewish, certainly not a German concoction.

20   What did I know? Nothing. Or, looked at another way, my real education, my life-long addiction to fiction, began with the trifling discovery
that the potato latke was not of Jewish origin, but something borrowed
from the German and now a taste that Jew and German shared in spite
of everything.

21   I felt easier about my affection for the German soldier Paul Baumer
once I was told by the women from the lending library that when Hitler
came to power in 1933 he had burned all of Erich Maria Remarque's

books and in 1938 he took away his German citizenship. Obviously Hitler had grasped that novels could be dangerous, something I learned when I was only 13 years old. He burned them; I began to devour them. I started to read at the breakfast table and on streetcars, often missing my stop, and in bed with benefit of a flashlight. It got me into trouble.

I grasped, for the first time, that I didn't live in the centre of the world 22 but had been born into a working-class family in an unimportant country far from the cities of light: London, Paris, New York. Of course this wasn't my fault, it was my inconsiderate parents who were to blame. But there was, I now realized, a larger world out there beyond St. Urbain Street in Montreal.

Preparing myself for the Rive Gauche, I bought a blue beret, but I 23 didn't wear it outside, or even in the house if anybody else was at home. I looked at but lacked the courage to buy a cigarette holder.

As my parents bickered at the supper table, trapped in concerns now 24 far too mundane for the likes of me — what to do if Dworkin raised the rent again, how to manage my brother's college fees — I sat with but actually apart from them in the kitchen, enthralled, reading for the first time, "All happy families are alike but an unhappy family is unhappy after its own fashion."[1]

Erich Maria Remarque, born in Westphalia in 1897, went off to war, 25 directly from school, at the age of 18. He was wounded five times. He lost all his friends. After the war he worked briefly as a schoolteacher, a stonecutter, a test driver for a tire company and an editor of Sportbild magazine. His first novel, *Im Westen Nichts Neues,* was turned down by several publishers before it was brought out by the Ullstein Press in Berlin in 1928. *All Quiet on the Western Front* sold 1.2 million copies in Germany and was translated in 29 languages, selling some four million copies throughout the world. The novel has been filmed three times; the first time, memorably by Lewis Milestone in 1930. The Milestone version, with Lew Ayres playing Paul Baumer, won Academy Awards for best picture and best direction.

Since *All Quiet on the Western Front* once meant so much to me, 26 I picked it up again with a certain anxiety. After all this time, I find it difficult to be objective about the novel. Its pages still evoke for me a back bedroom with a cracked ceiling and a sizzling radiator on St. Urbain Street: mice scrabbling in the walls, and a window looking out on the sheets frozen stiff on the laundry line.

Over the years the novel has lost something in shock value. The 27 original jacket copy of the 1929 Little, Brown & Company edition of

1. The opening sentence of *Anna Karenina* by Leo Tolstoy.

All Quiet on the Western Front warns the reader that it is "at times crude" and "will shock the supersensitive by its outspokenness." Contemporary readers, far from being shocked, will be amused by the novel's discretion, the absence of explicit sex scenes, the unbelievably polite dialogue of the men in the trenches.

28   The novel also has its poignant moments, both in the trenches and when Paul Baumer goes home on leave, an old man of 19, only to find insufferably pompous schoolmasters still recruiting the young with mindless prattle about the fatherland and the glory of battle. Strong characters are deftly sketched. Himmelstoss, the postman who becomes a crazed drillmaster. Tjaden, the peasant soldier. Kantorek, the schoolmaster.

29   On the front line the enemy is never the Frogs or the Limeys, but the insanity of the war itself. It is the war, in fact, and not even Paul Baumer, that is the novel's true protagonist. In a brief introduction to the novel Remarque wrote: "This book is to be neither an accusation nor a confession, and least of all an adventure, for death is not an adventure to those who stand face to face with it. It will try simply to tell of a generation of men who, even though they may have escaped its shells, were destroyed by the war."

30   Since the First World War we have become altogether too familiar with larger horrors. The Holocaust, Hiroshima, the threat of a nuclear winter. Death by numbers, cities obliterated by decree. At peace, as it were, we live the daily dread of the missiles in their silos, ours pointed at them, theirs pointed at us. None of this, however, diminishes the power of *All Quiet on the Western Front,* a novel that will endure because of its humanity, its honor and its refusal to lapse into sentimentality or strike a false note.

                                                                      (1986)

The Writer's Subject

1. What was Richler's attitude to novels before he had read *All Quiet on the Western Front*? What *did* he read, and why? (paras. 1-6)

2. Why did the young Richler react with anger when Remarque's novel was first lent to him? (paras. 7-8)

3. Why did Richler feel betrayed by "the last dreadful paragraphs" of the novel? Why had he expected a different ending? (paras. 11-15)

4. Why was Richler so distressed by the episode describing the making of potato cakes? (paras. 18-21)

5. Why does Richler twice use the word "dangerous" in connection with the reading of novels? (paras. 9, 21)

6. How did his reading of *All Quiet on the Western Front* change Richler's view of his own life? Why did he prepare himself for the "Rive Gauche" (the Left Bank, an area in Paris associated with the bohemian life)? (paras. 22-24)

7. Why, in Richler's view, has the novel lost something of its original "shock value"? What makes it, nevertheless, a work that will endure? (paras. 27-30)

The Writer's Style and Strategy

1. Discuss the appropriateness of the essay's title.

2. The essay was adapted from an introduction to a new edition of *All Quiet on the Western Front*. What elements of the essay reflect that function? What might the reader expect to find in the introduction to a reprinted novel?

3. Spending the first six paragraphs on his own conduct, Richler does not mention Remarque's novel until the seventh paragraph. What is Richler's purpose in adopting this strategy?

4. What is Richler burlesqueing in paragraph 10? What is the function of the paragraph in its context?

5. Discuss Richler's use of direct quotation from the novel and from its author's introduction. Why did he choose the passages he quotes?

6. What differences in tone are evident between the essay's opening section and its conclusion? Relate the shift in tone to the shape of Richler's essay.

Suggested Topics for Writing and Discussion

1. *All Quiet on the Western Front,* both as a novel and as a film, presents a powerful indictment of the waste and insanity of war. Choose another novel or film that seems to you to have a similar intention, and assess its treatment of the subject.

2. Richler feels that Remarque's novel may have lost some of its "shock value" for modern readers. Do you agree with his view that events in modern history may have hardened us to horror? Have film, literature, and the media made us more aware of the horrors of war and violence, or have they somehow dulled our moral and emotional responses?

3. Richler claims that Remarque's novel began the process of his "real education." From your own reading experience, select a work of literature that you found memorable, and attempt to account for its impact on you.

4. Richler was deeply affected by the ending of Remarque's novel, noting that it had shown him a picture of reality very different from what he had previously encountered in war movies. How faithfully, in your view, does the modern war movie reflect the reality of war?

The Historian's Opportunity
by Barbara Tuchman

Given the current decline of the novel and the parallel decline of poetry   1
and the drama, public interest has turned toward the literature of actuality. It may be that in a time of widening uncertainty and chronic
stress the historian's voice is the most needed, the more so as others
seem inadequate, often absurd. While the reasons may be argued, the
opportunity, I think, is plain for the historian to become the major interpreter in literary experience of man's role in society. The task is his
to provide both the matter to satisfy the public interest and those insights into the human condition without which any reading matter is
vapid.

Historians have performed this role before. Although we have no   2
figures on readership in classical Greece and Rome, it is evident from
their continuers and imitators and from later references that Herodotus,
Thucydides and Xenophon, Tacitus, Polybius, Josephus, Plutarch, Livy,
and the others were significant voices to their contemporaries. Since
the outbreak of World War II the statistics of the book trade reflect
the growing appetite of the public for biography, autobiography, science,
sociology, and history — especially contemporary history.

The last category, as we have lately been made rather tiresomely   3
aware, has its special problems, although in the long tradition of authorized biography a subject's family has usually found quieter means than
legal recourse for retaining control over personal matters. The simple
way to keep private affairs private is not to talk about them — to the
authorized, or even the "hired," writer.

I do not cite as evidence of the public interest in the literature of ac-   4 tuality the fact that since 1964 nonfiction, so called, has outsold fiction by two to one, because that merely reflects the mass buying of cookbooks and peace-of-mind books (the two front runners), plus voyeur books — that is, the sex life of everybody else — cartoon books, and how-to books on baby care, home decorating, curing arthritis, counting calories, golf, etiquette, and that recent sleeper, avoiding probate. Non-books aside, by whatever criterion you use — number of titles published and book-club choices, hardcovers and paperbacks, new titles and reprints — the categories concerned with reality all show greater increases than fiction.

5   People are turning to the books of reality for a truer image of man and society than is offered by contemporary novels. To look for the reason why fictional truth has gone askew is part of the historian's task. The novelists' failure is a consequence, I believe, of the historical experience of the twentieth century, which since the First World War has been one of man's cumulative disillusionment in himself. The idea of progress was the greatest casualty of that war, and its aftermath was cynicism, confirmed by a second round of world conflict and by the implications of the Nazis' gas chambers. Then the advent into man's hands of unlimited lethal power has been topped by the frightening pressure of overpopulation, so that now we live under the weight of a weird paradox which threatens us simultaneously with too many people in the world and too much power to destroy them. Finally, we are faced with mounting evidence — in pollution of air and water, in destruction of the balance of nature, in the coming ear-shattering boom of supersonic flight — that we cannot refrain from despoiling our environment.

6   The experience has been enough to destroy in many of our generation their inherited belief in human goodness. Gilbert Murray found the same despair of the world overtaking the Greeks after their own period of prolonged internecine warfare and ascribed it to a sense of "the pressure of forces that man could not control or understand."

7   Man in the twentieth century is not a creature to be envied. Formerly he believed himself created by the divine spark. Now, bereft of that proud confidence, and contemplating his recent record and present problems, he can no longer, like the Psalmist, respect himself as "a little lower than the angels." He cannot picture himself today, as Michelangelo did on the Sistine ceiling, in the calm and noble image of Adam receiving the spark from the finger of God. Overtaken by doubt of human purpose and divine purpose, he doubts his capacity to be good or even to survive. He has lost certainty, including moral and ethical certainty,

and is left with a sense of footloose purposelessness and self-disgust which literature naturally reflects. The result is what the *Times Literary Supplement* has named the "Ugh" school of fiction.

Writers who dislike their fellow men have taken over the literary 8 world. The mainstream of their work is epitomized by the recent novel advertised as an "engrossing" treatment of "more or less random adventures touching on thievery, homosexuality, pimping, sadism, voyeurism, a gang bang." Unaccountably, drug addiction was missing. As we all know, this is not exceptional, but run-of-the-mill, and the drama, in the dreary examples that reach the stage today, does its best to keep pace. The preferred characters of current fiction are the drifters and derelicts of life in whose affairs or ultimate fate it is impossible to sustain interest. They do not excite the question that is the heart of narrative — "What happens next?" — because one cannot care what happens to them.

Perhaps the fault is not in the novelists but in the times that their 9 characters are underlings; anti-heroes who reflect a general sense of man as victim. Perhaps the novelist today cannot honestly create a protagonist who is master of his fate and captain of his soul because man in the image of Henley seems obsolete. That man belonged to the self-confident nineteenth century, whereas the twentieth finds its exponent in losers, "beautiful losers" according to the title of a recent novel, although few seem to deserve the adjective. Oedipus was a loser and so was King Lear, but their losing was universal and profound, not pointless.

Since fiction and drama no longer present a true balance of human 10 activity and motive, it is not to be wondered that they are losing their audience. According to a recent report from the capital, "Official Washington does not read contemporary novels" for the reason given by a sub-Cabinet officer in these words: "I try to read them and give up. Why should I spend my time on [books] . . . where the central character spends 350 pages quivering about whether to cross the street or go to the toilet?"

He has a point. Reading, which is to say writing, is the greatest gift 11 with which man has endowed himself, by whose means we may soar on unlimited voyages. Are we to spend it picking through the garbage of humanity? Certainly the squalid and worthless, the mean and depraved are part of the human story just as dregs are part of wine, but the wine is what counts. Sexual perversion and hallucinatory drugs, as Eliot Fremont-Smith said of a recent novel, "are not what drives us, not what human history is about."

12   The task then devolves upon historians to tell what human history *is* about and what are the forces that *do* drive us. That is not to say that history excludes the squalid and depraved, but, being concerned as it is with reality and subject as it is to certain disciplines, it deals with these in proportion to the whole.

13   Historians start with a great advantage over fiction in that our characters, being public, are invested with power to affect destiny. They are the captain and kings, saints and fanatics, traitors, rogues and villains, pathfinders and explorers, thinkers and creators, even, occasionally, heroes. They are significant — if not necessarily admirable. They may be evil or corrupt or mad or stupid or even stuffed shirts, but at least, by virtue of circumstance or chance or office or character, they *matter*. They are the actors, not the acted upon, and are consequently that much more interesting.

14   Readers want to see man shaping his destiny or, at least, struggling with it, and this is the stuff of history. They want to know how things happened, why they happened, and particularly what they themselves have lived through, just as after a record heat or heavy snow the first thing one turns to in the morning paper is the account of yesterday's weather. And now more than ever, when man's place in the world has never been so subject to question, when "alienation" is the prevailing word, the public also hopes to find some guidelines to destiny, some pattern or meaning to our presence on this whirling globe. Whether or not, as individuals, historians believe in one pattern or another, or some of us in none, the evidence we have to present provides reassurance in showing that man has gone through his dark ages before.

15   When I was a young parent a series of books appeared on child behavior by Dr. Arnold Gesell and his associates of the Yale Clinic in which one discovered that the most aberrant, disturbing, or apparently psychotic behavior of one's own child turned out to be the common age pattern of the group innocently disporting itself behind Dr. Gesell's one-way observation screen. Nothing was ever so comforting. Historians provide a one-way screen on the past through which one can see man, at one time or another, committing every horror, indecency, or idiocy that he is capable of today. It is all already on his record, in kind if not in degree. I do not suggest that history can be as comforting as Gesell because the difference in degree that we face today is so great — in the speed and impact of the mechanisms we have created — that problems and dangers multiply faster than we can devise solutions. Henry

Adams' law of acceleration is proving perilously true. Nevertheless, Adams' law is one of those guidelines historians have to offer. The story and study of the past, both recent and distant, will not reveal the future, but it flashes beacon lights along the way and it is a useful nostrum against despair.

Historians cannot expect to take over the leading role in literature **16** without competition. Last summer Albert Rosenfeld, science editor of *Life*, wrote in an editorial that creative writers must turn to science to revive literature because "That is where the action is." There is a relevant and challenging truth in his statement. Science is formidably relevant and dynamic. "Great writing in any age," Rosenfeld continued, "casts some illumination on the major contemporary dilemmas." That is equally cogent. If science can evoke great creative writers who will do for space aeronautics or genetics or nuclear energy what Rachel Carson, for example, did for the sea around us, they will certainly win a large share of the public interest. The chief obstacle is language. Great writing in science must come from inside the discipline, and everything will depend on the rare talent which can break through the meshes of a technical vocabulary and express itself in words of common usage.

Here, too, we have a head start. Historians can — though not all do **17** — make themselves understood in everyday English, the language in use from Chaucer to Churchill. Let us beware of the plight of our colleagues, the behavioral scientists, who by use of a prolifering jargon have painted themselves into a corner — or isolation ward — of unintelligibility. *They* know what they mean, but no one else does. Psychologists and sociologists are the farthest gone in the disease and probably incurable. Their condition might be pitied if one did not suspect it was deliberate. Their retreat into the arcane is meant to set them apart from the great unlearned, to mark their possession of some unshared, unsharable expertise. No matter how illuminating their discoveries, if the behavioral scientists write only to be understood by one another, they must come to the end of the Mandarins.

Communication, after all, is what language was invented for. If history **18** is to share its insights with a public in need of them, it must practice communication as an art, as Gibbon did, or Parkman. History has, of course, other parts; like that other famous property, it is divisible into three: the investigative or research, the didactic or theory, and the narrated or communication. The elements that enter into communication are what I want to discuss, because history, it seems to me, is nothing if not communicated. Research provides the material, and theory a pattern of thought, but it is through communication that history is heard and understood.

19   At the risk of stating the obvious, it is worth remarking that success of communication depends upon the charm (I use the word in its most serious sense) of the narrative. "Writings are useless," declared Theodore Roosevelt, speaking as president of the American Historical Association in 1912, "unless they are read, and they cannot be read unless they are readable."

20   The history most successfully communicated, as far as the public is concerned, can in one sense be determined by the annual lists of the top best-sellers. Up to 1960 the all-time best-seller in history was H. G. Wells's *Outline of History,* first published in 1921, which stayed among the top ten for three years in a row and reappeared on the list in a cheaper edition in 1930. It is the only book of history up to 1960 to have sold more than two million copies — more, oddly enough, than *The Kinsey Report.* Since then the leading work in history has been William L. Shirer's *Rise and Fall of the Third Reich*, which has sold, at last report, close to three million copies in the United States alone.

21   These names suggest what the evidence confirms: During the 1920s and 1930s, when serious books had a better chance of reaching the top ten, the best-sellers in historical biography and straight history (as distinct from personal history and current events) included four academics, James Harvey Robinson, Charles Beard, Carl Van Doren, and James Truslow Adams three times over; and twelve non-academics, Emil Ludwig with four books, Hendrik van Loon with three, Lytton Strachey, Claude Bowers, Van Wyck Brooks, Andre Maurois, Francis Hackett, Stefan Zweig with two each, Will Durant, Frederick Lewis Allen, Margaret Leech, and Douglas Southall Freeman with one each. During the 1940s, when the war books took over, one academic, Arnold Toynbee (with his one-volume condensation) and one non-academic, Catherine Drinker Bowen, made the top ten. After that, except for Shirer and Frederic Morton's *The Rothchilds*, the swamping effect of the non-books begins and one has to look just beneath the top ten to the books which have been best-sellers during the course of the year without making the final list. Taking only the 1960s, these included three academics, Garrett Mattingly, Samuel Eliot Morison, Arthur Schlesinger, Jr., and nine independent writers, Winston Churchill, Bruce Catton, Alan Moorehead, Thomas Costain, Walter Lord, Cecil Woodham-Smith, and myself with two or more books each, Stewart Holbrook and George Kennan each with one.

To be a best-seller is not necessarily a measure of quality, but it *is*   22
a measure of communication. That the independent writers have done
better is hardly surprising, since communicating is their business; they
know how. To capture and hold the interest of an audience is their object, as it has been that of every storyteller since Homer. Perhaps the
academic historian suffers from having a captive audience, first in the
supervisor of his dissertation, then in the lecture hall. Keeping the reader
turning the page has not been his primary concern.

My intention is not to exacerbate the distinction between the profes-   23
sional historian and the so-called amateur but to clarify its terms. "Professional" — meaning someone who has had graduate training leading
to a professional degree and who practices within a university — is a
valid term, but "amateur" — used to mean someone outside the university without a graduate degree — is a misnomer. Graduate training certainly establishes a difference of which I, who did not have it, am deeply
aware, sometimes regretfully, sometimes thankfully. But I would prefer
to recognize the difference by distinguishing between academics and
independents, or between scholars and writers, rather than between professionals and amateurs, because the question is not one of degree of
professionalism but which profession. The faculty people are professional historians, we outside are professional writers. Insofar as they
borrow our function and we borrow their subject, each of us has a great
deal to learn from the other.

An objection often made to the independents is that they are insuffi-   24
ciently acquainted or careless with the facts. An extreme case is the
Cortez of Keats, staring at the Pacific with a wild surmise, silent upon
a peak in Darien. Keats, of course, got the name wrong but the idea
right. Through the power of marvelous phrasing and the exercise of
a poet's imagination he immortalized a historic moment. It is possible
that his vision of the man on the peak is more important, for conveying
history, than the name of the man. Poets aside, historians of course
should offer both. There is no need to choose between accuracy and
beauty; one should be clothed in the other.

In pockets of survival there may be some historians who still retain   25
the old notion imposed by scientific history that, as another president
of the American Historical Association, Walter Prescott Webb, put it,
"There is something historically naughty about good writing," that "a
great gulf exists between truth and beauty and the scholar who attempts
to bridge it deserves to fall in and drown," and that "the real scholar
must choose truth and somehow it is better if it is made so ugly that

nobody could doubt its virginity." If some still believe this, communication is not for them.

26   For the first element in communication, Webb gave the perfect triple criterion: a writer's belief that he has something to say, that it is worth saying, and that he can say it better than anyone else — and, he added, "not for the few but for the many." For coupled with compulsion to write must go desire to be read. No writing comes alive unless the writer sees across his desk a reader, and searches constantly for the word or phrase which will carry the image he wants the reader to see and arouse the emotion he wants him to feel. Without consciousness of a live reader, what a man writes will die on his page. Macaulay was a master of this contact with the reader. His sister Hannah cried when he read the *History of England* aloud to her. What writer could ask for more?

27   When it comes to content, inspiration, what Webb calls the moment of synthesis — the revealing flash of a synthesizing idea — is obviously a help. Webb describes his own moment of insight when the idea came to him that the emergence of Americans from the life of the forests to the life of the plains was of dramatic significance. Admiral Mahan had his moment when, from the study of Hannibal's failure to control sea communication with Carthage, the idea flashed on him of the influence of sea power on history. The moment is exciting but not, I think, essential. A theme may do as well to begin with as a thesis and does not involve, like the overriding theory, a creeping temptation to adjust the facts. The integrating idea or insight then evolves from the internal logic of the material, in the course of putting it together. From the gathering of the particulars one arrives at the general, at that shining grail we are all in search of, the historical generalization. To state it in advance does not seem necessary to me. The process is more persuasive and the integrating idea more convincing if the reader discovers it for himself out of the evidence laid before him.

28   All theses run the risk of obsolescence. The pathways of history, said the great historian of the frontier, Frederick Jackson Turner, are "strewn with the wrecks" of once known and acknowledged truths, discarded by a later generation. Revision and counter-revision roll against the shores of history as rhythmically as waves. Even so, a true inspiration or integrating idea such as Mahan's or Turner's will be valid and enlightening for its time, regardless of subsequent fortune.

29   Though some will debate it, intuition, too, is an aid. The intuitive historian can reach an understanding of long-past circumstance in much the same way as Democritus, the predecessor of Aristotle, arrived at

the idea of the atom. His mind, mulling over observed phenomena, worked out a theory of matter as composed of an infinite number of mobile particles. The process may have been cerebral, but its impetus was intuitive. Strict disciples of history as a science may scorn the intuitive process, but that attitude comes from being more Catholic than the Pope. True scientists know its value. It is an arrow shot into the air, which will often pierce the same target that the scientific historian with his nose on the ground will take months to reach on foot.

Of all the historian's instruments, belief in the grandeur of his theme   30
is the most compelling. Parkman, in his preface to *Montcalm and Wolfe*, describes his subject, the Seven Years' War in the American theater, as "the most momentous and far-reaching question ever brought to issue on this continent." Its outcome determined that there would be an American Revolution. "With it began a new chapter in the annals of the world." That is the way an author should feel about his subject. It ensures that no reader can put the book down.

Enthusiasm, which is not quite the same thing, has a no less leaven-   31
ing effect. It was recognized by Admiral Mahan, who, in the course of studying Britain's contest with Napoleon, developed a particular admiration for Pitt. "His steadfast nature," Mahan wrote, "aroused in me an enthusiasm which I did not seek to check; for I believe enthusiasm no bad spirit in which to realize history to yourself and to others."

Mahan's prescription disposes of the myth of "pure objectivity" when   32
used to mean "without bias." As John Gunther once said of journalism, "A reporter with no bias at all would be a vegetable." If such a thing as a "purely objective" historian could exist, his work would be unreadable − like eating sawdust. Bias is only misleading when it is concealed. After reading *The Proud Tower*, a onetime member of the Asquith government scolded me in a letter for misrepresenting as he thought, his party. "Your bias against the Liberals sticks out," he wrcte. I replied that it was better to have it stick out than be hidden. It can then be taken into account. I cannot deny that I acquired a distaste for Mr. Asquith as, for other reasons, I did for Henry Adams. There are some people in history one simply dislikes, and as long as they are not around to have their feelings hurt, I see no reason to conceal it. To take no sides in history would be as false as to take no sides in life.

A historian tries to be objective in the sense of learning as much as   33
possible, and presenting as sympathetically as possible the motives and conditions of both sides, because to do so makes the drama more intense − and more believable. But let us not pretend that this is being

without bias — as if historians were mere recorders who have given
up the exercise of judgment. Bias means a *leaning* which *is* the exercise of judgment as well as a source of insight. Admittedly, it is usually helped by emotional conditioning, but that is what makes for commitment. The great historians more often than not have been passionately
committed to a cause or a protagonist, as Mommsen was to Julius Caesar
or Michelet to the glorious power of the people.

34   How commitment can generate insight and heighten communication
is nowhere better shown than in G.M. Trevelyan's *Garibaldi and the
Thousand*, one of the finest works of history, I think, both for investigation and narrative, produced in this century. Trevelyan's commitment
to his hero is explicit. Describing the foot track from the Villa Spinola
down to the embarkation point in Genoa, he writes in a footnote, "I
had the honor of going down it" with a veteran of the Thousand. There
is no doubt where he stands. His feeling of personal involvement led
Trevelyan to visit every place connected with the Garibaldini, to walk
in their footsteps, to interview those still living, until he knew the persons,
terrain, view, sounds, smells, sights, distances, weather — in short,
the feel — of every scene of action he was to write about.

35   As the Thousand marched to the Battle of Calatafimi, Trevelyan writes,
"Their hearts were light with the sense that they were enviable above
all Italians, that their unique campaign was poetry made real." The quality
of emotion here is not, as so often, created out of the historian's feelings and foisted onto his characters, but drawn from the evidence. A
footnote gives the original from a letter of one of the Garibaldini to
his mother telling her, "*Questa spedizione è così poetica.*" ("This expedition is a poetical thing.") Approaching the battle, they pass through
a green valley at early morning. "In the bloom of the early Sicilian
summer," Trevelyan writes, "the vale fresh from last night's rain, and
sung over by the nightingale at dawn, lay ready to exhale its odors to
the rising sun. Nature seemed in tune with the hearts of Garibaldi and
his men." Here, too he worked from evidence in diaries and letters that
it had rained the night before and that the nightingale had sung. In these
two passages he has conveyed the sense of miraculous freshness and
noble enterprise which the Garibaldi expedition signalized for the liberal
spirit of the nineteenth century. He could accomplish this, first, because
of his quick sensitivity to source material, and second, because he himself
was in tune with the hearts of Garibaldi and his men.

36   Again, when Garibaldi's bugler blew reveille, "the unexpected music
rang through the noonday stillness like a summons to the soul of Italy."

In the verb of sound, "rang," the reader hears the bugle and in the phrase "like the summons to the soul of Italy" feels the emotion of the listener. Without knowing that he is being told, he has learned the meaning to history of the expedition.

To visit the scene before writing, even the scene of long-dead adven- 37 tures, is, as it were, to start business with money in the bank. It was said of Arthur Waley, the great Orientalist who died a few months ago, that he had never visited Asia, explaining that he was content with the ideal image of the East in his imagination. For a historian that would be a risky position. On the terrain motives become clear, reasons and explanations and origins of things emerge that might otherwise have remained obscure. As a source of understanding, not to mention as a corrective for fixed ideas and mistaken notions, nothing is more valuable than knowing the scene in person, and, even more so, living the life that belongs to it, Without that intimacy Francis Parkman would not have been the master he was.

Parkman's hero was really the forest. Through experience he learn- 38 ed passion for it, and fear, and understood both its savagery and beauty. In those long days of intermittent blindness when he was not allowed to write, his mind must have worked over remembered visions of the forest so that they come through on the page with extra clarity. As a scout paddles across the lake in autumn, "the mossed rocks double in the watery mirror" and sumachs on the shore glow like rubies against the dark green spruce. Or the frontier settler, returning at evening, sees a "column of blue smoke rising quietly in the still evening air" and runs to find the smoldering logs of his cabin and the scalped bodies of his murdered wife and children.

Vision, knowledge, experience will not make a great writer without 39 that extra command of language which becomes their voice. This, too, was Parkman's. When the English are about to descend the rapids of the upper St. Lawrence, they look on the river whose "reckless surges dashed and bounded in the sun, beautiful and terrible as young tigers at play." In choice of verbs and nouns and images that is a masterpiece. It is only physical description, to be sure, not a great thought, but it takes perfect command of words to express great thoughts in the event one has them.

Steeped in the documents he spent his life collecting, as he was steeped 40 in the forest, Parkman understood the hardship and endurance, grim energy, and implacable combat that underlay the founding of the American nation. He knew the different groups of combatants as if he had lived with each, and could write with equal sympathy of French or Indians, English or colonials. Consider his seventeenth-century French courtiers, "the butterflies of Versailles...facing death with careless gallantry, in their small three-cornered hats, powdered perukes, embroidered coats, and lace ruffles. Their valets served them with ices in the trenches, under the cannon of besieged towns." In this case the ices in the trenches is a specimen of the historian's selective insight at work. He has chosen a vivid item to represent a larger whole. It distills an era and a culture in a detail.

41   Distillation is selection, and selection, as I am hardly the first to affirm, is the essence of writing history. It is the cardinal process of composition, the most difficult, the most delicate, the most fraught with error as well as art. Ability to distinguish what is significant from what is insignificant is *sine qua non*.[1] Failure to do so means that the point of the story, not to mention the reader's interest, becomes lost in a morass of undifferentiated matter. What it requires is simply the courage and self-confidence to make choices and, above all, to leave things out.

42   In history as in painting, wrote the great stylist Macaulay, to put in everything achieves a less, rather than a more, truthful result. The best picture and best history, he said, are those "which exhibit such parts of the truth as most nearly produce the effect of the whole." This is such an obvious rule that it is puzzling why so many historians today seem to practice a reverse trend toward total inclusion. Perhaps the reason is timidity: fear of being criticized for having left something out, or, by injudicious selection, of not conforming to the dominant thesis of the moment. Here the independent writer has an advantage over the professional historian: He need not be afraid of the outstuck neck.

43   Finally, the historian cannot do without imagination. Parkman, intense as always in his effort to make the reader "feel the situation," chose to picture the land between the Hudson and Montreal as it would look to a wild goose flying northward in spring. He sees the blue line of the river, the dark mass of forests and shimmer of lakes, the geometric lines and mounds of man-made forts, "with the flag of the Bourbons like a flickering white speck" marking Ticonderoga, and the "mountain wilderness of the Adirondacks like a stormy sea congealed." On reading that passage I feel the excitement of the Count of Monte Cristo when he opened the treasure chest. It would not be remarkable for one of us who has traveled in airplanes to think of the device of the bird's-eye view, but Parkman had never been off the ground. It was a pure effort of imagination to put himself behind the eye of the goose, to see

1. sine qua non: "without which, nothing"

the flag as a flickering white speck and the mountains, in that perfect phrase, as "a stormy sea congealed."

Great as this is, the more necessary use of imagination is in applica- **44** tion to human behavior and to the action of circumstance on motive. It becomes a deliberate effort at empathy, essential if one is to understand and interpret the actions of historical figures. With antipathetic characters it is all the more necessary. The historian must put himself inside them, as Parkman put himself inside the wild goose, or as I tried to do inside Sir John French in an effort to understand the draining away of his will to fight. As soon as the effort was made, the explanation offered itself. I could feel the oppression, the weight of responsibility, the consciousness of the absence of any trained reserves to take the place of the BEF if it were lost.[2] The effort to get inside is, obviously enough, a path to insight. It is the *Einfühlung* that Herder demanded of historians: the effort to "feel oneself into everything." The interpreter of the Hebrew scriptures, as he put it, must be "a shepherd with shepherds, a peasant in the midst of an agricultural people, an oriental with the primitive dwellers of the East."

To describe the historian's task today in terms of narrative history **45** and two romantic practitioners, Parkman and Trevelyan, will seem old-fashioned at a time when interdisciplinary techniques, and horizontal subjects such as demography, and the computerized mechanics of quantification are the areas of fresh endeavor. These are methods of research, not of communication, for one reason because the people who use them tend to lose contact with ordinary language; they have caught the jargon disease. Their efforts are directed, I take it, toward uncovering underlying patterns in history and human behavior which presumably might help in understanding the past and managing the future, or even the present. Whether quantification will reveal anything which could not have been discerned by deduction is not yet clear. What seems to be missing in the studies that I have seen is a certain element of common sense.

The new techniques will, I am sure, turn up suggestive material and **46** open avenues of thought, but they will not, I think, transform history into a science, and they can never make it literature. Events happen: but to become history they must be communicated and understood. For that, history heeds writers − preferably great writers − a Trevelyan who can find and understand the *cosi poetica* in a soldier's letter and make the right use of it, a Parkman who can see and feel, and report with Shakespeare's gift of words; both, I need not add, assemblers of

2. BEF − British Expeditionary Force of World War I, headed in 1914 by Sir John French. Tuchman is referring in this paragraph to her Pulizer prize winning book, *The Guns of August*.

their own primary material. To be a really great historian, Macaulay said, "is the rarest of intellectual distinctions." For all who try, the opportunity is now and the audience awaits.

(1967)

The Writer's Subject

1. What does Tuchman mean by "the literature of actuality"? (paras. 1-4)

2. What cause and effect relation does Tuchman draw between "man's cumulative disillusionment in himself" (para. 5) and the state of contemporary fiction and drama? Why, in her view, are fiction and drama losing their audience? (paras. 5-11)

3. How, according to Tuchman, does the historian take account of "the squalid and worthless" differently from the contemporary novelist? (paras. 11-12)

4. How may the historian, in Tuchman's view, offer reassurance to the modern reader disturbed by the problems of contemporary life? (paras. 14-15)

5. What contrast does Tuchman draw between the writing of historians and that of behavioural scientists? (para. 17)

6. Why, in Tuchman's view, have the independent, non-academic historical writers been more successful with the reading public than the professional, academic historians? (paras. 20-24)

7. What are the most important attributes for a good historian, according to Tuchman? (paras. 26-44)

8. What is Tuchman's response to the idea that a historian should be completely objective and without bias? (paras. 32-33)

9. What qualities does Tuchman admire in the historians G.M. Trevelyan and Francis Parkman? (paras. 34-40)

10. What does Tuchman mean in asserting that "selection . . . is the essence of writing history"? (paras. 41-42)

11. What importance does Tuchman ascribe to the historian's ability to empathize with historical figures? (para. 44)

12. Of what value are computers and statistical approaches to the study of history, in Tuchman's view? (para. 45)

The Writer's Style and Strategy

1. How does Tuchman's title reflect her purposes in this essay?

2. What is Tuchman's thesis, and where is it most clearly stated?

3. What evidence does the essay provide of its origin as an address to the American Historical Association? What assumptions does Tuchman make about her audience?

4. Tuchman observes that the study of the past can throw light upon the present. Where does she exemplify this principle in the course of her discussion?

5. Show how Tuchman uses the works of other historians to illustrate the principles of good historical writing.

6. Tuchman alludes to W.E. Henley's poem "Invictus" (para. 9) and Keats's poem "On First Looking into Chapman's Homer" (para. 24). Look up the poems, and discuss the appropriateness of Tuchman's references to them for her argumentative purposes.

7. Tuchman believes that historians should "make themselves understood in everyday English" (para. 17). What qualities of "everyday English" does Tuchman's own writing display? Choose one or two paragraphs for the purpose of your analysis.

Suggested Topics for Writing and Discussion

1. Find a work of history by a noted historian of the nineteenth or twentieth century. Choose two or three pages for analysis and indicate whether the writer, in your opinion, exhibits the qualities that Tuchman maintains are needed for good historical writing.

2. Tuchman, writing this essay in 1967, says that most works of literature of the time were characterized by "the squalid and the worthless, the mean and depraved." Choose any well-known work of imaginative literature written in the last twenty years and indicate whether the work fits the generalized pattern described by Tuchman.

3. Tuchman says: "To be a best-seller is not necessarily a measure of quality, but it *is* a measure of communication." Consult a bestseller list in a national magazine or newspaper to locate a work of non-fiction which has been on the list for several months. Find two or three reviews of the book and report on its capacity to "communicate" its subject.

Influences

by Guy Vanderhaeghe

It was only after I published a book that I was forced to consider the question of influence on my writing. Until that point I had merely written. But reviewers made me aware of the problem of influence, drawing as they did convincing parallels between my short stories and the work of writers I had never read. Interviewers, too, were keen to unearth literary debts. Which writers and books, they asked, had most influenced me?   **1**

It was a question I wanted to answer honestly. But I was not sure I could. For one thing I had the impression I was really being asked which books and writers I admired most, asked that in the certainty that the answer to both questions was the same. That might be so, but isn't necessarily. *Ulysses,* for instance, is one of those universally admired works which has influenced writers less than one would think. *Remembrance of Things Past* is another.   **2**

What I was coming to suspect was that literary influences are more various and varied than I had imagined. In my case, the threads of these influences resolved themselves into a Gordian knot which stubbornly resisted all my efforts to untangle it. For instance, when asked to produce a list of those authors whom I particularly admired I was inevitably struck by the heterogeneity of the list I compiled. I could not but help imagine these authors incongruously yoked in conversation at literary cocktail parties. Flannery O'Connor and Anthony Powell? Christopher Isherwood and Rudy Wiebe? Alice Munro and Evelyn Waugh?   **3**

I could not see how these converging vectors of probable influence had shaped my writing. Worse, I felt I was suppressing another, perhaps   **4** equally important list of names. Names such as Zane Grey, Walter Scott, John Buchan, and Robert Louis Stevenson came immediately to mind. Yet I was afraid of being thought facetious if I gave these writers the nod of acknowledgement.

5   It was only when I read Vladimir Nabokov's autobiography *Speak, Memory* that I seriously began to define and elaborate a dim suspicion I had been harbouring: that "bad" writing is as influential in the development of a writer as "good" writing. A brief reference of Nabokov's to an article he had read as a child in the *Boy's Own Paper* strengthened that suspicion because it helped carry me back, back beyond my first acquaintance with Zane Grey, Stevenson, Buchan, and Scott, back to my earliest reading, to my introduction to the *Boy's Own Annual.*

6   During Nabokov's Edwardian childhood the *Boy's Own Paper* was one of those bellicose boys' magazines which tub-thumped for the British Empire and the "right little, tight little Island!" It may seem strange that such a paper found its way into the Nabokov home, but Vladimir Nabokov's father was a wealthy anglophile who insisted on English governesses, governesses who, in turn, insisted that their little Russian charges read and write English before they read and write Russian. Thus the *Boy's Own Paper.*

7   All this smacks a bit of Alice in Wonderland. There is surely something absurd in the notion of a young Russian aristocrat, citizen of a xenophobe empire, reading, in English, the rival claims to glory of a competing xenophobe empire. The only thing possibly more absurd is that almost exactly fifty years later, in 1957 or thereabouts, I was poring over a like-minded publication, the *Boy's Own Annual.* My volume too was Edwardian, an issue that Nabokov might conceivably have read on dark St. Petersburg winter evenings, a book that had lost its covers and was coming apart in my hands and which I, at the age of six, took to be a reasonably accurate account of the world outside my bailiwick. No one told me that the fabulous world described in its pages had expired in the mud of Flanders more than forty years before.

8   Or perhaps it was just that I refused not to believe in what I was reading. In any case, I held on to the illusion for something like three years before it evaporated. During that time I confined my reading basically to two books (aside from the insipid things assigned in school) and those books were an old school text of my mother's, *A History of the World,* and the previously mentioned volume of the *Boy's Own Annual.* In the beginning I found *A History of the World* the more intriguing because of its illustrations: photographs of antiquities such as

Mycenaean daggers and Etruscan coins, and reproductions of "historical" paintings which showed Egyptian charioteers dramatically dying, transfixed by Hittite arrows. The *Boy's Own Annual* supplanted the *History* in my affections only as my ability to read improved. Only then did it become the staple nourishment of my imagination. I never read, or had read to me, for instance, any of the chlldren's classics such as *Winnie the Pooh, The Jungle Book,* or *The Wind in the Willows.* In retrospect I can say it would have been a good thing if I had read other books, but at the time I certainly didn't suffer from these omissions. My pre-World War I issue of the *Boy's Own Annual* kept me entranced. I needed no other books. I was like a fundamentalist with his Bible.

The *Boy's Own Annual* fell into my hands by way of an elderly English **9** lady who was cleaning out her attic. This lady was typically English – or at least what North American readers of Agatha Christie mysteries might imagine as typically English. A widow, she lived for her huge garden, her budgerigars, and a cocker spaniel named Rusty. She presented me the tattered copy with the assurance that it was "just the thing for a lively young fellow." Against all odds it was.

The contents of the *Boy's Own,* as I remember it, divided fairly evenly **10** into three broad categories. Practical knowledge; historical yarns which even I recognized as historical; and "contemporary" tales which were, at the time I read them, already more than forty years old. The latter I insisted on thinking of as accurate reflections of life in the British Isles and Empire. With hindsight I conclude that this misconception of mine probably continued to flourish primarily because my parents didn't own a television. A TV set would have rubbed my nose in the grit of reality. But I also must have practised self-delusion on a grand scale, some part of my mind censoring all evidence that contradicted the *Boy's Own* picture of the world. Still, in my defence I can say that this was the age of Tarzan movies.

Anyway, who wouldn't wish to keep alive such magnificent delusions? **11** How well I recall the *Boy's Own* article on self-defence. Here was practical knowledge indeed, a step by step, blow by blow account of the proper use of one's walking stick in repulsing assailants. The reader was enjoined to strike *glancing* blows off threatening blackguards because glancing blows foil any attempts at seizing one's walking stick, wresting it from one's grasp, and turning it against one. (It being understood that blackguards were clearly not the kind of fellows to carry walking sticks of their own.) Recommended targets for such glancing blows were elbows, shins, and, of course, the crown of the head. As a bonus several policeman's grips were described and illustrated. When applied these grips promised to bring about the instant submission of felons. Young readers were reminded to use minimum force when practising such grips on their chums.

12 The article incited in me a powerful longing. I knew that there were no interesting blackguards stalking the streets of Esterhazy, Saskatchewan, of the type depicted in *Boy's Own*. Nor did I own an ashplant. However, that didn't mean I oughtn't to study the article very closely. Particularly since I had, on the spot, determined to go to England where there apparently was an abundance of blackguards, villains, and ruffians. All suitable for thrashing.

13 The rest of *Boy's Own* was, if possible, even better, stuffed plum-full to bursting with plucky youths. There were the plucky youths of the past: a ferreter-out of the Gunpowder Plot, an alarm-raiser at the Great Fire of London, an aider and abettor of the escape of Bonny Prince Charlie to France. Then there were the plucky youths I mistook for my contemporaries. My favourite among these was a lad who had stained his skin with berry juice, wrapped his head in a turban, and embarked on a steamer ferrying pilgrims to Mecca. His mission? To uncover a ring of Arab slavers dealing in British subjects. After making fog-bound London streets safe for respectable strollers I thought I might lend this chap a hand tidying up the Red Sea. My future bloomed.

14 If it was Nabokov's perfunctory comment about the *Boy's Own Paper* that resurrected memories which had lain mute under the dead weight of all the books that followed this one volume, books deposited year by year, strata upon strata, it was something else in *Speak, Memory* that made me consider whether my writing hadn't been flavoured by this early infatuation of mine with the *Boy's Own Annual.*

15 Reading Nabokov's autobiography I was struck by a curious thing. I noted that although Nabokov makes frequent reference to the authors of the great European and Russian masterpieces, he devotes more space to a man called Captain Mayne Reid than he does to either Blok, Pushkin, Tolstoy, Gogol, Kafka, Flaubert, Dostoevsky, or for that matter, any other writer.

16 Who was Captain Mayne Reid? Captain Mayne Reid (1818-83), Nabokov informs us, was a writer of Wild West romances. At the turn of the century translations of his work were enormously popular with Russian schoolchildren. Young Vladimir Nabokov was, however, because of the diligence of his governesses, fluent enough in English to have the privilege of reading them in the original language. His

favourite, he tells his readers, was *Headless Horseman.*

From what Nabokov has to say in *Speak, Memory* it is possible to   17
deduce that Mayne Reid completely captivated his young reader.
Nabokov even admits to re-reading *Headless Horseman* as an adult,
and he maintains that the book has its points. It is instructive to note
what these points are.

First of all Nabokov takes delight in the artificiality and intricacy of   18
Captain Mayne Reid's plots. Second, several passages of prose are quoted
with approval. There is the Whiskey decanter behind a Texan barman
which looks like "an iris sparkling behind his shoulder," and the barman
himself is improbably graced with "an aureole surrounding his perfumed
head." Now it is true that in all this Nabokovian applause there is more
than a trace of the familiar Nabokovian mockery. But two things came
to my mind also: Nabokov's own prose, touched as it is with the fantastic and a tincture of the archaic, and his own taste for studied
melodrama and gloriously coincidental plots. One has, after all, only
to think of how improbably the nymphet's mother was despatched in
Lolita to leave the field free for Humbert Humbert.

On such slender, even feeble evidence it would be foolhardy to argue   19
a connection between Reid and Nabokov, to see the romancer's taste,
filtered and purified by Nabokov's genius, later making a bow in the
shadows of Nabokov's novels. But I sensed that, if clearly unprovable,
it was still possible. Nabokov himself is frank in admitting that many
of the books he later read resonated with Reidian echoes. Dwelling on
Louise Pointdexter, a young lady equipped with lorgnette that he
discovered in *Headless Horseman,* Nabokov writes,

> That lorgnette I found afterward in the hands of Madame Bovary,
> and later Anna Karenin had it, and then it passed into the posses-
> sion of Chekhov's Lady with the Lapdog and was lost by her on
> the pier at Yalta. When Louise held it, it was directed toward the
> speckled shadows under the mesquites, where the horseman of her
> choice was having an innocent conversation with the daughter of
> a wealthy haciendado, Doña Isidora Covarubio de los Llanos (whose
> 'head of hair in luxuriance rivalled the tail of a wild steed').

In just this manner the turbaned heads of Moslem pilgrims that I had
met in the *Boy's Own Annual* sprang into view when I read *Lord Jim,*
and walking sticks in the hands of Henry James' characters were suddenly transformed from the innocent appurtenances of dandies into
menacing clubs.

20   There was something else, too. I had come to wonder if I had not
begun the process of learning to write long ago with the *Boy's Own*.
The one problem with the magazine was that it was a serial, and I
possessed only a single volume. Some of the stories had no beginning.
Worse, some had no end. Several of the more harrowing tales had ap-
pended to their last page a cruel joke: To be continued. My favourite
character, the berry-stained boy, I had to leave manacled in the bottom
of an Arab dhow on the point of being pitched overboard to sharks.
What, I asked myself in torments of anxiety, had happened to him?

21   I like to think now that he would have remained forever frozen in
that queer limbo of near death if I hadn't assumed the responsibility
of rescuing him. Because at some point in my childhood I came to realize
that what I was reading was fiction, a structure created by the imagination. If I were daring enough I might collaborate in the making of it.
Or as I saw it then: the boy can be saved. So at about the age of seven
or eight I set about saving him, manufacturing ploys and desperate acts
of desperate courage that would deliver him from implacable fate. In
other words, I began an apprenticeship. I was learning to write.

22   Perhaps all my subsequent fiction has been marked by this experience,
this revelation. Certain reviewers have remarked on my "traditionalism."
Others have gently chided me for my interest in plot and "story." Is
the *Boy's Own Annual* the obscure root of these tendencies? Have the
stratagems concocted to elude the wicked slavers become, in some sense,
second nature?

23   I don't know. The only testimony I can offer is the confession that
when I sit down to write it is only with the greatest effort of will I manage
to force the turbaned heads down, out of sight below the bulwarks of
the dhows, or manage to master the violent and intoxicating urge to
conclude every chapter with a clear suggestion of imminent peril.

24   It is, I suppose, only a matter of time before the will weakens and
the long serialization begun twenty-five years ago resumes under a slightly different guise. I find that once acquired the taste is hard to lose.

(1984)

The Writer's Subject

1. What difficulties did Vanderhaeghe encounter when he first considered the question of influences on his writing? (paras. 1-4)

2. Explain the meaning and relevance of Vanderhaeghe's allusion to a "Gordian knot." (para. 3)

3. In paragraphs 3 and 4 Vanderhaeghe describes two lists he made up, of writers he admired. Why was he "afraid of being thought facetious" if he acknowledged the writers on the second list?

4. What parallels does Vanderhaeghe draw between Nabokov's childhood reading and his own? Why does he find something absurd about their respective experiences? (paras. 5-7)

5. How does Vanderhaeghe's reference to "the mud of Flanders" reinforce his point about the vision of the world conveyed in the *Boy's Own Annual*? (para. 7)

6. Why, in speaking of his "self-delusion," does Vanderhaeghe say that "in my defence I can say that this was the age of Tarzan movies" (para. 10)?

7. Vanderhaeghe draws attention to the frequent references in Nabokov's autobiography to Captain Mayne Reid, a minor English writer of Wild West romances. What influence did Mayne Reid's work have on Nabokov? What parallel does Vanderhaeghe draw between Nabokov's reading experience and his own? (paras. 14-19)

8. How does Vanderhaeghe conclude that his own writing may have been shaped to some extent by his childhood reading of the single volume of the *Boy's Own Annual* in his possession? (paras. 20-24)

The Writer's Style and Strategy

1. What is Vanderhaeghe's thesis? How does he introduce it, and at what point does he make his thesis explicit? (paras. 1-5)

2. How does Vanderhaeghe convey the chauvinistic nature of the *Boy's Own Paper*? (paras. 6 and 7) What does the repeated phrase "xenophobe empire" tell you about the values of the *Boy's Own Paper*?

3. Why does Vanderhaeghe use the word "fabulous" to describe the world in the pages of the *Boy's Own Annual*? (para. 7)

4. How does Vanderhaeghe convey the flavour of the articles in the *Boy's Own Annual*? (para. 11) How does he create a sense of the romantic excitement he felt as a youthful reader of such articles? (paras. 12 and 13)

5. Vanderhaeghe begins his essay by saying that he wants to answer honest-
    ly the questions of interviewers concerning which writers and books most
    influenced him. What is the connection between Vanderhaeghe's statement
    of purpose and the essay's conclusion?

Suggested Topics for Writing and Discussion

1. Vanderhaeghe observes that "bad" writing may be as influential in the
    development of a writer as "good" writing. Drawing from your own reading
    experience, offer your views of what constitutes "bad" literature. Does
    "bad" literature have any redeeming qualities?

2. In discussing his misconceptions about reality derived from the *Boy's Own
    Annual,* Vanderhaeghe observes that these flourished in part because his
    parents did not own a TV set: "A TV set would have rubbed my nose
    in the grit of reality." To what extent, in your view, does television pre-
    sent us with a true picture of the real world?

3. Vanderhaeghe notes that as a child he did not read such children's classics
    as *Winnie the Pooh, The Jungle Book,* or *Wind in the Willows.* Choose
    one of these works, or another acknowledged children's classic, and offer
    your views about its possible appeal for young readers today.

4. Choose a contemporary magazine intended for children or teenagers, and
    analyze its contents. What assumptions does it make about its audience?
    What "picture of the world" does it create? How accurately does it reflect
    the values or circumstances of our society? In your assessment, you might
    consider whether the contents are likely to excite a young reader's curiosity
    and imagination.

How Should One Read a Book?
by Virginia Woolf

In the first place, I want to emphasize the note of interrogation at the 1
end of my title. Even if I could answer the question for myself, the
answer would apply only to me and not to you. The only advice, indeed, that one person can give another about reading is to take no advice, to follow your own instincts, to use your own reason, to come
to your own conclusions. If this is agreed between us, then I feel at
liberty to put forward a few ideas and suggestions because you will not
allow them to fetter that independence which is the most important quality
that a reader can possess. After all, what laws can be laid down about
books? The battle of Waterloo was certainly fought on a certain day;
but is *Hamlet* a better play than *Lear*? Nobody can say. Each must decide
that question for himself. To admit authorities, however heavily furred
and gowned, into our libraries and let them tell us how to read, what
to read, what value to place upon what we read, is to destroy the spirit
of freedom which is the breath of those sanctuaries. Everywhere else
we may be bound by laws and conventions — there we have none.

But to enjoy freedom, if the platitude is pardonable, we have of course 2
to control ourselves. We must not squander our powers, helplessly and
ignorantly, squirting half the house in order to water a single rose-bush;
we must train them, exactly and powerfully, here on the very spot. This,
it may be, is one of the first difficulties that faces us in a library. What
is "the very spot"? There may well seem to be nothing but a conglomera-
tion and huddle of confusion. Poems and novels, histories and memoirs,
dictionaries and blue-books; books written in all languages by men and
women of all tempers, races, and ages jostle each other on the shelf.

And outside the donkey brays, the women gossip at the pump, the colts gallop across the fields. Where are we to begin? How are we to bring order into this multitudinous chaos and so get the deepest and widest pleasure from what we read?

3   It is simple enough to say that since books have classes — fiction, biography, poetry — we should separate them and take from each what it is right that each should give us. Yet few people ask from books what books can give us. Most commonly we come to books with blurred and divided minds, asking of fiction that it shall be true, of poetry that it shall be false, of biography that it shall be flattering, of history that it shall enforce our own prejudices. If we could banish all such preconceptions when we read, that would be an admirable beginning. Do not dictate to your author; try to become him. Be his fellow-worker and accomplice. If you hang back, and reserve and criticise at first, you are preventing yourself from getting the fullest possible value from what you read. But if you open your mind as widely as possible, then signs and hints of almost imperceptible fineness, from the twist and turn of the first sentences, will bring you into the presence of a human being unlike any other. Steep yourself in this, acquaint yourself with this, and soon you will find that your author is giving you, or attempting to give you, something far more definite. The thirty-two chapters of a novel — if we consider how to read a novel first — are an attempt to make something as formed and controlled as a building: but words are more impalpable than bricks; reading is a longer and more complicated process than seeing. Perhaps the quickest way to understand the elements of what a novelist is doing is not to read, but to write; to make your own experiment with the dangers and difficulties of words. Recall, then, some event that has left a distinct impression on you — how at the corner of the street, perhaps, you passed two people talking. A tree shook; an electric light danced; the tone of the talk was comic, but also tragic; a whole vision, an entire conception, seemed contained in that moment.

But when you attempt to reconstruct it in words, you will find that it breaks into a thousand conflicting impressions. Some must be subdued; others emphasized; in the process you will lose, probably, all grasp upon the emotion itself. Then turn from your blurred and littered pages to the opening pages of some great novelist — Defoe, Jane Austen, Hardy. Now you will be better able to appreciate their mastery. It is not merely that we are in the presence of a different person — Defoe, Jane Austen, or Thomas Hardy — but that we are living in a different world. Here, in *Robinson Crusoe*, we are trudging a plain high road; one thing happens after another; the fact and the order of the fact is enough. But if the open air and adventure mean everything to Defoe they mean nothing to Jane Austen. Hers is the drawing-room, and people talking, and by the many mirrors of their talk revealing their characters. And if, when we have accustomed ourselves to the drawing-room and its reflections, we turn to Hardy, we are once more spun round. The moors are round us and the stars are above our heads. The other side of the mind is now exposed — the dark side that comes uppermost in solitude, not the light side that shows in company. Our relations are not towards people, but towards Nature and destiny. Yet different as these worlds are, each is consistent with itself. The maker of each is careful to observe the laws of his own perspective, and however great a strain they may put upon us they will never confuse us, as lesser writers so frequently do, by introducing two different kinds of reality into the same book. Thus to go from one great novelist to another — from Jane Austen to Hardy, from Peacock to Trollope, from Scott to Meredith — is to be wrenched and uprooted; to be thrown this way and then that. To read a novel is a difficult and complex art. You must be capable not only of great fineness of perception, but of great boldness of imagination if you are going to make use of all that the novelist — the great artist — gives you.

But a glance at the heterogeneous company on the shelf will show   5
you that writers are very seldom "great artists"; far more often a book makes no claim to be a work of art at all. These biographies and autobiographies, for example, lives of great men, of men long dead and forgotten, that stand cheek by jowl with the novels and poems, are we to refuse to read them because they are not "art"? Or shall we read them, but read them in a different way, with a different aim? Shall we read them in the first place to satisfy that curiosity which possesses us sometimes when in the evening we linger in front of a house where the lights are lit and the blinds not yet drawn, and each floor of the house shows us a different section of human life in being? Then we are consumed with curiosity about the lives of these people — the servants gossiping, the gentlemen dining, the girl dressing for a party, the old woman at the window with her knitting. Who are they, what are they, what are their names, their occupations, their thoughts, and adventures?

Biographies and memoirs answer such questions, light up innumerable   6
such houses; they show us people going about their daily affairs, toil-

ing, failing, succeeding, eating, hating, loving, until they die. And sometimes as we watch, the house fades and the iron railings vanish and we are out at sea; we are hunting, sailing, fighting; we are among savages and soldiers; we are taking part in great campaigns. Or if we like to stay here in England, in London, still the scene changes; the street narrows; the house becomes small, cramped, diamond-paned, and malodorous. We see a poet, Donne, driven from such a house because the walls were so thin that when the children cried their voices cut through them. We can follow him, through the paths that lie in the pages of books, to Twickenham; to Lady Bedford's Park, a famous meeting-ground for nobles and poets; and then turn our steps to Wilton, the great house under the downs, and hear Sidney read the *Arcadia* to his sister; and ramble among the very marshes and see the very herons that figure in that famous romance; and then again travel north with that other Lady Pembroke, Anne Clifford, to her wild moors, or plunge into the city and control our merriment at the sight of Gabriel Harvey in his black velvet suit arguing about poetry with Spenser. Nothing is more fascinating than to grope and stumble in the alternate darkness and splendour of Elizabethan London. But there is no staying there. The Temples and the Swifts, the Harleys and the St. Johns beckon us on; hour upon hour can be spent disentangling their quarrels and deciphering their characters; and when we tire of them we can stroll on, past a lady in black wearing diamonds, to Samuel Johnson and Goldsmith and Garrick; or cross the channel, if we like, and meet Voltaire and Diderot, Madame du Deffand; and so back to England and Twickenham — how certain places repeat themselves and certain names! — where Lady Bedford had her Park once and Pope lived later, to Walpole's home at Strawberry Hill. But Walpole introduces us to such a swarm of new acquaintances, there are so many houses to visit and bells to ring that we may well hesitate for a moment, on the Miss Berrys' doorstep, for example, when behold, up comes Thackeray; he is the friend of the woman whom Walpole loved; so that merely by going from friend to friend, from garden to garden, from house to house, we have passed from one end of English literature to another and wake to find ourselves here again in the present, if we can so differentiate this moment from all that have gone before. This, then, is one of the ways in which we can read these lives and letters; we can make them light up the many windows of the past; we can watch the famous dead in their familiar habits and fancy sometimes that we are very close and can surprise their secrets, and sometimes we may pull out a play or a poem that they have written and see whether it reads differently in the presence of the author. But this again rouses other questions. How far, we must ask ourselves, is a book influenced by its writer's life — how far is it safe to let the man interpret the writer? How far shall we resist or give way to the sympathies and antipathies that the man himself rouses in us — so sensitive are words, so receptive of the character of the author? These are questions that press upon us when we read lives and letters, and we must answer them for ourselves, for nothing can be more fatal than to be guided by the preferences of others in a matter so personal.

But also we can read such books with another aim, not to throw light **7** on literature, not to become familiar with famous people, but to refresh and exercise our own creative powers. Is there not an open window on the right hand of the bookcase? How delightful to stop reading and look out! How stimulating the scene is, in its unconsciousness, its irrelevance, its perpetual movement — the colts galloping round the field, the woman filling her pail at the well, the donkey throwing back his head and emitting his long, acrid moan. The greater part of any library is nothing but the record of such fleeting moments in the lives of men, women, and donkeys. Every literature, as it grows old, has its rubbish-heap, its record of vanished moments and forgotten lives told in filtering and feeble accents that have perished. But if you give yourself up to the delight of rubbish-reading you will be surprised, indeed you will be overcome, by the relics of human life that have been cast out to moulder. It may be one letter — but what a vision it gives! It may be a few sentences — but what vistas they suggest! Sometimes a whole story will come together with such beautiful humour and pathos and completeness that it seems as if a great novelist had been at work, yet it is only an old actor, Tate Wilkinson, remembering the strange story of Captain Jones; it is only a young subaltern serving under Arthur Wellesley and falling in love with a pretty girl at Lisbon; it is only Maria Allen letting fall her sewing in the empty drawing-room and sighing how she wishes she had taken Dr. Burney's good advice and had never eloped with her Rishy. None of this has any value; it is negligible in the extreme; yet how absorbing it is now and again to go through the rubbish-heaps and find rings and scissors and broken noses buried in the huge past and try to piece them together while the colt gallops round the field, the woman fills her pail at the well, and the donkey brays.

But we tire of rubbish-reading in the long run. We tire of searching **8** for what is needed to complete the half-truth which is all that the Wilkinsons, the Bunburys, and the Maria Allens are able to offer us. They had not the artist's power of mastering and eliminating; they could not tell the whole truth even about their own lives; they have disfigured the story that might have been so shapely. Facts are all that they can offer us, and facts are a very inferior form of fiction. Thus the desire grows upon us to have done with half-statements and approximations; to cease from searching out the minute shades of human character, to enjoy the greater abstractness, the purer truth of fiction. Thus we create the mood, intense and generalised, unaware of detail, but stressed by some regular, recurrent beat, whose natural expression is poetry; and that is the time to read poetry — when we are almost able to write it.

> Western wind, when wilt thou blow?
> The small rain down can rain.
> Christ, if my love were in my arms,
> And I in my bed again!

9   The impact of poetry is so hard and direct that for the moment there is no other sensation except that of the poem itself. What profound depths we visit then — how sudden and complete is our immersion! There is nothing here to catch hold of; nothing to stay us in our flight. The illusion of fiction is gradual; its effects are prepared; but who when they read these four lines stops to ask who wrote them, or conjures up the thought of Donne's house or Sidney's secretary; or enmeshes them in the intricacy of the past and the succession of generations? The poet is always our contemporary. Our being for the moment is centred and constricted, as in any violent shock of personal emotion. Afterwards, it is true, the sensation begins to spread in wider rings through our minds; remoter senses are reached; these begin to sound and to comment and we are aware of echoes and reflections. The intensity of poetry covers an immense range of emotion. We have only to compare the force and directness of

> I shall fall like a tree, and find my grave,
>   Only remembering that I grieve,

with the wavering modulation of

> Minutes are numbered by the fall of sands,
> As by an hour glass; the span of time
> Doth waste us to our graves, and we look on it;
> An age of pleasure, revelled out, comes home
> At last, and ends in sorrow; but the life,
> Weary of riot, numbers every sand,

Wailing in sighs, until the last drop down,
So to conclude calamity in rest,

or place the meditative calm of

whether we be young or old,
Our destiny, our being's heart and home,
Is with infinitude, and only there;
With hope it is, hope that can never die,
Effort, and expectation, and desire,
And something evermore about to be,

beside the complete and inexhaustible loveliness of

The moving Moon went up the sky,
And no where did abide:
Softly she was going up,
And a star or two beside —

or the splendid fantasy of

And the woodland haunter
Shall not cease to saunter
When, far down some glade,
Of the great world's burning,
One soft flame upturning
Seems, to his discerning,
Crocus in the shade.

to bethink us of the varied art of the poet; his power to make us at once actors and spectators; his power to run his hand into character as if it were a glove, and be Falstaff or Lear; his power to condense, to widen, to state, once and for ever.

"We have only to compare" — with those words the cat is out of the 10 bag, and the true complexity of reading is admitted. The first process, to receive impressions with the utmost understanding, is only half the process of reading; it must be completed, if we are to get the whole pleasure from a book, by another. We must pass judgment upon these multitudinous impressions; we must make of these fleeting shapes one that is hard and lasting. But not directly. Wait for the dust of reading to settle; for the conflict and the questioning to die down; walk, talk, pull the dead petals from a rose, or fall asleep. Then suddenly without our willing it, for it is thus that Nature undertakes these transitions, the book will return, but differently. It will float to the top of the mind as a whole. And the book as a whole is different from the book received currently in separate phrases. Details now fit themselves into their places. We see the shape from start to finish; it is a barn, a pigsty, or a cathedral. Now then we can compare book with book as we compare building with building. But this act of comparison means that our attitude has changed; we are no longer the friends of the writer, but his judges; and just as we cannot be too sympathetic as friends, so as judges we cannot be too severe. Are they not criminals, books that have wasted our time and sympathy; are they not the most insidious enemies of society, corrupters, defilers, the writers of false books, faked books, books that fill the air with decay and disease? Let us then be severe in our judgments; let us compare each book with the greatest of its kind. There they hang in the mind, the shapes of the books we have read solidified by the judgments we have passed on them — *Robinson Crusoe, Emma, The Return of the Native.* Compare the novels with these — even the latest and least of novels has a right to be judged with the best. And so with poetry — when the intoxication of rhythm has died down and the splendour of words has faded, a visionary shape will return to us and this must be compared with *Lear*, with *Phèdre*, with *The Prelude*; or if not with these, with whatever is the best or seems to us to be the best in its own kind. And we may be sure that the newness of new poetry and fiction is its most superficial quality and that we have only to alter slightly, not to recast, the standards by which we have judged the old.

11   It would be foolish, then, to pretend that the second part of reading, to judge, to compare, is as simple as the first — to open the mind wide to the fast flocking of innumerable impressions. To continue reading without the book before you, to hold one shadow-shape against another, to have read widely enough and with enough understanding to make such comparisons alive and illuminating — that is difficult; it is still more difficult to press further and to say, "Not only is the book of this sort, but it is of this value; here it fails; here it succeeds; this is bad; that is good." To carry out this part of a reader's duty needs such imagination, insight, and learning that it is hard to conceive any one mind sufficiently endowed; impossible for the most self-confident to find more than the seeds of such powers in himself. Would it not be wiser, then, to remit this part of reading and to allow the critics, the gowned and furred authorities of the library, to decide the question of the book's absolute value for us? Yet how impossible! We may stress the value of sympathy; we may try to sink our own identity as we read. But we know that we cannot sympathise wholly or immerse ourselves wholly;

there is always a demon in us who whispers, "I hate, I love," and we cannot silence him. Indeed, it is precisely because we hate and we love that our relation with the poets and novelists is so intimate that we find the presence of another person intolerable. And even if the results are abhorrent and our judgments are wrong, still our taste, the nerve of sensation that sends shocks through us, is our chief illuminant; we learn through feeling; we cannot suppress our own idiosyncrasy without impoverishing it. But as time goes on perhaps we can train our taste; perhaps we can make it submit to some control. When it has fed greedily and lavishly upon books of all sorts — poetry, fiction, history, biography — and has stopped reading and looked for long spaces upon the variety, the incongruity of the living world, we shall find that it is changing a little; it is not so greedy, it is more reflective. It will begin to bring us not merely judgments on particular books, but it will tell us that there is a quality common to certain books. Listen, it will say, what shall we call *this*? And it will read us perhaps *Lear* and then perhaps the *Agamemnon* in order to bring out that common quality. Thus, with our taste to guide us, we shall venture beyond the particular book in search of qualities that group books together; we shall give them names and thus frame a rule that brings order into our perceptions. We shall gain a further and a rarer pleasure from that discrimination. But as a rule only lives when it is perpetually broken by contact with the books themselves — nothing is easier and more stultifying than to make rules which exist out of touch with facts, in a vacuum — now at last, in order to steady ourselves in this difficult attempt, it may be well to turn to the very rare writers who are able to enlighten us upon literature as an art. Coleridge and Dryden and Johnson, in their considered criticism, the poets and novelists themselves in their unconsidered sayings, are often surprisingly relevant; they light up and solidify the vague ideas that have been tumbling in the misty depths of our minds. But they are only able to help us if we come to them laden with questions and suggestions won honestly in the course of our own reading. They can do nothing for us if we herd ourselves under their authority and lie down like sheep in the shade of a hedge. We can only understand their ruling when it comes in conflict with our own and vanquishes it.

If this is so, if to read a book as it should be read calls for the rarest **12** qualities of imagination, insight, and judgment, you may perhaps conclude that literature is a very complex art and that it is unlikely that we shall be able, even after a lifetime of reading, to make any valuable contribution to its criticism. We must remain readers; we shall not put on the further glory that belongs to those rare beings who are also critics. But still we have our responsibilities as readers and even our importance. The standards we raise and the judgments we pass steal into the air and become part of the atmosphere which writers breathe as they work. An influence is created which tells upon them even if it never finds its way into print. And that influence, if it were well instructed, vigorous and individual and sincere, might be of great value now when criticism is necessarily in abeyance; when books pass in review like the procession of animals in a shooting gallery, and the critic has only one second in which to load and aim and shoot and may well be pardoned if he mistakes rabbits for tigers, eagles for barndoor fowls, or misses altogether and wastes his shot upon some peaceful cow grazing in a further field. If behind the erratic gunfire of the press the author felt that there was another kind of criticism, the opinion of people reading for the love of reading, slowly and unprofessionally, and judging with great sympathy and yet with great severity, might this not improve the quality of his work? And if by our means books were to become stronger, richer, and more varied, that would be an end worth reaching.

13   Yet who reads to bring about an end, however desirable? Are there not some pursuits that we practise because they are good in themselves, and some pleasures that are final? And is not this among them? I have sometimes dreamt, at least, that when the Day of Judgment dawns and the great conquerors and lawyers and statesmen come to receive their rewards — their crowns, their laurels, their names carved indelibly upon imperishable marble — the Almighty will turn to Peter and will say, not without a certain envy when He sees us coming with our books under our arms, "Look, these need no reward. We have nothing to give them here. They have loved reading."

                                                                  (1932)

The Writer's Subject

1. Why does Woolf put her title in the form of a question?

2. What is the difficulty facing a reader in a library? (para. 2)

3. What, according to Woolf, should be the reader's attitude to the author whose work one is reading? (para. 3)

4. What, according to Woolf, is "the quickest way to begin to understand the elements of what a novelist is doing"? (paras. 3-4)

5. What accounts for the interest most readers have in works of biography and autobiography? (paras. 5-6)

6. What does Woolf mean by "the delight of rubbish-reading"? What is missing from such reading? (paras. 7-8)

7. What does Woolf mean by the statement, "The poet is always our contemporary"? (para. 9)

8. What are the two halves of the process of reading, as Woolf sees it? (para. 10) How does the second half of the process alter the reader's relationship with the writer which she describes in paragraph 3?

9. What importance does Woolf attach to individual taste? How is this taste formed? (para. 11)

10. At what stage in reading may the reader wish "to turn to the very rare writers who are able to enlighten us upon literature as an art"? (para. 11)

11. In what way may readers have an effect upon writers? (para. 12)

12. What, finally, is the reward of reading? (para. 13)

The Writer's Style and Strategy

1. How does Woolf organize her ideas in this essay? How does she divide and sub-divide her materials? What are the stages by which Woolf moves from her opening rejection of critical advice and judgment to her eventual assertion of their importance?

2. In paragraph 2, Woolf introduces the donkey, the women, and the colts outside the library window. What is her purpose, and what use does she make of them elsewhere in her essay?

3. What is Woolf's purpose in beginning over a third of her paragraphs with the word "But"?

4. What extended analogies does Woolf use to clarify her ideas about the appeal of biography? (paras. 5-6)

5. Discuss the ways in which Woolf makes use of example. What purposes do the examples serve in paragraph 4? in paragraph 6? in paragraph 7?

6. Discuss the effectiveness of Woolf's use of poetic quotation in paragraph 9.

7. Comment on Woolf's use of metaphorical language in paragraph 10. How does the writer's use of images here enhance her ideas?

8. Although Woolf's paragraphs are unusually long, they are all highly unified. Choose one paragraph and show how Woolf achieves this unity.

Suggested Topics for Writing and Discussion

1. Woolf speaks of the delight of "rubbish-reading." Choose two or three books that you think might be placed in such a category, and explain what pleasure a reader might derive from them.

2. Woolf says, "The poet is always our contemporary." Using the work of one poet not alive today, write an essay supporting this view.

3. Woolf says that books "return" to us at unexpected moments. Is there a book which has returned to you in this way? Try to account for its power over you.

4. Woolf ends her essay by saying that reading is its own reward. Do you agree?

Film and Television

At the movies
by William M. Arkin

Military action movies are big again, and the reason is simple: action   1
beats paralysis. Critics of the "Rambo" and "Rocky" genre contend that
the movies are a manipulative right-wing campaign to sell the idea that
the United States is militarily unprepared, cruel new propaganda tools
against the Soviet Union, or a manifestation of new U.S. nationalism.
But underneath these self-evident themes is a more serious warning
relating to the nuclear arms race: that the U.S. military is incompetent
and impotent, and that technocrats, bureaucrats, and scientists are the
enemy.

The story lines are certainly not new. They build upon a long U.S.   2
film history of lone-wolf heroes and one-man armies — Clint Eastwood,
Charles Bronson, *Dirty Dozen*, *Magnificent Seven*. The movies portray two popular hero types: individualists who will not be pushed around
and determined defenders of the social order. They portray the American
identity, real or imagined. Missing, however, are stories of military
units functioning together as a well-oiled machine, or images of a strong
national leader.

But it isn't only images that are affected by the movies; thinking can   3
shift as well. Julian Smith, in his book *Looking Away: Hollywood and
Vietnam*, examined how wars were dealt with in post-World War II
American cinema and the impact of movies on American thinking before
the Vietnam War. "Vietnam," he wrote, "may have been America's first
film-generated war, the first (and hopefully last) war to grow out of
attitudes supported, perhaps even created, by a generation of movies
depicting America's military omnipotence."

4   Once again, movies are having an enormous impact on U.S. society, especially *Star Wars* and *Rambo*. Even President Reagan, in his first exoatmospheric telephone call to the space shuttle, quoted a line from *Star Wars* to the astronauts: "May the force be with you." Reagan has captured the American imagination with his Strategic Defense Initiative and is basking in the movie's image. As Alan Brinkley wrote in the *New York Review of Books,* "Jimmy Carter's political errors were legion; but his greatest sin, in the eyes of the American Right, may have been his recognition that the problems of the modern world are complex and that solutions are not simple." The irony is that, while promoting a Star Wars defense system that is complex beyond workability, Reagan has succeeded in getting across the other, and opposite, *Star Wars* image: that the forces of good will triumph over the forces of evil by using savvy over technological superiority, flexibility over regimentation.

5   The same theme is found in *Rambo* and the whole series of movies for which it has become the symbol. These movies fall into two basic groups: fantasies about refighting and winning the Vietnam War, and those about wars that have not yet been declared. They almost consistently profile a force operating outside the strictures of society, single-handedly taking on the communists or other enemies, accomplishing what the entire U.S. military evidently could not do. The real-world sequels to these movies may still be in edit, but the simple messages seem to be infectious: computers and technology stand for complication against common sense, bureaucracies against people.

6   The first group includes such movies as *Uncommon Valor,* Chuck Norris's *Missing in Action 1* and *2,* and Sylvester Stallone's two Rambo films. They are about government betrayal in Vietnam, and thus about a loss of American honor. The other films deal directly with, or are allegories for, present and future military confrontations. They include *Red Dawn, Commando, Invasion U.S.A., Iron Eagle, Delta Force,* and *Rocky IV.*

7   After *Rambo, Rocky IV* has been the most popular recent film of this type. As in most of these movies, the United States is cast as the underdog against the Soviet Union, which has appropriated science in the form of a Soviet bionic boxer, who ultimately loses a battle against his more determined American foe. Ironically, Rocky the American is a base and backward peasant — a typical American stereotype of the Soviet people.

8   Interestingly, these and other movies — *Gorky Park, White Nights, Moscow on the Hudson* — do not promote fear of the Soviet Union so

much as they trivialize the Soviet threat. They show the Soviets as
somewhat less than 10-feet tall — "Ivan the Terrible Soldier" in Andrew
Cockburn's clever phrase. The lame anti-Soviet content of the movies
is echoed in the rash of comical anti-Soviet commercials on U.S.
television.

In some sense the message is: "What is the battle to the death that   9
we are preparing for all about?" In *Iron Eagle,* for instance, or *War
Games* of a few years back, the U.S. military is depicted as a collection of bumbling boy scouts who operate their gadgets but do not have
the brains to understand why. These movies add to the slowly percolating
image in Western society — aided by crashing cruise missiles and space
shuttles and $7,000 nuclear-hardened coffee makers — that the military
and its technology are out of control. But unlike other iconoclastic films
such as *Doctor Strangelove, Fail Safe,* and *Seven Days in May,* the new
films blame vaguely leftist, namby-pamby government technocrats and
bureaucrats who would not allow the United States to win in Vietnam.

Another message is, "Whom should we believe?" A fascinating theme   10
of the right-wing missing-in-action movies about retrieving mythical
U.S. soldiers long forgotten in prisoner of war camps in Vietnam is
that the government is withholding important information from the
public. Likewise, in *Red Dawn* and *Invasion U.S.A.,* the total lack of
U.S. defenses seems to contradict the image of restored strength which
the Reagan Administration is trying to sell.

The people who these movies imply should not be believed are liberals,   11
Democrats, intellectuals, eggheads, the Eastern establishment — call
them what you will: the "negativists" and "blame-America-first" crowd.
As *Newsweek* wrote last December, "Nobody much likes Stallone or
his works, that is to say, except the people." *Rambo* had the third-best
sales during opening weeks of any movie in history and it was not all
teenagers: half of those who attended it were over 25, and half of those
were women. The neanderthal *Washington Times* editorialized: "'Rambo'
hadn't been out a moment before the America-hating, guilt-ridden,
Eastern critic crowd dumped it as trash."

"America is sending an important message through Rambo," the   12
Washington Times continued, "and President Reagan should listen
carefully." What is the message? Writing in *New Society* magazine,
Adam Mars Jones compares the two enormously popular Rambo movies
(*First Blood* and more blood). In the first film, which takes place in
the United States, there is much less killing than in the second, which
takes the hero back to Vietnam. Mars-Jones observes: "The people

Rambo attacked [in the first movie] were Americans, and as such had a prima facie right to life. The people against whom Rambo (Sylvester Stallone) is deployed in the new film are not Americans, and he gives them reason to regret it."

13   Is that it? That Americans are in a vengeful mood, and that this is merely a new period of Red-bashing nationalism? There is no doubt that these movies make unabashed use of power. They shrilly promote a "wake-up-America" mentality, and as such have built upon the early Reagan rhetoric of U.S. weakness in the world. But under these messages is a sense of enormous anxiety about the future. And even with what they perceive to be the restoration of the United States' position as number one in the real world, the moviemakers can question the usefulness of weapons — including nuclear weapons — to secure American safety. When Rambo goes back into Vietnam, a series of incidents reduces his load until he is stripped down to little more than his biceps and crossbow. He is obviously more comfortable with the jungle than with technology. Gadgets are not necessary to the success of Rambo's mission.

14   Rambo's cunning gives American audiences some solace in the face of both the Soviet threat and perceptions of U.S. military incompetence. It is interesting to note that in spite of the hullabaloo over the planned ABC television mini series *Amerika*, which will portray a Soviet occupation of the United States, the least commercially successful of all these pictures have been those which deal with armed conflict in the United States. As Vincent Canby points out in the *New York Times,* the pictures which show "a World War III fought on native soil . . . have not done as well at the box office as the films with foreign locations. It could be that American audiences prefer not to fantasize about mayhem so close to home."

15   One explanation for the unpopularity of these fantasies is that, while people have in some ways accepted the Reagan Administration's image of the United States as underdog, they have not accepted either the real implications of that image or the solutions that are currently being offered. Confused by the contradictory messages of both the Administration and the film industry, the American audience is not interested in viewing either the collapse of the United States or mere bureaucratic, technocratic solutions to the country's presumed troubles.

(1986)

The Writer's Subject

1. How does Arkin's essay demonstrate his opening assertion that "Military

action movies are big again, and the reason is simple: action beats paralysis" (para. 1)?

2. What kinds of American heroes are celebrated by the movies Arkin discusses?

3. What is the theme common to both *Rambo* and *Star Wars*? What influence do these movies appear to be having on the American political scene?

4. What effects are movies such as *Rambo, Rocky IV,* and *Iron Eagle* having on American attitudes towards the Soviet Union? (paras. 6-8)

5. How, according to Arkin, do the military action movies reflect Americans' fears about their country's military inadequacies?

6. What inference may be drawn from Arkin's observation that, of the record-breaking crowds attending *Rambo* in its first weeks, half of those attending were women? (para. 11)

7. Why are the military action films with foreign locations apparently more successful at the box office than those set in America? (paras. 14-15)

The Writer's Style and Strategy

1. What methods does Arkin employ to develop his thesis?

2. How does Arkin classify the different kinds of action films he describes?

3. What does the phrase "the neanderthal *Washington Times*" reveal about Arkin's attitude to that paper? (para. 11)

4. In the course of his discussion, Arkin quotes from a variety of sources (e.g., Julian Smith, President Reagan, *Newsweek,* Vincent Canby). Examine the ways in which he uses such references to support his argument.

Suggested Topics for Writing and Discussion

1. Compare Arkin's essay with Bruno Bettelheim's essay, "The Art of Moving Pictures." Discuss the images of American society reflected in the movies, as perceived by each writer.

2. Choose a movie you have seen recently, and say what it tells the audience about the political and/or social attitudes of its country of origin. What "hidden message," if any, did you perceive in the film?

3. Compare any movie about World War II with a film about subsequent military conflicts (Korea, Vietnam, Central and South America, the Middle East). What differences are apparent in these films in the attitudes towards the waging of war, and towards the role of individuals in military action?

The Art of Moving Pictures
by Bruno Bettelheim

1 Whether we like it or not — and many may disagree with my thesis because painting, or music, or some other art is more important to them — the art of the moving image is the only art truly of our time, whether it is in the form of the film or television. The moving picture is our universal art, which comprises all others, literature and acting, stage design and music, dance and the beauty of nature, and, most of all, the use of light and of color.

2 It is always about us, because the medium is truly part of the message and the medium of the moving image is uniquely modern. Everybody can understand it, as everyone once understood religious art in church. And as people used to go to church on Sundays (and still do), so the majority today go to the movies on weekends. But while in the past most went to church only on some days, now everybody watches moving images every day.

3 All age groups watch moving pictures, and they watch them for many more hours than people have ever spent in churches. Children and adults watch them separately or together; in many ways and for many people, it is the only experience common to parents and children. It is the only art today that appeals to all social and economic classes, in short, that appeals to everybody, as did religious art in times past. The moving picture is thus by far the most popular art of our time, and it is also the most authentically American of arts.

4 When I speak here of the moving picture as the authentic American art of our time, I do not think of art with a capital A, nor of "high" art. Putting art on a pedestal robs it of its vitality. When the great

medieval and Renaissance cathedrals were erected, and decorated outside and in with art, these were popular works, that meant something
to everybody.

Some were great works of art, others not, but every piece was signifi-   5
cant and all took pride in each of them. Some gain their spiritual experience from the masterpiece, but many more gain it from the mediocre
works that express the same vision as the masterpiece but in a more
accessible form. This is as true for church music or the church itself
as for paintings and sculptures. This diversity of art objects achieves
a unity, and differences in quality are important, provided they all represent, each in its own way, the overarching vision and experience of
a larger, important cosmos. Such a vision confers meaning and dignity
on our existence, and is what forms the essence of art.

So among the worst detriments to the healthy development of the art   6
of the moving image are efforts by aesthetes and critics to isolate the
art of film from popular movies and television. Nothing could be more
contrary to the true spirit of art. Whenever art was vital, it was always
equally popular with the ordinary man and the most refined person.
Had Greek drama and comedy meant nothing to most citizens, the
majority of the population would not have sat all day long entranced
on hard stone slabs, watching the events on the stage; nor would the
entire population have conferred prizes on the winning dramatist. The
medieval pageants and mystery plays out of which modern drama grew
were popular entertainments, as were the plays of Shakespeare.
Michelangelo's David stood at the most public place in Florence, em-
bodying the people's vision that tyranny must be overthrown, while it
also related to their religious vision, as it represented the myth of
David and Goliath. Everybody admired the statue; it was simultaneously
popular and great art but one did not think of it in such disparate terms.
Neither should we. To live well we need both: visions that lift us up,
and entertainment that is down to earth, provided both art and entertainment, each in its different form and way, are embodiments of the
same visions of man. If art does not speak to all of us, common men
and elites alike, it fails to address itself to that true humanity that is
common to all of us. A different art for the elites and another one for
average man tears society apart; it offends what we most need: visions
that bind us together in common experiences that make life worth living.

When I speak of an affirmation of man, I do not mean the presenta-   7
tion of fake images of life as wonderfully pleasant. Life is best celebrated
in the form of battle against its inequities, of struggles, of dignity in

defeat, of the greatness of discovering oneself and the other.

8   Quite a few moving pictures have conveyed such visions. In *Kagemusha,* the great beauty of the historical costumes, the cloak-and-dagger story with its beguiling Oriental settings, the stately proceedings, the pageantry of marching and fighting armies, the magnificent rendering of nature, the consummate acting — all these entrance us and convince us of the correctness of the vision here: the greatness of the most ordinary of men. The hero, a petty thief who turns impostor, grows before our eyes into greatness, although it costs him his life. The story takes place in sixteenth-century Japan, but the hero is of all times and places: he accepts a destiny into which he is projected by chance and turns a false existence into a real one. At the end, only because he wants to be true to his new self, he sacrifices his life and thus achieves the acme of suffering and human greatness. Nobody wants him to do so. Nobody but he will ever know that he did it. Nobody but the audience observes it. He does it only for himself; it has no consequences whatsoever for anybody or anything else. He does it out of conviction; this is his greatness. Life that permits the lowest of men to achieve such dignity is life worth living, even if in the end it defeats him, as it will defeat all who are mortal.

9   Two other films, very different, render parallel visions that celebrate life, a celebration in which we, as viewers, vicariously participate although we are saddened by the hero's defeat. The first was known in the United States by its English name, *The Last Laugh,* although its original title, *The Last Man,* was more appropriate. It is the story of the doorman of a hotel who is demoted to cleaning washrooms. The other movie is *Patton.* In one of these films the hero stands on the lowest rung of society and existence; in the other, he is on society's highest level. In both pictures we are led to admire a man's struggle to discover who he really is, for, in doing so, he achieves tragic greatness. These three films, as do many others, affirm man and life, and so inspire in us visions that can sustain us.

10   My choice of these three films out of many is arbitrary. What I want to illustrate is their celebration of life in forms appropriate to an age in which self-discovery may exact the highest possible price. Only through incorporating such visions can we achieve satisfaction with our own life, and defeat and transcend existential despair.

11   What our society suffers from most today is the absence of consensus about what it and life in it ought to be. Such consensus cannot be

gained from society's present stage, or from fantasies about what it ought to be. For that the present is too close and too diversified, and the future too uncertain, to make believable claims about it. A consensus in the present hence can be achieved only through a shared understanding of the past, as Homer's epics informed those who lived centuries later what it meant to be Greek, and by what images and ideals they were to live their lives and organize their societies.

Most societies derive consensus from a long history, a language all 12 their own, a common religion, common ancestry. The myths by which they live are based on all of these. But the United States is a country of immigrants, coming from a great variety of nations. Lately, it has been emphasized that an asocial, narcissistic personality has become characteristic of Americans, and that it is this type of personality that makes for the malaise, because it prevents us from achieving a consensus that would counteract a tendency to withdraw into private worlds. In his study of narcissism, Christopher Lasch says that modern man, "tortured by self-consciousness, turns to new cults and therapies not to free himself of his personal obsessions but to find meaning and purpose in life, to find something to live for." There is wide-spread distress because national morale has declined, and we have lost an earlier sense of national vision and purpose.

Contrary to rigid religions or political beliefs, as are found in totali- 13 tarian societies, our culture is one of great individual differences, at least in principle and in theory. But this leads to disunity, even chaos. Americans believe in the value of diversity, but just because ours is a society based on individual diversity, it needs consensus about some overarching ideas more than societies based on the uniform origin of their citizens. Hence, if we are to have consensus, it must be based on a myth — a vision — about a common experience, a conquest that made us Americans, as the myth about the conquest of Troy formed the Greeks. Only a common myth can offer relief from the fear that life is without meaning or purpose. Myths permit us to examine our place in the world by comparing it to a shared idea. Myths are shared fantasies that form the tie that binds the individual to other members of his group. Such myths help to ward off feelings of isolation, guilt, anxiety, and purposelessness — in short, they combat isolation and anomie.

We used to have a myth that bound us together; in *The American* 14 *Adam,* R.W.B. Lewis summarizes the myth by which Americans used to live:

God decided to give man another chance by opening up a new world across the sea. Practically vacant, this glorious land had almost inexhaustible natural resources. Many people came to this new world. They were people of special energy, self-reliance, intuitive intelligence, and purity of heart. . . This nation's special mission in the world would be to serve as the moral guide for all other nations.

15   The movies used to transmit this myth, particularly the westerns, which presented the challenge of bringing civilization to places where before there was none. The same movies also suggested the danger of that chaos; the wagon train symbolized the community men must form on such a perilous journey into the untamed wilderness, which in turn became a symbol for all that is untamed within ourselves. Thus the western gave us a vision of the need for cooperation and civilization, because without it man would perish. Another symbol often used in these westerns was the railroad, which formed the link between wilderness and civilization. The railroad was the symbol of man's role as civilizer.

16   Robert Warshow delineates in *The Immediate Experience* how the hero of the western — the gunfighter — symbolizes man's potential: to become either an outlaw or a sheriff. In the latter role, the gunfighter was the hero of the past, and his opening of the West was our mythos, our equivalent of the Trojan War. Like all such heroes, the sheriff experienced victories and defeats, but, through these experiences, he grew wiser and learned to accept the limitations that civilization imposes.

17   This was a wonderful vision of man — or the United States — in the New World; it was a myth by which one could live and grow, and it served as a consensus about what it meant to be an American. But although most of us continue to enjoy this myth, by now it has lost most of its vitality. We have become too aware of the destruction of nature and of the American Indian — part of the reality of opening the West — to be able to savor this myth fully; and, just as important, it is based on an open frontier that no longer exists. But the nostalgic infatuation with the western suggests how much we are in need of a myth about the past that cannot be invalidated by the realities of today. We want to share a vision, one that would enlighten us about what it means to be an American today, so that we can be proud not only of our heritage but also of the world we are building together.

18   Unfortunately, we have no such myth, nor, by extension, any that reflects what is involved in growing up. The child, like the society,

needs such myths to provide him with ideas of what difficulties are involved in maturation. Fairy tales used to fill this need, and they would still do so, if we would take them seriously. But sugar-sweet movies of the Disney variety fail to take seriously the world of the child — the immense problems with which the child has to struggle as he grows up, to make himself free from the bonds that tie him to his parents, and to test his own strength. Instead of helping the child, who wants to understand the difficulties ahead, these shows talk down to him, insult his intelligence, and lower his aspirations.

While most of the popular shows for children fall short of what the 19 child needs most, others at least provide him with some of the fantasies that relieve pressing anxieties, and this is the reason for their popularity. Superman, Wonder Woman, and the Bionic Woman stimulate the child's fantasies about being strong and invulnerable, and this offers some relief from being overwhelmed by the powerful adults who control his existence. The Incredible Hulk affords a confrontation with destructive anger. Watching the Hulk on one of his rampages permits a vicarious experience of anger without having to feel guilty about it or anxious about the consequences, because the Hulk attacks only bad people. As food for fantasies that offer temporary relief, such shows have a certain value, but they do not provide material leading to higher integration, as myths do.

Science-fiction movies can serve as myths about the future and thus 20 give us some assurance about it. Whether the film is *2001* or *Star Wars,* such movies tell about progress that will expand man's powers and his experiences beyond anything now believed possible, while they assure us that all these advances will not obliterate man or life as we now know it. Thus one great anxiety about the future — that it will have no place for us as we now are — is allayed by such myths. They also promise that even in the most distant future, and despite the progress that will have occurred in the material world, man's basic concerns will be the same, and the struggle of good against evil — the central moral problem of our time — will not have lost its importance.

Past and future are the lasting dimensions of our lives; the present 21 is but a fleeting moment. So these visions about the future also contain our past; in *Star Wars,* battles are fought around issues that also motivated man in the past. There is good reason that Yoda appears in George Lucas's film: he is but a reincarnation of the teddy bear of infancy, to which we turn for solace; and the Yedi Knight is the wise old man, or the helpful animal, of the fairy tale, the promise from our

distant past that we shall be able to rise to meet the most difficult tasks
life can present us with. Thus any vision about the future is really based
on visions of the past, because that is all we can know for certain.

22   As our réligious myths about the future never went beyond Judgment
Day, so our modern myths about the future cannot go beyond the search
for life's deeper meaning. The reason is that only as long as the choice
between good and evil remains man's paramount moral problem does
life retain that special dignity that derives from our ability to choose
between the two. A world in which this conflict has been permanently
resolved eliminates man as we know him. It might be a universe peopled
by angels, but it has no place for man.

23   What Americans need most is a consensus that includes the idea of
individual freedom, as well as acceptance of the plurality of ethnic
backgrounds and religious beliefs inherent in the population. Such consensus must rest on convictions about moral values and the validity of
overarching ideas. Art can do this because a basic ingredient of the
aesthetic experience is that it binds together diverse elements. But only
the ruling art of a period is apt to provide such unity: for the Greeks,
it was classical art; for the British, Elizabethan art; for the many petty
German states, it was their classical art. Today, for the United States,
it has to be the moving picture, the central art of our time, because
no other art experience is so open and accessible to everyone.

24   The moving picture is a visual art, based on sight. Speaking to our
vision, it ought to provide us with the visions enabling us to live the
good life; it ought to give us insight into ourselves. About a hundred
years ago, Tolstoy wrote, "Art is a human activity having for its purpose
the transmission to others of the highest and best feelings to which men
have risen." Later, Robert Frost defined poetry as "beginning in delight
and ending in wisdom." Thus it might be said that the state of the art
of the moving image can be assessed by the degree to which it meets
the mythopoetic task of giving us myths suitable to live by in our time
− visions that transmit to us the highest and best feelings to which men
have risen − and by how well the moving images give us that delight
which leads to wisdom. Let us hope that the art of the moving image,
this most authentic American art, will soon meet the challenge of becoming truly the great art of our age.

(1981)

The Writer's Subject

1. Why does Bettelheim regard the moving picture as the "only art truly of our time" (paras. 1-4)?

2. What is the point of the analogy between going to the movies and going to church? (para. 2)

3. Why does Bettelheim insist that mediocre works of art are as important as masterpieces in conferring "meaning and dignity on our existence" (para. 5)? Why does Bettelheim argue against an art for the élite?

4. What common qualities of heroes does Bettelheim identify in the movies *Kagemusha, The Last Laugh,* and *Patton*? Why does he attach such importance to movies of this kind? (paras. 8 and 9)

5. Why, according to Bettelheim, does a society need common myths? (paras. 10-14)

6. Bettelheim says that Americans used to be bound together by a myth. What was this myth? In what ways was this myth expressed in the Western movie? Why has the Western lost its vitality as myth? (paras. 15-17)

7. What mythic qualities are embodied in science fiction movies, according to Bettelheim? (paras. 20-21)

8. Why does Bettelheim compare the art of the moving picture in the United States to classical art in Greece and Elizabethan art in Britain? (para. 23)

The Writer's Style and Strategy

1. Bettelheim asserts that the efforts of aesthetes and critics to distinguish the art of film from popular movies and television are "contrary to the true spirit of art" (para. 6). What method does he use to support his argument?

2. "Vision" is a key word in this essay. Examine Bettelheim's use of this word, and show its importance to his central argument.

3. What use does Bettelheim make of examples to demonstrate his point that, for modern audiences, science fiction films have taken over the role of myth?

4. Show the relationship between the opening and closing sentences of the essay, and comment on their different emphases.

Suggested Topics for Writing and Discussion

1. Choose a science fiction film with which you are familiar and argue for it as myth.

2. According to Bettelheim, the American myth focused on a new world, a myth often embodied in Westerns. What myth do you think characterizes the Canadian experience? In what form has this myth found expression?

3. Do you agree with Bettelheim's assertion that movies of the Disney variety "talk down to [the child], insult his intelligence, and lower his aspirations"? Use specific examples to explain your view.

4. The heroes of television programs, films and books can tell us a great deal about the values and attitudes of our society. Choose one hero from a contemporary television program, film or book and explain what that hero tells us about our values and attitudes. Be specific and detailed in your response.

The Grand Illusion
by Robert Fulford

There is something slightly inhuman and robotic about the reporters 1
who deliver the news to us on television. As a class they do not represent humanity. TV news people are never ugly. They are never old and
seldom middle-aged. They are rarely overweight or bald and they do
not wear striking or ungainly clothing. They are never unhappy or ill
at ease. They are, without exception, middle class: no national TV
reporter speaks with a regional or working-class accent, or for that matter
a Rosedale honk or a Westmount whine. Whatever eccentricities they
may have are suppressed. They are chosen not to reflect the audience
but to reflect the way producers believe — perhaps with good reason
— that we want to see our society represented. They appear to be picked as carefully as actors in a play — except that directors of plays often
look for striking or anomalous characteristics and TV news producers
never do.

The script for television news varies only slightly from performance 2
to performance and from actor to actor. As interviewers, TV reporters
ask roughly the same questions of successful politicians and grief-stricken
widows ("How do you feel?"). When they address the audience they
maintain an even, cool tone and a direct, noncommittal gaze. They are
affable but never effusive. Their intonation betrays neither delight nor
anger. They are surprised by nothing. They are apparently never excited. Someone being interviewed may shout or burst into tears — that
makes "good television" — but the reporter will remain calm. In general
TV reporters take their subjects, particularly politicians, less seriously
than the subjects take themselves. Often they speak of the people they
cover with a certain easy disdain. Sometimes, as with Peter Trueman

of Global or Roger Mudd of NBC, this reflects the cynicism of long experience; sometimes it appears to be nothing more than a mannerism picked up from other reporters, an attitudinal twitch.

3   The standard TV news item begins brightly, perhaps a bit urgently: the reporter has something important to tell us. Then, in ninety seconds or less, the material is packaged and put in its place and the item ends tidily − always in the same way. Covering a routine fire or the most terrifying hostage-taking, the reporter never fails to conclude with the same earnest glance into the camera, the same dying fall ("Mike Duffy, CBC News, Ottawa"). The reporter is saying: no matter what happens, we are in control.

4   Long ago Marshall McLuhan argued that the facts and ideas we absorb through a medium of communication matter less than the nature of the medium itself. What counts is the form, because the form will determine how we see the world. If we read two or three newspapers a day, then the newspapers − whether we like it or not - shape our way of thinking; if we are confirmed magazine readers, then our minds are influenced by the specific approach of magazines to their subjects. In McLuhan's famous phrase, the medium is the message. Not all of us, of course, read either newspapers or magazines, but nearly all of us watch the news on television and some of us see TV news three or four times a day. Arguably, the TV newscast is the most influential form of mass communication. In Canada it may be even more influential than in the United States, because Canadians have about twice as much news to watch as Americans − we can see theirs as well as ours − and this summer a viewer in Vancouver or Montreal may be equally sophisticated about the Democratic primaries and the Liberal leadership campaign. In Canada, TV news provides one set of facts (American) overlaid on another (Canadian). Perhaps in no other country is so much TV news available, and so much consumed. But when we watch TV news, what do we experience? Aside from the facts themselves, and the occasional idea or overt opinion, what message does television news deliver to us? What attitude does it pass on?

5   One obvious fact about TV reporters is that they convey information much more skilfully than newspaper reporters. The daily newspaper is centuries old, but newspaper reporters − as opposed to editorial writers, columnists, and feature writers − have still not worked out an adequate and convincing way to present data. In the nineteenth century, newspapers developed the "inverted pyramid" news story, in which the crucial facts appear in the heading and the first paragraph. The

material grows less and less consequential until, in the last few paragraphs, when many readers have stopped reading, the least interesting facts are finally dropped in.

That form was set in the early years of the telegraph system, so that **6** if a message were interrupted in the middle the essential facts would still be conveyed. It was maintained through the days when newspapers published many editions; inverted-pyramid news stories could be changed several times through the day and could be hastily cut from the bottom up without the loss of the most essential details. In recent decades newspapers have eliminated many of their editions and there's now much more time to prepare a news page; but such is the atavism of newspaper editors that the inverted pyramid has persisted and still dominates most news pages. It remains, as it was in the beginning, a clumsy and unsatisfactory form of communication. It makes daily newspapers much more boring than they need to be.

By contrast, the TV news report — no more than about three decades **7** old — is a work of art. It has a beginning, a middle, and an end. Its practitioners appear to know instinctively that they must present a thesis, allow for an antithesis, then make a stab at a synthesis. The result is a structured and carefully crafted little drama, without unexplained facts or unanswered questions. Television news stories are much more persuasive than their newspaper equivalents because they appear to make good sense and the reporters appear to be completely in control of their material. The style of TV reporting makes us believe that the whole story has been told, whereas the style of newspaper reporting - with its loose ends and incomplete thoughts — makes us believe we are receiving only a partial account. The effect is partly subconscious but no less real for that.

In structure, TV news stories are closer to the reports in *Time* magazine **8** than to newspaper stories. TV news stories also borrow from commercials: they have some of the same urgency and pacing. In fact, the news people and the producers of commercials appear to learn from each other. In the most professional TV news operations, each report is polished to the point of apparent perfection. Even when an item must be drastically cut — for instance, when items from *The National* are trimmed to fit into the news roundup at 11 p.m. — the style persists. In their most truncated state, TV news stories retain their format; only the most careful viewer will notice the seams.

The superiority of TV news is, of course, purely aesthetic. Newspapers **9** are much more useful. The people who put them out are more knowledgeable than TV reporters, spend more time on research, and earn more respect from the people they write about. TV gets on the air with the news faster than newspapers and displays it more convincingly; but, paradoxically, newspaper editors make society's decisions about what is important. In the United States *The Washington Post* and *The New York Times*, rather than ABC or CBS, decide which public officials must be pilloried, which issue must be pursued; in Canada *The Globe and Mail* fills a similar office.

10   After watching the media for some years from his perch in the prime minister's office, Jim Coutts declared that "Print in Canada still sets the basic day-to-day news and public-affairs agenda for the electronic media — and not the other way around. How often in Ottawa you see the circle operate. A story begins at *The Globe and Mail*. It goes out overnight on the Canadian Press wire, hits radio and television by morning, and re-appears as a question in the House of Commons at two p.m. It goes from there via television cameras to the local and national prime time evening TV news - while the *Globe* and other print media are already launching Round II."

11   Newspapers of course provide far more information than TV, and readers use that information more selectively. Each of us functions privately as an editor. We re-edit the newspaper by passing over stories or whole sections we don't want to read and concentrating on those items that matter to us. Increasingly, newspapers are edited for specialists — those who urgently need many facts on certain subjects. The Montreal *Gazette*, for example, will include far more about local politics than any television station would consider worth carrying; presumably there are people who need to know the details of local government and the *Gazette* may be valuable to them for that alone. Sometimes a newspaper story — on a zoning issue, for example, or a long-running royal commission — will be comprehensible only to those who have followed previous stories.

12   On television everything must be understood by everyone, even those who have not seen previous broadcasts. In a sense TV is the most democratic of media because it assumes that we can all understand whatever subject it decides to cover and implies that those subjects it doesn't cover aren't worth worrying about. It involves all of us in the ritual of finding form and order in disparate and otherwise baffling facts. The central myth of TV news is the breathtakingly audacious idea that *everything* can be understood.

13   Television reporters don't get above themselves, don't exceed their

authority. They never claim superior knowledge — in fact, they don't even hint that they know anything except the facts they are delivering. They are aware, and perhaps the audience is too, that all but very few TV reporters are innocent children when set beside knowledgeable newspaper reporters.

What the TV people have in place of knowledge or wisdom is techni- 14 que and an unerring sense of ritual. They can fit the world together, make sense of it, in a way that other journalists cannot. They make life a dramatic pageant, a series of interesting and satisfying vignettes. They never bore us with the more cumbersome details of reality or the awkward corners of events. The underlying message of their broadcasts is that one plausibly described little event is very much like another.

In this way television news responds to one of our most profound 15 needs: it reduces the chaos of the day to something approaching order. The anthropologist Clifford Geertz has explained that human beings are "symbolizing, conceptualizing, meaning-seeking" animals who wish to "make sense out of our experience, to give it form and order." It is this form that the TV reporter is reaching for as he fits his film and his commentary into a carefully organized "story". Geertz's studies of various primitive tribes convince him that humanity's need for order and explanation is "evidently as real and as pressing as the more familiar biological needs," sustenance and sex. There was a time when many of us routinely satisfied this pattern-seeking need through religion; for people from whose lives religious belief has departed, the manipulation of information about the world provides a kind of substitute. TV manipulates information better than any other medium, and however sceptical we are in most other ways we tend to believe in TV news during the time we are watching it. Indeed, I think we badly want to believe in it.

Those people who appear on our television sets every night, show- 16 ing us their film and explaining what it means, occupy a unique place where the history of technology and the history of culture come together. Technology has made their work possible. Culture — which now acknowledges that almost everything in the universe is uncertain - has made their work extremely important to us, perhaps even necessary. Their central function is to make an incomprehensible world seem, for a few minutes, comprehensible.

(1984)

The Writer's Subject

1. On what grounds does Fulford maintain that "There is something slightly inhuman and robotic" about news reporters? (para. 1)

2. Why is "form" such an important element in the communication of facts and ideas? What is meant by McLuhan's famous phrase, "the medium is the message" (para 4)?

3. Discuss the contrast Fulford draws between the structure and style of news reports prepared for television and the approach taken in newspaper articles. What essential differences does he perceive?

4. "The superiority of TV news is, of course, purely aesthetic. Newspapers are much more useful." What does Fulford mean by "aesthetic" here? What evidence does he bring in support of the second of these contentions? (paras. 7-12)

5. In what way, according to Fulford, has television news become a "kind of substitute" for religion? What human needs does it appear to satisfy? (para. 15)

The Writer's Style and Strategy

1. Fulford writes from the perspective of a print journalist rather than a television journalist. How is his bias revealed?

2. Discuss the diction and the tone of paragraph 3. How does Fulford slant his argument?

3. How does Fulford develop his comparison of news reports on television with those in the print media? (paras. 6-8)

4. Paragraph 10 consists almost entirely of a quotation from Jim Coutts, an aide in the Prime Minister's Office. What is Fulford's purpose in quoting such a highly placed government official?

5. How does the phrase "the myth of TV news" in paragraph 12 convey Fulford's attitude?

Suggested Topics for Writing and Discussion

1. "In Canada, TV news provides one set of facts (American) overlaid on another (Canadian)." Using broadcasts of the evening news on one or two Canadian networks, explain whether you agree with Fulford's assessment of TV news in Canada.

2. Choose one news item of current national or international importance being reported in the press and on television. Compare the ways in which each medium presents the information, and offer your view about their respective strengths and weaknesses.

3. According to Fulford, TV displays news more convincingly than newspapers, "but, paradoxically, newspaper editors make society's decisions about what is important." Choose one or two controversial issues (e.g., an international issue, such as terrorism; an environmental issue, such as acid rain; or a local issue, such as cutbacks in educational funding). Discuss the part that television news or printed news has played in shaping your opinions of these issues.

Who Killed King Kong?

by X.J. Kennedy

1   The ordeal and spectacular death of *King Kong*, the giant ape, undoubtedly has been witnessed by more Americans than have ever seen a performance of *Hamlet, Iphigenia at Aulis,* or even *Tobacco Road.* Since RKO-Radio Pictures first released *King Kong,* a quarter-century has gone by; yet year after year, from prints that grow more rain-beaten, from sound tracks that grow more tinny, ticket-buyers by thousands still pursue Kong's luckless fight against the forces of technology, tabloid journalism and the DAR. They see him chloroformed to sleep, see him whisked from his jungle isle to New York and placed on show, see him burst his chains to roam the city (lugging a frightened blonde), at last to plunge from the spire of the Empire State Building, machine gunned by model airplanes.

2   Though Kong may die, one begins to think his legend unkillable. No clearer proof of his hold upon the popular imagination may be seen than what emerged one catastrophic week in March 1955, when New York WOR-TV programmed Kong for seven evenings in a row (a total of sixteen showings). Many a rival network vice-president must have scowled when surveys showed that Kong — the 1933 B-picture — had lured away fat segments of the viewing populace from such powerful competitors as Ed Sullivan, Groucho Marx and Bishop Sheen.

3   But even television has failed to run *King Kong* into oblivion. Coffee-in-the-lobby cinemas still show the old hunk of hokum, with the apology that in its use of composite shots and animated models the film remains technically interesting. And no other monster in movie history has won so devoted a popular audience. None of the plodding mummies, the

stultified draculas, the whitecoated Lugosis with their shiny pinball-machine laboratories, none of the invisible stranglers, berserk robots, or menaces from Mars has ever enjoyed so many resurrections.

Why does the American public refuse to let *King Kong* rest in peace? It is true, I'll admit, that Kong outdid every monster movie before or since in sheer carnage. Producers Cooper and Schoedsack crammed into it dinosaurs, headhunters, riots, aerial battles, bullets, bombs, bloodletting. Heroine Fay Wray, whose function is mainly to scream, shuts her mouth for hardly one uninterrupted minute from first reel to last. It is also true that Kong is larded with good healthy sadism, for those whose joy it is to see the frantic girl dangled from cliffs and harried by pterodactyls. But it seems to me that the abiding appeal of the giant ape rests on other foundations. **4**

Kong has, first of all, the attraction of being manlike. His simian nature gives him one huge advantage over giant ants and walking vegetables in that an audience may conceivably identify with him. Kong's appeal has the quality that established the Tarzan series as American myth — for what man doesn't secretly imagine himself a huge hairy howler against whom no other monster has a chance? If Tarzan recalls the ape in us, then Kong may well appeal to that great-granddaddy primordial brute from whose tribe we have all deteriorated. **5**

Intentionally or not, the producers of *King Kong* encourage this iden- **6** tification by etching the character of Kong with keen sympathy. For the ape is a figure in a tradition familiar to moviegoers: the tradition of the pitiable monster. We think of Lon Chaney in the role of Quasimodo, of Karloff in the original *Frankenstein*. As we watch the Frankenstein monster's fumbling and disastrous attempts to befriend a flower-picking child, our sympathies are enlisted with the monster in his impenetrable loneliness. And so with Kong. As he roars in his chains, while barkers sell tickets to boobs who gape at him, we perhaps feel something more deep than pathos. We begin to sense something of the problem that engaged Eugene O'Neill in *The Hairy Ape*: the dilemma of a displaced animal spirit forced to live in a jungle built by machines.

King Kong, it is true, had special relevance in 1933. Landscapes of **7** the depression are glimpsed early in the film when an impresario, seeking some desperate pretty girl to play the lead in a jungle movie, visits souplines and a Woman's Home Mission. In Fay Wray — who's been caught snitching an apple from a fruitstand — his search is ended. When he gives her a big feed and a movie contract, the girl is magic-carpeted out of the world of the National Recovery Act. And when, in the film's climax, Kong smashes that very Third Avenue landscape in which Fay had wandered hungry, audiences of 1933 may well have felt a personal satisfaction.

8   What is curious is that audiences of 1960 remain hooked. For in the heart of urban man, one suspects, lurks the impulse to fling a bomb. Though machines speed him to the scene of his daily grind, though IBM comptometers ("freeing the human mind from drudgery") enable him to drudge more efficiently once he arrives, there comes a moment when he wishes to turn upon his machines and kick hell out of them. He wants to hurl his combination radioalarmclock out the bedroom window and listen to its smash. What subway commuter wouldn't love − just for once − to see the downtown express smack head-on into the uptown local? Such a wish is gratified in that memorable scene in Kong that opens with a wideangle shot: interior of a railway car on the Third Avenue El. Straphangers are nodding, the literate refold their newspapers. Unknown to them, Kong has torn away a section of trestle toward which the train now speeds. The motorman spies Kong up ahead, jams on the brakes. Passengers hurtle together like so many peas in a pail. In a window of the car appear Kong's bloodshot eyes. Women shriek. Kong picks up the railway car as if it were a rat, flips it to the street and ties knots in it, or something. To any commuter the scene must appear one of the most satisfactory pieces of celluloid ever exposed.

9   Yet however violent his acts, Kong remains a gentleman. Remarkable is his sense of chivalry. Whenever a fresh boa constrictor threatens Fay, Kong first sees that the lady is safely parked, then manfully thrashes her attacker. (And she, the ingrate, runs away every time his back is turned.) Atop the Empire State Building, ignoring his pursuers, Kong places Fay on a ledge as tenderly as if she were a dozen eggs. He fondles her, then turns to face the Army Air Force. And Kong is perhaps the most disinterested lover since Cyrano: his attentions to the lady are utterly without hope of reward. After all, between a five-foot blonde and a fifty-foot ape, love can hardly be more than an intellectual flirtation. In his simian way King Kong is the hopelessly yearning lover of Petrarchan convention. His forced exit from his jungle, in chains, results directly from his single-minded pursuit of Fay. He smashes a Broadway theater when the notion enters his dull brain that the flashbulbs of photographers somehow endanger the lady. His perilous shinnying up a skyscraper to pluck Fay from her boudoir is an act of the kindliest of hearts. He's impossible to discourage even though the love of his life can't lay eyes on him without shrieking murder.

The tragedy of King Kong then, is to be the beast who at the end   **10**
of the fable fails to turn into the handsome prince. This is the conviction that the scriptwriters would leave with us in the film's closing line.
As Kong's corpse lies blocking traffic in the street, the entrepreneur
who brought Kong to New York turns to the assembled reporters and
proclaims: "That's your story, boys — it was beauty and the beast!"
But greater forces than those of the screaming Lady have combined
to lay Kong low, if you ask me. Kong lives for a time as one of those
persecuted near-animal souls bewildered in the middle of an industrial
order, whose simple desires are thwarted at every turn. He climbs the
Empire State Building because in all New York it's the closest thing
he can find to the clifftop of his jungle isle. He dies, a pitiful dolt, and
the army brass and publicity men cackle over him. His death is the only
possible outcome to as neat a tragic dilemma as you can ask for. The
machine guns do him in, while the manicured human hero (a nice clean
Dartmouth boy) carries away Kong's sweetheart to the altar. O, the
misery of it all. There's far more truth about upper-middle-class
American life in *King Kong* than in the last seven dozen novels of John
P. Marquand.

A Negro friend from Atlanta tells me that in movie houses in colored   **11**
neighborhoods throughout the South, Kong does a constant business.
They show the thing in Atlanta at least every year, presumably to the
same audiences. Perhaps this popularity may simply be due to the fact
that Kong is one of the most watchable movies ever constructed, but
I wonder whether Negro audiences may not find some archetypical appeal in this serio-comic tale of a huge black powerful free spirit whom
all the hardworking white policemen are out to kill.

Every day in the week on a screen somewhere in the world, King   **12**
Kong relives his agony. Again and again he expires on the Empire State
Building, as audiences of the devout assist his sacrifice. We watch him
die, and by extension kill the ape within our bones, but these little deaths
of ours occur in prosaic surroundings. We do not die on a tower, New
York before our feet, nor do we give our lives to smash a few flying
machines. It is not for us to bring to a momentary standstill the civilization in which we move. King Kong does this for us. And so we kill
him again and again, in much-spliced celluloid, while the ape in us
expires from day to day, obscure, in desperation.

The Writer's Subject

1. What evidence does Kennedy bring in support of his contention that "no other monster in movie history has won so devoted a popular audience" as Kong? (paras. 1-3)

2. Summarize what Kennedy believes to be the reasons for "the abiding appeal of the giant ape."

3. Why does Kennedy refer to the Tarzan series as an American myth? What connection does this myth have with *King Kong*? (para. 5)

4. What does Kennedy mean by "the tradition of the pitiable monster"? (para. 6)

5. Why, in Kennedy's view, did the film have particular appeal to audiences during the Depression? (para. 7)

6. Why does Kennedy believe that the violent episode he describes in paragraph 8 would be satisfying to audiences in modern cities?

7. What use does Kennedy make of the well known fairytale, "Beauty and the Beast"? (para. 10)

8. What larger social significance does Kennedy perceive in the ordeal and the inevitable death of Kong? (para. 10)

9. To what does Kennedy attribute the popularity of King Kong with black audiences? (para. 11)

10. What does Kennedy mean when he says, in paragraph 12, that Kong's celluloid death is a "sacrifice"? Relate his comment to his choice of title.

The Writer's Style and Strategy

1. What details of phrasing and diction in the first four paragraphs reveal Kennedy's attitude to *King Kong* as film?

2. In paragraph 3 Kennedy compares Kong to other movie monsters. How does his description of Kong's rivals convey his sense of their inferiority?

3. What use does Kennedy make of analogy in paragraph 6 to convey Kong's "pitiable" qualities?

4. Discuss the organization of paragraph 8. How does Kennedy relate his assertion about modern urban man to the scene he describes from *King Kong*?

5. What is the tone of paragraph 9, and how is it established? Why does Kennedy describe Kong as "a gentleman" with a "sense of chivalry," and as "the hopelessly yearning lover of Petrarchan convention"?

6. The tone and language of this essay are informal, even colloquial, for the most part, but they change dramatically in the closing paragraphs (compare, for example, paragraphs 4 and 12). Why does Kennedy adopt this strategy?

7. Identify the major stages of Kennedy's discussion. At what point does he move from his introduction to his principal arguments? How is the reader prepared for the conclusion?

Suggested Topics for Writing and Discussion

1. Kennedy points to a number of reasons for the success of *King Kong*, including psychological, political and social. Choose a popular movie and discuss those elements which might claim for the film a deeper significance.

2. Choose a genre other than monster movies (e.g., Westerns, science fiction movies, spy thrillers, ninja and kung-fu movies) and account for the genre's popularity.

3. Many of the modern equivalents of *King Kong* are notable for their realistic violence and brutality, aided by the use of special effects. Do you think there is a case for the censoring of such films?

4. Locate reviews of the "remake" of *King Kong* which appeared in 1980 and the "sequel," *King Kong Lives!* which appeared in 1986. What do these reviews suggest about the continuing popularity of *King Kong*?

STAR WARS: A Trilogy

A Space Iliad:
The STAR WARS War: I
by Arthur Lubow

If you want a loyal friend or a lethal weapon, try a machine. But when 1
the revolution is sliding down the incinerator chute and there's only five
seconds left to save it, you had better rely on the Life Force.

That's the unexpected message of *Star Wars*, a movie which manages 2
to slap technology's face while celebrating the glories of gadgetry. This
double-jointed maneuver gives the film its springy bounce. An anti-
modern message in an ultra-modern wrapper: what could be more
stylish? What could be more fun?

Much of *Star Wars'* success is simply the overflow from its excesses. 3
Loaded with enough special features to equip a dozen lesser vehicles,
hurtling along at a velocity close to light speed, George Lucas's movie
breaks down all barriers of resistance. Like a radio serial, it begins at
the middle, quickly summarizing previous events and starting right in
with some sizzling action. The race is on, and there are no pit stops.
No reflective pauses or digressing subplots are permitted to slow the
progression of adventures. Any hints of romance are condensed into
an offhand mumble of affection or a second's kiss before a daring leap.
This is a boy's movie.

At times, it seems like three or four boy's movies, grafted into a 4
superhardy hybrid. The charred house and skeletons of Luke Skywalker's
aunt and uncle might have been left by Indians in a Western. Luke and
princess Leia's rope-swing across an urban canyon would have done
Tarzan proud. And the bombers at the movie's end are World War II
planes covered with galactic graffiti. Lucas has ordered up every heroic
ingredient in the catalogue. To the mixture he has added a pinch of Her-

mann Hesse and a dash of Flash Gordon. The combination tickles the palate.

5   After the first viewing, dazzled by the binary sunlight of the brilliant special effects, you might thank the technicians for your two hours of enjoyment. Certainly they deserve their inevitable awards. The protoplasmic degenerates at the spaceside bar almost steal the show. The film is meticulous in its details, from the scruffy beat-up surfaces of the spaceships to the individual languages concocted for each creature. Throwaways like the futuristic food processor and the metallic cigars make a celluloid civilization slightly more believable. The holographic chess game between See Threepio and the Wookie, the tentacle that pulls Luke into the muck, and the dogfights between the rebel bombers and the imperial fighters provide the same rush of exhilaration that you get in other movies from a great performance or a witty stretch of dialogue. It's the excitement of witnessing a masterly achievement. In a movie starring machines, you'd expect that excitement to come from the special effects department and not from central casting. Although the close-ups of Artoo-Detoo blinking and whimpering are remarkably moving, Al Pacino has nothing to worry about.

6   The technical achievements of *Star Wars* are so exciting that it's easy to overestimate their importance. The film's screenplay, for instance, can be dismissed as secondary. Is it anything more than a collage of old movies and comic strips? The script is like some ordinary fir tree, plucked arbitrarily from a forest and festooned with strands of gorgeous lights. Or so you think at first. But there's a sharp mind behind this mindlessness. Lucas knows exactly what he's doing.

7   Among the countless quotations from hack movies and comic books, one scene stands out as different. Several critics have remarked that the closing sequence of *Star Wars,* in which Luke, Han Solo, and the Wookie Chewbacca walk down a grand aisle to receive their medals, is a restaging of the march of Hitler, Himmler, and Lutze to the Nuremberg memorial monument in Leni Riefenstahl's *Triumph of the Will.* The quote is appreciated as a high-spirited joke by a former film student. If it means anything, it's merely a skeptical footnote to the heroism celebrated throughout the movie. Like Paramount's ad campaign for *King Kong* — "The most exciting original motion picture event of all time" — the reference to *Triumph of the Will* is a whispered selfcriticism, a bite without teeth, a flaw smoothed away with a witticism.

8   *Star Wars* would seem to be light-years away from a celebration of Nazi power. Yet its subject is indeed the triumph of the will, and a

reviewer from the *Volkischer Beobachter* would find much to praise. "History is a sequence of many virile decisions," Josef Goebbels wrote in his novel, *Michael*. "Armies are not victorious, but men within armies." George Lucas has similar ideas about individual heroism. Who could ask for a better Ubermensch than Obi-Wan Kenobi? (One can only imagine the titan who sired Luke.) Obi-Wan's strength lies in the power of his will. "The Force can have a strong influence on the weakminded," he remarks after hypnotically browbeating some imperial Storm Troopers. His call to self-sacrifice lures young Skywalker ("I can't get involved, I've got work to do") from a life of bourgeois stultification. Tomorrow belongs to Luke.

What we are watching is but another battle in the epic struggle be- 9 ween Mammon and idealism, matter and spirit. The one city depicted in *Star Wars* could be Hitler's vision of Weimar Berlin. Naturally, Luke is a farm boy of pure yeoman stock. He is justifiably sickened by the jabbering Jawas, bright-eyed itinerant merchants whom the Führer would have found familiar. No better are the Sand people, barbaric gypsies who lack culture and humanity. Against this sordid world of ugliness and corruption stand the power and the glory of the Force.

Obi-Wan defines the Force as the "energy field created by all living 10 things . . . it binds the galaxy together." The Force is a version of Bergson's *élan vital* and Jung's collective unconscious. More to the point, it is an expression of a basic Nazi tenet: the fundamental unity of nature, the "ultimate interconnections" of all living things. To acquire enormous powers, you need only tap the Force. "The ability to destroy a planet is insignificant beside the power of the Force," says the arch-villain, Darth Vader. Unfortunately for the evil Galactic Empire, the asthmatic Darth Vader is a prophet unheeded. The imperial technocrats favor science over this "ancient religion." They would agree with the pragmatic smuggler, Han Solo: "Hokey religions and ancient weapons are no match for a good blaster."

The Death Star is the greatest achievement of modern science. It is 11 destroyed by the power of the Force. A friend of mine says that when Luke blows up the Death Star, it's as if rockthrowing kids have over-run the Pentagon. Goebbels too would have been thrilled. As he wrote: "The old ones . . . defend their power to the last. But one day they will be defeated after all. Youth finally must be victorious." The heroic individual triumphs against the old, corrupt system. In *Star Wars,* Luke is able to penetrate the Death Star's defenses because the Empire has protected itself against machines, not heroes. As the rebel teacher says:

"The Empire doesn't consider a one-man fighter to be a threat."

12   When he enters the final run of his bombing mission, Luke hears the voice of his sainted teacher, Obi-Wan. "Use the Force, Luke," the voice urges. "Let go of the computer. Luke, trust me." Obi-Wan had already given Luke more extensive advice in person. "Let go your conscious self and act on instinct," he instructed. "Your eyes can deceive you. Don't trust them. Stretch out with your feelings." The time has come to test this philosophy. And, glory be — mysticism works. It's not only holier than science; it's more effective. Shucking off his technological blinders, Luke disconnects his homing computer, opens his inner eyes, and drops the bomb right down the shaft. Civilization survives. The Force prevails.

13   What are we to make of this mumbo-jumbo? Is it significant that beneath this film's futuristic skin there beats an unregenerate reactionary heart? The movie that duplicates the achievement of automation — replacing human protagonists with machines — is stridently anti-technological. *Star Wars* is a paean to mysticism and an attack on modern science. That message has a powerful appeal. It was the essence of the Nazi myth, and that's worth pointing out — not because the analogy makes *Star Wars* a "fascist movie" (its good humor and lack of rancor insure that it's not), but because it explains some of the buzz of excitement from the audiences leaving the movie theater. The Nazi mixture of heroism, self-sacrifice, and mysticism is heady stuff. When the old *Liebfraumilch* is poured into new bottles, it packs a powerful wallop.

(1977)

The Writer's Subject

1. What contradiction does Lubow point out in his introductory paragraphs? How does this contradiction anticipate his main point about the movie's underlying meaning?

2. What elements of *Star Wars* lead Lubow to say, "This is a boy's movie"? (paras. 3 and 4)

3. Explain Lubow's assertion that "Lucas has ordered up every heroic ingredient in the catalogue" (para. 4).

4. Lubow praises the special effects; why then does he warn against "overestimating their importance"? (para. 6)

5. What connection does Lubow draw between *Star Wars* and Riefenstahl's film *Triumph of the Will*? (paras. 7 and 8)

6. What similarities does Lubow see between Nazi ideology and the ideas underlying *Star Wars*? Why is "the Force," in his view, "an expression of a basic Nazi tenet" (paras. 7-11)?

7. Why, according to Lubow, does *Star Wars* suggest that mysticism is more effective than science? (para. 12)

8. Why does this "stridently anti-technological" film have such a powerful appeal, in Lubow's view?

The Writer's Style and Strategy

1. What expectations are raised by the title of this essay?

2. The first part of Lubow's essay applauds the fast pace and technical achievements of *Star Wars*; the second part is an examination of the film's informing ideas. How does Lubow effect the transition between the two parts of the discussion?

3. Discuss Lubow's use of metaphors and comparisons in paragraphs 3 and 4. How do they demonstrate the assertion at the beginning of paragraph 3, "Much of *Star Wars'* success is simply the overflow from its excesses"?

4. Why does Lubow allude to "a reviewer from the *Volkischer Beobachter*," a German newspaper of the 1920s and 1930s? (para. 8)

5. Lubow draws a detailed analogy between Nazi ideology and the ideas underlying *Star Wars*. How does he make this analogy convincing? (paras. 8-13)

6. After outlining the triumph of "the Force" in *Star Wars*, Lubow asks, "What are we to make of this mumbo-jumbo?" (para. 13) What does this question tell the reader about Lubow's attitude to his subject? Where else is this attitude revealed?

7. Discuss the appropriateness of the metaphor with which Lubow concludes his essay.

Suggested Topics for Writing and Discussion

See the questions on this and other essays on *Star Wars* at the end of this section.

Star Drek: The STAR WARS War: II
by Terry Curtis Fox

1   *Star Wars* is the *Tom Jones* of 1977. Critics who believe analysis belongs on the couch love it; the audience which made science fiction the last pulp genre has led the lines to a box-office smash. The survival chances of *Star Wars,* on the other hand, are slim. The film defeats serious consideration. No matter how one looks at it, George Lucas has not only made a movie which is mindless where it would be mind-boggling, he has made a movie which is totally inept.

2   Never mind special effects. If you've seen one plastic starship you've seen them all. As for midgets in cute-suits, who remembers the amputees in *Soylent Green*? Consider instead the laser-sword which Lucas painfully spends forty-five minutes defining as an elegantly human weapon, emblematic of the life-sustaining Force. Not only is there nothing elegant, much less exciting, in the light-sword fight between Lord Darth Vader (David Prowse) and Ben/Obi-Wan Kenobi (Alec Guinness), but Luke Skywalker (Mark Hamill), the Force's young receiver, never gets to use the thing at all. Lucas has painfully constructed a payoff which never arrives.

3   The same is true of the movie's major climax, the race between Luke and Vader to see whether the rebels or the imperials will blow the other up first. The scene represents an act of skill on Luke's part (he's got one shot which must be right on target), a sky-chase on Vader's side, and a moment of redemption for Han Solo (Harrison Ford), the mercenary smuggler who makes a last-minute decision to look out for Luke and not just himself, thus saving Luke from Vader.

Not only does Lucas blow the impact of Luke's act — it's so 4
technological it's completely removed (why not use the already symbolic laser-sword?) — but the chase is so devoid of spherical geography
it is impossible to tell if Luke is really in danger or exactly how Han
saves his friend.

And that's just entertainment. When it comes to extending the genre, 5
Lucas hasn't done a thing. Consider Luke's return from the desert to
find his surrogate parents blown away by an Imperial raiding party.
The shot itself is a direct quote from *The Searchers* and, one expects,
a particularly relevant quote at that. Martin Pauley's discovery of his
massacred family not only occurs after a diversionary chase through
a desert, but it forces Pauley to begin the redefinition of family which
lies at the heart of that film.

Luke's encounter should mean something. In the desert, after all, he 6
has met Ben/Obi-Wan, the man who becomes his second surrogate father
and who gives him both a true history and a heroic future. Luke has
been searching for a connection to his father's life, but he is afraid to
follow Ben/Obi-Wan since it means abandonment of his aunt and uncle
at harvest time. The two surrogate fathers are in serious opposition —
by choosing one, Luke must disown the other.

But unlike *The Searchers,* which Lucas quotes, the death of Luke's 7
"family" causes neither pain nor a confrontation with difficult decisions.
Rather than raising problems, it solves them. With his old surrogate
parents conveniently killed off, Luke can follow his new surrogate father
to the ends of the universe. Between good and evil is an easy choice.

Even more revealing is the film's end quote — a hero's welcome for 8
Luke, Han, and company which is a direct lift from Leni Riefenstahl's
Triumph of the Will. Although there is talk about the death of a "republic"
and the dismantling of a "senate," the alternative in *Star Wars* is at best
a parliamentary monarchy. Not only does this world rely upon heroes,
it is devoutly subservient to Princess Leia Organa (Carrie Fisher). The
rebel forces seem to want restoration, not revolution.

This is not an idle ideological complaint. Unlike the detective novel, 9
science fiction has yet to find its Hammett. Of the current generation
of writers, only two, Roger Zelazny and Samuel R. Delany, are in-
herently interesting because of their style. From H.P. Lovecraft's *Cthulhu*
to Frank Herbert's *Dune,* SF is a genre whose strength comes from its
imaginative powers, its ability to create societies in which alternative
laws of action and behavior can be displayed.

Lucas, who was so successful at creating a social structure in both 10

THX 1138 and *American Graffiti,* seems here to have abandoned his most interesting talent. Subsumed by technology, he's lost control not only of his mechanics and metaphors but of his vision as well.

11   Examine, for a moment, the much praised robot comedy team of See Threepio (Anthony Daniels) and Artoo-Detoo (Kenny Baker). Like the spelling out of their names, See Threepio and Artoo-Detoo are in the throes of what Travis McGee calls "the terminal cutes." They've got everything but fur — everything, that is, except the ability to comment on human activity which makes real comedy teams (not to mention better anthropomorphizations) worthwhile.

12   Unlike HAL in *2001: A Space Odyssey* the robots of *Star Wars* are not the most human characters in the film. They are exactly what they pretend to be — mechanical figures endowed with a limited number of human characteristics. Like the dog with which W.C. Fields refused to appear, the robot-comics reveal nothing: they exist solely to steal scenes.

13   The fun-fun-fun brigade claims this is just the point. Looking at the movie closely is like throwing water on the Wicked Witch of the West — so why make it dissolve? Because Lucas has (or had) more potential and, box-office records notwithstanding, so did the film. I'd rather spend my time with a Barry Smith *Conan the Barbarian.* Smith is in control of both his material and medium; Lucas is not.

14   *2001* had acid. What's *Star Wars'* excuse?

(1977)

The Writer's Subject

1. According to Fox, what kinds of audience account for the box office success of *Star Wars*? (para. 1)

2. What flaws does Fox point to in the film's plot and use of special effects? (paras. 1-4)

3. What criticism does Fox make of Lucas's use of the earlier film, *The Searchers?* What, in Fox's view, does the *Star Wars* episode lack that gave *The Searchers* its power? (paras. 6-7)

4. Consider Fox's view of the robots in *Star Wars*. How are his views different from those of Lubow and Rosenbaum (the other writers on *Star Wars* in this reader)?

5. What is the "fun-fun-fun brigade" (para. 13)? Why does Fox take issue with this audience?

The Writer's Style and Strategy

1. In paragraph 1, Fox says of *Star Wars*, "The film defeats serious consideration." Is this an appropriate opening strategy for the essay that follows?

2. What is the predominant tone of the essay? By what means is it established?

3. To what audience does Fox direct his discussion? What elements of the essay suggest that he is writing for this particular audience?

4. Discuss the appropriateness of Fox's title.

Suggested Topics for Writing and Discussion

See the questions on this and other essays on *Star Wars* at the end of this section.

The Solitary Pleasures of STAR WARS
by Jonathan Rosenbaum

1   'A long time ago in a galaxy far, far away . . .' reads the opening title, over vast interstellar reaches of wide-screen space. 'I've seen the future and it works!' declares a happy teenager on his way out of the movie to a TV reporter in Los Angeles — oddly parroting what Lincoln Steffens said about Russia over fifty years ago, before Ford Motors gave the slogan a second lease of life. 'Another galaxy, another time,' begins the novel's prologue more non-committally, carefully hedging all bets. But confusion between past and future, however useful to the tactics of George Lucas' *Star Wars,* seems almost secondary to the overriding insistence that whenever this giddy space opera is taking place, it can't possibly be anywhere quite so disagreeable as the present.

2   'Rather than do some angry, socially relevant film,' Lucas has said, 'I realised there was another relevance that is even more important — dreams and fantasies, getting children to believe there is more to life than garbage and killing and all that real stuff like stealing hubcaps — that you could still sit and dream about exotic lands and strange creatures.' Although garbage and killing are anything but absent from *Star Wars,* and stealing hubcaps is around in spirit if not in letter, Lucas' aspiration is easy enough to comprehend, even after the social interests of his *THX 1138* and *American Graffiti.* The disconcerting thing for a good many critics about his latest box-office monolith is that it doesn't seem to *mean* anything other than what it unabashedly is: a well-crafted, dehumanised update of *Flash Gordon* with better production values, no ironic overtones and a battery of special effects.

3   Consider the plot, which any well-behaved computer fed with the right

amount of pulp could probably regurgitate: Luke Skywalker (Mark Hamill), farm youth living with uncle and aunt on the remote planet Tatooine, son of a vanquished Jedi warrior of the Old Republic — an order overturned by the evil Galactic Empire, headed by former Jedi warrior Darth Vader and the malignant Grand Moff Tarkin (Peter Cushing) — accidentally intercepts part of a sound-and-image message sent by beautiful princess Leia Organa (Carrie Fisher), a rebel senator from planet Alderaan held captive by the Empire, to Ben 'Obi-Wan' Kenobi (Alec Guinness), legendary Jedi warrior now living as an outlaw in the Tatooine mountains. . . .

Following the squat robot who carries the message — R2-D2, who **4** is usually accompanied by C-3PO, a tall vocal sidekick that mumbles like an English butler — Luke meets Kenobi, who bequeaths him his father's light sabre and, after uncle and aunt are promptly killed in an Empire raid, enlists his aid in Leia's rescue. Meanwhile, he trains the youth in the mystical powers of the Force, a spiritual order which bestows extra-sensory talents. Hiring the hardened mercenary Han Solo (Harrison Ford) and his non-human servant Chewbacca in the grubby Mos Eisley Spaceport to pilot them, Luke and Kenobi set off on a string of adventures, during which the latter is killed in a duel with Vader and Leia is freed. Luke then accompanies the rebel freedom fighters in an offensive against Death Star, the Empire's seemingly impregnable battle station, and single-handedly succeeds in blowing it to attractively bubbly, sparkling and satisfying smithereens.

All this is very clean and bloodless. Vader crunches a few audible **5** bones; aunt and uncle are burned to black cinders in homage to *The Searchers*; Kenobi executes a smooth forearm amputation with his sabre in the Mos Eisley saloon, and meets his own sabre death by vanishing into thin air, to be absorbed within the Force; the rest is mainly fireworks and pinball machines. The smirking idealism of Luke, the sullen cynicism of Han, the shrewish irritability of Leia, the growls and whines of Chewbacca, the fussy chattering of C-3PO and the electronic chirping of R2-D2 are all set up as 'cute' objects of delighted audience ridicule. Hamill, Ford and Fisher are made to look like surfers at an s-f masquerade ball; Cushing, the only visibly human villain, comes off as a rather improbable blend of Ming the Merciless and Jean-Luc Godard, in physiognomy as well as emotional tone. And apart from the steadfast Alec Guinness, who is respectfully allowed to assume a vaguer and more benign flatness as archetypal father figure, nearly everyone else is a monster, whether lovable (domestic) or disgusting (threatening),

with the borderline between human and non-human often indistinguishable. (The gibbering, scavenging Jawas on Tattooine are a
striking case in point: brown-robed and black-gloved, their only visible
features are firefly eyes.)

6   The deliberate silliness of all this — like the intricate silliness that
has always been part of Disney's stock-in-trade — leaves the audience
free to react from a safe voyeuristic distance, enjoying 'pure' sensations
that are unencumbered by any moral or emotional investments. Indeed,
the cursory treatment of 'romantic interest' (with Leia still prevaricating
at the end between both male leads via bored winks) leaves the way
open for a very different sort of titillation. In the exhilarating space
battles, with their odourless ecstasies of annihilation, and the various
space-gun skirmishes, with their fancy dismemberings and eliminations,
this essentially becomes an occasion for sexual release devoid of any
partner. Like the remote-control TV channel selectors that children love
to play with, and the mechanical shooting games found in arcades, *Star
Wars* offers solitary, narcissistic pleasures more than communal or
romantic myths to keep its audience cheering.

7   Admittedly, Westerns, samurai sagas, Arthurian legends, Disney
bestiaries, DeMille spectaculars and World War II epics have been borrowed from as liberally as earlier s-f. The climactic Death Star attack
is modelled directly after a compilation of air battle clips from over
fifty war films, and even the final procession of Luke, Han and Chewbacca down a long aisle to receive their medals has been identified by
Arthur Lubow as a conscious 'restaging of the march of Hitler, Himmler
and Lutze to the Nuremberg monument' in *Triumph of the Will*. But
the point of this approach is to make all the myths it plunders equally
trivial and 'usable' as nostalgic plot fodder, even if most of the emotions are absent. One would probably have to go back to the 1940s,
as Lucas did, to find such a guiltless celebration of unlimited warfare,
but one needs to escape history entirely in order to set up oppositions
of good and bad — reflected in black and white patternings of costume
and decor — as unambiguous. On the level of racial ideology, this knowing mindlessness is even shrewder. While the original 1936 *Flash Gordon*
serial could allude to the 'Yellow Peril' directly through Ming the Merciless without any sort of embarrassment, the styling of the Jawas as
stingy Jewish merchants — 'Munchkin Shylocks', in Richard Corliss'
apt phrase — is much more oblique and subtle; one might even have
to see the relationship of 'Jawa' to the Hebrew 'Yaweh' in order to catch
the clue.

Following the fashion set by *2001* in some aspects of its design — **8**
robots programmed to be more 'personable' than any of the actors, in-
depth trajectories of slab-like missiles entering the lower foreground
of shots and sliding away diagonally (including the three long paragraphs
preceding the action) — *Star Wars* postulates itself as the anti-*2001* in
nearly every other respect, and not only because fantasy is systematically
substituted for technology. If Kubrick's central subject was intelligence,
Lucas' is predicated on blind instinct: Luke's initiation into the Force,
like the spectator's into the film, is basically a matter of surrendering
to conditioned reflexes and letting the cosmic *mise en scène* take over.
And where *2001*'s sense of spectacle was contemplative, *Star Wars'* is
near-Pavlovian in its careful measurements of give and take, making
it impossible on a practical level to isolate many of the special effects
from the editing.

Working on the assumption that the enchantment of any creature, land- **9**
scape, gadget or set decreases in ratio to the length of time it's on the
screen — a withholding premise already evident in the Krel episodes
of *Forbidden Planet* and the brief, last-minute glimpses of a perishing
city in *This Island Earth* — the movie is constructed like a teasing comic
strip storyboard. Nothing incidental or scenic is allowed to retard the
rapidly paced narrative, but is merely packed along en route (like the
twin moons of Tatooine, or the binoculars Luke uses while scouting
for R2-D2). A rare exception is made for diverse beasties in the inventive Mos Eisley Western saloon sequence, where spectacle momentarily
triumphs over event.

Less imaginative in its other-worldly architecture than *The 5000* **10**
Fingers of Dr. T — an all but forgotten Stanley Kramer production of
the 1950s which, unlike *Star Wars,* incorporated an escape from an
unbearable present in its plot — Lucas' smorgasbord of styles is often
more a matter of quantity than quality, as in the dense profusion of red
laser beams which periodically streak across the screen. An effort is
made, however, to make some of the locations (the scrapheap inside
the Jawas' Sandcrawler, Mos Eisley, Han's pirate starship) untidy enough
to seem lived in. Sound, including the nearly continuous music, serves
the elliptical pacing throughout: intimations of Tarkin's imminent torture
of Leia are limited to a brief shot of a syringe and the loud sliding shut
of a door; the beast that pulls Luke down into the slimy muck of a shrink-
ing garbage bin is more heard than seen; and the whistling sounds of
the attacking rebel starships work a lot better as drama than as science.

For a film so devoid of any dialectic, one is tempted to speculate what **11** its absolute antithesis might be. Would the recent films of Grand Moff Godard — low-budget, experimental, pleasurable to the mind rather than to the reflexes — be far off the mark? Yet if any parallel can be found between the film world and Lucas' Manichean universe, it is the blitzkrieg of media fanfare celebrating *Star Wars* and its countless spin-off industries — not the trifling efforts to get Godard's films seen or acknowledged anywhere — that corresponds to the Empire's efforts to snuff out every form of resistance. And the consortium that is current-ly contriving to inundate everyone's mind with a few profitable monoliths and assign the rebel forces of cinema to cheerful oblivion is not merely a group of big business men, but a movement composed of critics, editors and media programmers and broadcasters — all of whom collaborate with other consumers in making *Star Wars* (which is already threaten-ing to topple *Jaws* as the all-time money-maker) more than a simple movie, but an appreciable dent in the landscape.

12   What has any of this to do with esoteric items like *Numéro Deux* and *Ici et Ailleurs,* whose more fragile transactions might as well be occur-ring on another planet? Simply the fact that both are concerned with advancing knowledge in the here and now, and this is generally taken to be such a distasteful activity that even defenders of such films generally feel compelled to describe their experiences as ones of necessary 'unpleasure'. The mere title of an earlier Godard film, *Le Gai Savoir,* already sounds anachronistic within the present climate. Who but a sick person, runs the implied argument, could take pleasure in a documen-tary shot of Palestinian soldiers in *Ici et Ailleurs,* followed by a title saying that 'Nearly all these actors are dead'? Better to take a calculated step backward in knowledge, sever communal and historical ties, hoot at heroes and villains alike, blow up invisible, imaginary enemies from a safe video distance and, enjoy it all as good, clean, healthy fun mark-ing time until the next real opportunities for automatic, xenophobic destruction arrive. This is the 'relevance' of *Star Wars* that a Lucas finds 'more important'; and several million filmgoers are heartily agreeing.

(1977)

The Writer's Subject

1. What aspect of Rosenbaum's argument is highlighted by the title of his essay?

2. What are Rosenbaum's chief criticisms of the plot and characters of *Star Wars*? (paras. 3-5)

3. What, according to Rosenbaum, gives *Star Wars* a "voyeuristic" appeal? (para. 6)

4. Why does Rosenbaum condemn George Lucas's many allusions in *Star Wars* to scenes or images from earlier movies? (para. 7)

5. In what way, according to Rosenbaum, does *Star Wars* reveal a kind of mindless racism? (para. 7)

6. What disturbs Rosenbaum about the huge publicity campaign accompanying the distribution of *Star Wars*? (para. 11)

7. Why in Rosenbaum's view are low-budget, "esoteric" films like those of Jean-Luc Godard less popular than *Star Wars*? (para. 12)

The Writer's Style and Strategy

1. Rosenbaum's essay first appeared in the film journal *Sight and Sound*. What elements of his approach suggest that he is writing for an audience with some knowledge of film-making and the history of cinema?

2. In what way does the opening paragraph lay the groundwork for Rosenbaum's subsequent argument?

3. What is Rosenbaum's purpose in quoting George Lucas's own words in paragraph 2? What use does he make of this quotation at the end of the essay?

4. As is customary in film critiques, Rosenbaum provides a brief account of the plot and characters of *Star Wars* (paras. 3-5). How does he make his own views clear in the course of this summary?

5. Explain the appropriateness of the analogies with which Rosenbaum concludes paragraph 6.

6. Give several examples to show how Rosenbaum uses comparison or contrast to other movies as a means of reinforcing his attack on the shortcomings of *Star Wars*.

7. Discuss the effectiveness of Rosenbaum's conclusion. How does it look back to the essay's opening, both in tone and in content?

Suggested Topics for Writing and Discussion

1. One means by which a film critic may judge a film's achievement is by

comparing it with other films similar in subject, genre, or treatment. Write a review of a film you have seen recently, assessing the degree of its success or failure by comparing it to another film of the same kind.

2. The critic Terry Curtis Fox takes exception to *Star Wars* because it is "just entertainment," and Jonathan Rosenbaum criticizes the film for lack of meaning. Does a film have to "mean" something in order to have a serious claim on our attention? Use a specific example to support your view.

3. Both Fox and Rosenbaum attack Lucas's simplistic treatment of the conflict between good and evil. Choose a recent film which focusses on this conflict; how would you assess its treatment of this theme? Was it, in your opinion, dealt with in a simplistic way? A subtle way?

4. Film critics must be conscious of the tastes and interests of their audience. Write two 500-word reviews of a film you have seen recently, one review intended for a college audience, the other for a more general audience. (Before you begin, create a "profile" of each group of hypothetical readers. Consider the adjustments which you will have to make in "aiming" the review at the particular audience.)

5. Locate the movie page in your local daily newspaper (an edition that has lots of ads for movies, perhaps a weekend section). What do the advertisements tell you about the appeals made by the movie's publicists? What assumptions do they seem to make about the potential audience the ads are aimed at? Where possible, compare a film's publicity to the film itself. Were your expectations fulfilled, or was the publicity an example of advertising "hype"?

6. Find another essay or review on *Star Wars* and compare it with one of the essays on the film in this reader. (Magazines and newspapers for 1977 will give you reviews written when the film was "current.") Consider differences in emphasis, opinion, interpretation, and style.

7. Fox wrote in 1977 that "The survival chances of *Star Wars* . . . are slim," yet the film is commonly referred to by later reviewers of films and by others writing about films. What in your view accounts for the continuing interest in *Star Wars*? (You may wish to look at the remarks on *Star Wars* made by Bruno Bettelheim in "The Art of Moving Pictures" (1981) and by William Arkin in "At the Movies" (1986), two essays in this reader.)

8. In "The Art of Moving Pictures," Bruno Bettelheim argues that science fiction movies provide "myths" for modern audiences. Choose a science fiction film other than *Star Wars* and identify those features of character, plot and theme that impart to the film mythic qualities.

Nature and Mankind

The Obligation to Endure
by Rachel Carson

The history of life on earth has been a history of interaction between 1
living things and their surroundings. To a large extent, the physical form
and the habits of the earth's vegetation and its animal life have been
moulded by the environment. Considering the whole span of earthly
time, the opposite effect, in which life actually modifies its surroundings, has been relatively slight. Only within the moment of time
represented by the present century has one species — man — acquired
significant power to alter the nature of his world.

During the past quarter century this power has not only increased 2
to one of disturbing magnitude but it has changed in character. The most
alarming of all man's assaults upon the environment is the contamination of air, earth, rivers, and sea with dangerous and even lethal
materials. This pollution is for the most part irrecoverable; the chain
of evil it initiates not only in the world that must support life but in
living tissues is for the most part irreversible. In this now universal
contamination of the environment, chemicals are the sinister and little
recognized partners of radiation in changing the very nature of the world
— the very nature of its life. Strontium 90, released through nuclear
explosions into the air, comes to earth in rain or drifts down as fallout,
lodges in soil, enters into the grass or corn or wheat grown there, and
in time takes up its abode in the bones of a human being, there to remain until his death. Similarly, chemicals sprayed on croplands or forests
or gardens lie long in soil, entering into living organisms, passing from
one to another in a chain of poisoning and death. Or they pass mysteriously by underground streams until they emerge and, through the alchemy

of air and sunlight, combine into new forms that kill vegetation, sicken cattle, and work unknown harm on those who drink from once pure wells. As Albert Schweitzer has said, "Man can hardly even recognize the devils of his own creation."

3   It took hundreds of millions of years to produce the life that now inhabits the earth — eons of time in which that developing and evolving and diversifying life reached a state of adjustment and balance with its surroundings. The environment, rigorously shaping and directing the life it supported, contained elements that were hostile as well as supporting. Certain rocks gave out dangerous radiation; even within the light of the sun, from which all life draws its energy, there were short-wave radiations with power to injure. Given time — time not in years but in millennia — life adjusts, and a balance has been reached. For time is the essential ingredient; but in the modern world there is no time.

4   The rapidity of change and the speed with which new situations are created follow the impetuous and heedless pace of man rather than the deliberate pace of nature. Radiation is no longer merely the background radiation of rocks, the bombardment of cosmic rays, the ultraviolet of the sun that have existed before there was any life on earth; radiation is now the unnatural creation of man's tampering with the atom. The chemicals to which life is asked to make its adjustment are no longer merely the calcium and silica and copper and all the rest of the minerals washed out of the rocks and carried in rivers to the sea; they are the synthetic creations of man's inventive mind, brewed in his laboratories, and having no counterparts in nature.

5   To adjust to these chemicals would require time on the scale that is nature's; it would require not merely the years of a man's life but the life of generations. And even this, were it by some miracle possible, would be futile, for the new chemicals come from our laboratories in an endless stream; almost five hundred annually find their way into actual use in the United States alone. The figure is staggering and its implications are not easily grasped — 500 new chemicals to which the bodies of men and animals are required somehow to adapt each year, chemicals totally outside the limits of biologic experience.

6   Among them are many that are used in man's war against nature. Since the mid-1940's over 200 basic chemicals have been created for use in killing insects, weeds, rodents, and other organisms described in the modern vernacular as "pests": and they are sold under several thousand different brand names.

7   These sprays, dusts, and aerosols are now applied almost universal-

ly to farms, gardens, forests, and homes — nonselective chemicals that have the power to kill every insect, the "good" and the "bad," to still the song of birds and the leaping of fish in the streams, to coat the leaves with a deadly film, and to linger on in soil — all this though the intended target may be only a few weeds or insects. Can anyone believe it is possible to lay down such a barrage of poisons on the surface of earth without making it unfit for all life? They should not be called "insecticides," but "biocides."

The whole process of spraying seems caught up in an endless spiral. 8 Since DDT was released for civilian use, a process of escalation has been going on in which ever more toxic materials must be found. This has happened because insects, in a triumphant vindication of Darwin's principle of the survival of the fittest, have evolved super races immune to the particular insecticide used. Hence a deadlier one has always to be developed — and then a deadlier one than that. It has happened also because, for reasons to be described later, destructive insects often undergo a "flareback," or resurgence, after spraying, in numbers greater than before. Thus the chemical war is never won, and all life is caught in its violent crossfire.

Along with the possibility of the extinction of mankind by nuclear 9 war, the central problem of our age has therefore become the contamination of man's total environment with such substances of incredible potential for harm — substances that accumulate in the tissues of plants and animals and even penetrate the germ cells to shatter or alter the very material of heredity upon which the shape of the future depends.

Some would-be architects of our future look toward a time when it 10 will be possible to alter the human germ plasm by design. But we may easily be doing so now by inadvertence, for many chemicals, like radiation, bring about gene mutations. It is ironic to think that man might determine his own future by something so seemingly trivial as the choice of an insect spray.

All this has been risked — for what? Future historians may well be 11 amazed by our distorted sense of proportion. How could intelligent beings seek to control a few unwanted species by a method that contaminated the entire environment and brought the threat of disease and death even to their own kind? Yet this is precisely what we have done. We have done it, moreover, for reasons that collapse the moment we examine them. We are told that the enormous and expanding use of pesticides is necessary to maintain farm production. Yet is our real problem not one of *overproduction*? Our farms, despite measures to remove acreages from production and to pay farmers *not* to produce, have yielded such a staggering excess of crops that the American taxpayer in 1962 is paying out more than one billion dollars a year as the total carrying cost of the surplus-food storage program. And is the situation helped when one branch of the Agriculture Department tries to reduce production while another states, as it did in 1958, "It is believed generally that reduction of crop acreages under provisions of the Soil Bank will stimulate interest in use of chemicals to obtain maximum production on the land retained in crops." ?

12   All this is not to say there is no insect problem and no need of control. I am saying, rather, that control must be geared to realities, not to mythical situations, and that the methods employed must be such that they do not destroy us along with the insects.

13   The problem whose attempted solution has brought such a train of disaster in its wake is an accompaniment of our modern way of life. Long before the age of man, insects inhabited the earth — a group of extraordinarily varied and adaptable beings. Over the course of time since man's advent, a small percentage of the more that half a million species of insects have come into conflict with human welfare in two principal ways: as competitors for the food supply and as carriers of human disease.

14   Disease-carrying insects become important where human beings are crowded together, especially under conditions where sanitation is poor, as in time of natural disaster or war or in situations of extreme poverty and deprivation. Then control of some sort becomes necessary. It is a sobering fact, however, as we shall presently see, that the method of massive chemical control has had only limited success, and also threatens to worsen the very conditions it is intended to curb.

15   Under primitive agricultural conditions the farmer had few insect problems. These arose with the intensification of agriculture — the devotion of immense acreages to a single crop. Such a system set the stage for explosive increases in specific insect populations. Single-crop farming does not take advantage of the principles by which nature works; it is agriculture as an engineer might conceive it to be. Nature has introduced great variety into the landscape, but man has displayed a passion for simplifying it. Thus he undoes the built-in checks and balances by which nature holds the species within bounds. One important natural check is a limit on the amount of suitable habitat for each species. Obviously then, an insect that lives on wheat can build up its population

to much higher levels on a farm devoted to wheat than on one in which wheat is intermingled with other crops to which the insect is not adapted.

The same thing happens in other situations. A generation or more 16 ago, the towns of large areas of the United States lined their streets with the noble elm tree. Now the beauty they hopefully created is threatened with complete destruction as disease sweeps through the elms, carried by a beetle that would have only limited chance to build up large populations and to spread from tree to tree if the elms were only occasional trees in a richly diversified planting.

Another factor in the modern insect problem is one that must be viewed 17 against a background of geologic and human history: the spreading of thousands of different kinds of organisms from their native homes to invade new territories. This worldwide migration has been studied and graphically described by the British ecologist Charles Elton in his recent book *The Ecology of Invasions*. During the Cretaceous Period, some hundred million years ago, flooding seas cut many land bridges between continents and living things found themselves confined in what Elton calls "colossal separate nature reserves." There, isolated from others of their kind, they developed many new species. When some of the land masses were joined again, about 15 million years ago, these species began to move out into new territories – a movement that is not only still in progress but is now receiving considerable assistance from man.

The importation of plants is the primary agent in the modern spread 18 of species, for animals have almost invariably gone along with the plants, quarantine being a comparatively recent and not completely effective innovation. The United States Office of Plant Introduction alone has introduced almost 200,000 species and varieties of plants from all over the world. Nearly half of the 180 or so major insect enemies of plants in the United States are accidental imports from abroad, and most of them have come as hitchhikers on plants.

In new territory, out of reach of the restraining hand of the natural 19 enemies that kept down its numbers in its native land, an invading plant or animal is able to become enormously abundant. Thus it is no accident that our most troublesome insects are introduced species.

These invasions, both the naturally occurring and those dependent 20 on human assistance, are likely to continue indefinitely. Quarantine and massive chemical campaigns are only extremely expensive ways of buying time. We are faced, according to Dr. Elton, "with a life-and-death need not just to find new technological means of suppressing this plant or that animal"; instead we need the basic knowledge of animal populations and their relations to their surroundings that will "promote an even balance and damp down the explosive power of outbreaks and new invasions."

21   Much of the necessary knowledge is now available but we do not use it. We train ecologists in our universities and even employ them in our government agencies but we seldom take their advice. We allow the chemical death rain to fall as though there were no alternative, whereas in fact there are many, and our ingenuity could soon discover many more if given opportunity.

22   Have we fallen into a mesmerized state that makes us accept as inevitable that which is inferior or detrimental, as though having lost the will or the vision to demand that which is good? Such thinking, in the words of the ecologist Paul Shepard, "idealizes life with only its head out of water, inches above the limits of toleration of the corruption of its own environment. . . . Why should we tolerate a diet of weak poisons, a home in insipid surroundings, a circle of acquaintances who are not quite our enemies, the noise of motors with just enough relief to prevent insanity? Who would want to live in a world which is just not quite fatal?"

23   Yet such a world is pressed upon us. The crusade to create a chemically sterile, insect-free world seems to have engendered a fanatic zeal on the part of many specialists and most of the so-called control agencies. On every hand there is evidence that those engaged in spraying operations exercise a ruthless power. "The regulatory entomologists . . . function as prosecutors, judge and jury, tax assessor and collector and sheriff to enforce their own orders," said Connecticut entomologist Neely Turner. The most flagrant abuses go unchecked in both state and federal agencies.

24   It is not my contention that chemical insecticides must never be used. I do contend that we have put poisonous and biologically potent chemicals indiscriminately into the hands of persons largely or wholly ignorant of their potentials for harm. We have subjected enormous numbers of people to contact with these poisons, without their consent and often without their knowledge. If the Bill of Rights contains no guarantee that a citizen shall be secure against lethal poisons distributed either by private individuals or public officials, it is surely only because our forefathers, despite their considerable wisdom and foresight, could conceive of no such problem.

25   I contend, furthermore, that we have allowed these chemicals to be used with little or no advance investigation of their effect on soil, water,

wildlife, and man himself. Future generations are unlikely to condone our lack of prudent concern for the integrity of the natural world that supports all life.

There is still very limited awareness of the nature of the threat. This 26 is an era of specialists, each of whom sees his own problem and is unaware of or intolerant of the larger form into which it fits. It is also an era dominated by industry, in which the right to make a dollar at whatever cost is seldom challenged. When the public protests, confronted with some obvious evidence of damaging results of pesticide applications, it is fed little tranquilizing pills of half truth. We urgently need an end to these false assurances, to the sugar coating of unpalatable facts. It is the public that is being asked to assume the risks that the insect controllers calculate. The public must decide whether it wishes to continue on the present road, and it can do so only when in full possession of the facts. In the words of Jean Rostand, "The obligation to endure gives us the right to know."

(1962)

The Writer's Subject

1. What does Carson mean by "the chain of evil" initiated by chemical pollution? (para. 2) How does she illustrate her point?

2. Why does Carson believe that modern man cannot adjust to the various chemicals he has introduced into the environment? (paras. 3-5)

3. Why does Carson say that insecticides should be called "biocides"? (para. 7)

4. Why does Carson believe that the chemical war against insects may never be won? (para. 8)

5. What does Carson mean by saying that "control must be geared to realities, not to mythical situations" (para. 12)?

6. How do modern agricultural practices help to increase specific insect populations rather than curb them? (para. 15)

7. Carson says that man has the knowledge necessary to control troublesome insects without polluting the environment. Why, in her view, has man not used this knowledge?

8. What changes in attitudes and government policies does Carson imply must take place if the dangers of chemical pollution are to be checked?

The Writer's Style and Strategy

1. What is the tone of this essay? How is it established?

2. The essay is both an exposition of the effects of chemicals and an argument against their uncontrolled use. Identify those elements which are primarily expository and those which are particularly calculated to appeal to the reader's emotions.

3. Carson makes use of a number of devices to lend weight and add emphasis to her argument: rhetorical questions, the citing of authorities, references to statistical information. Find an example of each of these and comment on its effectiveness.

Suggested Topics for Writing and Discussion

1. This essay is taken from Rachel Carson's book *Silent Spring,* published in 1962. In what respects are we still threatened by the dangers which Carson pointed out a quarter of a century ago?

2. We are a society accustomed to the free use of chemicals in the home as well as in industry and agriculture. Drawing on your own experience, show how chemical products play a part in our daily lives. To what extent do any of these products constitute a threat to human life or the natural environment?

3. Compare the concerns of Carson in "The Obligation to Endure" with those of Bronowski in "The Real Responsibilities of the Scientist." Both are concerned with the need to keep the public well informed about scientific research. How might this be accomplished?

4. Carson says that ours is "an era dominated by industry, in which the right to make a dollar at whatever cost is seldom challenged." Do you agree with Carson's assessment?

The Bird and the Machine

by Loren Eiseley

I suppose their little bones have years ago been lost among the stones   1
and wind of those high glacial pastures. I suppose their feathers blew
eventually into the piles of tumbleweed beneath the straggling cattle
fences and rotted there in the mountain snows, along with dead steers
and all the other things that drift to an end in the corners of the wire.
I do not quite know why I should be thinking of birds over the *New
York Times* at breakfast, particularly the birds of my youth half a continent away. It is a funny thing what the brain will do with memories
and how it will treasure them and finally bring them into odd juxtapositions with other things, as though it wanted to make a design, or get
some meaning out of them, whether you want it or not, or even see it.

It used to seem marvelous to me, but I read now that there are machines   2
that can do these things in a small way, machines that can crawl about
like animals, and that it may not be long now until they do more things
− maybe even make themselves − I saw that piece in the *Times* just
now. And then they will, maybe − well, who knows − but you read
about it more and more with no one making any protest, and already
they can add better than we and reach up and hear things through the
dark and finger the guns over the night sky.

This is the new world that I read about at breakfast. This is the world   3
that confronts me in my biological books and journals, until there are
times when I sit quietly in my chair and try to hear the little purr of
the cogs in my head and the tubes flaring and dying as the messages
go through them and the circuits snap shut or open. This is the great
age, make no mistake about it; the robot has been born somewhat ap-

propriately along with the atom bomb, and the brain they say now is just another type of more complicated feedback system. The engineers have its basic principles worked out; it's mechanical, you know; nothing to get superstitious about; and man can always improve on nature once he gets the idea. Well, he's got it all right and that's why, I guess, I sit here in my chair, with the article crunched in my hand, remembering those two birds and that blue mountain sunlight. There is another magazine article on my desk that reads "Machines Are Getting Smarter Every Day." I don't deny it, but I'll stick with the birds. It's life I believe in, not machines.

4   Maybe you don't believe there is any difference. A skeleton is all joints and pulleys, I'll admit. And when man was in his simpler stages of machine building in the eighteenth century, he quickly saw the resemblances. "What," wrote Hobbes, "is the heart but a spring, and the nerves but so many strings, and the joints but so many wheels, giving motion to the whole body?" Tinkering about in their shops it was inevitable in the end that men would see the world as a huge machine "subdivided into an infinite number of lesser machines."

5   The idea took on with a vengeance. Little automatons toured the country — dolls controlled by clockwork. Clocks described as little worlds were taken on tours by their designers. They were made up of moving figures, shifting scenes, and other remarkable devices. The life of the cell was unknown. Man, whether he was conceived as possessing a soul or not, moved and jerked about like these tiny puppets. A human being thought of himself in terms of his own tools and implements. He had been fashioned like the puppets he produced and was only a more clever model made by a greater designer.

6   Then in the nineteenth century, the cell was discovered, and the single machine in its turn was found to be the product of millions of infinitesimal machines — the cells. Now, finally, the cell itself dissolves away into an abstract chemical machine, and that into some intangible, inexpressible flow of energy. The secret seems to lurk all about, the wheels get smaller and smaller, and they turn more rapidly, but when you try to seize it the life is gone — and so, by popular definition, some would say that life was never there in the first place. The wheels and the cogs are the secret and we can make them better in time — machines that will run faster and more accurately than real mice to real cheese.

7   I have no doubt it can be done, though a mouse harvesting seeds on an autumn thistle is to me a fine sight and more complicated, I think, in his multiform activity than a machine "mouse" running a maze. Also,

I like to think of the possible shape of the future brooding in mice, just as it brooded once in a rather ordinary mousy insectivore who became man. It leaves a nice fine indeterminate sense of wonder that even an electronic brain hasn't got, because you know perfectly well that if the electronic brain changes, it will be because of something man has done to it. But what man will do to himself he doesn't really know. A certain scale of time and a ghostly intangible thing called change are ticking in him. Powers and potentialities like the oak in the seed, or a red and awful ruin. Either way, it's impressive; and the mouse has it, too. Or those birds, I'll never forget those birds — yet before I measured their significance, I learned the lesson of time first of all. I was young then and left alone in a great desert — part of an expedition that had scattered its men over several hundred miles in order to carry on research more effectively. I learned there that time is a series of planes existing superficially in the same universe. The tempo is a human illusion, a subjective clock ticking in our own kind of protoplasm.

As the long months passed, I began to live on the slower planes and 8 to observe more readily what passed for life there. I sauntered, I passed more and more slowly up and down the canyons in the dry baking heat of midsummer. I slumbered for long hours in the shade of huge brown boulders that had gathered in tilted companies out on flats. I had forgotten the world of men and the world had forgotten me. Now and then I found a skull in the canyons, and these justified my remaining there. I took a serene cold interest in these discoveries. I had come, like many naturalists before me, to view life with a wary and subdued attention. I had grown to take pleasure in the divested bone.

I sat once on a high ridge that fell away before me into a waste of 9 sand dunes. I sat through hours of a long afternoon. Finally, as I glanced beside my boot an indistinct configuration caught my eye. It was a coiled rattlesnake, a big one. How long he had sat with me I do not know. I had not frightened him. We were both locked in the sleep-walking tempo of the earlier world, baking in the same high air and sunshine. Perhaps he had been there when I came. He slept on as I left, his coils, so ill-discerned by me, dissolving once more among the stones and gravel from which I had barely made him out.

Another time I got on a higher ridge, among some tough little wind- 10 warped pines half covered over with sand in a basinlike depression that caught everything carried by the air up to those heights. There were a few thin bones of birds, some cracked shells of indeterminable age, and the knotty fingers of pine roots bulged out of shape from their long and agonizing grasp upon the crevices of the rock. I lay under the pines in the sparse shade and went to sleep once more.

11   It grew cold finally, for autumn was in the air by then, and the few things that lived thereabouts were sinking down into an even chillier scale of time. In the moments between sleeping and waking I saw the roots about me and slowly, slowly, a foot in what seemed many centuries, I moved my sleep-stiffened hands over the scaling bark and lifted my numbed face after the vanishing sun. I was a great awkward thing of knots and aching limbs, trapped up there in some long, patient endurance that involved the necessity of putting living fingers into rock and by slow, aching expansion bursting those rocks asunder. I suppose, so thin and slow was the time of my pulse by then, that I might have stayed on to drift still deeper into the lower cadences of the frost, or the crystalline life that glistens pebbles, or shines in a snowflake, or dreams in the meteoric iron between the worlds.

12   It was a dim descent, but time was present in it. Somewhere far down in that scale the notion struck me that one might come the other way. Not many months thereafter I joined some colleagues heading higher into a remoter windy tableland where huge bones were reputed to protrude like boulders from the turf. I had drowsed with reptiles and moved with the century-long pulse of trees; now, lethargically, I was climbing up some invisible ladder of quickening hours. There had been talk of birds in connection with my duties. Birds are intense, fast-living creatures — reptiles, I suppose one might say, that have escaped out of the heavy sleep of time, transformed fairy creatures dancing over sunlit meadows. It is a youthful fancy, no doubt, but because of something that happened up there among the escarpments of that range, it remains with me a lifelong impression. I can never bear to see a bird imprisoned.

13   We came into that valley through the trailing mists of a spring night. It was a place that looked as though it might never have known the foot of man, but our scouts had been ahead of us and we knew all about the abandoned cabin of stone that lay far up on one hillside. It had been built in the land rush of the last century and then lost to the cattlemen again as the marginal soils failed to take to the plow.

14   There were spots like this all over that country. Lost graves marked by unlettered stones and old corroding rim-fire cartridge cases lying where somebody had made a stand among the boulders that rimmed the valley. They are all that remain of the range wars; the men are under the stones now. I could see our cavalcade winding in and out through

the mist below us: torches, the reflection of the truck lights on our collecting tins, and the far-off bumping of a loose dinosaur thigh bone in the bottom of a trailer. I stood on a rock a moment looking down and thinking what it cost in money and equipment to capture the past.

We had, in addition, instructions to lay hands on the present. The 15 word had come through to get them alive — birds, reptiles, anything. A zoo somewhere abroad needed restocking. It was one of those reciprocal matters in which science involves itself. Maybe our museum needed a stray ostrich egg and this was the payoff. Anyhow, my job was to help capture some birds and that was why I was there before the trucks.

The cabin had not been occupied for years. We intended to clean it 16 out and live in it, but there were holes in the roof and the birds had come in and were roosting in the rafters. You could depend on it in a place like this where everything blew away, and even a bird needed some place out of the weather and away from coyotes. A cabin going back to nature in a wild place draws them till they come in, listening at the eaves, I imagine, pecking softly among the shingles till they find a hole, and then suddenly the place is theirs and man is forgotten.

Sometimes of late years I find myself thinking the most beautiful sight 17 in the world might be the birds taking over New York after the last man has run away to the hills. I will never live to see it, of course, but I know just how it will sound because I've lived up high and I know the sort of watch birds keep on us. I've listened to sparrows tapping tentatively on the outside of air conditioners when they thought no one was listening, and I know how other birds test the vibrations that come up to them through the television aerials.

"Is he gone?" they ask, and the vibrations come up from below, "Not 18 yet, not yet."

Well, to come back, I got the door open softly and I had the spotlight 19 all ready to turn on and blind whatever birds there were so they couldn't see to get out through the roof. I had a short piece of ladder to put against the far wall where there was a shelf on which I expected to make the biggest haul. I had all the information I needed, just like any skilled assassin. I pushed the door open, the hinges squeaking only a little. A bird or two stirred — I could hear them — but nothing flew and there was a faint starlight through the holes in the roof.

I padded across the floor, got the ladder up and the light ready, and 20 slithered up the ladder till my head and arms were over the shelf. Everything was dark as pitch except for the starlight at the little place back of the shelf near the eaves. With the light to blind them, they'd never make it. I had them, I reached my arm carefully over in order to be ready to seize whatever was there and I put the flash on the edge of the shelf where it would stand by itself when I turned it on. That way I'd be able to use both hands.

21 Everything worked perfectly except for one detail — I didn't know what kind of birds were there. I never thought about it at all, and it wouldn't have mattered if I had. My orders were to get something interesting. I snapped on the flash and sure enough there was a great beating and feathers flying, but instead of my having them, they, or rather he, had me. He had my hand, that is, and for a small hawk not much bigger than my fist he was doing all right. I heard him give one short metallic cry when the light went on and my hand descended on the bird beside him; after that he was busy with his claws and his beak was sunk in my thumb. In the struggle I knocked the lamp over on the shelf, and his mate got her sight back and whisked neatly through the hole in the roof and off among the stars outside. It all happened in fifteen seconds and you might think I would have fallen down the ladder, but no, I had a professional assassin's reputation to keep up, and the bird, of course, made the mistake of thinking the hand was the enemy and not the eyes behind it. He chewed my thumb up pretty effectively and lacerated my hand with his claws, but in the end I got him, having two hands to work with.

22 He was a sparrow hawk and a fine young male in the prime of life. I was sorry not to catch the pair of them, but as I dripped blood and folded his wings carefully, holding him by the back so that he couldn't strike again, I had to admit the two of them might have been more than I could have handled under the circumstances. The little fellow had saved his mate by diverting me, and that was that. He was born to it and made no outcry now, resting in my hand hopelessly but peering toward me in the shadows behind the lamp with a fierce, almost indifferent glance. He neither gave nor expected mercy and something out of the high air passed from him to me, stirring a faint embarrassment.

23 I quit looking into that eye and managed to get my huge carcass with its fist full of prey back down the ladder. I put the bird in a box too small to allow him to injure himself by struggle and walked out to welcome the arriving trucks. It had been a long day, and camp still to make in the darkness. In the morning that bird would be just another episode. He would go back with the bones in the truck to a small cage in a city where he would spend the rest of his life. And a good thing,

too. I sucked my aching thumb and spat out some blood. An assassin has to get used to these things. I had a professional reputation to keep up.

In the morning, with the change that comes on suddenly in that high 24 country, the mist that had hovered below us in the valley was gone. The sky was a deep blue, and one could see for miles over the high outcroppings of stone. I was up early and brought the box in which the little hawk was imprisoned out on to the grass where I was building a cage. A wind as cool as a mountain spring ran over the grass and stirred my hair. It was a fine day to be alive. I looked up and all around and at the hole in the cabin roof out of which the other little hawk had fled. There was no sign of her anywhere that I could see.

"Probably in the next county by now," I thought cynically, but before 25 beginning work I decided I'd have a look at my last night's capture.

Secretively, I looked again all around the camp and up and down and 26 opened the box. I got him right out in my hand with his wings folded properly and I was careful not to startle him. He lay limp in my grasp and I could feel his heart pound under the feathers but he only looked beyond me and up.

I saw him look that last look away beyond me into a sky so full of 27 light that I could not follow his gaze. The little breeze flowed over me again, and nearby a mountain aspen shook all its tiny leaves. I suppose I must have had an idea then of what I was going to do, but I never let it come up into consciousness. I just reached over and laid the hawk on the grass.

He lay there a long minute without hope, unmoving, his eyes still 28 fixed on that blue vault above him. It must have been that he was already so far away in heart that he never felt the release from my hand. He never even stood. He just lay with his breast against the grass.

In the next second after that long minute he was gone. Like a flicker 29 of light, he had vanished with my eyes full on him but without actually seeing a premonitory wing beat. He was gone straight into that towering emptiness of light and crystal that my eyes could scarcely bear to penetrate. For another long moment there was silence. I could not see him. The light was too intense. Then from far up somewhere a cry came ringing down.

I was young then and had seen little of the world, but when I heard 30 that cry my heart turned over. It was not the cry of the hawk I had captured; for, by shifting my position against the sun I was now seeing farther up. Straight out of the sun's eye, where she must have been soaring restlessly above us for untold hours, hurtled his mate. And from far up, ringing from peak to peak of the summits over us, came a cry of such unutterable and ecstatic joy that it sounds down across the years and tingles among the cups on my quiet breakfast table.

31   I saw them both now. He was rising fast to meet her. They met in a great soaring gyre that turned to a whirling circle and a dance of wings. Once more, just once, their two voices, joined in a harsh wild medley of question and response, struck and echoed against the pinnacles of the valley. Then they were gone forever somewhere into those upper regions beyond the eyes of men.

32   I am older now, and sleep less, and have seen most of what there is to see and am not very much impressed any more, I suppose, by anything. "What Next in the Attributes of Machines?" my morning headline runs. "It Might Be the Power to Reproduce Themselves."

33   I lay the paper down and across my a mind a phrase floats insinuatingly: "It does not seem that there is anything in the construction, constituents, or behavior of the human being which it is essentially impossible for science to duplicate and synthesize. On the other hand. . . ."

34   All over the city the cogs in the hard, bright mechanisms have begun to turn. Figures move through computers, names are spelled out, a thoughtful machine selects the fingerprints of a wanted criminal from an array of thousands. In the laboratory an electronic mouse runs swiftly through a maze toward the cheese it can neither taste nor enjoy. On the second run it does better than a living mouse.

35   "On the other hand. . . ." Ah, my mind takes up, on the other hand the machine does not bleed, ache, hang for hours in the empty sky in a torment of hope to learn the fate of another machine, nor does it cry out with joy nor dance in the air with the fierce passion of a bird. Far off, over a distance greater than space, that remote cry from the heart of heaven makes a faint buzzing among my breakfast dishes and passes on and away.

                                                                                    (1955)

The Writer's Subject

1. What fears about the "new world" does Eiseley express in the first three paragraphs?

2. Eiseley says that man has come to see himself as a mechanism. What, in Eiseley's opinion, are the limitations of this view? (paras. 4-7)

3. Eiseley describes time as "a series of planes existing superficially in the same universe" and speaks of his own experience in the desert where he "began to live on the slower planes." How did Eiseley become aware of these "slower planes of time" (para. 7-11)?

4. In speaking of time at the beginning of paragraph 12, what does Eiseley mean by "one might come the other way"?

5. What feelings are stirred in Eiseley by the resistance of the male sparrow hawk? (paras. 22-23)

6. Why did Eiseley let the bird go?

7. In his description of the release of the sparrow hawk, Eiseley gives special prominence to the sky. Why? (paras. 24-31)

8. Why does Eiseley place his reflections in the mundane setting of his breakfast table?

The Writer's Style and Strategy

1. Eiseley treats the machine age in ironic terms. How is this irony conveyed? (paras. 2-3)

2. How does Eiseley move from general observations about men and machines to the more personal element of his narrative?

3. How does Eiseley's use of co-ordinated clauses in paragraph 11 help to convey his experience of the slowing down of time?

4. What is Eiseley's attitude to the expedition's secondary task, that the researchers "lay hands on the present" (para. 15)? How is this attitude conveyed?

5. Why does Eiseley refer to himself at several points as a skilled assassin with a professional reputation to keep up (paras. 19, 21, and 23)? What is the significance of his description of himself as a "huge carcass with a fistful of prey" (para. 23)?

6. Discuss the tone and language of the final paragraph. What makes the paragraph a fitting conclusion to Eiseley's reflections?

7. Comment on Eiseley's title. What emphasis does he gain by using the definite article?

Suggested Topics for Writing and Discussion

1. Eiseley seems disturbed at the notion that he must send the sparrow hawk to the city, to spend the rest of its life in a zoo. What is your own attitude to zoos? Do you think they serve a useful function?

2. Eiseley expresses concern at scientists' attempts to duplicate life forms. Do you believe that scientists should be given unrestricted freedom to pursue their experiments in genetic engineering and artificial intelligence?

3. Relate an incident which led to a change in your perspective. Use specific details of the experience to develop your narrative.

4. Eiseley is not enamoured of man's achievements in the modern age. Do you share his view? Choose one achievement of modern technology and show whether its benefits outweigh its drawbacks.

Roughing It in the Bush

My Plans for Moose Hunting in the Canadian Wilderness

by Stephen Leacock

The season is now opening when all those who have a manly streak 1
in them like to get out into the bush and "rough it" for a week or two
of hunting and fishing. For myself, I never feel that the autumn has
been well spent unless I can get out after the moose. And when I go
I like to go right into the bush and "rough it" — get clear away from
civilization, out in the open, and take fatigue or hardship just as it comes.

So this year I am making all my plans to get away for a couple of 2
weeks of moose hunting along with my brother George and my friend
Tom Gass. We generally go together because we are all of us men who
like the rough stuff and are tough enough to stand the hardship of living in the open. The place we go to is right in the heart of the primitive
Canadian forest, among big timber, broken with lakes as still as glass,
just the very ground for moose.

We have a kind of lodge up there. It's just a rough place that we put 3
up, the three of us, the year before last, built out of tamarack logs faced
with a broad axe. The flies, while we were building it, were something
awful. Two of the men that we sent in there to build it were so badly
bitten that we had to bring them out a hundred miles to a hospital. None
of us saw the place while we were building it, — we were all busy at
the time, — but the teamsters who took in our stuff said it was the worst
season for the black flies that they ever remembered.

Still we hung to it, in spite of the flies, and stuck at it till we got 4
it built. It is, as I say, only a plain place but good enough to rough

it in. We have one big room with a stone fireplace, and bedrooms round the sides, with a wide verandah, properly screened, all along the front. The verandah has a row of upright tamaracks for its posts and doesn't look altogether bad. In the back part we have quarters where our man sleeps. We had an ice-house knocked up while they were building and water laid on in pipes from a stream. So that on the whole the place has a kind of rough comfort about it, – good enough anyway for fellows hunting moose all day.

5   The place, nowadays, is not hard to get at. The government has just built a colonization highway, quite all right for motors, that happens to go within a hundred yards of our lodge.

6   We can get the railway for a hundred miles, and then the highway for forty, and the last hundred yards we can walk. But this season we are going to cut out the railway and go the whole way from the city in George's car with our kit with us.

7   George has one of those great big cars with a roof and thick glass sides. Personally none of the three of us would have preferred to ride in a luxurious darned thing like that. Tom says that as far as he is concerned he'd much sooner go into the bush over a rough trail in a buckboard, and for my own part a team of oxen would be more the kind of thing that I'd wish.

8   However the car is there, so we might as well use the thing especially as the provincial government has built the fool highway right into the wilderness. By taking the big car also we can not only carry all the hunting outfit that we need but we can also, if we like, shove in a couple of small trunks with a few clothes. This may be necessary as it seems that somebody has gone and slapped a great big frame hotel right there in the wilderness, not half a mile from the place we go to. The hotel we find a regular nuisance. It gave us the advantage of electric light for our lodge (a thing none of us care about), but it means more fuss about clothes. Clothes, of course, don't really matter when a fellow is roughing it in the bush, but Tom says that we might find it necessary to go over to the hotel in the evenings to borrow coal oil or a side of bacon or any rough stuff that we need; and they do such a lot of dressing up at these fool hotels now that if we do go over for bacon or anything in the evening we might just as well slip on our evening clothes, as we could chuck them off the minute we get back. George thinks it might not be a bad idea, – just as a way of saving all our energy for getting after the moose, – to dine each evening at the hotel itself. He knew some men who did that last year and they told him that

the time saved for moose hunting in that way is extraordinary. George's idea is that we could come in each night with our moose, — such and such a number as the case might be — either bringing them with us or burying them where they die, — change our things, slide over to the hotel and get dinner and then beat it back into the bush by moonlight and fetch in the moose. It seems they have a regular two dollar table d'hôte dinner at the hotel, — just rough stuff of course but after all, as we all admit, we don't propose to go out into the wilds to pamper ourselves with high feeding: a plain hotel meal in a home-like style at two dollars a plate is better than cooking up a lot of rich stuff over a camp fire.

If we *do* dine at the hotel we could take our choice each evening be-   **9** tween going back into the bush by moonlight to fetch in the dead moose from the different caches where we had hidden them, or sticking round the hotel itself for a while. It seems that there is dancing there. Nowadays such a lot of women and girls get the open air craze for the life in the bush that these big wilderness hotels are crowded with them. There is something about living in the open that attracts modern women and they like to get right away from everybody and everything; and of course hotels of this type in the open are nowadays always well closed in with screens so that there are no flies or anything of that sort.

So it seems that there is dancing at the hotel every evening, — nothing   **10** on a large scale or pretentious, — just an ordinary hardwood floor, — they may wax it a little for all I know — and some sort of plain, rough Italian orchestra that they fetch up from the city. Not that any of us care for dancing. It's a thing that personally we wouldn't bother with. But it happens that there are a couple of young girls that Tom knows that are going to be staying at the hotel and of course naturally he wants to give them a good time. They are only eighteen and twenty (sisters) and that's really younger than we care for, but with young girls like that, — practically kids, — any man wants to give them a good time. So Tom says, and I think quite rightly, that as the kids are going to be there we may as well put in an appearance at the hotel and see that they are having a good time. Their mother is going to be with them too, and of course we want to give her a good time as well; in fact I think I will lend her my moose rifle and let her go out and shoot a moose. One thing we are all agreed upon in the arrangement of our hunting trip, is in not taking along anything to drink. Drinking spoils a trip of that sort. We all remember how in the old days we'd go out into a camp in the bush (I mean before there used to be any highway or any hotel) and carry in rye whiskey in demijohns (two dollars a gallon it was) and sit around the camp fire drinking it in the evenings.

11   But there's nothing in it. We all agree that the law being what it is, it is better to stick to it. It makes a fellow feel better. So we shall carry nothing in. I don't say that one might not have a flask or something in one's pocket in the car; but only as a precaution against accident or cold. And when we get to our lodge we all feel that we are a darned sight better without it. If we *should* need anything, — though it isn't likely, — there are still three cases of old Scotch whiskey, kicking around the lodge somewhere; I think they are kicking round in a little cement cellar with a locked door that we had made so as to use it for butter or anything of that sort. Anyway there are three, possibly four, or maybe, five, cases of Scotch there and if we should for any reason want it, there it is. But we are hardly likely to touch it, — unless we hit a cold snap, or a wet spell; — then we might; or if we strike hot dry weather. Tom says he thinks there are a couple of cases of champagne still in the cellar; some stuff that one of us must have shot in there just before prohibition came in. But we'll hardly use it. When a man is out moose hunting from dawn to dusk he hasn't much use for champagne, not till he gets home anyway. The only thing that Tom says the champagne might come in useful for would be if we cared to ask the two kids over to some sort of dinner; it would be just a rough kind of camp dinner (we could hardly ask their mother to it) but we think we could manage it. The man we keep there used to be a butler in England, or something of the sort, and he could manage some kind of rough meal where the champagne might fit in.

12   There's only one trouble about our plans for our fall camp that bothers us just a little. The moose are getting damn scarce about that place. There used, so they say, to be any quantity of them. There's an old settler up there that our man buys all our cream from who says that he remembers when the moose were so thick that they would come up and drink whiskey out of his dipper. But somehow they seem to have quit the place. Last year we sent our man out again and again looking for them and he never saw any. Three years ago a boy that works at the hotel said he saw a moose in the cow pasture back of the hotel and there were the tracks of a moose seen last year at the place not ten miles from the hotel where it had come to drink. But apart from these two exceptions the moose hunting has been poor.

13   Still, what does it matter? What we want is the *life*, the rough life just as I have described it. If any moose comes to our lodge we'll shoot

him, or tell the butler to. But if not, — well, we've got along without
for ten years, I don't suppose we shall worry.

1923

The Writer's Subject

1. What image of himself does the narrator create in the first two paragraphs?

2. At what point in the essay does the reader see that the narrator is not all
   that he professes to be?

3. What are the "rough comforts" that the narrator reluctantly feels that he
   and his companions must take advantage of?

4. Under what conditions does the narrator indicate that he and his companions
   might partake of a little alcohol? (paras. 10-11)

5. How important to the narrator and his friends is the prospect of shooting
   a moose?

The Writer's Style and Strategy

1. This is clearly a humorous essay. What seems to you to be its chief
   humorous effect? How is this effect achieved?

2. What expectations are set up by the title of the essay? Comment on the
   subtitle.

3. In paragraphs 3 and 4, the narrator uses such phrases as "a kind of lodge,"
   "just a rough place," "only a plain place," and "a kind of rough comfort."
   Why does the narrator use such vague phrases? Find other examples.

4. What effect does the narrator wish to create by his references to "the fool
   highway" and "these fool hotels" (para. 8)?

5. How does the narrator suggest again and again that the unfortunate luxuries of life in the bush are not of his choosing? How does Leacock's use
   of expletive constructions (i.e., "it is," "there are," "it seems that") convey
   the narrator's apparent reluctance?

6. Discuss the appropriateness to the essay as a whole of the concluding
   paragraph.

Suggested Topics for Writing and Discussion

1. Though Leacock's essay is humorous, it touches on the serious subject of man's encroachment on the wilderness. Discuss one form of man's encroachment (e.g., tourism, hunting, logging) and show how it threatens a particular wilderness area.

2. The myth of "the great outdoors" as an important part of North American life is still kept alive in films and on television. Discuss one TV programme or movie and show how it perpetuates this myth.

3. Camping has come a long way from the original idea of "getting away from it all" with a tent and a campfire. Write an essay showing the extent to which modern camping equipment and supplies have taken the "roughing it" element out of camping.

4. Write a humorous account of a camping or holiday experience.

The Nature of the North
by Farley Mowat

Somewhere far to the north of Newfoundland, the St. Lawrence Seaway,   1
Place Ville Marie, the Macdonald-Cartier Freeway, the bald-headed
prairie and Stanley Park lies an unreal world conceived in the mind's
eye, born out of fantasy and cauled in myth. It is a weird and terrible
land where nothing is as it may seem. Home of the ice worm and the
igloo, of mad trappers and mushing Mounties, of pingos and polar bears,
of the legions of the damned that were conjured into being by Robert
Service, its voice is the baleful whisper of the aurora borealis, the eerie
howl of Jack London's malemutes and the whining dirge of C.B.C. wind
machines. It is a "white hell", "the ultimate desolation", a "howling
wasteland", "the Land that God Forgot" and "the Land God Gave to
Cain." It is a region almost wholly of our contriving, and we have made
of it so inimical a world that the truly alien moon, even as seen on television screens and in picture magazines, seems to have more reality.

This North, this Arctic of the mind, this frigid concept of a flat and   2
formless void of ice and snow congealed beneath the impenetrable
blackness of the polar night, is pure illusion. Behind it lies a lost world
obscured in drifts of literary drivel, obliterated by blizzards of bravado
and buried under an icy weight of obsessive misconceptions. The magnificent reality behind the myth has been consistently rejected by Canadians since the day of our national birth and is rejected still. Through
almost a century the Far North has meant to Canadians either a
nightmarish limbo or an oppressive polar presence looming darkly over
southern Canada and breathing icily down our necks. During most of
that century the handful of people who called themselves Canadians

were engrossed in the occupation of the apparently limitless spaces on the southern fringes of the country. When that space was finally circumscribed and its limits reached, Canadians did not look northward to the challenge of the unknown half of their share of the continent. The northern myth seemed more than they could face, even as it had in the past. They shunned it then − they shun it still. With the exception of a very few outstanding individuals, most of them employed by the Geological Survey of Canada, the exploration of the High North was accomplished, not by Canadians, but by British, French, Scandinavian, German, American and even Portuguese adventurers − men who mastered the myth, faced the reality, and took their knowledge home with them to their native lands. Those who followed in the paths of the explorers and made use of their discoveries, the traders and merchant exploiters, were English, Scotch, French and American, and the companies that employed them (such as the Hudson's Bay Company, Revillon Frères, Canalaska Trading Company) operated out of London, Paris, New York and Seattle. Even the missionaries, coming in time-honoured manner in the wake of trade, were aliens. Moravians from Germany, and Grenfell from England, worked the Labrador coast; throughout the rest of the North, Oblate priests from Belgium and France competed for souls with Anglican priests straight out from England. Meanwhile the seas of the Canadian North were being exploited by Scotch and American whalers. In the Yukon the placer gold fields were overrun by men of half a hundred lands − and there were precious few Canadians among them. White trappers, moving in on the Eskimos and Indians, were almost exclusively northern Europeans. Even Canada's standard-bearers of a token sovereignty in the Arctic, the North West (later the Royal Canadian) Mounted Police, got most of their first recruits from England, Scotland, Newfoundland and even farther afield.

3   The pattern is old and well established. A century after the nation's birth, about three-quarters of the exploration and exploitation of the Canadian North is being carried out by consortiums controlled by American, European and Japanese companies. Military occupation of the North, while nominally a joint undertaking, remains effectively American. Until the middle of the twentieth century almost the only Canadians in the Arctic were Indians and Eskimos; but they were people born to the reality and in any case were, and are, "Canadians" only by courtesy.

4   Only since the early 1950's have southern Canadians begun to glance over their shoulders northward. As yet only a handful have made the effort to penetrate to the reality behind the myth and to actually go north,

not to make a quick buck and then flee south as if the very hounds of hell were on their heels, but to attempt to make themselves integral parts of a gigantic and exciting world spurned by the nation that pretends to own it.

They are very few indeed. Apart from government employees and 5 similar transients employed by mines and military installations, there are not more than a few thousand Canadians of other than Eskimo or Indian ancestry living in a land that is larger than the ten provinces. And most of these few are concentrated in southern Yukon Territory and around Great Slave Lake. In the central and eastern reaches, themselves ten times as vast as Texas, only a few hundred southern Canadians make the North their abiding home.

These are the true pioneers in a nation that is fond of boasting about 6 her pioneering spirits. Men like Bob Williamson at Rankin Inlet, Terry Ryan at Cape Dorset, Ross Peyton at Pangnirtung, Ernie Lyall at Spence Bay, Fred Ross at Cambridge Bay, Tom Butters at Inuvik, Allan Innis-Taylor at Dawson, Bob Engles at Yellowknife, Don Stuart at Hay River — these are of the few, the dedicated ones, who have committed their lives to a land the rest of us reject. They are trying desperately to neutralize the apathy and ignorance of southern Canda, to destroy the suffocating myth so that we others may come to know the North for what it really is. So that we may come to recognize it as a part of our nation.

Men like these believe that la dolce vita is the way of death for any 7 country. They would have us face resolutely north to a world that offers us — if we are men and women enough to recognize and grasp the opportunity — not only the material wealth we crave, but a fighting chance of finding the greatness of spirit that Canada so signally lacks.

* * *

The first difficulty that must be mastered in coming to grips with the 8 Far North is to decide just where "north" begins and to ascertain its boundaries. Modern man has tried to evade the issue by separating the northern regions into sections, like a layer cake, so that he can deal with each part as a separate entity. Ask a scientist for a definition of "north" and you are instantly ears deep in boreal, subarctic and arctic zones, in isotherms, degree-days and permafrost limits. The truth is that the region has no arbitrary southern boundary except insofar as one exists in us as a state of mind. The situation is akin to that of an astronaut shot up in a rocket. At what point does he enter space? At no point, but only when he has become aware that he has entered an alien environment.

9   Since Canadians generally regard the Far North as an alien environment, they enter it when they leave their familiar world of the South behind them. The entry takes place in the upper reaches of the broad band of sombre coniferous forest that stretches across the entire breadth of Canada. Beginning near the Yukon — British Columbia border, this transition region slopes southeastward to Hudson Bay near Churchill where it swings sharply south, paralleling the coast around James Bay. It then angles northeastward across Ungava to reach the Atlantic in the general vicinity of Nain on the Labrador coast. At its southernmost point (the top of James Bay) there are polar bears, seals, tundra, and caribou. The North embraces the arctic zone but it is not limited to that region, nor to the Yukon and the Northwest Territories. It includes a sliver of northern Alberta, rather more of northern Saskatchewan, a goodly bite of northern Manitoba, a nibble of Ontario, a large part of Quebec, and the upper portion of Labrador.

10   It comprises a huge section of the earth's surface. Measuring from the north tip of Ellesmere Island (less than five hundred miles from the North Pole), the northern land mass strikes southward nearly two thousand miles to Cape Henrietta Maria on Hudson Bay — roughly the distance between Montreal and Calgary! And from the Alaska-Yukon border to Cape Dyer on the coast of Baffin Bay it stretches about the same distance east and west. It encompasses about one million, seven hundred thousand square miles — nearly half the total area of Canada.

11   The Canadian North reaches from Atlantic to Pacific but, more important, it extends almost to the heart of the Arctic Ocean. Canada fronts on this third ocean, which is a true mediterranean sea, in exactly the same way that North Africa fronts on the European Mediterranean. This is a startling idea but one we would be well advised to get used to since Asia, Europe and North America all face each other across the almost land-locked polar sea and it is here that the three continents lie closest together. The orientation we get from looking at standard maps that show the North Pole at the top of beyond is arbitrary and wrong. This is not the way the world really is. The polar region is actually the centre of the northern hemisphere, and the geographic centre of Canada is in the Keewatin tundra 250 miles north-northwest of Churchill. Consequently when we turn our back on the North in the belief that there isn't much of interest in that direction, we are turning our backs on Europe and Asia, as well as on a great part of our own country. So far only the military men, preoccupied with death and destruction, have

grasped this vital fact. When and if Canadians have the sense to appreciate its peaceful significance we may become a nation at the centre, instead of remaining a sycophantic satellite at the back door of the United States.

One of the particularly cockeyed misconceptions we have about our 12 North is that it is all of a piece — or, at the most, of two pieces: a bleak expanse of frozen sea and a dreary wilderness of frozen plain. The truth is that the Arctic displays as much variety as any other great natural realm on earth. Stretching from central Labrador to Baffin Island, the up-tilted eastern edge of the Canadian Shield forms a shaggy range of glacier-encrusted mountains that are as formidable, as massively overwhelming in appearance, as anything in the Rockies. There is nothing to match them in eastern North America; yet they are almost unknown to us. They form the eastern wall of the North. Far to the westward, beyond the Mackenzie River, rise range after range of mountains that culminate in the St. Elias Range whose glacier-shrouded peaks soar to nearly twenty thousand feet in Canada and twenty-four thousand in Alaska. This is the western wall. Between these walls sprawls the worn and pitted face of the Canadian Shield composed of some of the oldest rocks on earth and so eroded by the work of the eons that only the time-smoothed stubs of its once-mighty mountains remain as undulating hills, giving relief to the naked, ancient rock. Here, in the shield country, lies the greatest assemblage of lakes upon our planet. Between the western edge of the Shield and the risers of the Yukon Cordillera lies a broad tongue of lowlands that extends north from the Great Central Plains of North America, and down it one of the world's greatest rivers, the Mackenzie, carries the waters of the Peace, the Liard, and many lesser rivers to the Arctic Ocean.

North of the mainland lies the Arctic Archipelago, some nine hun- 13 dred thousand square miles of lands constituting the largest island group in the world. These islands, too, have their variety. Some are mountainous, others are low and grassy plains, still others are bald stone and gravel deserts. Surrounding them lies a complex of sounds and channels as intricate as the most sophisticated maze.

Contained within the arctic lands of Canada is the vast inland sea of 14 Hudson Bay, in which the British Isles could be sunk without a trace. East of the main northern land mass a tremendous river carried on the Labrador Current flows down through Baffin Bay and Davis Strait, stretching an arctic tentacle as far south as Nova Scotia. The polar ocean is itself a species of "land", for it is perpetually ice covered and, though the ice moves, men can and do travel over it, and four-engine aircraft can land upon it.

15   Although the bone structure of most of the North, the Canadian Shield, is perhaps five million years old, much of the land looks raw and new. This is because a mere ten thousand years ago the entire region, except for the northwestern corner, lay buried beneath a gigantic ice sheet. The dome of the Keewatin District ice sheet was two miles thick. Its own titanic weight made the ice sheet plastic and it flowed implacably in all directions outwards from several high-domed centers. It scoured and gouged the ancient rocks, shearing off the surface soil layers and leaving behind an incredibly intricate pattern of water-filled valleys, basins, and deep coastal fiords. When the ice eventually melted it left the land littered with debris that ranged from barn-sized boulders to vast fields of shattered rock, and it embossed the naked bones of the country with a complex design of morainic ridges, drumlins, and long sinuous eskers of sand and gravel.

16   The ice had another, unseen effect. It deep-froze the rock beneath it, producing what we call permafrost. In the extreme northern islands permafrost penetrates fifteen hundred feet into the primeval rock. Even as far south as northern Manitoba the ancient frost remains, unyielding, only a few feet below the shallow surface layers that thaw in summer.

17   Remnants of the ice sheet itself also survive. In the wall of the eastern mountains some sixty thousand square miles of ice crown the heights and fill great valleys. Other remnants of ice persist in the mountains of the west.

18   Another generally held misconception about the North is that its climate is so hostile that only polar bears and Eskimos can endure it. Yet winter blizzards on the western prairies can match, in ferocity if not in intensity, the worst weather the North produces. Northern residents who have subsequently endured a winter at Saskatoon or Winnipeg have been heard to refer with nostalgia to the North as "the banana belt". Surprisingly, it is a dry world with very little rain or snowfall. Winter snows often lie deeper in Toronto or Montreal than in most parts of the North. Although not even the Yellowknife Chamber of Commerce would call northern winters balmy, summers can be lovely. There are only two true seasons: winter and summer, the transitions between them being so brief as to be negligible. Near and north of the Arctic Circle the midsummer sun never sets and temperatures sometimes persist in the comfortable sixties and higher for days on end. In winter above the Arctic Circle the sun vanishes for weeks or months, but this "long

night" is seldom really dark. The Northern Lights often give a pervading luminosity and the glitter of the stars in a lucid atmosphere combined with bright moonlight provides enough light for almost normal activity, including hunting.

The concept of the Far North as a lifeless land is another of our more **19** grotesque illusions. Its southern fringes include the upper reaches of the taiga forests — mainly black and white spruce, larch, birch and poplar. The northward-marching trees of the taiga grow sparser and more stunted until they fade out in the vast open plains called tundra. There is no absolute line of demarcation between taiga and tundra — no real "timberline". The two regions interpenetrate like the clasped fingers of gigantic hands. There are pockets of tundra deep inside the forest, and oases of trees far out on the sweep of the tundra. Nor is the tundra all of a kind. There is alpine tundra high on mountain slopes, shrub tundra close to the taiga region, sedge tundra to the north, moss-and-lichen tundra still farther north and, on the extreme northern islands, fell-field tundra where vegetation finally gives up its stubborn attempt to occupy the remote lands that lie surrounded by unyielding polar ice. But in summertime most tundra regions boast an array of flowering plants of infinite number and delight. Although they are small, they mass in such profusion that they suffuse hundreds of square miles with shifting colour. They form a Lilliputian jungle where hunting spiders, bumblebees, small and delicate moths and butterflies abound. Black flies and mosquitoes abound too, alas, and there is no evading the fact that they are the bane of summer in the North.

Birds breed almost everywhere. Mammals of many species, ranging **20** from squat, rotund lemmings to massive muskox occupy the lands. The seas are home to whales, seals, obese walrus and sinuous white bears. The seas are also rich in fishes as are the numberless inland lakes. For those with eyes to see, the North is vitally and vividly alive. Long, long ago, men of other races out of another time recognized this truth and learned to call the northern regions "home".

(1967)

The Writer's Subject

1. What does Mowat mean by his assertion that the North is "a region almost wholly of our contriving" (para. 1)?

2. Why, in Mowat's view, have Canadians consistently rejected "the magnificent reality behind the myth" of the North? (para. 2)

3. Mowat outlines the pattern of early exploration and development of the Canadian North, pointing out how little was the contribution made by Canadians themselves. What, in his view, is the current situation?

4. What contrast does Mowat draw in paragraphs 4-7 between southern Canadians and those who live and work in the North? Why does he believe that southern Canadians must "face resolutely north"?

5. What analogy does Mowat use in paragraph 8 to show the difficulty of establishing where the North begins?

6. What is the "vital fact" about the Canadian North that is so far understood only by the military?

7. What are the principal misconceptions about the North that Mowat addresses from paragraph 12 onwards? What evidence does he produce to dispose of these misconceptions?

The Writer's Style and Strategy

1. Why does Mowat begin the essay with a list of the various images associated with the North?

2. What effect is he seeking by using such phrases as "mad trappers and mushing Mounties" or "the whining dirge of C.B.C. wind machines"? What is the point Mowat is making with the five phrases in quotation marks? (para. 1)

3. What is the tone of the first two sentences of paragraph 2? What figure of speech does Mowat use in the second sentence of paragraph 2? What response does Mowat hope to arouse in the reader by this strategy?

4. What words or phrases convey most clearly Mowat's critical attitudes to southern Canadians?

5. What audience has Mowat in mind for this essay? Provide specific evidence for your point of view.

6. Much of this essay is devoted to a description of the North. How does the descriptive element of this essay serve Mowat's argumentative purpose?

7. Discuss the means by which Mowat establishes the size and magnificence of the Arctic landscape in paragraphs 12-15. Comment on his use of adjectives, particularly superlatives.

8. How does Mowat convey the rich variety of plant life on the tundra in paragraph 19? Identify instances of personification, simile, and metaphor in this paragraph, and comment on the description of the flowering plants as "a Lilliputian jungle."

Suggested Topics for Writing and Discussion

1. Find a recent newspaper or magazine article about Canada's North and discuss how it confirms or contradicts Mowat's thesis that Southern Canadians have constructed a false myth about the North.

2. Mowat says somewhat bitterly that Canada lacks greatness of spirit. Do you agree?

3. Choose a nation, national group or geographic region (e.g., China, the Russians, the Sahara) and discuss the stereotypical images and myths associated with it. Can you, as Mowat has done, account for the formation of such myths and offer an opposing view?

4. In paragraph 4, Mowat says that it is only since the 1950s that southern Canadians have "begun to glance over their shoulders northward"; he implies that Canadians habitually face south. Indeed, he goes on to condemn Canada as a "sycophantic satellite" of the United States. Has the situation changed since Mowat wrote this essay in 1967? Does the North figure more prominently in our national consciousness, or is our orientation still primarily to the south?

A Planet for the Taking
by David Suzuki

1 Canadians live under the remarkable illusion that we are a technologically advanced people. Everything around us denies that assumption. We are, in many ways, a Third World country, selling our natural resources in exchange for the high technology of the industrialized world. Try going through your home and looking at the country of origin of your clothes, electrical appliances, books, car. The rare technological product that does have Canada stamped on it is usually from a branch plant of a multinational company centred in another country. But we differ from traditional Third World countries. We have a majority population of Caucasians and a very high level of literacy and affluence. And we have been able to maintain our seemingly advanced social state by virtue of an incredible bounty of natural resources.

2 Within the Canadian mystique there is also a sense of the vastness of this land. The prairies, the Arctic, the oceans, the mountains are ever present in our art and literature. This nation is built on our sense of the seeming endlessness of the expanse of wilderness and the output of nature and we have behaved as if this endlessness were real. Today we speak of renewable resources but our "harvest" procedures are more like a mining operation. We extract raw resources in the crudest of ways, gouging the land to get at its inner core, spewing our raw wastes into the air, water and soil in massive amounts while taking fish, birds, animals and trees in vast quantities without regard to the future. So we operate under a strange duality of mind: we have both a sense of the importance of the wilderness and space in our culture and an attitude that it is limitless and therefore we needn't worry.

Native cultures of the past may have been no more conservation- 3
minded than we are but they lacked the technology to make the kind
of impact that we do today. Canadians and Americans share one of the
great natural wonders, the Great Lakes, which contain 20 per cent of
the world's fresh water, yet today even this massive body of water is
terribly polluted and the populations of fish completely mixed-up by
human activiity. We speak of "managing" our resources, but do it in
a way that resembles the sledgehammer-on-the-head cure for a headache.
On the west coast of Canada, Natives lived for millennia on the incredible abundance of five species of salmon. Today, the massive runs are
gone and many biologists fear that the fish may be in mortal jeopardy
because of both our fishing and management policies. Having improved
fishing techniques this century to the point of endangering runs yet still
knowing very little of the biology of the fish, we have assumed that
we could build up the yield by simply dumping more back. But it wasn't
known that sockeye salmon fry, for example, spend a year in a freshwater
lake before going to sea. Millions of sockeye fry were dumped directly
into the Fraser River where they died soon after. In Oregon, over-fishing
and hydroelectric dams had decimated coho populations in the Columbia River. In one year, over 8 million fry were released of which only
seven were ever caught. No one knows what's happening to the rest.

We act as if a fish were a fish, a duck a duck or a tree a tree. If we 4
"harvest" one, we renew it by simply adding one or two back. But what
we have learned is that all animals and plants are not equivalent. Each
organism reflects the evolutionary history of its progenitors; in the case
of salmon, each race and subrace of fish has been exquisitely honed
by nature to return to a very specific part of the Pacific watershed.
Similarly, in the enormous area of prairie pothole country in the centre
of the continent, migratory birds do not just space themselves out according to the potholes that are empty. Scientists have discovered that
the birds have been selected to return to a very restricted part of that
area. And of course, our entire forestry policy is predicated on the
ridiculous idea that a virgin stand of fir or cedar which has taken millennia to form and clings to a thin layer of topsoil can be replaced after
clear-cut logging simply by sticking seedlings into the ground. How
can anyone with even the most rudimentary understanding of biology
and evolution ignore the realities of the complex interaction between
organisms and the environment and attempt to manipulate wild populations as if they were tomato plants or chickens?

I believe that in large part our problems rest on our faith in the power 5 of science and technology. At the beginning of this century, science, when applied by industry and medicine, promised a life immeasurably better and there is no doubt that society, indeed the planet, has been transformed by the impact of new ideas and inventions of science. Within my lifetime, I've seen the beginning of television, oral contraception, organ transplants, space travel, computers, jets, nuclear weapons, satellite communication, and polio vaccine. Each has changed society forever and made the world of my youth recede into the pages of history. But we have not achieved a technological utopia. The problems facing us today are immense and many are a direct consequence of science and technology. What has gone wrong?

6   I believe that the core of our 20th century dilemma lies in a fundamental limitation of science that most scientists, especially those in the life sciences, fail to recognize. Most of my colleagues take it for granted that our studies will ultimately be applicable to the "big picture," that our research will have beneficial payoffs to society eventually. That is because the thrust of modern science has been predicated on the Newtonian idea that the universe is like an enormous machine whose entire system will be reconstructed on the basis of our understanding of the parts. This is the fundamental reductionist faith in science: the whole is equal to the sum of its parts. It does make a lot of sense — what distinguishes science from other activities that purport to provide a comprehensive "world view" is its requirement that we focus on a part of nature isolated to as great an extent as possible from the rest of the system of which it is a part. This has provided enormous insights into that fragment of nature, often accompanied by power to manipulate it. But when we attempt to tinker with what lies in the field of our view, the effects ripple far beyond the barrel of the microscope. And so we are constantly surprised at the unexpected consequences of our interference. Scientists only know nature in "bits and pieces" and assume that higher levels of organization are simply the expression of the component parts. This is what impels neurobiologists to study the chemical and electrical behaviour of single neurons in the faith that it will ultimately lead to an understanding of what creativity and imagination are, a faith that I don't for a moment think will ever be fulfilled (although a lot of useful information will accrue).

7   Physicists, who originally set this view in motion, have this century, with the arrival of relativity and quantum theory, put to rest the notion that we will ever be able to reconstruct the entire universe from fundamental principles. Chemists know that a complete physical descrip-

tion of atoms of oxygen and hydrogen is of little value in predicting the behaviour of a water molecule. But biologists scream that any sense that there are properties of organization that don't exist at lower levels is "vitalism", a belief that there is some mystical life force in living organisms. And so biochemists and molecular biologists are intent on understanding the workings of organisms by learning all they can about sub-cellular organization.

Ironically, ecology, long scorned by molecular biologists as an inex- 8 act science, is now corroborating physics. In studying ecosystems, we are learning that a simple breakdown into components and their behaviour does not provide insight into how an entire collection of organisms in a natural setting will work. While many ecologists do continue to "model" ecosystems in computers in the hope that they will eventually derive a predictive tool, their science warns of the hazard of treating it too simply in management programs.

At present, our very terminology suggests that we think we can manage 9 wild plants and animals as though they were domesticated organisms. We speak of "herds" of seals, of "culling," "harvesting," "stocks." The ultimate expression of our narrow view (and self-interested rationalizations) is seen in how we overlook the enormous environmental impact of our pollution, habitat destruction and extraction and blame seals and whales for the decline in fish populations or wolves for the decrease in moose — and then propose bounties as a solution!

But Canadians do value the spiritual importance of nature and want 10 to see it survive for future generations. We also believe in the power of science to sustain a high quality of life. And while the current understanding of science's power is, I believe, misplaced, in fact the leading edges of physics and ecology may provide the insights that can get us off the current track. We need a very profound perceptual shift, and soon.

(1985)

The Writer's Subject

1. On what grounds does Suzuki argue that Canada is in some respects a Third World country? (para. 1)

2. What is the "duality of mind" which Suzuki identifies in Canadians? (para. 2)

3. What evidence does Suzuki produce to support his assertion that our management of natural resources has been based on ignorance of "the realities of the complex interaction between organisms and the environment"? (paras. 3-4)

4. What, according to Suzuki, is the fundamental misconception about science that is largely responsible for many of our current problems? What are the consequences of that misconception? (para. 6)

5. What distinction does Suzuki draw between the attitudes of biologists and those of other scientists? (para. 7)

6. What hope does Suzuki offer for an improved understanding of our natural environment in the future?

The Writer's Style and Strategy

1. What audience is Suzuki addressing in this essay? What relationship does he establish with that audience?

2. Suzuki presents an unequivocal condemnation of our mismanagement of natural resources, but his first paragraph seems unrelated to this topic. What is the function of the first paragraph, and how does it prepare us for what follows?

3. What method does Suzuki employ in paragraphs 3 and 4 to present his attack on resource policies?

4. As a scientist discussing the impact of science, Suzuki might be expected to employ an objective tone. What, in fact, is Suzuki's tone in this essay? What words or phrases help to create this tone and thus convey Suzuki's attitude to his subject?

Suggested Topics for Writing and Discussion

1. Suzuki says in his final sentence, "We need a very profound perceptual shift, and soon." Suggest ways in which this perceptual shift might be made to come about more quickly.

2. Suzuki describes the impact of scientific ideas and inventions which have transformed society in this century. Choose one scientific or technological development of the twentieth century and show the impact it has had upon a particular area of society (e.g., the television and the family; computers and education; the airplane and travel; food processing and eating habits).

3. A number of societies have been established with the purpose of protecting the environment (e.g., Greenpeace, Sea Shepherd Conservation Society, Society Promoting Environmental Conservation). Choose one such group and outline its objectives. How successful has it been in meeting those objectives?

A River Pilot Looks at the Mississippi
by Mark Twain

1   The face of the water, in time, became a wonderful book — a book that was a dead language to the uneducated passenger, but which told its mind to me without reserve, delivering its most cherished secrets as clearly as if it uttered them with a voice. And it was not a book to be read once and thrown aside, for it had a new story to tell every day. Throughout the long twelve hundred miles there was never a page that was void of interest, never one that you could leave unread without loss, never one that you would want to skip, thinking you could find higher enjoyment in some other thing. There never was so wonderful a book written by man; never one whose interest was so absorbing, so unflagging, so sparklingly renewed with every re-perusal. The passenger who could not read it was charmed with a peculiar sort of faint dimple on its surface (on the rare occasions when he did not overlook it altogether); but to the pilot that was an *italicized* passage; indeed, it was more than that, it was a legend of the largest capitals, with a string of shouting exclamation-points at the end of it, for it meant that a wreck or a rock was buried there that could tear the life out of the strongest vessel that ever floated. It is the faintest and simplest expression the water ever makes, and the most hideous to a pilot's eye. In truth, the passenger who could not read this book saw nothing but all manner of pretty pictures in it, painted by the sun and shaded by the clouds, whereas to the trained eye these were not pictures at all, but the grimmest and most dead-earnest of reading-matter.

2   Now when I had mastered the language of this water, and had come

to know every trifling feature that bordered the great river as familiar-
ly as I knew the letters of the alphabet, I had made a valuable acquisi-
tion. But I had lost something, too. I had lost something which could
never be restored to me while I lived. All the grace, the beauty, the
poetry, had gone out of the majestic river! I still keep in mind a certain
wonderful sunset which I witnessed when steamboating was new to me.
A broad expanse of the river was turned to blood; in the middle distance
the red hue brightened into gold, through which a solitary log came
floating, black and conspicuous; in one place a long, slanting mark lay
sparkling upon the water; in another the surface was broken by boiling, tumbling rings, that were as many-tinted as an opal; where the ruddy
flush was faintest, was a smooth spot that was covered with graceful
circles and radiating lines, ever so delicately traced; the shore on our
left was densely wooded, and the somber shadow that fell from this
forest was broken in one place by a long, ruffled trail that shone like
silver; and high above the forest wall a clean-stemmed dead tree wav-
ed a single leafy bough that glowed like a flame in the unobstructed
splendor that was flowing from the sun. There were graceful curves,
reflected images, woody heights, soft distances; and over the whole
scene, far and near, the dissolving lights drifted steadily, enriching it
every passing moment with new marvels of coloring.

I stood like one bewitched. I drank it in, in a speechless rapture. The 3
world was new to me, and I had never seen anything like this at home.
But as I have said, a day came when I began to cease from noting the
glories and the charms which the moon and the sun and the twilight
wrought upon the river's face; another day came when I ceased altogether
to note them. Then, if that sunset scene had been repeated, I should
have looked upon it without rapture, and should have commented upon
it, inwardly, after this fashion: "This sun means that we are going to
have wind tomorrow; that floating log means that the river is rising,
small thanks to it; that slanting mark on the water refers to a bluff reef
which is going to kill somebody's steamboat one of these nights, if it
keeps on stretching out like that; those tumbling 'boils' show a dissolving bar and a changing channel there; the lines and circles in the slick
water over yonder are a warning that that troublesome place is shoal-
ing up dangerously; that silver streak in the shadow of the forest is the
'break' from a new snag, and he has located himself in the very best
place he could have found to fish for steamboats; that tall dead tree,
with a single living branch, is not going to last long, and then how is
a body ever going to get through this blind place at night without the

friendly old landmark?"

4   No, the romance and beauty were all gone from the river. All the
value any feature of it had for me now was the amount of usefulness
it could furnish toward compassing the safe piloting of a steamboat.
Since those days, I have pitied doctors from my heart. What does the
lovely flush in a beauty's cheek mean to a doctor but a "break" that ripples above some deadly disease? Are not all her visible charms sown
thick with what are to him the signs and symbols of hidden decay? Does
he ever see her beauty at all, or doesn't he simply view her professionally,
and comment upon her unwholesome condition all to himself? And
doesn't he sometimes wonder whether he has gained most or lost most
by learning his trade?

                                                                        (1875)

The Writer's Subject

1. Why did Twain find the river so absorbing and interesting? (para. 1)

2. What contrast does Twain draw between the perceptions of a passenger
    and those of a river pilot? (para. 1)

3. What does Twain feel he lost when he had "mastered the language of this
    water"? (para. 2)

4. How did Twain respond to a beautiful sunset on the river when steam-
    boating was still a new experience? How did his response change with
    experience? (paras. 3-4)

5. Why does Twain say that he pities doctors? (para. 4) What is the relation
    between this observation and his account of his river-boat experiences?

The Writer's Style and Strategy

1. How does Twain use an extended metaphor in paragraph 1 to describe
    the features of the river?

2. How does Twain effect a transition from paragraph 1 to paragraph 2?

3. Paragraphs 2 and 3 present two different views of the river. How does
    Twain organize the details of the contrast?

4. How does the language of paragraph 2 convey the sense of "rapture" that
    Twain first felt about the river at sunset? What details in paragraph 3 convey
    a change of tone?

5. Discuss the function of the concluding paragraph. By what means does Twain reinforce the connection between this paragraph and what has preceded it?

Suggested Topics for Writing and Discussion

1. Twain shows how a writer may convey his feelings about a landscape by a careful selection of detail and descriptive words. Describe a place or landscape in such a way as to help the reader share your feelings about the scene (e.g., a city seen from an airplane; a mountain range; a building).

2. Twain's closing comment suggests that professional training and education involve losses as well as gains. Choose a career or profession that interests you, and speculate what gains and losses it may entail.

3. Choose a place or a person that impressed you in childhood, and write an essay contrasting your early impressions with those you hold now.

Death of a Pig
by E.B. White

1   I spent several days and nights in mid-September with an ailing pig and
I feel driven to account for this stretch of time, more particularly since
the pig died at last, and I lived, and things might easily have gone the
other way round and none left to do the accounting. Even now, so close
to the event, I cannot recall the hours sharply and am not ready to say
whether death came on the third night or the fourth night. This uncertainty afflicts me with a sense of personal deterioration; if I were
in decent health I would know how many nights I had sat up with a pig.

2   The scheme of buying a spring pig in blossomtime, feeding it through
summer and fall, and butchering it when the solid cold weather arrives,
is a familiar scheme to me and follows an antique pattern. It is a tragedy
enacted on most farms with perfect fidelity to the original script. The
murder, being premeditated, is in the first degree but is quick and skillful,
and the smoked bacon and ham provide a ceremonial ending whose
fitness is seldom questioned.

3   Once in a while something slips — one of the actors goes up in his
lines and the whole performance stumbles and halts. My pig simply
failed to show up for a meal. The alarm spread rapidly. The classic
outline of the tragedy was lost. I found myself cast suddenly in the role
of pig's friend and physician — a farcical character with an enema bag
for a prop. I had a presentiment, the very first afternoon, that the play
would never regain its balance and that my sympathies were now wholly
with the pig. This was slapstick — the sort of dramatic treatment that
instantly appealed to my old dachshund, Fred, who joined the vigil,
held the bag, and, when all was over, presided at the interment. When

we slid the body into the grave, we both were shaken to the core. The loss we felt was not the loss of ham but the loss of pig. He had evidently become precious to me, not that he represented a distant nourishment in a hungry time, but that he had suffered in a suffering world. But I'm running ahead of my story and shall have to go back.

My pigpen is at the bottom of an old orchard below the house. The 4 pigs I have raised have lived in a faded building that once was an icehouse. There is a pleasant yard to move about in, shaded by an apple tree that overhangs the low rail fence. A pig couldn't ask for anything better - or none has, at any rate. The sawdust in the icehouse makes a comfortable bottom in which to root, and a warm bed. This sawdust, however, came under suspicion when the pig took sick. One of my neighbors said he thought the pig would have done better on new ground − the same principle that applies in planting potatoes. He said there might be something unhealthy about that sawdust, that he never thought well of sawdust.

It was about four o'clock in the afternoon when I first noticed that 5 there was something wrong with the pig. He failed to appear at the trough for his supper, and when a pig (or a child) refuses supper a chill wave of fear runs through any household, or ice-household. After examining my pig, who was stretched out in the sawdust inside the building, I went to the phone and cranked it four times. Mr Dameron answered. "What's good for a sick pig?" I asked (There is never any identification needed on a country phone; the person on the other end knows who is talking by the sound of the voice and by the character of the question.)

"I don't know, I never had a sick pig," said Mr. Dameron, "but I can 6 find out quick enough. You hang up and I'll call Henry."

Mr. Dameron was back on the line again in five minutes. "Henry 7 says roll him over on his back and give him two ounces of castor oil or sweet oil, and if that doesn't do the trick give him an injection of soapy water. He says he's almost sure the pig's plugged up, and even if he's wrong, it can't do any harm."

I thanked Mr. Dameron. I didn't go right to the pig, though. I sank 8 into a chair and sat still for a few minutes to think about my troubles, and then I got up and went to the barn, catching up on some odds and ends that needed tending to. Unconsciously I held off, for an hour, the deed by which I would officially recognize the collapse of the performance of raising a pig; I wanted no interruption in the regularity of feeding, the steadiness of growth, the even succession of days. I wanted no interruption, wanted no oil, no deviation. I just wanted to keep on

raising a pig, full meal after full meal, spring into summer into fall.
I didn't even know whether there were two ounces of castor oil in the
place.

9   Shortly after five o'clock I remembered that we had been invited out
to dinner that night and realized that if I were to dose a pig there was
no time to lose. The dinner date seemed a familiar conflict: I move in
a desultory society and often a week or two will roll by without my
going to anybody's house to dinner or anyone's coming to mine, but
when an occasion does arise, and I am summoned, something usually
turns up (an hour or two in advance) to make all human intercourse
seem vastly inappropriate. I have come to believe that there is in hostesses
a special power of divination, and that they deliberately arrange dinners to coincide with pig failure or some other sort of failure. At any
rate, it was after five o'clock and I knew I could put off no longer the
evil hour.

10   When my son and I arrived at the pigyard, armed with a small bottle
of castor oil and a length of clothesline, the pig had emerged from his
house and was standing in the middle of his yard, listlessly. He gave
us slim greeting. I could see that he felt uncomfortable and uncertain.
I had brought the clothesline thinking I'd have to tie him (the pig weighed
more than a hundred pounds) but we never used it. My son reached
down, grabbed both front legs, upset him quickly, and when he opened
his mouth to scream I turned the oil into his throat — a pink, corrugated
area I had never seen before. I had just time to read the label while
the neck of the bottle was in his mouth. It said Puretest. The screams,
slightly muffled by oil, were pitched in the hysterically high range of
pig-sound, as though torture were being carried out, but they didn't last
long: it was all over rather suddenly, and, his legs released, the pig
righted himself.

11   In the upset position the corners of his mouth had been turned down,
giving him a frowning expression. Back on his feet again, he regained
the set smile that a pig wears even in sickness. He stood his ground,
sucking slightly at the residue of oil; a few drops leaked out of his lips
while his wicked eyes, shaded by their coy little lashes, turned on me
in disgust and hatred. I scratched him gently with oily fingers and he
remained quiet, as though trying to recall the satisfaction of being scratched when in health, and seeming to rehearse in his mind the indignity
to which he had just been subjected. I noticed, as I stood there, four
or five small dark spots on his back near the tail end, reddish brown
in color, each about the size of a housefly. I could not make out what

they were. They did not look troublesome but at the same time they did not look like mere surface bruises or chafe marks. Rather they seemed blemishes of internal origin. His stiff white bristles almost completely hid them and I had to part the bristles with my fingers to get a good look.

Several hours later, a few minutes before midnight, having dined well 12 and at someone else's expense, I returned to the pighouse with a flashlight. The patient was asleep. Kneeling, I felt his ears (as you might put your hand on the forehead of a child) and they seemed cool, and then with the light made a careful examination of the yard and the house for signs that the oil had worked. I found none and went to bed.

We had been having an unseasonable spell of weather — hot, close 13 days, with the fog shutting in every night, scaling for a few hours in midday, then creeping back again at dark, drifting in first over the trees on the point, then suddenly blowing across the fields, blotting out the world and taking possession of houses, men, and animals. Everyone kept hoping for a break, but the break failed to come. Next day was another hot one. I visited the pig before breakfast and tried to tempt him with a little milk in his trough. He just stared at it, while I made a sucking sound through my teeth to remind him of past pleasures of the feast. With very small, timid pigs, weanlings, this ruse is often quite successful and will encourage them to eat; but with a large, sick pig the ruse is senseless and the sound I made must have made him feel, if anything, more miserable. He not only did not crave food, he felt a positive revulsion to it. I found a place under the apple tree where he had vomited in the night.

At this point, although a depression had settled over me, I didn't sup- 14 pose that I was going to lose my pig. From the lustiness of a healthy pig a man derives a feeling of personal lustiness; the stuff that goes into the trough and is received with such enthusiasm is an earnest of some later feast of his own, and when this suddenly comes to an end and the food lies stale and untouched, souring in the sun, the pig's imbalance becomes the man's, vicariously, and life seems insecure, displaced, transitory.

As my own spirits declined, along with the pig's, the spirits of my 15 vile old dachshund rose. The frequency of our trips down the footpath through the orchard to the pigyard delighted him, although he suffers greatly from arthritis, moves with difficulty, and would be bedridden if he could find anyone willing to serve him meals on a tray.

He never missed a chance to visit the pig with me, and he made many 16 professional calls on his own. You could see him down there at all hours, his white face parting the grass along the fence as he wobbled and stumbled about, his stethoscope dangling — a happy quack, writing his villainous prescriptions and grinning his corrosive grin. When the enema bag appeared, and the bucket of warm suds, his happiness was complete, and he managed to squeeze his enormous body between the two lowest rails of the yard and then assumed full charge of the irrigation. Once, when I lowered the bag to check the flow, he reached in and hurriedly drank a few mouthfuls of the suds to test their potency. I have noticed that Fred will feverishly consume any substance that is associated with trouble — bitter flavor is to his liking. When the bag was above reach, he concentrated on the pig and was everywhere at once, a tower of strength and inconvenience. The pig, curiously enough, stood rather quietly through this colonic carnival, and the enema, though ineffective, was not as difficult as I had anticipated.

17   I discovered, though, that once having given a pig an enema there is no turning back, no chance of resuming one of life's more stereotyped roles. The pig's lot and mine were inextricably bound now, as though the rubber tube were the silver cord. From then until the time of his death I held the pig steadily in the bowl of my mind; the task of trying to deliver him from his misery became a strong obsession. His suffering soon became the embodiment of all earthly wretchedness. Along toward the end of the afternoon, defeated in physicking, I phoned the veterinary twenty miles away and placed the case formally in his hands. He was full of questions, and when I casually mentioned the dark spots on the pig's back, his voice changed its tone.

18   "I don't want to scare you," he said, "but when there are spots, erysipelas has to be considered."

19   Together we considered erysipelas, with frequent interruptions from the telephone operator, who wasn't sure the connection had been established.

20   "If a pig has erysipelas can he give it to a person?" I asked.

21   "Yes, he can," replied the vet.

22   "Have they answered?" asked the operator.

23   "Yes, they have," I said. Then I addressed the vet again. "You better come over here and examine the pig right away."

24   "I can't come myself," said the vet, "but McFarland can come this evening if that's all right. Mac knows more about pigs than I do anyway. You needn't worry too much about the spots. To indicate erysipelas they would have to be deep hemorrhagic infarcts."

"Deep hemorrhagic what?" I asked.   25

"Infarcts," said the vet.   26

"Have they answered?" asked the operator.   27

"Well," I said, "I don't know what you'd call these spots, except they're   28
about the size of a housefly. If the pig has erysipelas I guess I have
it, too, by this time, because we've been very close lately."

"McFarland will be over," said the vet.   29

I hung up. My throat felt dry and I went to the cupboard and got   30
a bottle of whiskey. Deep hemorrhagic infarcts — the phrase began
fastening its hooks in my head. I had assumed that there could be nothing
much wrong with a pig during the months it was being groomed for
murder; my confidence in the essential health and endurance of pigs
had been strong and deep, particularly in the health of pigs that belonged
to me and that were part of my proud scheme. The awakening had been
violent and I minded it all the more because I knew that what could
be true of my pig could be true also of the rest of my tidy world. I
tried to put this distasteful idea from me, but it kept recurring. I took
a short drink of the whiskey and then, although I wanted to go down
to the yard and look for fresh signs, I was scared to. I was certain I
had erysipelas.

It was long after dark and the supper dishes had been put away when   31
a car drove in and McFarland got out. He had a girl with him. I could
just make her out in the darkness — she seemed young and pretty. "This
is Miss Owen," he said. "We've been having a picnic supper on the shore,
that's why I'm late."

McFarland stood in the driveway and stripped off his jacket, then   32
his shirt. His stocky arms and capable hands showed up in my flashlight's
gleam as I helped him find his coverall and get zipped up. The rear
seat of his car contained an astonishing amount of paraphernalia, which
he soon overhauled, selecting a chain, a syringe, a bottle of oil, a rubber tube, and some other things I couldn't identify. Miss Owen said
she'd go along with us and see the pig. I led the way down the warm
slope of the orchard, my light picking out the path for them, and we
all three climbed the fence, entered the pighouse, and squatted by the
pig while McFarland took a rectal reading. My flashlight picked up
the glitter of an engagement ring on the girl's hand.

"No elevation," said McFarland, twisting the thermometer in the light.   33
"You needn't worry about erysipelas." He ran his hand slowly over the
pig's stomach and at one point the pig cried out in pain.

"Poor piggledy-wiggledy!" said Miss Owen.   34

35   The treatment I had been giving the pig for two days was then repeated,
somewhat more expertly, by the doctor, Miss Owen and I handing him
things as he needed them — holding the chain that he had looped around
the pig's upper jaw, holding the syringe, holding the bottle stopper, the
end of the tube, all of us working in darkness and in comfort, working
with the instinctive teamwork induced by emergency conditions, the
pig unprotesting, the house shadowy, protecting, intimate. I went to
bed tired but with a feeling of relief that I had turned over part of the
responsibility of the case to a licensed doctor. I was beginning to think,
though, that the pig was not going to live.

36   He died twenty-four hours later, or it might have been forty-eight
— there is a blur in time here, and I may have lost or picked up a day
in the telling and the pig one in the dying. At intervals during the last
day I took cool fresh water down to him and at such times as he found
the strength to get to his feet he would stand with head in the pail and
snuffle his snout around. He drank a few sips but no more; yet it seemed
to comfort him to dip his nose in water and bobble it about, sucking
in and blowing out through his teeth. Much of the time, now, he lay
indoors half buried in sawdust. Once, near the last, while I was attending him I saw him try to make a bed for himself but he lacked the
strength, and when he set his snout into the dust he was unable to plow
even the little furrow he needed to lie down in.

37   He came out of the house to die. When I went down, before going
to bed, he lay stretched in the yard a few feet from the door. I knelt,
saw that he was dead, and left him there: his face had a mild look, ex-
pressive neither of deep peace nor of deep suffering, although I think
he had suffered a good deal. I went back up to the house and to bed,
and cried internally — deep hemorrhagic intears. I didn't wake till nearly
eight the next morning, and when I looked out the open window the
grave was already being dug, down beyond the dump under a wild apple. I could hear the spade strike against the small rocks that blocked
the way. Never send to know for whom the grave is dug, I said to myself,
it's dug for thee. Fred, I well knew, was supervising the work of digging, so I ate breakfast slowly.

38   It was Saturday morning. The thicket in which I found the gravedig-
gers at work was dark and warm, the sky overcast. Here, among alders
and young hackmatacks, at the foot of the apple tree, Lennie had dug
a beautiful hole, five feet long, three feet wide, three feet deep. He
was standing in it, removing the last spadefuls of earth while Fred patroll-

ed the brink in simple but impressive circles, disturbing the loose earth of the mound so that it trickled back in. There had been no rain in weeks and the soil, even three feet down, was dry and powdery. As I stood and stared, an enormous earthworm which had been partially exposed by the spade at the bottom dug itself deeper and made a slow withdrawal, seeking even remoter moistures at even lonelier depths. And just as Lennie stepped out and rested his spade against the tree and lit a cigarette, a small green apple separated itself from a branch overhead and fell into the hole. Everything about this last scene seemed overwritten — the dismal sky, the shabby woods, the imminence of rain, the worm (legendary bedfellow of the dead), the apple (conventional garnish of a pig).

But even so, there was a directness and dispatch about animal burial, **39** I thought, that made it a more decent affair than human burial: there was no stopover in the undertaker's foul parlor, no wreath nor spray; and when we hitched a line to the pig's hind legs and dragged him swiftly from his yard, throwing our weight into the harness and leaving a wake of crushed grass and smoothed rubble over the dump, ours was a business-like procession, with Fred, the dishonorable pallbearer, staggering along in the rear, his perverse bereavement showing in every seam in his face; and the post-mortem performed handily and swiftly right at the edge of the grave. so that the inwards that had caused the pig's death preceded him into the ground and he lay at last resting squarely on the cause of his own undoing.

I threw in the first shovelful, and then we worked rapidly and without **40** talk, until the job was complete. I picked up the rope, made it fast to Fred's collar (he is a notorious ghoul), and we all three fled back up the path to the house, Fred bringing up the rear and holding back every inch of the way, feigning unusual stiffness. I noticed that although he weighed far less than the pig, he was harder to drag, being possessed of the vital spark.

The news of the death of my pig traveled fast and far, and I received **41** many expressions of sympathy from friends and neighbors, for no one took the event lightly and the premature expiration of a pig is, I soon discovered, a departure which the community marks solemnly on its calendar, a sorrow in which it feels fully involved. I have written this account in penitence and in grief, as a man who failed to raise his pig, and to explain my deviation from the classic course of so many raised pigs. The grave in the woods is unmarked, but Fred can direct the mourner to it unerringly and with immense good will, and I know he and I shall often revisit it, singly and together, in seasons of reflection and despair, on flagless memorial days of our own choosing.

(1947)

The Writer's Subject

1. From White's reference to "the pigs I have raised" (para. 4), it is clear that he was no novice in the business of fattening up and slaughtering pigs. Why, then, is he so affected by the illness and death of the pig described in this essay?

2. Why did the pig's illness mean that "the classic outline of the tragedy was lost" (para. 3)? What "tragedy" is White referring to here?

3. Explain the importance of White's statement that "the loss we felt was not the loss of ham but the loss of pig" (para. 3).

4. What is revealed by White's reluctance to administer the castor oil? (para. 8)

5. Discuss the role of Fred the dachshund. Why did he seem to enjoy the pig's illness and death? Why does White call him "a happy quack"? (para. 16)

6. Why did White become obsessed with the task of saving the pig from its misery? (para. 17)

7. Why was White so disturbed by the preliminary diagnosis of erysipelas? In what way did this news affect his attitude to life? (paras. 18-30)

8. Why did everything about the pig's burial seem "overwritten" in White's eyes? (para. 38)

9. White states that he is writing his account of the pig's death "in penitence and in grief" (para. 41). Why should he feel penitent? Do you think he means this statement to be taken seriously?

The Writer's Style and Strategy

1. White's essay is a subtle blend of humour, irony, and pathos. Find examples of these differing tones in the essay, and explain their appropriateness.

2. Why does White "run ahead of his story" in the first three paragraphs? What function is performed by these paragraphs?

3. Discuss White's use of analogy in paragraphs 2 and 3. How does the analogy contribute to our understanding of White's feelings about the death of his pig?

4. Discuss the terms in which White describes the pig. What is conveyed by the use of the pronoun "he" rather than "it" in White's references to the animal? Why does he twice draw analogies between the pig and a child? (paras. 5, 12)

5. Examine the effect of each of the following statements in their respective contexts:
   (a) "I found myself cast suddenly in the role of pig's friend and physician — a farcical character with an enema bag for a prop" (para. 3).
   (b) "A pig couldn't ask for anything better — or none has, at any rate" (para. 4).
   (c) "I went back up to the house and to bed, and cried internally — deep hemorrhagic intears" (para. 37).
   (d) "'Poor piggledly-wiggledy!' said Miss Owen" (para. 34).
   (e) "Never send to know for whom the grave is dug, I said to myself, it's dug for thee" (para. 37).

6. In the concluding paragraph, White states that the whole community feels sorrow at "the premature expiration of a pig." How does he create a sense of that community in the course of his essay?

7. Discuss the essay's final paragraph. What makes it a fitting conclusion to the account that has preceded it?

Suggested Topics for Writing and Discussion

1. Most people have at one time or another suffered the loss of a pet. Working from a real or an imaginary experience, describe your own response to such an event.

2. As White explains in his essay, the breeding and butchering of animals for food is a commonplace feature of life on a farm. In recent years, however, animal activists have questioned man's right to exploit animals, even in this way. Do you believe that man has the right to use animals as he sees fit?

3. As White presents him, Fred the dachshund is more than a dog; he is a character in the drama of the pig's death. Describe an animal you have known that might be regarded as "a character."

Patterns of Social Behaviour

Of Marriage and Single Life
by Francis Bacon

He that hath wife and children hath given hostages to Fortune, for they are impediments to great enterprises either of virtue or mischief. Certainly the best works and of greatest merit for the public have proceeded from the unmarried or childless men, which both in affection and means have married and endowed the public. Yet it were great reason that those that have children should have greatest care of future times, unto which they know they must transmit their dearest pledges. Some there are who though they lead a single life, yet their thoughts do end with themselves and account future times impertinences. Nay, there are some other that account wife and children but as bills of charges. Nay more, there are some foolish rich covetous men that take a pride in having no children, because they may be thought so much the richer. For perhaps they have heard some talk, "Such an one is a great rich man," and another except to it, "Yea, but he hath a great charge of children," as if it were an abatement to his riches. But the most ordinary cause of a single life is liberty, especially in certain self-pleasing and humorous minds which are so sensible of every restraint as they will go near to think their girdles and garters to be bonds and shackles. Unmarried men are best friends, best masters, best servants, but not always best subjects, for they are light to run away, and almost all fugitives are of that condition. A single life doth well with Church men, for charity will hardly water the ground where it must first fill a pool. It is indifferent for judges and magistrates, for if they be facile and corrupt, you shall have a servant five times worse than a wife. For soldiers I find the generals, commonly in their hortatives, put men in mind of their wives and children. And I think the despising of marriage amongst the Turks maketh the vulgar soldier more base. Certainly wife and children are a kind of discipline of humanity; and single men, though they be many times more charitable, because their means are less exhaust, yet, on the other side, they are more cruel and hard hearted, (good to make severe inquisitors) because their tenderness is not so oft called upon. Grave natures, led by custom and therefore constant, are commonly loving husbands; as was said of Ulysses, *"Vetulam suam praetulit im-mortalitati."*[1] Chaste women are often proud and forward, as presuming upon the merit of their chastity. It is one of the best bonds, both of chastity and obedience, in the wife if she think her husband wise, which she will never do if she find him jealous. Wives are young men's mistresses, companions for middle age, and old men's nurses. So as a man may have a quarrel to marry when he will. But yet he was reputed one of the wise men, that made answer to the question, When a man should marry? "A young man not yet, an elder man not at all." It is often seen that bad husbands have very good wives; whether it be that it raiseth the price of their husbands' kindness when it comes, or that the wives take a pride in their patience. But this never fails, if the bad husbands were of their own choosing, against their friends' consent; for then they will be sure to make good their own folly.

(1613)

1. "He preferred his old wife to immortality."

The Writer's Subject

1. At the beginning of this essay, Bacon seems to give the advantage to the single life. How does he go on to qualify this view?

2. What is the single man's view of marriage and family, according to Bacon?

3. Why are unmarried men "not always best subjects"?

4. Why does Bacon think that churchmen should be single, whereas soldiers should be married?

5. Why, in Bacon's view, do single men make good inquisitors?

6. What qualities does Bacon suggest are necessary in a good wife?

7. What advice does Bacon offer about the best time for a man to marry?

The Writer's Style and Strategy

1. Explain the metaphor in the first sentence.

2. This essay is a loosely constructed contrast between marriage and the single life. In what ways does Bacon impose order on what might otherwise seem a series of unconnected observations?

3. What does Bacon's comment about single men's views of "their girdles and garters" reveal about his attitude to the single life? (In the Renaissance, "girdles and garters" were belts and stocking fasteners worn by men.)

4. The sentence beginning, "grave natures, led by custom . . ." acts as a transition between Bacon's discussion of married or single men and his observations on good husbands and good wives. What is the function of the allusion to the Homeric story of Ulysses and Penelope in this sentence?

Suggested Topics for Writing and Discussion

1. Write a brief essay on marriage versus the single life, twentieth-century style.

2. In "Of Marriage and Single Life," Bacon writes about marriage and the single life, but only as it affects men. Write an essay in which you explain why a woman should or should not get married. Use appropriate examples to support your arguments in favour of marriage or the single life for women.

3. Is there, in your view, any "best time" to marry?

A Hearing
by Hugh Brody

1   In June, Joseph and his family set up their summer camp on the Reserve. Four small households camped together in a patch of woodland only a few hundred yards from Joseph's house. There Atsin and David stretched a small tarpaulin between the trees and a sloping ridge pole. This provided shelter from rain, but, being open-sided, was cool. Sam Crown and Jimmy Wolf, Joseph and Liza, and Reza, Shirley and Tommy all pitched tents around a central fireplace. Atsin had a fire in front of his camp, but he and David — along with everyone else who lived or visited there — spent much of their time sitting, chatting, and eating by Joseph's fire.

2   The hot days of summer had their own special mood. Every morning one or two of the younger men went to find the horses, following their tracks along the riverside or into the hay and oat fields where they liked to feed. Once they had chased them back to camp, the hunters tethered the ones they thought they might need during the day. But it was often too hot to hunt; days slipped by without much activity. The men lay for hours, a short distance from the fires, half asleep, getting up to eat, visit a neighbour, or play cards. Liza, Reza, and Shirley fried bannock on the campfire above which they carefully hung meat to smoke and to protect it from flies. On very still days they also built smoke fires to keep away the flies and wasps that persistently bit the horses. Children roamed the hillsides and river banks looking for berries, swimming, or hunting rabbits and grouse.

3   Thomas and Abe Fellow worked almost every day on the Reserve ranch, riding off to herd cattle, move a bull from one meadow to another,

or look for horses that had strayed into the surrounding woods. Some days Sam and Atsin suggested a hunt, and then we would ride down the Midden River valley or drive to promising areas within fifteen miles of the Reserve. In summer, bull moose and buck mule deer are in prime condition, and hunting spots were chosen with them in mind. But tracking in great heat and through thick undergrowth and clouds of mosquitoes is hard work. Although enough kills were made to maintain an adequate supply of fresh meat, we spent most days dozing in the shade of the campsite.

In early August, almost everyone on the Reserve went to the Fort 4 St. John rodeo. In mid-August, Joseph's brother and sister-in-law visited for two weeks, camping with us in the small wood by Joseph's house. At this time berries were ripening in abundance — first strawberries, then gooseberries, blueberries, and saskatoon berries. Everyone picked them as they found them, the children sometimes returning to camp with hats or plastic bags full of blueberries. Thomas's sister-in-law stewed panfuls of them in fat; that way, everyone said, you can eat as much as you want without any risk of diarrhoea.

In August, the heat was often intense. During the middle of the day 5 even the mosquitoes kept to the cool shade of the undergrowth. The stillness was broken only by groups of children who walked and rode to a deep swimming hole a mile from camp. There they splashed and swam, sometimes riding into the water until their horses were out of their depth and then clinging on as the animal swam, or plunging off when a horse lunged and bucked in protest. A few older men and women at times came and watched these games, but many people spent their days in almost total inactivity. Summer is a time for resting.

So July and August passed quickly, quietly, and pleasantly. We twice 6 moved camp from one part of the woodland to another. A porcupine, one or two mule deer, and grouse contributed to the excellence of our . diet. From time to time someone went fishing within a half mile of the camp and returned with a sucker or a few rainbow trout. But there were also mishaps. Joseph was stung on the face by a wasp and spent two days with a painfully swollen cheek. Jimmy Wolf cut himself on the leg when angrily swatting at a bee with his hunting knife. One of the horses developed sores on its back and could not be ridden. These and similar events lent small features to a hazy, undifferentiated passage of time.

Then, in early September, thoughts turned yet again to Quarry and 7 Bluestone, and the need to build up stocks of meat. Joseph spoke of the marmot that would be easy to shoot as they basked, fat from a summer of feeding, on rocks high in the foot hills. He also said they might now find caribou in the mountains. It was at this time that the Blueberry Reserve was evacuated. A pipe in a nearby gas-cleaning plant had fractured and the reserve had been enveloped in the middle of the night in a cloud of hydrogen-sulphide gas. Thanks to haste, nobody was killed; but the community was forced to live temporarily in summer tents a few miles east of the Alaska Highway. This alarming event caused much discussion. Joseph and others at the Reserve had relatives who lived at Blueberry, and there had long been rumours of impending drilling for oil or gas on the Reserve itself.

8   But as summer turned to another autumn, the events at Blueberry were overshadowed by talk of the Alaska Highway Pipeline, and about a plan to hold hearings in each of the communities that might suffer some of the consequences of this enormous project. An employee of the Northern Pipeline Agency (an office set up by the federal government to prepare social and environmental conditions as well as to facilitate pipeline construction) visited the Reserve. He left a sheaf of papers at the house of the Chief. Then, some weeks later, a long and difficult document was also left, which set out, in provisional form, the terms and conditions that might govern the pipeline's construction. Finally, a notice was fixed to the door of the meeting hall that announced a date on which a public hearing into these terms and conditions would be held.

9   It is possible that a few people on the Reserve saw, or even tried to read, the documents, although no one did at Joseph's camp. If they had tried, they would have made little sense of the tortured bureaucratese by which every idea in the documents was obscured. Perhaps agency officials had attempted to discuss the ideas that they were advancing. If so, the people's interest or understanding was too slight for such ideas to become topics of conversation in our camp. The Alaska Highway Pipeline was seen as a vast, unwelcome, and perplexing menace. But no one knew quite where it was supposed to go; few knew what it would carry; no one knew if its possible dangers had been considered. The construction project that developers had hailed, and environmentalists bewailed, as the largest and most significant in the history of free enterprise was little more than a vague and distant enigma to the people who were supposedly to be its first and absolute victims.

10   Some chiefs and other representatives of the Indians of northeast British Columbia had visited Ottawa the year before to appear before a parliamentary subcommittee, where they had spoken out against the

pipeline. But the connection between that visit and the papers left in the Chief's home was not clear. White officials were always saying that bits of paper were of special importance, but right now there were other important matters at hand: the beginning of the autumn hunt, marmot, caribou. . . .

In September, Joseph's household, along with several others, return- 11 ed to Quarry for the first autumn hunt; but the weather broke and for two weeks the hunters endured almost continuous rain, eventually returning to the Reserve. By this time the hearing had become a more pressing issue. Northern Pipeline Agency officials had drawn up a provisional timetable, and political anxieties about how the whole process was to be effected were becoming intense. Yet the many meetings and disputes about the hearing took place in offices in Vancouver, Calgary, and Ottawa, and did not bear in any direct way upon the people. In early October, however, the Indians were told that representatives of the company planning to construct the pipeline, officials of the Northern Pipeline Agency, political and legal workers from the Union of British Columbia Indian Chiefs, along with an independent presiding chairman, and the press would converge upon the Reserve in November. Then, they said, they would listen to the people. A schedule set out the dates on which a hearing would take place at each of the reserves and at several of the towns and white communities throughout the region.

These community hearings were characterized by the Northern 12 Pipeline Agency as an opportunity for the Indians and others to respond to the terms and conditions which they, at the agency, had already drafted. This limitation would not be rigidly enforced, since it was bound to result either in endless misunderstandings or a reduction of the hearings to discussion that, for many people, might well be unintelligible. The preparation of terms and conditions — the rules that were supposed to reflect the Indian interest — had also taken place before any close attention had been given to the Indian point of view.

The people at the Reserve nonetheless anticipated their hearing with 13 great interest. Doubts may have arisen in the minds of their political representatives. Reports and papers left in the reserves by various officials may have gone unread. But the people themselves insisted that the coming meeting was of great importance. There was an ever-growing sense of occasion. No one had taken much trouble to ask the Indians what they thought about pipelines or any other frontier activity, and a hearing seemed to many like the first real chance to express their long-neglected points of view. As the event came nearer, the Fort St. John radio station repeatedly announced the days and times of different hearings. Everyone at the Reserve including Joseph began to look forward to the occasion.

14   The morning of the hearing was sunny and cold. No one was quite sure when it was supposed to begin. The notice on the door of the Hall gave the time as 10 A.M., but some people insisted that nothing much was going to happen before noon. At Joseph's house there was some excitement. On the previous afternoon, Atsin and Sam had discovered the freshly prepared den of a black bear. Branches and earth had been piled up around the den's entrance: the bear was about to bed down for the winter. The way the branches had been pulled and heaped left the men sure that they would be able to force the animal from its den and kill it in the entranceway, where it could easily be dragged out. The sooner they went back to the new den, said Atsin, the better. At this time of year, after a whole summer of feeding and the early autumn cold, the meat and fur should both be in excellent condition and there would be plenty of fat. Joseph added that he could use some bear grease, the best thing for softening and protecting the leather of his saddles and bridles.

15   Joseph, Atsin, and Sam were adamant: we should go and get the bear right away. Maybe we would be able to get back in time for the meeting; maybe the meeting should wait until later in the day; or maybe we could get the talking over with quickly, and be on our way to the den by early afternoon. It was a perfect day for hunting. Who could possibly want to spend it listening to talk? What was there to say about the pipeline anyway? After a long discussion, we finally agreed that the bear hunt could wait until first thing the following morning. Joseph and Atsin decided to stay for the hearing. Sam Wolf, however, said he would never listen to talk when he could be out hunting. He pointedly prepared his equipment and set off on foot to look for moose. Brian Akattah and I went to the hall to put up the maps the people of the Reserve had drawn to show the extent of their hunting and trapping territories. Everyone else patiently waited at home for the hearing to begin.

16   It was a long wait. The chairman came early, to be shown the Reserve, but it was midday before a busload of officials drove up to the hall. Specialists on social and economic impacts, a secretary to oversee proceedings, people whose job it was to record every word that was spoken, all climbed out and began to assemble their equipment. In separate cars came the men from West Coast Transmission — the company that would build the British Columbian section of the line — with their diagrams

of the pipeline, the press, and representatives of the Union of Chiefs.

Inside the hall, chairs and tables were arranged, maps pinned on the   17
walls. In the kitchen, beside the main meeting room, the women of the
Reserve were cooking. They had prepared two kinds of moose stew,
venison steaks, and a bountiful supply of bannock. Rich aromas filled
the hall and indicated that however numerous and alien the outsiders
and their technology might be, the Reserve was going to do its best
to turn the hearing into its own kind of occasion.

By the time the hall was finally ready for the hearing to begin, there   18
were at least as many outsiders to listen, report, or observe as there
were Indians prepared to speak. The visitors were talkative and jovial
and quickly chose their seats. The Indians were quiet and reluctant even
to enter the room. The chairman took his place at the altar-table on
which, just over a year ago, Stan had drawn his hunting map. The two
transcribers sat among a tangle of equipment. The Reserve women stayed
in the kitchen, out of sight and busy with their work, but able to see
and hear through a hatch and doorway which opened into the hall.
Joseph, Jimmy Wolf, Abe Fellow, Robert Fellow, and Clare Akattah,
with other community elders and leaders, had been urged into sitting
at a table to one side of the chairman. They looked uncomfortable. No
doubt they were wondering what was expected of them and were puzzled
by the microphones an official kept rearranging in front of them —
technology that hardly seemed necessary in so small a room.

In this unpromising way, the meeting at length began. The chairman   19
started by trying to explain its purpose. He spoke about the Alaska
Highway Pipeline and sought to give some rudimentary history of the
litigation by which it was being facilitated. Nervously, in an attempt
to overcome the problems of language and culture, and conscious of
the extreme lack of background information among the people who sat
there trying to make sense of it all, he laid out the reason for the hearing. He talked about terms and conditions and explained what kinds
of rules there would be. He tried, also, to describe the differences between the roles of the governments, agencies, and construction companies. And he emphasized his wish to hear all that the people of the
Reserve might have to say about the pipeline, or any of the other
developments to which it related.

The elders at the table watched and listened. They quickly felt some   20
sympathy for the chairman, an elderly man with a quiet voice and gentle
manner, who was wearing beaded moccasins. By keeping their focus
on him, they lessened the disturbing effects of the other strangers and

could feel that they were able to talk and be listened to in a personal, human way.

21   But it was not easy for them. The chairman was followed by the Northern Pipeline Agency's secretary and a representative of West Coast Transmission who introduced their colleagues and said what each of them did. The introductions were not translated into Beaver. At this time, in any case, only a small number of the people had come to sit in the hall. They continued to stand in the doorway, in the kitchen, or to wait outside. When the chairman did at last ask the Indians to offer their points of view, Joseph began to talk. His clarity and confidence filled the hall and transformed its atmosphere. He spoke in Beaver, with an interpreter. The unfamiliarity of the sounds and the richness of his tone cast a spell over the proceedings. The absurdities and awkwardness of the event faded away. Here, at last, was an Indian voice. After every few sentences, Joseph paused and let the interpreter translate. In English, the words were not easy to grasp, and its being rendered in the third person made the sense no clearer. But the points were not lost:

> He was saying in our country there was no such thing as money before the white man came; our only way to make a living is to hunt and there is no such thing as money to get from one another and big bulldozers that come over, go across our country.

> He is saying as long as there is the sun that goes over, that he shall never stop hunting in this country and wherever he likes to do, as long as the sun is still there.

> He is saying that the white man pushed his way into our country, that he stakes up all the land and a long time ago there was no people and then now there is so many. . . .

> He is saying if the pipeline goes through, the game will never be here and is there no way that we can stop this pipeline from going through and when the game goes away how would the people make their survival for meat?

> He says if the white man makes more roads, what if they get on my trapline and if they cut all the trees down, where would I go for hunting and where would I get the fur?

Then another of the elders made his statement. Again the Beaver language filled the room. Again the translation was uncertain, but the hesitant and broken English combined with the resonance of the Beaver to powerful effect.

One after the other the people spoke. Atsin tried to convey the im- 22
portance of Quarry and, determined to speak in English, made a cryptic,
struggling, but moving statement. Robert Fellow spoke in a mixture
of Beaver and English about the progressive destruction of the timber
on his trapline and tried to explain how this is driving away the squir-
rel, marten, and lynx. Clare Akattah talked about her ten-year-old son
and the happiness he gets from trapping. Brian Akattah explained the
significance of the people's hunting maps and pointed out that his family
— like others on the Reserve — needed to have their trapline. His mother
spoke in support of him and, in one sentence, encapsulated what everyone
had been trying to say: "There is no way you can make paper into
moccasins."

After the Reserve people had spoken, the representatives of West Coast 23
Transmission explained their project. With the use of a pipeline map,
they gave numbers, routes and scraps of history: 444 miles of 56-inch
diameter pipe along a 125-foot right-of-way; nine construction camps
at 50-mile intervals; four compressor stations, the nearest to be 46 miles
away; at Mile 92 of the Highway there is already a compressor station.
West Coast Transmission's other pipelines were built in the area in 1956,
1961, and 1964. Several gathering lines have been built around Fort
St. John and Fort Nelson to connect the main lines with scattered gas
fields. The proposed Alaska Highway pipeline, permissions granted,
will be started in 1982 or 1983; the section on muskeg would be built
in winter, the other parts in summer and fall; pipe would be brought
into the area by the British Columbia Railroad, and off-loaded at Fort
St. John, Beatton River, or Fort Nelson; this would be done in winter
and the pipe then stored at compressor station sites to be distributed
to construction points along the line.

Then the Northern Pipeline Agency representative spoke. Pipelines 24
cause problems. There must be rules; the people here, and in all the
other communities in the region, must say what rules they think they
need. West Coast Transmission will have to follow the rules. Problems
with traplines or any other issues can now be voiced. The job is to finalize
rules, but there can be more discussion. "Our purpose in being here,"
he said, "is to listen to you so that we can set the best rules possible,
but at the same time, recognizing that those rules have to be reasonable."

These men did not speak for long. Perhaps they sensed the impossi- 25
bility of their task. Their statements were not translated. They may have
been untranslatable. The divide between the details they offered and
the people's voices was too enormous. West Coast Transmission and

the Northern Pipeline Agency men came as employees of remote organizations to discuss a pipeline. They were on a business trip, doing a job. The men and women of the Reserve spoke of their homes, their lives and, moved to do so by profound apprehensions about the future,

26   they struggled against language barriers and nervousness.

    By 2 P.M. everyone had spoken. Joseph and Abe Fellow made final statements. The chairman expressed his thanks and admiration and adjourned the meeting. The West Coast Transmission men began packing up their map. Agency officials bantered cheerfully with one another. The transcribers coiled up their wires and packed away their machines. The Union of British Columbia Indian Chiefs' representatives and organizers exchanged the happy opinion that the hearing had been a success. Meanwhile, work in the kitchen continued. A few individuals had slipped in there to eat. Children crowded around their mothers, curious to glimpse the proceedings in the hall without being caught by the strangers' eyes. When the hearing adjourned, everyone was urged to help themselves to steaming dishes of stews, steaks, bannock. It was a lavish welcome, an invitation to share. If speeches and explanations had not captured the attention of the visitors, or had caused them to be at all uneasy, here was a feast to reassure everyone and, in its way, to give special emphasis to the importance of what the Indians had said.

27   It was all very convivial. The chairman and his associates, however, were eager to be on their way. Tired and satisfied, they regarded the hearing as ended. Once the social niceties were over and done with, the visitors could return to their homes and hotels in town satisfied that a job had been well done. Another hearing was scheduled for the next day. The formal business of making statements and placing them on the record was over. Children now ran in and out, and the two worlds of kitchen and hall had become the combined setting for a feast.

28   But the people had more to say. The Whites may have completed their work, but now that everyone was eating the Indians' food and talking to one another without agonizing and distorting formality, the hearing could get under way on the Indians' terms. Relaxed and scattered around the hall and kitchen in small groups, the visitors and officials failed to notice when Jimmy Wolf's brother Aggan and Aggan's wife Annie brought a moosehide bundle into the hall. Neither Aggan nor Annie had spoken earlier in the day, but they went directly to the table at which the elders had sat. There they untied the bundle's thongs and began very carefully to pull back the cover. At first sight the contents seemed to be a thick layer of hide, pressed tightly together. With great care, Aggan

took this hide from its cover and began to open the layers. It was a magnificent dream map.

The dream map was as large as the table top, and had been folded 29 tightly for many years. It was covered with thousands of short, firm, and variously coloured markings. The people urged the chairman and other white visitors to gather round the table. Abe Fellow and Aggan Wolf explained. Up here is heaven; this is the trail that must be followed; here is a wrong direction; this is where it would be worst of all to go; and over there are all the animals. They explained that all of this had been discovered in dreams.

Aggan also said that it was wrong to unpack a dream map except 30 for very special reasons. But the Indians' needs had to be recognized; the hearing was important. Everyone must look at the map now. Those who wanted to might even take photographs. They should realize, however, that intricate routes and meanings of a dream map are not easy to follow. There was not time to explain them all. The visitors crowded around the table, amazed and confused. The centre of gravity had suddenly shifted away from procedural concerns, pipelines and terms and conditions, to the Indians' world.

A corner of the map was missing and one of the officials asked how 31 it had come to be damaged. Aggan answered: someone had died who would not easily find his way to heaven, so the owner of the map had cut a piece of it and buried it with the body. With the aid of even a fragment, said Aggan, the dead man would probably find the correct trail, and when the owner of the map died, it would all be buried with him. His dreams of the trail to heaven would then serve him well.

Prompted by the map, the elders spoke again about the way their life 32 is changing, and the extent to which frontier developments have damaged their lands. They complained, too, about the weakness of dreamers to-day: would the young people be able to use these essential skills? Some of these thoughts had been spoken into the microphones and, in inchoate form, had become part of the official record. But now there was no recording, nothing that made the words official. The people now spoke in their own ways, and with real confidence. Most important of all, they said what they wanted and needed. The officials and visitors expressed delight and interest, but it is difficult to know how much they understood. Did the dream map come from too remote a cultural domain? Did the fractured and hesitant English in which the Beaver people spoke too completely obscure their points? Or, taking place after the hearing had been adjourned, off the record, was the conversation around the

map seen as no more than a further display of agreeable hospitality?
It is never easy to judge the political significance of informal events.
Evoking a strange and distant world, the Indians who showed the dream
map could have failed to make their point simply because they were
now using their own, very unfamiliar idioms.

33   All the men and women who spoke, whether at the microphones, in
seemingly sociable conversations over plates of food, or while the dream
map was being shown, said that their lives depended on traplines. They
said that logging should be carried out in such a way as to leave enough
habitat for squirrels and marten. They said that sports hunters must be
kept out of the Indians' hunting territories. Many also insisted that the
Alaska Highway pipeline either should not be built at all, or should
somehow be built in a way that would not drive away the region's moose.
They spoke of oppression in the past and disregard for their interests
in the present. The substance of their remarks, along with the gentle
tones they used, made it clear that the people had not given up hope,
either of being listened to or of leading the kind of life that strengthens
their economy and culture. They had tried to explain their concerns
in many different ways. They took part in the outsiders' hearing and
used it to explain their point of view, but they also prepared moose
meat stew and showed a dream map. Despite a century of experience
that might urge them to do otherwise, the Indians took the hearing
seriously.

34   Many of the Whites who spent the day in the Reserve hall said they
were deeply moved. The chairman repeatedly thanked the people for
their words and generosity, and thanked the elders for sharing their
wisdom. Yet discussion of the dream map soon petered out, and the
officials hurried into their bus, anxious to drive back to town. The people
of the Reserve were puzzled. Where had their visitors gone? The meeting
was just getting under way. Thinking that there must be some
misunderstanding, they asked everyone to come back into the hall,
though representatives of the pipeline construction company had long
since driven away.

35   Inside the hall, the elders explained that whenever a dream map is
taken out, someone must play a drum and chant. The visitors would,
of course, want to share in this. And one of the elders made the room
echo with the soft but insistent rhythm of the drum, and sang. No one
understood the words, and the singer was too shy to explain. He sat
in a corner and relied on the power of the rhythm to hold everyone's
attention. At the end of the first song he stopped and looked up. Perhaps

someone else would now drum? The evening was just beginning.

But as soon as the drumming stopped the officials expressed their 36
thanks and escaped again to their bus. They were tired, they said, and
it really was time they were back in town. From their point of view
the meeting had ended more than an hour before. The people in the
hall let them go. Perhaps they were no longer surprised by this
demonstration of the white man's haste and incomprehension. No one
criticized or complained. The drummer began another song. The sound
of the bus driving away broke into the music, but soon the noise of
its engine faded into the distance. When the second song ended, the
men said that it was a pity there had been no time to play the stick game.
They had looked forward to it.

People lingered in the hall. A young man visiting from another village 37
drummed and sang for a while. Others ate. The elders talked about
dreams and dreaming, and the maps of the Indians' hunting territories
were taken from the wall. The hall began to seem very empty. It was
still early. Outside a group of men talked about the meeting and the
weather. "Tomorrow will be fine and cold," said Joseph. "We'll go and
look for the bear early."

By the next morning it was hard to remember all that had happened 38
at the hearing. Atsin led us to the bear's den. He and Sam Crown judged
the lie of its interior by the shapes and textures of the ground, and then
they dug and pounded until the animal appeared at the entrance. Sam
shot it. Joseph and Robert Fellow skinned and butchered the bear while
the others set off on a moose hunt. The sports-hunting season was over.
The people again had the woods to themselves. No one said whether
or not they felt they had gained anything by all the talk of the previous
day. It is difficult to mix hunting with politics. But when they discovered
a sports hunter's equipment cache and old campsite a few miles from
the bear kill, their expressions of indignation were nothing if not political.
As he uncovered cans of fuel, ropes, and tarpaulins, and looked around
to see if a kill had been made, Atsin declared over and over again that
white men had no right to hunt there, on the Indians' land. When Joseph
heard about the cache he said: "Pretty soon we'll fix it all up. We've
made maps and everyone will see where we have our land."

(1981)

The Writer's Subject

1. Brody quotes Clare Akhata as saying "There is no way you can make paper into moccasins" (para. 22). How does this statement "encapsulate" what everyone had been trying to say at the hearing?

2. Brody describes what both the Indians and the white men say at the hearing. What differences are apparent in their ways of presenting their respective positions?

3. What details in the account show that the Indians take the hearing seriously?

4. What is the importance of the fractured pipe incident in Brody's narrative? (para. 7)

5. What details in the essay help us understand the Indians' sense of time? The white man's sense of time?

6. What is the importance of the Indians' debate about whether to attend the hearing or kill the bear? (paras. 14-15)

7. This essay is taken from a book entitled *Maps and Dreams,* and maps play an important part in this essay itself. What different significances do the Indians and the white men attach to maps at the hearing? What is the force of the concluding sentence of the essay?

The Writer's Style and Strategy

1. Why does Brody spend the first few pages of this essay giving a detailed account of Indian life in the summer months?

2. How does Brody make the reader aware of where his sympathies lie?

3. What use does Brody make of the *verbatim* rendering of the translation of Joseph's words at the hearing? Compare this translation with the explanation of their project by the representatives from West Coast Transmission.

4. What details of the hearing emphasize the contrasting attitudes and behaviours of the white men and the Indians?

Suggested Topics for Writing and Discussion

1. This essay centres on a clash of cultures. Discuss examples or instances of cultural conflicts that may exist within your own community.

2. Using your college library, find out what you can about the Alaska Pipeline Hearings and the outcome of the project.

3. Brody's essay is, in part, about the impact of technological change on a traditional way of life, a situation also common in other areas of the world (e.g., mining and logging operations in the Amazon, and hydroelectric projects such as the James Bay project in Quebec or the Aswan Dam project in Egypt). Choose an example of this kind of technological impact and discuss its effect on the way of life of a specific cultural group.

4. In his essay, "Tyranny of the Clock," George Woodcock discusses modern industrial man's view of time as a "commodity." Compare this view of time with that of the Indians as described by Brody.

Murder Among the Lovebirds
by Janet Flanner

1   Maybe our grandmothers were right and female standards are, on all
sides, not so high as they used to be. Certainly an eclectic comparison
between the mediocre murder recently committed by the nineteen-year-
old Parisian flapper Mlle. Violette Nozière and the stylish assassination achieved by the consummate Mme. Germaine d'Anglemont, aged
forty-eight, indicates a deplorable decline in the younger generation.
Mme. d'Anglemont shot her lover like a lady, because she was jealous;
Violette Nozière killed her father like a cannibal, because she wanted
to eat and drink up the savings that were his French life and blood.

2   Even in their private lives − or as private as could be, considering
that both females lived on love for sale − Germaine d'Anglemont cut
the grander figure, since, though an uneducated foundling, in her long
life she had learned to dine with royalty, own a smart house, accept
diamonds, and take such an intelligent interest in politics that senators
and deputies had been her slaves. And even the gentleman she finally
shot was a chief magistrate.

3   Though her doting parents had educated her over their heads and means
in a Paris private school, in her brief career Violette Nozière had learned
merely how to drink bad cocktails with penniless collegiates, was at
home only on the Boul' Mich', gave her mother's engagement ring to
a lover rather than received any gem from him, and certainly never
met any member of the government until, on trial for parricide, she
made the acquaintance of her judge.

4   Germain d'Anglemont was the last of the silk-ruffled, scented, hard-
lipped, handsome prewar courtesans, and she made a fortune. Violette

was, one fears, not the last of the fake-silver-foxed, hard-toothed, modern young monsters of mediocre looks and without any sense of the business of life. Being up to date, her crime cruelly lacked the grand manner.

Since she was faintly intellectual, Violette Nozière characteristically 5 chose poison and patience as her weapons. Though she did not succeed till August 1934 in putting her father into his grave and her mother into the hospital, she practised up on murdering them in March by giving them, "as a nice new tonic" with their evening coffee, six and three tablets of veronal, respectively, which they hungrily swallowed, since both were passionate patent-medicine gourmets.

At shortly past midnight after the March evening, contented with their 6 coma, their daughter set fire to the flat's modest parlor curtains, walked across the hall, roused a neighbor with a scream of "Fire!" and a brainy afterscream of, "I think the electricity must have short-circuited." The local fire brigade was called, and the next day M. and Mme. Nozière made the second page of the Parisian newspapers for the first and last time – thereafter they were unfortunately to be front-page stuff – for being unconscious from suffocation in what was called "A Bizarre Conflagration." Murder in an odd form was on its way to the Rue de Madagascar, where the three Nozières dwelt till they started on their separate paths toward cemetery, clinic and prison.

In the five months which followed, the immodest Violette did nothing 7 unusual – for her. She continued her afternoon and evening life on the large sidewalks and in the small hotels of the Boulevard Saint-Michel where, from the age of fifteen, she had been playing hooky from the costly female seminary for which her parents had scrimped so that she might star in mathematics. But though majoring in geometry, Vi knew less about Euclid than about a lot of other men. At her trial, it was brought out that she was not only a nympho – but also a mythomaniac – or a natural tart plus a born liar.

On the Café d'Harcourt terrace, she picked up men with a dual pur- 8 pose, the second being to tell them fantastic fibs – that she was an heiress, that her grandmother owned a château, that an aunt had millions, an uncle billions, that she herself was noble, that she was a trigonometry professor, and that her father was a director in the French railways. He was, in a way. He was the locomotive engineer on the Paris-Vichy fast train; her grandmother's country place was a cottage where, after her granddaughter's arrest, the old peasant humbly died of shame among her cabbages. Indeed, only two things unusual were performed by Vi during those fatal five months. She continued to try to kill her mother occasionally: at any rate, whenever the girl prepared breakfast for her, *maman* was deathly sick after, so Vi must have been putting something into the coffee — besides the chicory, that is. (Her father, having just fallen out of his engine cab onto his head, was momentarily in the hospital and so drank his bad coffee without ill results.)

9   Violette's second odd act was to fall in love: the emotion was great, since she eventually killed for it; the object was slight — an eighteen-year-old gigolo law student with sleek hair, slack morals, and American horn-rimmed spectacles, worn like a foolish foreign trade-mark on his French phiz. His name was Jean Dabin; his father, in Vi's mythology, was also probably a railway director — i.e., in reality, a whistle-blowing petty station-master on the Paris belt railroad.

10   Violette's love for Jean was the only true passion in her life, except that for murder. To him she gave all she had — herself plus one hundred francs a day, which she got from other men by night. She also promised to give him a secondhand Bugatti and a first-rate September holiday, for, as she said, she was shortly expecting to inherit one hundred and eighty thousand francs, or the exact sum her father had saved up from a lifetime of driving the Paris-Vichy express.

11   On August 23, her patience and poison and passion finally focused. Violette Nozière repeated what she had tried out in March, except that she increased her father's dose to twenty powdered veronal tablets and her mother's to six. This time she also gave herself a small dose of milk of magnesia, as she was feeling liverish. Then she curled up in a chair for a nap by her parent's couch while they died — she hoped. At two a.m. when she called the same neighbor, she this time screamed — since she had turned on the kitchen range without lighting it — "Gas!" and, as a new addition, "I think the pipe has burst."

12   The neighbor was, of all men to call in twice, an electrician and gas fitter by trades. Whatever he had failed to smell in March, this time he smelled not only gas but a rat. So did Vi, at dawn in the city hospital, sitting tenderly by her mother's bedside; the authorities had refused to let her sit tenderly by her father's slabside in the morgue. Sensing danger, she calmly rose and walked out into the new Paris day and what for one week seemed limbo, since no one could find her. By dinner, her news photo as "Wanted for Parricide" was posted all over Paris. Police hunted her everywhere, except at the Bal Tabarin (where she spent the first night after her crime gracefully waltzing) and on the Boulevard de la Madeleine, where a white-faced, neurotic, not very pretty young creature plied her trade while whispering crazily to her customers that

her father was a railway director, her grandmother owned a château, and that she herself was an heiress . . . to one hundred and eighty thousand francs . . . oh, yes, she was surely an heiress by now. . . . On the sixth day she was trapped into a second rendezvous by a gallant young male who had recognized her face on the pillow from the newspaper he'd tossed on the chair. Arrested, she told the truth, probably for the first time in her life. At any rate she said she was glad she'd killed her father, who, she claimed, was a satyr, though her relief at hearing that her mother was yawning back from the jaws of death may have been a lie.

Her trial for murder in the autumn of 1934 was melodramatic. It 13 opened in the Paris Assizes with a five-minute silence for King Alexander of Yugoslavia, who had also just been murdered in Marseilles. In the three days which followed, Violette fainted frequently, was occasionally nearly lynched by angry crowds, and was constantly hectored in court by her mother, who was sentimentally suing her for damages for having robbed her of the sweetest husband woman ever knew.

In addition to other details, the jury was swayed by the fact that Violette 14 had also robbed what she thought was her mother's corpse of a thousand francs pinned to the maternal corset. With lust for money to spend on her lover in cafés (for bad Martinis) accredited as her miserable motive, the jury judged her guilty of the uncivilized crime of parricide, whereupon the judge read what remains the most medieval death sentence preserved in modern French law: "She is to have her head cut off in death upon a public place in Paris. She shall be taken there barefooted, clad only in her chemise and with her head covered by a black veil. Before the execution shall be done, let the clerk in a clear voice read aloud this Judgment." Though women are no longer guillotined in France, and if they were, no matter whom they had killed, they would be allowed to die dressed and with their boots on, the rare sentence was followed by unusual silence in court, suddenly broken by Violette's vulgarly shouting, "Curse my father, curse my mother!"

To the outraged gendarme who dragged her away, she shouted in 15 one of her illuminating afterthoughts, "Fetch my handbag with my powder, rouge, money. I must have dropped it in the prisoner's box." What was most precious she had clearly left behind her in court. Thus passed from youth into lifelong imprisonment the best-educated, worst-mannered young murderess in French annals. But it was the fact of the girl's having rudely slept in the intimate presence of the dead and dying that caused the French jury to cut her off from civilized society as long as she might live.

16   The jury in the same Paris court which had just tried Germaine d'Anglemont for having shot her late love, Causeret, had only cut her off from civilized society for eleven months. And even that period of sequestration was a cultivated *passetemps*, since she spent it as prison librarian; both before and after murdering, dear Germaine was ever the bookworm. Her crime, trial, sentence, were all as cynical and sociable as her origin. Born a love child humbly named Huot, whose father only made her acquaintance when she was aged eleven, at twelve Germaine had won the catechism prize in her orphan asylum, at fourteen had her first flirtation, at fifteen her first carriage and pair and the stylish name of D'Anglemont, which she picked out of a dime novel. The week before Mlle. Huot became Mme. d'Anglemont, she had been noted − pretty and shabby − in the then famous Jardin de Paris Café, the noting being done by a tableful which included Catulle Mendès, the poet; Henry Bernstein, the playwright: Prince Fouad, now King of Egypt: and other gentlemen of the 1905 *belle époque*, one of whom asked her how she got there.

17   She said she had run away from home penniless and had got into the café by pawning her umbrella for three francs with the *vestiaire*. The gentlemen handed her five hundred francs (one hundred dollars in those lovely days) to get some decent clothes, three francs to get her umbrella, and invited her to dine. Her second lover, according to the list the Paris judge indelicately read out at her murder trial thirty-four years later, was a Dutch millionaire named Van Horschoot; the third was an Argentine tutor the Dutchman had hired to complete the girl's education − though she seemed to know a great deal already; the fourth love was the Prince Franz Josef of the royal house of Bavaria, who died of a broken heart because she wouldn't marry him.

18   Among the innumerable others she did not marry were the Polish Count Wielsinski, who, instead of a wedding ring, could give her only diamonds and pearls; the Agha Khan, who merely gave her a diamond (though it was eighteen karats); Camille Picard, today Deputy from the Vosges; a M. France, who was seventy and in sugar; a M. Astruc, at whom she once threw an expensive Gothic statue of the Virgin; and a Dr. Morgilewski (whom she never saw again for thirteen years, till the fatal day when she telephoned him to come round professionally as she seemed to have shot one of his successors). The mass of Parliamentarians she also enmeshed finally dwindled down, in her

forties, to the late-lamented Chief Magistrate Causeret, young, promising politician, fickle, married, father of children — and what was worse, son of the prime Rector Causeret of Clermont University.

"If I've omitted any of your lovers, pray excuse me, Madame," the 19 Judge said ironically at her trial. "The list is already so long, You were a *courtisane de haut vol* — a highflier; you are also, alas, a good shot." It was her custom to practise in the shooting gallery near the Rond-Point where Ivar Kreuger bought his fatal suicide gun: she kept two pistols in her boudoir alongside the statue of Sainte Thérèse — all three useful as weapons to a woman in a jealous rage. For it was for jealousy that she murdered Causeret. She had him followed through the streets of Paris by a hunchback female detective (a masseuse, when spying was scarce), who reported that he had gone to a department store to buy suspicious silk pajamas, instead of going, as he had announced, to talk politics with an old gentleman.

At noon, five minutes after Causeret had returned to her smart Place 20 Beauvais flat to lunch, there was still nothing to eat on the dining-room table, but there was a corpse with only a bullet in its stomach in the boudoir. As Germaine later admitted to the jury, she'd been a little hasty — the handsomest apology a murderess ever made.

At her trial the jury also was hasty; in one minute they saw it would 21 be useless to condemn her, since they also saw, all around the court, the visiting politicos who would demand and obtain her pardon. The jury therefore judged her guilty but with a cynically strong recommendation for mercy, which to the judge's mind meant a sentence of eleven months. Thus the quality of mercy was for once strained, since six years is a normal clement "stretch" for French female killers. Along with her eleven months, Germaine d'Anglemont also got bouquets of flowers in court, and her male friends shook hands, kissing hers.

In her trial, justice was not done. Yet injustice would have been ac- 22 complished had not a D'Anglemont's punishment been infinitely less than a Nozière's. For in a way these two were test cases, illustrating the modern French attitude toward murder, which can be summed up thus: the manner of killing is as important as the manner of living.

(1936)

The Writer's Subject

1. What were the principal differences in character and background of the two women described by Flanner? (paras. 1-4)

2. Why, according to Flanner, did Violette Nozière want to murder her parents? (paras. 7-10)

3. How was Violette eventually captured? (para. 12)

4. What was Germaine d'Anglemont's motive for murdering her lover? (para. 19)

5. Why was Germaine's sentence so much lighter than Violette's, even though both women were convicted of murder? (para. 21)

6. Why does Flanner believe that an injustice would have been done "had not a D'Anglemont's punishment been infinitely less than a Nozière's" (para. 22)?

The Writer's Style and Strategy

1. A writer, particularly a journalist, will often choose an "angle" from which to approach a subject. What "angle" is established in the opening paragraph? How does it determine the shape of the account that follows?

2. Flanner's essay first appeared in the *New Yorker,* a weekly magazine. Judging by Flanner's treatment of her subject, what conclusions might you draw about the *New Yorker*'s readership?

3. The tone of Flanner's essay is ironic throughout. What does the tone reveal about Flanner's attitude to the two women she describes, and to the society which condemned them?

4. Why does Flanner refer to Violette as "Vi" at many points in her essay? (paras. 7-12)

5. Flanner uses a variety of devices in her prose, including parallel or contrasting sentence elements, nouns or noun clauses in series, parenthetical comments, unexpected juxtapositions, colloquialisms, and alliteration. Pick out examples of each of these in paragraphs 6-11, and indicate how their use contributes to the ironic effect sought by Flanner.

6. Why does Flanner describe some of Germaine d'Anglemont's innumerable lovers? (paras. 17-18) How does that description prepare the reader for the essay's concluding paragraphs?

7. How does Flanner's title reflect the tone of the essay as a whole?

Suggested Topics for Writing and Discussion

1. Germaine d'Anglemont served a sentence of only eleven months before she was released. Today in North America, though murderers must generally serve much longer sentences, many become eligible for early release through parole. Do you think that a murderer should ever be released from jail?

2. Find two or three published accounts of a recent murder trial in local newspapers and national magazines. What differences are apparent in the various accounts of the proceedings? How is the character of the murderer drawn in each of your sources?

3. In discussing the sentencing of two murderers, Flanner demonstrates the application, a rather extreme one, of a double standard. Using an instance from public or private life, discuss another situation in which a double standard seems to apply.

Women's Clothes — Towards Emancipation

by Alison Lurie

The Superficially Liberated Woman

1   The more conventional late-Victorian and Edwardian woman, though she was no longer supposed to be childish and frail, was far from liberated by modern standards. Though her appearance was queenly, like most queens of recent years her freedom was hedged round with duties and restrictions. She was often called "divine" — and, as is the custom with goddesses, stood on a pedestal, which is an inconvenient place to stand if you want to do anything other than be worshipped. If you move at all, you are in danger of falling off — of becoming, in the popular phrase of the time, a "fallen woman."

2   The first wave of feminism, as historians of costume have pointed out, did not liberate most women from the bulky and elaborate clothes of the period. Indeed in many ways the female fashions of the time were more oppressive than those of midcentury. The corset had previously ended at or just below the waist, accommodating the many pregnancies of the early-Victorian woman. Now advances in medical science had decreased infant mortality, and it was no longer necessary or fashionable to have many children. The late-Victorian corset lengthened to midthigh, severely restricting locomotion. Gradually it began to push the chest forward and the hips back, creating the S-bend figure with its low-slung monobosom and protruding monorump. Over the corset were worn a corset cover, a camisole, several petticoats, and dresses with trailing skirts and trains. All these garments were richly trimmed with lace, ruffles, tucks, ribbons and embroidery; they were in constant danger of being rumpled or soiled, often giving a literal meaning

to the current euphemism "soiled dove."

The ordinary woman who held a job or emancipated opinions might   3
wear, instead of a lace-trimmed gown, a more plainly cut wool or linen
suit (the "tailor-made") with a shirtwaist, tie and straw boater that imitated those of men. But this imitation was superficial. Beneath her clothes
her corset was as uncomfortable and confining as ever, and when she
lifted her heavy floor-length skirt she showed a froth of delicate petticoats and lacy stockings. The message of this costume was clear: the
masculine efficiency or intellectual force were only external; underneath
she was still a member of the frailer sex. To wear such clothes, however,
did not necessarily mean acceptance of the status quo. Some feminists
wore them deliberately in order to confuse or disarm their opponents:
indeed, several of the leaders of the Emancipation Movement were
famous for their stylishness. This stratagem was also used during the
second wave of women's liberation, by Gloria Steinem among others.

The Modern Girl

In the early twentieth century substantial gains in dress reform were   4
achieved. Slowly, women began to liberate themselves from the duty
of acting as walking advertisements of their own helplessness and their
male relatives' wealth. (The struggle was an uphill one, however, and
it is by no means over.) There was also a gradual relaxation of the corset and a rise in the skirt, which cleared the ground by 1905, and by
1912 was above the ankle. Once women could breathe a little more easily
and had no trains to trip over they were better able to take part in sports.
Some, though to our eyes still absurdly handicapped, joined in professional competition. By the end of World War I women's clothes had
become relatively unconfining, but they were still sex-typed, and by
no means as comfortable as those of men. Various counterrevolutionary
efforts were made — notably, the introduction of the hobble skirt in
1910 — but these were generally unsuccessful. As in all transitional
periods, however, they provided a useful guide to the political and social
views of the women who wore them.

The clothes of the 1920s were thought at the time to represent an   5
extreme of freedom for women, and certainly they were a relief to anyone
old enough to have worn the styles of twenty years earlier. For one
thing, they drastically reduced the time spent in washing, ironing and
mending, and also in simply getting dressed and undressed. The woman
who bobbed her waist-length hair, for instance, saved several hours
a week that had previously been employed in brushing it out, washing

and drying it, braiding it at night and putting it up in a pompadour over pads of wire mesh and false hair every morning.

6   Twenties' dresses often had little-boy collars or ties, but these were no more than piquant additions to a recognizably feminine costume; they declared that their wearer was charmingly boyish, but not that she was a boy. The fulminations of contemporary critics against mannish women and womanish men seem exaggerated today. In photographs of the twenties men and women do look more alike; but this is because they both look more like children, and the difference between the sexes is less pronounced in childhood. Even in her Buster Brown or Peter Pan collar the flapper of the 1920s (like the Gibson Girl of a generation earlier in her mannish shirt and tie) is only male from the waist up. Below it, her skirt, silk stockings and pumps proclaim that basically she is a female.

Wearing the Pants

7   Reform of the bottom half of women's costume got seriously underway in the 1890s, when the introduction of the bicycle was followed by the introduction of the divided skirt for female bicyclists. Though at first it was called unfeminine and even shocking, the divided skirt was in fact voluminously modest. Eventually it was generally accepted — possibly because no one could mistake it for masculine dress.

8   Real trousers took much longer to become standard female wear. It was not until the 1920s that women and girls began to wear slacks and even shorts for sports and lounging. The new style was greeted with disapproval and ridicule. Women were told that they looked very ugly in trousers, and that wanting to wear The Pants — in our culture, for centuries, the symbolic badge of male authority — was unnatural and sexually unattractive. Nevertheless the fashion spread, and by the mid-1930s a woman could go on a picnic, play tennis or dig in the garden in clothes that did not handicap her. This freedom, however, was limited to the private and informal side of life. Wearing slacks to the office or to a party was out of the question, and any female who appeared on a formal occasion in a trouser suit was assumed to be a bohemian eccentric and probably a lesbian. Most schools and colleges insisted on skirts for classes and in the library until the 1960s; and even today this custom occasionally survives. At the Frick Collection Library in New York women may not be admitted unless they are wearing skirts; a particularly ancient and unattractive skirt is kept at the desk for the use of readers ignorant of this rule.

The woman who wore slacks or shorts before 1960, too, was only   9
outwardly liberated. Underneath her clothes she was more pinched and
squeezed and trussed-up than she had been in the twenties. Her bra hauled
her breasts up toward the shoulders and forced them into the currently
fashionable shape, often with the help of wires or deceptive padding.
The straps of this bra usually cut into the flesh, leaving sore red lines
on her shoulders and around her body to match the sore red lines left
lower down by her tight elastic girdle. Even slim women wore girdles,
since the fashionable figure had almost no hips or derrière, and a bouncy
rear end was thought vulgar. There was also no other decent way to
hold up the obligatory stockings: unless your skirt was very full, any
garter belt would show an embarrassing outline beneath it.

To Freedom and Partway Back

The fifties and early sixties were the years of the baby boom, togetherness 10
and the feminine mystique; and, as usually happens in patriarchal
periods, female and male clothes were sharply distinguished. The New
Look Woman and the Man in the Gray Flannel Suit were almost as
distinct in silhouette as their grandparents. Nevertheless it was in this
period that trousers for women began to edge their way into respec-
tability. At first they took rather peculiar and unbecoming forms. The
popular "toreador" or "Capri" pants, for instance, came in odd, glaring
colors and ended a tight, awkward six inches above the ankle as if they
had shrunk in the wash. They were often worn under maternity or mock-
maternity smocks, producing a costume that resembled that of a medieval
page. It was accompanied by shoes as narrow and sharply pointed —
and no doubt as uncomfortable — as those fashionable in the fourteenth
and fifteenth centuries. This outfit was appropriate, since the harassed,
untrained middle-class mother of the baby-boom years — unlike her
own parents — had no servants, and was reduced to waiting hand and
foot on her husband and too many children.

   In the late 1960s trousers for women finally became elegant as well 11
as respectable, and underwear vanished or mutated into harmless forms.
Even before the second wave of women's liberation got underway, the
long struggle for comfort and freedom in female dress seemed to have
been won at last. The introduction of panty hose freed women from
the ugly and often painful rubber and metal and plastic hardwear they
had been using to hold up their stockings. It was again permissible to
have curves below the waist as well as above; and millions of girdles
went into the trash can, where they were soon joined by millions of

padded and wired bras. During the 1970s pants suits and slacks were worn to work, to parties, to the theater, in elegant restaurants and on international planes, by women of all ages. They were usually accompanied by comfortable low-heeled shoes or boots. Fashion editors asserted, and women believed, that the bad old days were over forever.

12   In the last few years, however, there have been ominous signs of retrenchment and a counterrevolutionary movement seems to be gaining force. If one is pessimistic it is possible to see the sixties and seventies as merely a period of temporary victory. Indeed, the entire history of female fashion from 1910 to the present can be viewed as a series of more or less successful campaigns to force, flatter or bribe women back into uncomfortable and awkward styles, not only for purposes of Vicarious Ostentation and security of sexual ownership, but also and increasingly in order to handicap them in professional competition with men. The hobble skirt, the girdle, the top-heavy hats of the teens and the forties, the embarrassingly short dresses of the twenties and the sixties, all have aided this war effort. Today its most effective strategic devices are fashionable footwear and the demand for slimness.

The Shoe as a Strategic Weapon

13   Attempts to limit female mobility by hampering locomotion are ancient and almost universal. The foot-binding of upper-class Chinese girls and the Nigerian custom of loading women's legs with pounds of heavy brass wire are extreme examples, but all over the world similar stratagems have been employed to make sure that once you have caught a woman she cannot run away, and even if she stays around she cannot keep up with you. What seems odd is that all these devices have been perceived as beautiful, not only by men but by women. The lotus foot, which seems to us a deformity, was passionately admired in China for centuries, and today most people in Western society see nothing ugly in the severely compressed toes produced by modern footwear. The high-heeled, narrow-toed shoes that for most of this century have been an essential part of woman's costume are considered sexually attractive, partly because they make the legs look longer — an extended leg is the biological sign of sexual availability in several animal species — and because they produce what anthropologists call a "courtship strut." They also make standing for any length of time painful, walking exhausting and running impossible. The halting, tiptoe gait they produce is thought provocative — perhaps because it guarantees that no woman wearing them can outrun a man who is chasing her. Worst of all, if

they are worn continually from adolescence on, they deform the muscles of the feet and legs so that it becomes even more painful and difficult to walk in flat soles.

Literally as well as figuratively modern women's shoes are what keep **14** Samantha from running as fast as Sammy. As anyone who has worn them can testify, it is hard to concentrate on your job when your feet are killing you — especially if you are faint with hunger because you had only half a grapefruit and coffee for breakfast so as to stay a glamorous ten pounds below your natural healthy weight. For a while in the sixties and seventies it was not necessary to be handicapped in this way unless you chose to be. During the last few years, however, women have begun wearing tight high-heeled shoes again, even with pants, and the most fashionable styles are those that, like clogs and ankle-strap sandals, give least support to the feet and make walking most difficult.

Counterrevolution and Ambiguity

There have been other signs recently that all is not well with the in- **15** dependent woman. One is the gradual demotion of the pants suit for both daytime and evening wear. By now it has become a low-status indicator, especially when made of polyester, and is seldom seen in middle-class circumstances. It has been replaced by the "skirted suit" recommended as the proper costume for white-collar success, which must of course be worn with panty hose and heels. Another ominous sign is the narrowing of the skirt to the point where ordinary gestures like sitting on a low sofa or stepping over a puddle become difficult.

Prudence Glynn, a former fashion editor of the London *Times,* was **16** one of the first to point out the internal contradictions of much post-feminist fashion. The platform shoes and clogs that became popular during the seventies, for instance, are usually made on a wide last which does not compress the foot; however, they produce a clumping, awkward gait and are not only hard to manage but dangerous, often leading to serious injury. As Prudence Glynn puts it, "By their height they cater to an instinct in women to be taller and thus of more consequence vis-à-vis men. By their construction, which makes walking extremely difficult, they cater to an instinct to remain vulnerable."

Another popular style of the time, known as the Annie Hall Look **17** after the clothes worn by Diane Keaton in the film of the same name, was ambiguous in a more complex way. Essentially it involved the wear-ing of actual men's clothing: elegant three-piece suits, vests, shirts, ties and hats in pale colors — beige, off-white, tan and gray — often with a twenties look. Everything was worn very large and loose — collars open, shirts ballooning out, sleeves and trouser legs rolled up. These clothes were accompanied by huge handbags and kooky, childish costume jewelry: ceramic and wood and painted-tin ice cream cones and rainbows and Mickey Mice.

18   The wearing of men's clothes can mean many different things. In the thirties, sophisticated actresses such as Marlene Dietrich in top hat and tails and elegantly cut suits projected sophistication, power and a dangerous eroticism. The slacks and sweaters of the war period, and the jeans and pants outfits of the sixties and early seventies, were serious gestures toward sexual equality.

19   The Annie Hall style is a double message. It announces that its wearer is a good sport, a pal: not mysteriously and delicately female, but an easy-going, ready-for-anything tomboy type, almost like one of the guys. She will not demand to be protected from the rain or make a fuss about having to stand up at a football game. She probably enjoys active sports and is good at them (though not annoyingly, competitively good). Besides, you can see from her Snoopy pin that she has a sense of humor and is just a kid at heart.

20   At the same time, however, these clothes convey an ironic antifeminist message. Because they are worn several sizes too large, they suggest a child dressed up in her daddy's or older brother's things for fun, and imply "I'm only playing; I'm not really big enough to wear a man's pants, or do a man's job." This is a look of helpless cuteness, not one of authority; it invites the man to take charge, even when he is as incompetent himself as the characters played by Woody Allen.

                                                                    (1981)

The Writer's Subject

1. What connection does Lurie make between women's clothes and the degree of female emancipation in late-Victorian society? (paras. 1-3)

2. To what extent did dress reform in the 1920s close the gap between the sexes? (paras. 4-6)

3. What, according to Lurie, was the early reaction to the wearing of slacks or shorts by women? (paras. 7-9) How far did this trend in women's clothes really represent liberation?

4. Lurie notes that in the sixties women's trousers were often worn with smocks, "producing a costume that resembled that of a medieval page" (para. 10). Why does she call such an outfit "appropriate"?

5. Why, according to Lurie, was the introduction of pantyhose so important to women's clothing styles? (para. 11)

6. What contrast does Lurie draw between the fashions of the sixties and seventies, and those of the last few years? What does she mean by the statement that "a counterrevolutionary movement seems to be gaining force" (para. 12)?

7. How does Lurie interpret the styles of footwear customarily worn by women? Why is she disturbed by the modern fashion for high-heeled shoes? (paras. 13-14)

8. In the last four paragraphs of the essay, Lurie discusses the wearing of men's clothes by women. Why does this fashion seem to her to "convey an ironic antifeminist message"?

The Writer's Style and Strategy

1. Lurie's account is a mixture of social history, sociological commentary, and polemic. Where does Lurie move away from history and analysis to make her own position clear? How does she do so?

2. Discuss the language of paragraph 12. What is the extended metaphor through which Lurie presents the history of changes in women's fashions?

3. Discuss the structure and development of Lurie's paragraphs. Where does she usually place the topic sentence? (See, for example, paras. 8-11.)

4. From time to time Lurie shifts from the impersonality of the third person to "you." Discuss the purpose and effectiveness of this shift in point of view in paragraphs 13 and 14.

5. How does Lurie demonstrate that women have been handicapped by fashion? (paras. 13-15)

6. Examine Lurie's description of the "Annie Hall look" in paragraphs 17-20. What is Lurie's attitude to this fashion, and how is it conveyed?

Suggested Topics for Writing and Discussion

1. Lurie sees a direct connection between women's clothes and the degree of women's independence in a male-dominated society. To what extent do you agree with her findings? Are the current fashions, as were those in 1981 when this essay was written, a sign that "all is not well with the independent woman"?

2. Lurie's analysis focuses on women's fashions. What might a similar study of men's clothes tell us about the status of men in modern society?

3. Lurie discusses ways in which women's clothing "sex-types" them. Discuss other ways in which society encourages boys or girls (or both) to fix their sexual identities.

4. When *Dress for Success,* a book on women's clothing, appeared in 1976, it soon established a "dress code" for professional women. A spate of such books followed and, in fact, even became a target for satire — as in 1984's collection of Gary Trudeau's cartoons entitled *Dressed for Failure, I See. Dressing Thin* (1981), *Dressing Rich: A Guide to Classic Chic for Women with More Taste than Money* (1984), and *Dressing Up: How to Look and Feel Absolutely Perfect for Any Social Occasion* (1984) were included in the books for women; *Dressing Right* (1976) and *Dressing to Win: How to Have More Money, Romance, and Power in Your Life* (1984) were among those for men. Using your local library or bookstore, locate one such book and analyze its appeal. Write an essay outlining the book's assumptions about the audience's interests.

De Mortuis
by J.H. Plumb

The British have hilarious fun over the quaint funerary habits of the   1
Americans. The death of Hubert Eaton, the world's greatest entrepreneur
of death, and the recent discovery of a funeral home for pets, by a
wandering British journalist, released another gale of satirical laughter
in the English press. The mockery was hearty and sustained; yet was
it deserved? Well, certainly much of Mr. Eaton's Forest Lawn is hard
to take — the wet, nursery language for the hard facts of dying ("the
loved one" for the corpse, "leave taking" for burying, and "slumber"
for death), the cosmetic treatment (the contortions of death waxed away,
replaced by rouge and mascara and fashionably set hair) — all of this
is good for a gruesome joke. The place names of Forest Lawn appall
— Lullabyland, Babyland. The piped guff, the music that flows like
oil, and the coy fig-leaved art give one goose flesh.

   One turns, almost with relief, to a harsh fifteenth-century represen-   2
tation of the dance of death — livid corpses, jangling bones, and skulls
that haunt. How wholesome, after Hubert Eaton, seem the savage depic-
tions by Bonfigli of the ravages of plague, or even the nightmares of
death painted by Hieronymus Bosch. And how salutary in our own age
to turn from Forest Lawn to the screaming, dissolving bodies of a Francis
Bacon painting, for surely this is how life ends for most of us, in pain,
in agony.

   And if Forest Lawn nauseates, what of the Pets Parlor? "Blackie"   3
combed and brushed, stretched out on the hearth rug before a log fire,
waits for his sorrowing owners. The budgerigar is wired to its perch.
The Ming Room houses the Siamese cats, and if you want to do your

kitty proud, you can spend three hundred dollars or so on a stately lay-ing out, a goodly coffin (if you're worried about its fun in the afterlife, you can put an outsize rubber mouse in with it), and naturally a special plot in Bide-A-Wee, the memorial park for pets. President Nixon's dog, Checkers, had the treatment: he lies among the immortals in Bide-A-Wee, like Hubert in Forest Lawn.

4   However, this will become a mere second-class death if deep-freezing really catches on, as it shows every sign of doing. The Life Extension Society is spreading, and the entrepreneurs have smelled the profit in immortality. As soon as the breath goes, get yourself encapsulated in liquid nitrogen and stored in one of the specially constructed freezers that are springing up all over America from Phoenix to New York. And so wait for the day when they can cure what you died of, or replace what gave way — the heart, the brain, the liver, or the guts — or re-juvenate your cells.

5   None of this is cheap: the capsule costs four thousand dollars, and then there are the freezing costs and who knows what they may be in fifty years, so it would be imprudent not to make ample provision. Forest Lawn may be death for the rich; this is death for the richer, death for the Big Time. But in America there are a lot of very rich, so maybe soon now, outside all the large cities, there will be refrigerators as huge as pyramids, full of the frozen dead. This surely must be a growth industry.

6   Perhaps by the year 2000 Hubert Eaton will seem but a modest pioneer of the death industry, for who does not crave to escape oblivion? The rich have always tried to domesticate death, to make death seem like life. The American way of death is not novel: seen in proper historical perspective it reaches back not only down the centuries but down the millennia, for it is a response to a deep human need.

7   Some of the earliest graves of men, dating from paleolithic times, contained corpses decked out with bits of personal finery and sprinkled with red ocher, perhaps the symbol of blood and life, done in the hope of a future resurrection. After the neolithic revolution, which created much greater resources and considerable surplus wealth, men went in for death in a very big way. Doubtless the poor were thrown away, burned or exposed or pushed into obscurity, back to the anonymous mind from which they came.

8   The rich and the powerful, high priests and kings, could not die; they merely passed from one life to another. Because the life hereafter was but a mirror image of life on earth, they took with them everything

they needed — jewels, furniture, food, and, of course, servants. In the Royal Graves at Ur, some of the earliest and most sumptuous of tombs ever found, a row of handmaidens had been slaughtered at the burial — death's necessities were life's. No one, of course, carried this elaboration of funerary activity further than the Egyptians. And the tombs of Pharaohs and the high officials of the Egyptian kingdom make Forest Lawn seem like a cheap cemetery for the nation's down-and-outs.

What should we think of vast stone mausoleums outside Washington, **9** stuffed with personal jewelry from Winston's, furniture from Sloane's, glassware by Steuben, food from Le Pavillon, etc., etc., and in the midst of it all the embalmed corpse of a Coolidge or a Dulles? We should roar with laughter. We should regard it as vulgar, ridiculous, absurd. Pushed back three millennia, such habits acquire not only decorum but also majesty, grandeur, awe.

The Egyptians were as portentous in death as in life, and their grave **10** goods only occasionally give off the breath of life, unlike the Etruscans who domesticated death more completely and more joyously than any other society. A rich caste of princes built tombs of singular magnificence, filling them with amphorae, jewels, and silver. And they adorned their walls with all the gaiety that they had enjoyed alive. There was nothing solemn about their attitude to death. In their tombs they hunted, played games, performed acrobatics, danced, feasted; their amorous dalliance was both wanton and guiltless. Deliberately they banished death with the recollected gusto of life. No society has brought such eroticism, such open and natural behavior, to the charnel house. But in the annals of death, Etruscans are rare birds.

How different the grandiose tombs of medieval barons, with their **11** splendid alabaster or marble effigies. There they lie, larger than life, grave, portentous, frozen in death, a wife, sometimes two, rigidly posed beside them, and beneath, sorrowing children, kneeling in filial piety, the whole structure made more pompous with heraldic quarterings. Yet these are but another attempt to cheat death, to keep alive in stone what was decaying and crumbling below. And even here a breath of life sometimes creeps in. The Earl and Countess of Arundel lie side by side, dogs beneath the feet, pillows under the head, he in armor, she in her long woolen gown. But, movingly enough, they are holding hands. The sons of Lord Teynham cannot be parted, even in death, with their hawk and hound. Nor were these tombs so cold, so marmoreal, when they were first built. They were painted, the faces as alive with color as the corpses in the parlors of Forest Lawn.

12   Seen in the context of history, Forest Lawn is neither very vulgar
nor very remarkable, and the refrigerators at Phoenix are no more surprising than a pyramid in Palenque or Cairo. If life has been good, we,
like the rich Etruscans, want it to go on and on and on, or at the very
least to be remembered. Only a few civilizations have evaded expensive funerary habits for their illustrious rich, and these usually poverty
stricken ones. For all their austerity, the Hindus, burning bodies and
throwing the ashes into the Ganges, have maintained distinction in their
pyres. Not only were widows coaxed or thrown onto the flames, but
rare and perfumed woods were burned to sweeten the spirit of the rich
Brahman as it escaped from its corrupt carapace. Cremation à la Chanel!

13   What is tasteless and vulgar in one age becomes tender and moving
in another. What should we say if we decorated our tombs with scenes
from baseball games, cocktail bars, and the circus, or boasted on the
side of our coffins of our amatory prowess, as erect and as unashamed
in death as in life. And yet when the Etruscans do just these things,
we are moved to a sense of delight that the force of life could be so
strong that men and women reveled in it in their graves.

14   So the next time you stroll through Forest Lawn, mildly repelled by
its silly sentimentality, think of those Etruscans; you will understand
far more easily why seven thousand marriages a year take place in this
California graveyard. After all, like those Arundels, Eros and Death
have gone hand in hand down the ages. The urge to obliterate death
is the urge to extend life, and what more natural than that the rich should
expect renewal. How right, how proper, that Checkers should be waiting
in Slumberland.

                                                                    (1967)

The Writer's Subject

1. What is Plumb's thesis, and where is it most clearly stated?

2. What aspects of American funerary practice provoked "satirical laughter" in the British press?

3. What is suggested about American attitudes to death in the first five paragraphs of the essay?

4. Why does Plumb seem to find the grim paintings of death described in paragraph 2 "wholesome" or "salutary" in comparison with the practices of Forest Lawn?

5. What parallels does Plumb draw between American burial practices and those of earlier civilizations? To what conclusions do these comparisons lead him, with respect to the apparent vulgarity of places like Forest Lawn?

6. How did the Etruscans banish death "with the recollected gusto of life" (para. 10)? What connection does Plumb draw between Etruscan burial practices in particular and those found in Forest Lawn? (paras. 13-14)

7. Why is Plumb not surprised that "seven thousand marriages a year take place in this California graveyard" (para. 1)?

The Writer's Style and Strategy

1. What examples of euphemism does Plumb include in the first paragraph?

2. What tone is established in the opening paragraph of the essay? Where is there a clear shift in tone, and what occasions that shift?

3. What is conveyed of the writer's attitude to American funerary practices by such statements as "the entrepreneurs have smelled the profit in immortality" (para. 4), or "This surely must be a growth industry" (para. 5)?

4. How does Plumb convey his sense of the absurdities involved in the burial of pets? (para. 3)

5. Show what use Plumb makes of comparison and contrast as a strategy to structure his argument. In this connection, what function is performed by paragraph 6?

6. In his use of historical evidence, Plumb alludes to the tombs of medieval barons and gives several examples. (para. 11) Discuss how the use of examples and descriptive details at this point develops Plumb's thesis.

7.   Discuss the effectiveness of the essay's conclusion. How well does it round off Plumb's discussion? What does its tone reveal about his attitude?

8.   Why does Plumb use a Latin title for this essay?

Suggested Topics for Writing and Discussion

1.   Plumb describes some of the methods by which modern Americans try to "domesticate death." What aspects of funerary practice in your own community seem to you to have the same purpose?

2.   Plumb treats cryogenics (a term to describe the deep-freezing of the dead, taken over from the branch of physics dealing with very low temperatures) somewhat sardonically; he focusses almost exclusively on its high costs. What is your own view of this process? Do you think that any ethical or religious considerations may be involved?

3.   Many cemeteries in North America now forbid the erection of funerary monuments; they require instead that graves be marked only with a horizontal stone so that the effect of a park is achieved. What is your view of this practice? Do you think cemeteries should be showplaces? Parks? Quiet places for the dead and their surviving family and friends?

4.   Cemeteries are often fascinating places, especially as tourist attractions. Using travel guides from your local library or bookstore, find out what you can about some of the famous cemeteries of Europe and prepare your own "mini-guide to the best resting places." You may want to look up some of the following: Père-Lachaise in Paris — burial place of Frederick Chopin, Oscar Wilde, Jim Morrison and many other celebrated figures; the Protestant Cemetery in Rome — burial place of John Keats and Percy Bysshe Shelley's ashes; the Central Cemetery in Vienna — burial place of Mozart, Beethoven, Brahms, and Schubert; Highgate Cemetery in London — burial place of Karl Marx and George Eliot.

Nostalgia
by Witold Rybczynski

*However, insofar as there is such reference to a historic
past, the peculiarity of "invented" traditions is that the
continuity with it is largely factitious.*

Eric Hobsbawm
The Invention of Tradition

We've all seen this comfortable man; his face looks out from the adver-   1
tising pages of magazines. His graying hair, which is close-cropped,
belies his age — he is only forty-three — just as his frayed shirt and
faded Levi's belie his eight-figure income. The latter is barely hinted
at by the silver Rolex discreetly half-hidden by the jacket sleeve, and
by the hand-made cowboy boots. What he does for a living is not immediately clear. Well, we do know that despite his worn work clothes
he doesn't pick lettuce; migrant workers don't wear muted wool-and-
mohair sport jackets. He could be a professional athlete — a purveyor
of light beer and deodorant — but his clothes are too low-key, and in
any case he lacks a mustache. Still, whatever he does do, it seems to
agree with him — a half-smile crosses his tanned face. But his glance
is neither the vacuous stare of the professional clotheshorse nor the self-
satisfied grin of the celebrity; this man looks content. "Look at me,"
he is saying, "I could dress any way I want, but I don't need to impress
anyone, not even you. I feel good just like this." Since all ads, whether
for cigarettes or for cancer research, are selling something, we can only
conclude that what this man is selling is comfort.

Of course, this man is comfortable. Why shouldn't he be? He owns   2
90 percent of a business whose annual sales total a billion dollars. His
personal after-tax income in 1982 was said to be fifteen million dollars.
He has all the perks that success of this kind brings: an upper Fifth
Avenue duplex (more about that later), an estate in Westchester, another
on Jamaica, a beach house on Long Island, a ten-thousand-acre ranch
in Colorado, and a private jet to travel among them.

What does he do, this business mogul, this multimillionaire, this com-   3 fortable man? He thinks up ways for people to dress. Fifty years ago he might have been a tailor or a dressmaker; if he had lived in France he would have been called a couturier. But to call Ralph Lauren a tailor is like calling the Bechtel Corporation a builder. The word does not convey the sheer size or the international scale of the operation. A tailor makes clothes; Lauren's corporation franchises manufacturers on four continents who turn out products that are sold in more than three hundred shops carrying his name, as well as in specialty boutiques in department stores in the United States, Canada, England, Italy, Switzerland, Scandinavia, Mexico, and Hong Kong. As it has grown, his business has also diversified. It started modestly, with neckties, but soon expanded to men's wear, then clothes for women, lately a special line for children. Now perfumes, soaps, cosmetics, shoes, luggage, belts, wallets, and eyeglasses all bear his imprimatur. Lauren's is that most modern of professions: he is the total fashion designer.

4   The first thing that strikes us about Lauren's clothes is how American they look. They are based on recognizable homegrown images: the western ranch, the prairie farm, the Newport mansion, the Ivy League college. The feeling of déjà vu is intentional: Lauren is an orchestrator of images. Although his clothes are not faithful replicas of period dress, their appearance does reflect popular ideas about various romantic periods of American history. We have seen them all before, in paintings, in photographs, on television, and, especially, in films.

5   Lauren understands films. One of his early designs for men's evening wear consisted of a black dinner suit, wing-collared shirt, white gloves, and a white silk muffler. Reporting on the show, *The New York Times* described this outfit as having "stepped out of a Leslie Howard movie"; Lauren himself appeared in black pinstripes and reminded the reporter of Douglas Fairbanks. The cinematic simile was appropriate, since Lauren had just designed the men's costumes for a film version of *The Great Gatsby.* For a brief time, Twenties-influenced fashion became popular; dress-for-success, Lauren called it. A few years later, many of his designs were featured in the film *Annie Hall*; the comfortable, relaxed clothes worn by its stars, Woody Allen and Diane Keaton, became the look of the year. This inclination to be a costumer, along with a career built as much on advertising as on fashion shows and *Vogue* magazine, has not assured Lauren a secure position in the fashion world. It is unlikely that there will ever be a Ralph Lauren retrospective of the Metropolitan Museum, as there was in 1984 for Yves Saint Laurent.

6   Whether or not fashion design is an art is arguable, but there is no

doubt that today it is a very big business. It all started in 1967, when Yves Saint Laurent, the boy wonder of haute couture who had succeeded Christian Dior as Paris's leading dressmaker, opened Rive Gauche, a chain of shops that sold expensive but mass-produced clothes with the now-famous YSL label. Rive Gauche proved to be a great success (there are now more than 170 outlets around the world), and soon other couturiers such as Courrèges and Givenchy were lending — that is, selling — their talents to the *prêt à porter* trade. Even the conservative Chanel succumbed to this trend, although the house did so only after the death of its founder.

Haute couture had provided the fashion industry with glamour, but 7 ready-to-wear clothing now became its bread and butter.* In the process many designers acquired a distinctly commercial relationship to the products that they endorsed; if you've seen athletes peddling golf clothes or tennis shoes you get the idea. It is difficult to believe that Pierre Cardin, for instance, would ever be caught dead wearing much of the perfume or the clothing (made in a Bombay sweatshop) that carries his cachet. It is obvious that the fashion pates often have little, if anything, to do with the design of "their" products; in any case, their reputations, like those of Arnold Palmer or Bjorn Borg, are made elsewhere. In that sense, at least, mass marketing, lucrative though it may be, is only a sideline.

Unlike Cardin and Saint Laurent, whose careers were founded in the 8 exclusive dress salons, Lauren was never a couturier; from the beginning he was concerned with mass-produced clothing, and so he acquired an understanding of popular instead of elite tastes. His renown as a designer has been the result of his commercial success, not vice versa. His influence on the way that Americans dress is often overlooked, precisely because it has been indirect. Most of the women who copied Diane Keaton's loose tweed jackets or oversized men's shirts in 1977 were unaware that they were imitating Lauren originals. The 1980s fashion for Ivy League clothes — the so-called preppy look — was also Lauren-inspired.

What does this have to do with domestic comfort? In 1984, Ralph 9 Lauren announced that he was entering the home furnishings field. The only surprise is that it took him so long. The relationship between clothing and interior decoration is venerable. Look at a Hogarth paint-

*The dressmaker Charles Frédéric Worth invented the term "haute couture" in 1858. For a long time it could only be used by fashion houses that were recognized by the French government Office pour Art et Création. Curiously, haute couture was *not* the highest accreditation; the work of the most select fashion houses was referred to as "couture création."

ing of an early Georgian interior. The soft curves of the carved furniture were a counterpart to the rich costumes of the time and com-
plemented the voluminous gowns of the women and the lace fronts and
elaborate wigs of the men. The slightly pompous interiors of the nineteenth century also reflected clothing fashions; skirted chairs and gathered
draperies imitated the details of how cloth was used in skirts and gowns,
and wallpaper copied the designs used in fabrics. The richness of Art
Deco furniture mirrored its owners' luxurious costumes.

10   And how does Ralph Lauren intend to dress the modern home? The
line of furnishings — it is called a Collection — provides everything
needed to decorate the home. The Collection is meant to be, in the words
of Lauren's publicists, a total home environment. You can now put on
a Lauren dressing gown, slip on a pair of Lauren slippers, shower with
Lauren soap, dry with a Lauren towel, walk across a Lauren rug, glance
at the Lauren wallpaper, and slip between Lauren sheets, beneath a
Lauren comforter, to sip warm milk from a Lauren glass. You can now
be a part of the ad.

11   It is doubtful, however, that this is "the next plateau of life-style
marketing," as one enthusiastic distributor has called it. For one
thing, the Collection will have a limited clientele. The Lauren furnishings, which are not mass-produced, are expensive, and are being sold
only in fashionable department stores in major cities like Chicago, Dallas
and Los Angeles. For another, despite Lauren's long list of products
the Collection is limited and does not include a full range of furniture
— thus far only a few wicker pieces are available. Nevertheless, it is
worthwhile examining how a corporation whose success is based on
understanding the public's taste for clothing interprets popular images
of the home.

12   I go to Bloomingdale's, New York's store for the upper-middle-class
consumer, to witness this next plateau. "Fashion is a function of life-
style," a voice says as I get off the escalator. Startled, I turn. There
he is, the comfortable man, star of his own furnishings video. Across
from the television monitor is the entrance to the Ralph Lauren Home
Furnishings boutique, which consists of a number of rooms displaying
the Lauren products. They remind me of the Shelburne Museum, in
Vermont, where furnishings and objects are displayed in actual houses
as part of recreated room settings. This gives the historical rooms the
impression of being inhabited. In Bloomingdale's, the Lauren rooms
are also fully recreated, with walls, ceilings, even windows, and look
more like movie sets than store displays.

It turns out that the Collection is not one line but four. The four have **13**
names: "Log Cabin," "Thoroughbred," "New England," and "Jamaica."
The walls of the "Log Cabin" are chinked with white plaster, and the
ceiling is supported by rough-hewn beams. Buffalo Check and
Woodsman Plaid blankets cover the massive pegged timber bed. The
bedclothes are soft brushed flannel with matching pillow shams, sheets,
and bedskirts. The rugged furniture is obviously handmade, and goes
nicely with the American Indian hearth rug on the floor. A pair of Bean
boots stands by the bed; on the side table is a copy of everyone's favorite
summer-cottage reading, the *National Geographic* magazine. The
general effect is one of moneyed rusticity, the furnishings equivalent
of designer jeans.

"Jamaica" is across the aisle. It is obviously designed for the Sunbelt. **14**
A giant bamboo four-poster bed, draped with what looks like voile but
could be mosquito netting, stands in the center of a cool white room.
The colors of the Italian linens, Swiss embroidery, and chambray com-
forters are feminine — pink and blue. The bedclothes and table linens
are trimmed with ruffles and embroidered with floral bouquet designs.
If the inhabitant of "Log Cabin" is out shooting moose, the owners of
this home must be on the verandah sipping Planter's Punch.

The decor of "Thoroughbred" is equally genteel — a country **15**
gentleman's room of dark colors highlighted by the polished brass of
the bedstead and the gleaming mahogany wall paneling. Pheasant and
hunting motifs abound, as do paisley prints and tartans.* Wall cover-
ings are checks, tattersalls, and foulards. The effect is a bit overwhelming, like being caught inside Rex Harrison's closet. At the foot of the
bed are a pair of riding boots. The publicity stills showed two beagle
hounds dozing among the tweeds. I look for them in the cozy setting,
but that must be where Bloomingdale's drew the line. "Thoroughbred"
includes a distinctly anglophile table setting: teapots, egg cups, and a
covered muffin dish, as well as plates ornamented with scenes of mounted
polo players. "A dream England filtered through preppy America," an
uncharitable British journalist called it.

"New England" contains staid Early American furniture; this could **16**

---

*Lauren is certainly unaware, as are most people, of the recent origin of the "traditional"
Scottish tartan. The idea of associating specific tartans with different families occurred during
the first part of the nineteenth century — not in the mists of Celtic antiquity — and, like the
kilt itself, was a modern invention. The introduction of tartans was the result of Queen Victoria's cult of the Highlands, as evidenced at Balmoral Castle, her Scottish country home, and
of a sales campaign by cloth manufacturers who were seeking to develop larger markets for
their products.

be the bedroom of a restored Vermont country inn. The colors are muted, the wall fabrics are solid and candy-striped to match the Oxford-cloth bedclothes. It is the least theatrical of the four; Yankee sobriety doesn't lend itself to dramatization.

17   The four themes have a lot in common. They are inspired by Lauren's own homes — the Jamaican hideaway, the ranch, the New England farm. They are aimed at the growing number of people who have second, and even third homes — by the lake, next to the ski slope, or on the beach — and so they follow rural models. At the same time, the comfortable informality of these furnishings is likely to be just as appropriate to apartments and townhouses as to weekend retreats. The furnishings are also an extension of Lauren's clothing designs, which have been called "western and outdoorsy or conservative and tweedy." In that sense these are settings, for which the costumes have already been designed. This tendency to coordinate clothes and furnishings is to be continued in two other themes not featured in Bloomingdale's — "Mariner" and "Safari." The former is to establish an appropriately yachtsmanlike setting; the latter will convey, according to the designer, the feeling "of a hunter getting out of his Range Rover and aiming his elephant gun."

18   The settings have something else in common, something which has become the hallmark of the Lauren look. One of his early and more extravagant outfits for men consisted of a Donegal tweed jacket with black belt and bellows pockets, worn with white flannel trousers, and complete with collar pin and English shoes of saddle leather. "You just know that the gentleman wearing it belongs to a private club and drives a Rolls-Royce, or at least wants to give that impression," wrote a fashion reporter, who dubbed this the "Vanderbilt look." In much of his recent clothing designs, Lauren has managed to restrain a tendency to evoke the symbols and the style of turn-of-the-century wealth, but the major influence on the treatment of the furnishing themes continues to be what an associate calls the look of "old money."* Old, in most cases, means falling between 1890 and 1930. The log cabin setting, for instance, has the affected, cedar-stump rusticity that used to characterize rich men's hunting lodges at the end of the last century — although Lauren, a supporter of wildlife preservation, has carefully omitted the stuffed animal heads mounted on the wall. The "old world elegance and refinement" of the Jamaican furnishings brings to mind the relaxed pace

*The friction between new and old money took a bizarre turn recently, when it was reported that Lauren had brought legal action for infringing on "his" corporate symbol against an organization that had the temerity to use the figure of a man on a horse swinging a mallet as its insignia. The object of his suit was the United States Polo Association, founded in 1900.

of life in the white porticoed homes of the island during its colonial period. The country gentleman's retreat evoked by "Thoroughbred" could be Lord Sebastian Flyte's room in Evelyn Waugh's *Brideshead Revisited*. But this is not period decor in the conventional sense — it lacks the consistent and specific details of neo-Georgian or French Antique, to name two popular styles. Lauren is not so much interested in recalling the authentic appearance of a historical period as he is in evoking the atmosphere of traditional hominess and solid domesticity that is associated with the past.

This acute awareness of tradition is a modern phenomenon that reflects **19** a desire for custom and routine in a world characterized by constant change and innovation. Reverence for the past has become so strong that when traditions do not exist, they are frequently invented. There are other examples than the Scottish tartan. After England adopted a national anthem in the mid-eighteenth century, most European nations quickly followed suit. The results were sometimes curious. Denmark and Germany, for instance, simply set their own words to the English music. Switzerland still sings "Ruft die, mein Vaterland" to the strains of "God Save the King," and until Congress adopted an official national anthem — in 1931 — Americans sang "My Country 'Tis of Thee" to the same regal music. The "Marseillaise" is original, and authentic; it was written during the French Revolution. But Bastille Day was first celebrated in 1880, a hundred years after the actual event.

Another example of invented tradition is the popular fashion for so- **20** called Early American or Colonial furniture. In most people's imagination it represents a link to the values of the Founding Fathers, the Spirit of '76, an integral part of the national heritage. The truth is that the Colonial style owes its existence not to an unbroken continuity passed from colonial father to republican son, but to the much more recent Centennial celebrations of 1876. The Centennial encouraged the founding of many so-called patriotic societies, such as the Sons (now defunct) and the Daughters (still active) of the American Revolution, the Colonial Dames of America, and the Society of Mayflower Descendants. This new interest in genealogy was due partly to the Centennial itself, and partly to efforts by the established middle class to distance itself from the increasing number of new, predominantly non-British immigrants. This process of cultural authentification was fortified by furnishing homes in the so-called Colonial style, thus underlining the link to the past. Like most invented traditions, the Colonial revival was also a reflection of its own time — the nineteenth century. Its visual

taste was influenced by the then current English architectural fashion
– Queen Anne – which had nothing to do with the Pilgrim Fathers,
but whose cozy hominess appealed to a public sated by the extravagances
of the Gilded Age.

21   Lauren's invented traditions are derived from the literary and cinematic
imagination. The English country life suggested by "Thoroughbred" was
already in decline when Waugh wrote about it, forty years ago. Today,
where fox-hunting still exists, it is practiced almost in secret, to avoid
the attacks of various environmental and animal-welfare groups.
"Mariner" conjures up the Newport of F. Scott Fitzgerald, but although
his blazer-clad sailors lolled about on sixty-foot teak-decked ketches
– crewed by hired help – most of us have to be content with a car-
topped fiberglass dinghy. "Safari" recalls a time when wealthy Americans
and Europeans could go to Africa and shoot their hearts out; today,
if they go they are less likely to be carrying a Mannlicher – as Hemingway did – than a Minolta. The real postindependence Jamaica is
less old-world charm than packaged tours, dope, and threatening
Rastafarians. As for the simple fireside pleasures implicit in "Log Cabin,"
these have been replaced, or at least augmented, by hang gliders and
mountain bikes.

22   What is also striking about these handsome interiors is the absence
of so many of the things that characterize modern life. We look in vain
for clock-radios, electric hair dryers, or video games. There are pipe
racks and humidors in the bedrooms, but no cordless telephones, no
televisions. There may be snowshoes hanging on the cabin wall, but
there are no snowmobile boots by the door. In the tropical setting we
glimpse an overhead fan instead of an air-conditioning unit. The
mechanical paraphernalia of contemporary living has been put away,
and replaced by brass-cornered gun boxes, silver bedside water carafes,
and leather-bound books.

23   Admittedly, these tableaux are not real interiors but only backdrops
designed to set off the fabrics, tableware, and bedclothes that form the
Furnishings Collection; it is unlikely that anyone would ever furnish
his or her home to look like the Lauren publicity brochures. But that
is beside the point; advertisements often represent a not altogether real,
stylized world, but one which does reflect society's view of how things
ought to be. These themes have been chosen to evoke popular images
that are informal and comfortable, reminiscent of wealth, stability, and
tradition. What they leave out is as revealing as what they include.

24   There is little doubt that these carefully arranged rooms would be

compromised by the introduction of modern objects. Like a director filming a costume epic who blanks out the telephone wires and the drone of the overhead jet, Lauren has kept the twentieth century at bay. There is no polypropylene thermal underwear drying in front of the stone fireplace, no electric toaster on the table, to intrude on the traditional coziness of "Log Cabin," just as there is no personal computer on the desk in "Thoroughbred." How do we fit reality into this dream world? One way is to not even try. The headquarters of Estée Lauder Incorporated, a large cosmetics corporation, are located in the General Motors Building in New York. The main offices are conventional; the chairman's office is not — it resembles the small drawing room of a Loire château. Estée Lauder's desk is Louis XVI, as are two of the side chairs. The two wing chairs are Second Empire, the couch is Belle Epoque, and the lamp holder is French Bouillotte (obviously, the candles have been replaced by electrical bulbs). The only modern objects are two telephones. The office of Malcolm S. Forbes, owner of *Forbes* magazine, does not make even that compromise with modernity. No telephones disturb the top of his elegant Georgian partner's desk, which is flanked by a pair of Queen Anne corner chairs and a fine Chippendale-style wing chair. A chandelier hangs from the ceiling and illuminates the mahogany-paneled room, originally built in the nineteenth century and free from any reminders of the twentieth. This is as much a place for drinking a glass of vintage port as for transacting business.

This sort of historical verisimilitude is difficult to achieve, and obviously expensive. In any case, outside Mr. Forbes's and Mrs. Lauder's offices are the telex machines, flickering word processors, ergonomically designed stenographer's chairs, steel file cabinets, and fluorescent strip lighting that are necessary for the proper functioning of a modern corporation. One reason that all this equipment is outside is that it is not easy to integrate it into a Louis XVI salon or a Georgian study. Only a few modern devices lend themselves to being camouflaged in period clothing. A Baume & Mercier carriage clock, for instance, has an octagonal case of pearwood with brass fittings, that contains a quartz movement. A strictly modern device like a photocopier, on the other hand, has no precedents, it can only be disguised, and were this ever attempted the result would be about as satisfying as when television sets are made up to look like Colonial credenzas.

So the modern world is kept at bay. These office interiors, like the settings of the Lauren Collection, present the appearance of a way of life that no longer exists. Their reality is no deeper than the flocked covering on the wall; a cynic would point out that the lady in the Louis XVI office was actually born in Queens, and Mr. Forbes in Brooklyn (Lauren, that other anglophile, grew up in the Bronx). But whether the way of life is remembered, or simply imagined, it nevertheless signifies a widely held nostalgia. Is it simply a curious anachronism, this desire for tradition, or is it a reflection of a deeper dissatisfaction with the surroundings that our modern world has created? What are we missing that we look so hard for in the past?

(1986)

The Writer's Subject

1. Why does Rybczynski call Ralph Lauren a "total fashion designer"? (para. 3)

2. What is distinctly American about the look of Lauren's clothes? (para. 4)

3. In what respects, according to Rybczynski, does Lauren differ from such famous couturiers as Yves St. Laurent or Pierre Cardin? (paras. 5-8)

4. What does Rybczynski mean by calling the relationship between clothing and interior decoration "venerable"? (para. 9)

5. What do the different rooms in Lauren's "Collection" in Bloomingdale's have in common? What is the nature of their appeal, according to Rybczynski? (paras. 17-18)

6. What, according to Rybczynski, is Lauren's goal in making use of "period" designs? (paras. 18-23)

7. To what does Rybczynski attribute the modern awareness of and desire for tradition? (para. 19) What does he mean by "invented" traditions? (paras. 19-21)

8. What has been left out of Lauren's interiors? (paras. 22-24)

The Writer's Style and Strategy

1. Why does Rybczynski begin by describing Ralph Lauren as he appears in magazine advertisements?

2. What is Rybczynski's purpose in the repetition of "comfort" and "comfortable" in the first two paragraphs?

3.   Discuss the meaning and the intended effect of the following statements, in their respective contexts:
     a) "Now perfumes, soaps, cosmetics, shoes, luggage, belts, wallets, and eyeglasses all bear his imprimatur" (para. 3);
     b) "The feeling of déjà vu is intentional: Lauren is an orchestrator of images" (para. 4);
     c) "You can now be a part of the ad" (para. 10).

4.   Rybczynski gives detailed descriptions of the four Lauren rooms in Bloomingdale's. (paras. 12-18) What elements of diction or phrasing suggest the writer's attitude to those rooms?

5.   What are the main stages of Rybczynski's discussion? How does he effect transitions from one stage to the next?

6.   How does Rybczynski use contrast to drive home his point about "invented traditions" in paragraph 21?

7.   Examine the last three paragraphs of the essay. Why does Rybczynski move away from a study of Ralph Lauren? Does the conclusion present us with a change of focus, or is another strategy involved?

8.   While this essay is complete in itself, it is also the first chapter in Rybczynski's book, *Home: A Short History of an Idea*. What features of the essay suggest such a relationship? In this regard, look particularly at the last paragraph.

Suggested Topics for Writing and Discussion

1.   Rybczynski says that Lauren's designs follow rural models. What, in your view, accounts for the appeal of the rural model, especially what Rybczynski calls "moneyed rusticity"?

2.   Rybczynski says that "acute awareness of tradition is a modern phenomenon that reflects a desire for custom and routine in a world characterized by constant change and innovation" (para. 19). How important is tradition in your own family or community? Give examples to illustrate your view.

3.   Rybczynski's essay is concerned with nostalgia as it is expressed in home furnishings. Write an essay in which you focus on two or three things that have nostalgic value for you and explain, if you can, the basis of their significance.

4.   Analyze an ad for fashion — either in clothing or home furnishings — and discuss what the ad suggests to the audience. Give attention to background as well as foreground details in the ad.

5. Analyze the current trends in fashion evident in the clothes of a particular
    group (e.g., college students, business executives, teenagers), and sug-
    gest what image the wearers seek to project.

Courtship Through the Ages
by James Thurber

Surely nothing in the astonishing scheme of life can have nonplussed   1
Nature so much as the fact that none of the females of any of the species
she created really cared very much for the male, as such. For the past
ten million years Nature has been busily inventing ways to make the
male attractive to the female, but the whole business of courtship, from
the marine annelids up to man, still lumbers heavily along, like a complicated musical comedy. I have been reading the sad and absorbing
story in Volume 6 (Cole to Dama) of the *Encyclopaedia Britannica*.
In this volume you can learn all about cricket, cotton, costume design-
ing, crocodiles, crown jewels, and Coleridge, but none of these subjects is so interesting as the Courtship of Animals, which recounts the
sorrowful lengths to which all males must go to arouse the interest of
a lady.

We all know, I think, that Nature gave man whiskers and a mustache   2
with the quaint idea in mind that these would prove attractive to the
female. We all know that, far from attracting her, whiskers and
mustaches only made her nervous and gloomy, so that man had to go
in for somersaults, tilting and lances, and performing feats of parlor
magic to win her attention; he also had to bring her candy, flowers,
and the furs of animals. It is common knowledge that in spite of all
these "love displays" the male is constantly being turned down, insulted,
or thrown out of the house. It is rather comforting, then, to discover
that the peacock, for all his gorgeous plumage, does not have a particularly easy time in courtship; none of the males in the world do. The
first peahen, it turned out, was only faintly stirred by her suitor's beautiful

train. She would often go quietly to sleep while he was whisking it
around. The *Britannica* tells us that the peacock actually had to learn
a certain little trick to wake her up and revive her interest: he had to
learn to vibrate his quills so as to make a rustling sound. In ancient
times man himself, observing the ways of the peacock, probably tried
vibrating his whiskers to make a rustling sound; if so, it didn't get him
anywhere. He had to go in for something else; so, among other things,
he went in for gifts. It is not unlikely that he got this idea from certain
flies and birds who were making no headway at all with rustling sounds.

3   One of the flies of the family Empidae, who had tried everything,
finally hit on something pretty special. He contrived to make a glisten-
ing transparent balloon which was even larger than himself. Into this
he would put sweetmeats and tidbits and he would carry the whole
elaborate envelope through the air to the lady of his choice. This amused
her for a time, but she finally got bored with it. She demanded silly
little colorful presents, something that you couldn't eat but that would
look nice around the house. So the male Empis had to go around gathering flower petals and pieces of bright paper to put into his balloon. On
a courtship flight a male Empis cuts quite a figure now, but he can hardly
be said to be happy. He never knows how soon the female will demand
heavier presents, such as Roman coins and gold collar buttons. It seems
probable that one day the courtship of the Empidae will fall down, as
man's occasionally does, of its own weight.

4   The bowerbird is another creature that spends so much time courting
the female that he never gets any work done. If all the male bowerbirds
became nervous wrecks within the next ten or fifteen years, it would
not surprise me. The female bowerbird insists that a playground be built
for her with a specially constructed bower at the entrance. This bower
is much more elaborate than an ordinary nest and is harder to build;
it costs a lot more, too. The female will not come to the playground
until the male has filled it up with a great many gifts: silvery leaves,
red leaves, rose petals, shells, beads, berries, bones, dice, buttons, cigar
bands, Christmas seals, and the Lord knows what else. When the female
finally condescends to visit the playground, she is in a coy and silly
mood and has to be chased in and out of the bower and up and down
the playground before she will quit giggling and stand still long enough
even to shake hands. The male bird is, of course, pretty well done in
before the chase starts, because he has worn himself out hunting for
eyeglass lenses and begonia blossoms. I imagine that many a bowerbird, after chasing a female for two or three hours, says the hell with

it and goes home to bed. Next day, of course, he telephones someone else and the same trying ritual is gone through with again. A male bower-bird is as exhausted as a night-club habitué before he is out of his twenties.

The male fiddler crab has a somewhat easier time, but it can hardly   5
be said that he is sitting pretty. He has one enormously large and powerful claw, usually brilliantly colored, and you might suppose that all he had to do was reach out and grab some passing cutie. The very earliest fiddler crabs may have tried this, but, if so, they got slapped for their pains. A female fiddler crab will not tolerate any caveman stuff; she never has and she doesn't intend to start now. To attract a female, a fiddler crab has to stand on tiptoe and brandish his claw in the air. If any female in the neighborhood is interested - and you'd be surprised how many are not — she comes over and engages in light badinage, for which he is not in the mood. As many as a hundred females may pass the time of day with him and go on about their business. By night-fall of an average courting day, a fiddler crab who has been standing on tip-toe for eight or ten hours waving a heavy claw in the air is in pretty sad shape. As in the case of the males of all species, however, he gets out of bed next morning, dashes some water on his face, and tries again.

The next time you encounter a male web-spinning spider, stop and   6
reflect that he is too busy worrying about his love life to have any desire to bite you. Male web-spinning spiders have a tougher life than any other males in the animal kingdom. This is because the female web-spinning spiders have very poor eyesight. If a male lands on a female's web, she kills him before he has time to lay down his cane and gloves, mistaking him for a fly or a bumblebee who has tumbled into her trap. Before the species figured out what to do about this, millions of males were murdered by ladies they called on. It is the nature of spiders to perform a little dance in front of the female, but before a male spinner could get near enough for the female to see who he was and what he was up to, she would lash out at him with a flat-iron or a pair of garden shears. One night, nobody knows when, a very bright male spinner lay awake worrying about calling on a lady who had been killing suitors right and left. It came to him that this business of dancing as a love display wasn't getting anybody anywhere except the grave. He decided to go in for web-twitching, or strand-vibrating. The next day he tried it on one of the nearsighted girls. Instead of dropping in on her sudden-ly, he stayed outside the web and began monkeying with one of its strands. He twitched it up and down and in and out with such a lilting

rhythm that the female was charmed. The serenade worked beautifully; the female let him live. The *Britannica*'s spider-watchers, however,
report that this system is not always successful. Once in a while, even
now, a female will fire three bullets into a suitor or run him through
with a kitchen knife. She keeps threatening him from the moment he
strikes the first low notes on the outside strings, but usually by the time
he has got up to the high notes played around the center of the web,
he is going to town and she spares his life.

7   Even the butterfly, as handsome a fellow as he is, can't always win
a mate merely by fluttering around and showing off. Many butterflies
have to have scent scales on their wings. Hepialus carries a powder
puff in a perfumed pouch. He throws perfume at the ladies when they
pass. The male tree cricket, Oecanthus, goes Hepialus one better by
carrying a tiny bottle of wine with him and giving drinks to such doxies
as he has designs on. One of the male snails throws darts to entertain
the girls. So it goes, through the long list of animals, from the bristle
worm and his rudimentary dance steps to man and his gift of diamonds
and sapphires. The golden-eye drake raises a jet of water with his feet
as he flies over a lake; Hepialus has his powder puff, Oecanthus his
wine bottle, man his etchings. It is a bright and melancholy story, the
age-old desire of the male for the female, the age-old desire of the female
to be amused and entertained. Of all the creatures on earth, the only
males who could be figured as putting any irony into their courtship
are the grebes and certain other diving birds. Every now and then a
courting grebe slips quietly down to the bottom of a lake and then, with
a mighty "Whoosh!," pops out suddenly a few feet from his girl friend,
splashing water all over her. She seems to be persuaded that this is a
purely loving display, but I like to think that the grebe always has a
faint hope of drowning her or scaring her to death.

8   I will close this investigation into the mournful burdens of the male
with the *Britannica*'s story about a certain Argus pheasant. It appears
that the Argus displays himself in front of a female who stands perfectly still without moving a feather....The male Argus the *Britannica* tells
about was confined in a cage with a female of another species, a female
who kept moving around, emptying ashtrays and fussing with lamp-
shades all the time the male was showing off his talents. Finally, in
disgust, he stalked away and began displaying in front of his water
trough. He reminds me of a certain male (Homo sapiens) of my acquaintance who one night after dinner asked his wife to put down her
detective magazine so that he could read a poem of which he was very

fond. She sat quietly enough until he was well into the middle of the thing, intoning with great ardor and intensity. Then suddenly there came a sharp, disconcerting slap! It turned out that all during the male's display, the female had been intent on a circling mosquito and had finally trapped it between the palms of her hands. The male in this case did not stalk away and display in front of a water trough; he went over to Tim's and had a flock of drinks and recited the poem to the fellas. I am sure they all told bitter stories of their own about how their displays had been interrupted by females. I am also sure that they all ended up singing "Honey, Honey, Bless Your Heart."

(1939)

The Writer's Subject

1. What is Thurber's thesis? (para. 1)

2. Why did the male have to resort to various activities in order to attract the attention of the female? (para. 2) What means did he adopt to win attention?

3. What are the characteristic approaches to the female employed by the male Empis? the bowerbird? the fiddler crab? the web-spinning spider, the butterfly? the tree cricket? (paras. 3-7) What equivalents in human behavior are suggested by Thurber's discussion of these species?

4. Why does Thurber refer to *Britannica* at several points in his essay?

5. What incongruities are particularly striking in the story of the Argus pheasant? (para. 8)

6. What is Thurber's point in ending his essay with the statement that he is sure that his friend's companions "all ended up singing 'Honey, Honey, Bless your Heart.'" (para. 8)?

7. What features in Thurber's essay suggest that this account is, like the story of courtship he tells, "bright and melancholy" (para. 7)?

The Writer's Style and Strategy

1. What in the introductory paragraph suggests that Thurber is taking a humorous approach to his subject?

2. What is the implied audience for this essay?

3. What is Thurber's strategy in using "I," "we," and "you" throughout this essay? What is his particular purpose in beginning the first two sentences of paragraph 2 with "We all know . . ."?

4. What means does Thurber use to develop his thesis?

5. How does Thurber effect transitions between paragraphs?

6. How does it become clear that Thurber, in his description of courtship displays, is as concerned with man as with animals?

7. Choose two or three examples of ways in which Thurber surprises the reader and creates humour.

8. Although Thurber uses "female," "lady," and "ladies," he never uses "woman." Why not?

9. How does Thurber create an informal, conversational tone?

10. Comment on Thurber's title.

Suggested Topics for Writing and Discussion

1. Thurber remarks humorously that the male had "to go in for somersaults, tilting with lances, and performing feats of parlour magic to win [the female's] attention; he also had to bring her candy, flowers, and the furs of animals." Discuss current "courting" practices of young men.

2. Thurber suggests that the female of the species expects the male "to display" in order to gain her interest. Do you think that women are, in fact, brought up to expect these activities from men?

3. Thurber talks about the ways in which males try to win the attention of females. Write an essay in which you discuss the ways in which women attempt to get the attentions of men.

4. Thurber uses a number of examples from the animal kingdom to illustrate the human activity of courtship. Choose another animal or insect and write a humorous account of its mating activities, following Thurber's approach.

5. Although Thurber could safely assume in 1942 that his audience would generally be amused, this assumption might not be so certain today. Discuss the possible responses of a feminist audience to Thurber's essay.

The Tyranny of the Clock
by George Woodcock

1   In no characteristic is existing society in the West so sharply distinguished from the earlier societies, whether of Europe or of the East, as in its conception of time. To the ancient Chinese or Greek, to the Arab herdsman or the Mexican peon of today, time is represented by the cyclic processes of nature, the alternation of day and night, the passage from season to season. The nomads and the farmers measured and still measure their day from sunrise to sunset, and their year in terms of seed-time and harvest, of the falling leaf and ice thawing on the lakes and rivers. The farmer worked according to the elements, the craftsman for as long as he felt it necessary to perfect his product. Time was seen as a process of natural change, and men were not concerned in its exact measurement. For this reason civilizations highly developed in other respects had the most primitive means of measuring time: the hourglass with its trickling sand or dripping water, the sundial, useless on a dull day, and the candle or lamp whose unburnt remnant of oil or wax indicated the hours. All these devices were approximate and inexact, and were often rendered unreliable by the weather or the personal laziness of the tender. Nowhere in the ancient or the mediaeval world were more than a tiny minority of men concerned with time in the terms of mathematical exactitude.

2   Modern, western man, however, lives in a world which runs according to the mechanical and mathematical symbols of clock time. The clock dictates his movements and inhibits his actions. The clock turns time from a process of nature into a commodity that can be measured and bought and sold like soap or sultanas. And because, without some

means of exact timekeeping, industrial capitalism could never have developed and could not continue to exploit the workers, the clock represents an element of mechanical tyranny in the lives of modern men more potent than any individual exploiter or than any other machine. It is therefore valuable to trace the historical process by which the clock influenced the social development of modern European civilization.

It is a frequent circumstance of history that a culture or a civilization 3 develops the device that will later be used for its destruction. The ancient Chinese, for example, invented gunpowder, which was developed by the military experts of the West and eventually lcd to the Chinese civilization itself being destroyed by the high explosives of modern warfare. Similarly, the super achievement of the craftsmen of the mediaeval cities of Europe was the invention of the clock, which, with its revolutionary alteration of the concept of time, materially assisted the growth of the Middle Ages.

There is a tradition that the clock appeared in the eleventh century, 4 as a device for ringing bells at regular intervals in the monasteries, which, with the regimented life they imposed on their inmates, were the closest social approximation in the Middle Ages to the factory of today. The first authenticated clock, however, appeared in the thirteenth century, and it was not until the fourteenth century that clocks became common as ornaments of the public building in German cities.

These early clocks, operated by weights, were not particularly ac- 5 curate, and it was not until the sixteenth century that any great reliability was attained. In England, for instance, the clock at Hampton Court, made in 1540, is said to have been the first accurate clock in the country. And even the accuracy of the sixteenth-century clocks is relative, for they were equipped only with hour-hands. The idea of measuring time in minutes and seconds had been thought out by the early mathematicians as far back as the fourteenth century, but it was not until the invention of the pendulum in 1657 that sufficient accuracy was attained to permit the addition of a minute-hand, and the second-hand did not appear until the eighteenth century. These two centuries, it should be observed, were those in which capitalism grew to such an extent that it was able to take advantage of the techniques of the Industrial Revolution to establish its economic domination over society.

The clock, as Lewis Mumford has pointed out, is the key machine 6 of the machine age, both for its influence on technics and for its influence on the habits of men. Technically, the clock was the first really automatic machine that attained any importance in the life of man.

Previous to its invention, the common machines were of such nature that their operation depended on some external and unreliable force, such as human or animal muscles, water, or wind. It is true that the Greeks had invented a number of primitive automatic machines, but these were used, like Hero's steam engine, either for obtaining "supernatural" effects in the temples or for amusing the tyrants of Levantine cities. But the clock was the first automatic machine that attained public importance and a social function. Clock-making became the industry from which men learnt the elements of machine-making and gained the technical skill that was to produce the complicated machinery of the Industrial Revolution.

7   Socially the clock had a more radical influence than any other machine, in that it was the means by which the regularization and regimentation of life necessary for an exploiting system of industry could be best assured. The clock provided a means by which time — a category so elusive that no philosophy has yet determined its nature — could be measured concretely in the more tangible terms of space provided by the circumference of a clock dial. Time as duration became disregarded, and men began to talk and think always of "lengths" of time, just as if they were talking of lengths of calico. And time, being now measurable in mathematical symbols, was regarded as a commodity that could be bought and sold in the same way as any other commodity.

8   The new capitalists, in particular, became rabidly time-conscious. Time, here symbolizing the labour of the workers, was regarded by them almost as if it were the chief raw material of industry. "Time is money" was one of the key slogans of capitalist ideology, and the timekeeper was the most significant of the new types of official introduced by the capitalist dispensation.

9   In the early factories the employers went so far as to manipulate their clocks or sound their factory whistles at the wrong times in order to defraud the workers of a little of this valuable new commodity. Later such practices became less frequent, but the influence of the clock imposed a regularity on the lives of the majority of men that had previously been known only in the monasteries. Men actually became like clocks, acting with a repetitive regularity which had no resemblance to the rhythmic life of a natural being. They became, as the Victorian phrase put it, "as regular as clockwork." Only in the country districts where the natural lives of animals and plants and the elements still dominated existence did any large proportion of the population fail to succumb to the deadly tick of monotony.

At first this new attitude to time, this new regularity of life, was im-   10
posed by the clock-owning masters on the unwilling poor. The factory
slave reacted in his spare time by living with a chaotic irregularity which
characterized the gin-sodden slums of early-nineteenth-century in-
dustrialism. Men fled to the timeless worlds of drink or Methodist inspiration. But gradually the idea of regularity spread downwards and
among the workers. Nineteenth-century religion and morality played
their part by proclaiming the sin of "wasting time." The introduction
of mass-produced watches and clocks in the 1850s spread time-
consciousness among those who had previously merely reacted to the
stimulus of the knocker-up or the factory whistle. In the church and
the school, in the office and the workshop, punctuality was held up as
the greatest of the virtues.

Out of this slavish dependence on mechanical time which spread in-   11
sidiously into every class in the nineteenth century, there grew up the
demoralizing regimentation which today still characterizes factory life.
The man who fails to conform faces social disapproval and economic
ruin − unless he drops out into a non-conformist way of life in which
time ceases to be of prime importance. Hurried meals, the regular morning and evening scramble for trains or buses, the strain of having to
work to time schedules, all contribute, by digestive and nervous disturbance, to ruin health and shorten life.

Nor does the financial imposition of regularity tend, in the long run,   12
to greater efficiency. Indeed, the quality of the product is usually much
poorer, because the employer, regarding time as a commodity which
he has to pay for, forces the operative to maintain such a speed that
his work must necessarily be skimped. Quantity rather than quality
becoming the criterion, the enjoyment is taken out of the work itself,
and the worker in his turn becomes a "clock-watcher," concerned only
with when he will be able to escape to the scanty and monotonous leisure
of industrial society, in which he "kills time" by cramming in as much
time-scheduled and mechanical enjoyment of cinema, radio, and
newspaper as his wage packet and his tiredness will allow. Only if he
is willing to accept the hazard of living by his faith or his wits can the
man without money avoid living as a slave to the clock.

The problem of the clock is, in general, similar to that of the machine.   13
Mechanized time is valuable as a means of co-ordinating activities in
a highly developed society, just as the machine is valuable as a means
of reducing unnecessary labour to a minimum. Both are valuable for
the contribution they make to the smooth running of society, and should

be used in so far as they assist men to co-operate efficiently and to eliminate monotonous toil and social confusion. But neither should be allowed to dominate men's lives as they do today.

14   Now the movement of the clock sets the tempo of men's lives — they become the servants of the concept of time which they themselves have made, and are held in fear, like Frankenstein by his own monster. In a sane and free society such an arbitrary domination of man's functions by either clock or machine would obviously be out of the question. The domination of man by man-made machines is even more ridiculous than the domination of man by man. Mechanical time would be relegated to its true function of a means of reference and co-ordination, and men would return again to a balanced view of life no longer dominated by time-regulation and the worship of the clock. Complete liberty implies freedom from the tyranny of abstractions as well as from the rule of men.

(1939)

The Writer's Subject

1. How did the concept of time in older societies differ from that of modern Western society? (para. 1)

2. How, according to Woodcock, did the development of the clock make possible the rise of industrial capitalism? (paras. 6-8)

3. What impact has the development of clock time had on the life of the modern worker, in Woodcock's view? (paras. 9-12)

4. At several points Woodcock uses the word "commodity" to describe the modern concept of time. What are the implications of this term, and how does its use further Woodcock's thesis?

5. What comparison does Woodcock make between the clock and the machine? (paras. 13-14)

The Writer's Style and Strategy

1. Discuss the appropriateness of Woodcock's choice of title.

2. Is there a rhetorical as well as an expository purpose behind Woodcock's explanation in paragraph 1 of how time was recorded by older societies?

3. Examine Woodcock's description of modern Western concepts of time in paragraph 2. How does his choice of words convey his attitude here? Does the diction seem "slanted" in any way?

4. Woodcock proposes to "trace the historical process by which the clock influenced the social development of modern European civilization" (para. 2). What principle seems to determine his choice of historical evidence? How does he use the history of the Industrial Revolution to further his argumentative purposes?

5. Discuss the ways in which Woodcock describes employers and workers throughout the essay. How does he make clear where his sympathies lie?

6. What use does Woodcock make of such clichés as "Time is money" or "as regular as clockwork" to further his argument?

7. Trace the stages by which Woodcock's argument moves from past to present, and from specific to general.

Suggested Topics for Writing and Discussion

1. Do you agree with Woodcock's view that we have become slaves to "mechanical time"? Draw on your own daily life to support your point of view.

2. Woodcock describes factory workers in the eighteenth and nineteenth centuries as slaves who were brutally exploited by ruthless capitalists. Find out what you can about conditions in factories, mills, or mines in the nineteenth century; using one or two particular examples, show whether or not Woodcock's assertions are justified.

3. Although Woodcock's essay is largely devoted to attacking "the tyranny of the clock," in paragraph 13 he acknowledges the importance of mechanical time in the smooth running of society. Write an essay on the beneficial aspects of mechanical time, illustrating your argument with specific examples.

4. Woodcock and Mumford argue that the clock is "the key machine of the machine age . . . for its influence on the habits of men " (para. 6) . Discuss the effects of one other machine upon our daily lives.

Politics and Morality

On Party-Lying

by Joseph Addison

Defendit numerus, junctaeque umbone phalanges.[1]
                                                                    Juvenal

There is something very Sublime, tho' very Fanciful, in *Plato's* Descrip- 1
tion of the Supreme Being, that *Truth is his Body, and Light his
Shadow.* According to his Definition, there is nothing so contradictory to his Nature as Error and Falshood. The Platonists have so just
a Notion of the Almighty's Aversion to every thing which is false and
erroneous, that they looked upon *Truth* as no less necessary than *Virtue,* to qualifie an Human Soul for the Enjoyment of a separate State.
For this Reason, as they recommended Moral Duties to qualifie and
season the Will for a future Life, so they prescribed several Contempla-
tions and Sciences to rectifie the Understanding. Thus *Plato* has called
Mathematical Demonstrations the Catharticks or Purgatives of the Soul,
as being the most proper Means to cleanse it from Error, and to give
it a Relish of Truth, which is the natural Food and Nourishment of the
Understanding, as Virtue is the Perfection and Happiness of the Will.

There are many Authors who have shewn wherein the Malignity of 2
a *Lie* consists, and set forth, in proper Colours, the Heinousness of the
Offence. I shall here consider one Particular Kind of this Crime, which
has not been so much spoken to: I mean, that abominable Practice of
Party-lying. This Vice is so very predominant among us at present,
that a Man is thought of no Principles, who does not propagate a certain
System of Lies. The Coffee-Houses are supported by them, the Press
is choaked with them, eminent Authors live upon them. Our Bottle-
Conversation is so infected with them, that a Party-Lie is grown as

---

1. *Motto.* Juvenal, *Satires,* 2. 46: They are protected by their numbers and the close shields
   of their phalanx.

fashionable an Entertainment, as a lively Catch or a merry Story: The Truth of it is, half the great Talkers in the Nation would be struck dumb, were this Fountain of Discourse dryed up. There is, however, one Advantage resulting from this detestable Practice; the very Appearances of Truth are so little regarded, that Lies are at present discharged in the Air, and begin to hurt no Body. When we hear a Party-story from a Stranger, we consider whether he is a Whig or a Tory that relates it, and immediately conclude they are Words of Course, in which the honest Gentleman designs to recommend his Zeal, without any Concern for his Veracity. A Man is looked upon as bereft of common Sense, that gives Credit to the Relations of Party-Writers, nay his own Friends shake their Heads at him, and consider him in no other Light than as an officious Tool or a well-meaning Ideot. When it was formerly the Fashion to husband a Lie, and trump it up in some extraordinary Emergency, it generally did Execution, and was not a little serviceable to the Faction that made use of it; but at present every Man is upon his Guard; the Artifice has been too often repeated to take Effect.

3   I have frequently wondered to see Men of Probity, who would scorn to utter a Falshood for their own particular Advantage, give so readily into a Lie when it is become the Voice of their Faction, notwithstanding they are thoroughly sensible of it as such. How is it possible for those, who are Men of Honour in their Persons, thus to become Notorious Liars in their Party? If we look into the Bottom of this Matter, we may find, I think, three Reasons for it, and at the same time discover the Insufficiency of these Reasons to justifie so Criminal a Practice.

4   In the first place, Men are apt to think that the Guilt of a Lie, and consequently the Punishment, may be very much diminished, if not wholly worn out, by the Multitudes of those who partake in it. Though the Weight of a Falshood would be too heavy for *one* to bear, it grows light in their Imaginations, when it is shared among *many*. But in this Case a Man very much deceives himself; Guilt, when it spreads through Numbers, is not so properly divided as multiplied: Every one is criminal in proportion to the Offence which he commits, not to the Number of those who are his Companions in it. Both the Crime and the Penalty lie as heavy upon every Individual of an offending Multitude, as they would upon any single Person, had none shared with him in the Offence. In a Word, the Division of Guilt is like that of Matter; though it may be separated into infinite Portions, every Portion shall have the whole Essence of Matter in it, and consist of as many Parts as the whole did afore it was divided.

But in the second place, though Multitudes, who join in a Lie, can- 5
not exempt themselves from the Guilt, they may from the Shame of
it. The Scandal of a Lie is in a manner lost and annihilated, when dif-
fused among several Thousands; as a Drop of the blackest Tincture wears
away and vanishes, when mixed and confused in a considerable Body
of Water: The Blot is still in it, but is not able to discover it self. This
is certainly a very great Motive to several Party-Offenders, who avoid
Crimes, not as they are prejudicial to their Virtue, but to their Reputation. It is enough to show the Weakness of this Reason, which palliates
Guilt without removing it, that every Man, who is influenced by it,
declares himself in effect an infamous Hypocrite, prefers the Appearance
of Virtue to its Reality, and is determined in his Conduct neither by
the Dictates of his own Conscience, the Suggestions of true Honour,
nor the Principles of Religion.

The third and last great Motive for Mens joining in a popular Falshood, 6
or, as I have hitherto called it, a Party-Lie, notwithstanding they are
convinced of it as such, is the doing Good to a Cause which every Party
may be supposed to look upon as the most meritorious. The Unsound-
ness of this Principle has been so often exposed, and is so universally
acknowledged, that a Man must be an utter Stranger to the Principles,
either of natural Religion or Christianity, who suffers himself to be
guided by it. If a Man might promote the supposed Good of his Country by the blackest Calumnies and Falshoods, our Nation abounds more
in Patriots than any other of the Christian World. When *Pompey* was
desired not to set Sail in a Tempest that would hazard his Life, *It is
necessary for me,* says he, *to Sail, but it is not necessary for me to
Live*: Every Man should say to himself, with the same Spirit, It is my
Duty to speak Truth, tho' it is not my Duty to be in an Office. One of
the Fathers has carried this Point so high, as to declare *he would not
tell a Lie though he were sure to gain Heaven by it*: However extravagant
such a Protestation may appear, every one will own, that a Man may
say very reasonably *he would not tell a Lie, if he were sure to gain
Hell by it*; or, if you have a mind to soften the Expression, that he would
not tell a Lie to gain any Temporal Reward by it, when he should run
the hazard of losing much more than it was possible for him to gain.

(1712)

The Writer's Subject

1. Comment on the appropriateness of the epigraph to the content of the essay.

2. While lamenting the prevalence of lying, Addison sees one advantage in its general acceptance; what is this advantage? (para. 2)

3. What are the reasons which Addison gives for the acceptance of party-lying by "Men of Probity"? (paras. 3-6)

4. What is Addison's own attitude to party-lying, and to lying in general? Where is this attitude given most explicit expression?

The Writer's Style and Strategy

1. What is the function of the opening paragraph? How does Addison effect a transition from this paragraph to his principal subject, party-lying?

2. In paragraph 2, Addison says ". . . a Man is thought of no Principles, who does not propagate a certain System of Lies." What is the figure of speech used here?

3. What is meant by the phrase "Our Bottle-Conversation" in paragraph 2?

4. Find an example of metaphor in paragraph 2 and explain its usefulness in emphasizing Addison's point.

5. Discuss the organization of paragraphs 3 through 6, and show how Addison deals with the arguments of those he is attacking.

6. Explain the analogy in the second sentence of paragraph 5, and discuss its effectiveness.

7. "If a Man might promote the supposed Good of his Country by the blackest Calumnies and Falshoods, our Nation abounds more in Patriots than any other of the Christian World" (para. 6). What is the tone of this statement?

Suggested Topics for Writing and Discussion

1. In what respects are Addison's views on politics similar to those expressed by George Orwell in his essay "Politics and the English Language"?

2. "Party-lying" is as common in our own time as in Addison's. The most notorious recent examples are the "Watergate Affair" during Richard Nixon's presidency and the "Iran arms deal" during that of Ronald Reagan. Find out what you can about one of these episodes in American politics, and offer your views about what the incident revealed concerning the morality of the political scene at the time.

3. Addison attacks those who lie for what they believe to be a good cause (para. 6). Do you believe that there may in fact be any cause worth lying for? (You may wish to look at what Bronowski has to say in "The Real Responsibilities of the Scientist" concerning scientists who lie for what they consider to be good reasons.)

The Writer's Responsibility

by Margaret Atwood

1   The subject we have come together to address is one which increases in importance as the giants of this world move closer and closer to violent and fatal confrontation. Broadly put, it is: what is the writer's responsibility, if any, to the society in which he or she lives? The question is not a new one; it's been with us at least since the time of Plato; but more and more the answers of the world's governments have taken the form of amputation: of the tongue, of the soul, of the head.

2   We in Canada are ill-equipped to come to grips even with the problem, let alone the solution. We live in a society in which the main consensus seems to be that the artist's duty is to entertain and divert, nothing more. Occasionally our critics get a little heavy and start talking about the human condition, but on the whole the audience prefers art not to be a mirror held up to life but a Disneyland of the soul, containing Romanceland, Spyland, Pornoland and all the other Escapelands which are so much more agreeable than the complex truth. When we take an author seriously, we prefer to believe that her vision derives from her individual and subjective and neurotic tortured soul — we like artists to have tortured souls — not from the world she is looking at. Sometimes our artists believe this version too, and the ego takes over. *I, me* and *mine* are our favourite pronouns; *we, us* and *ours* are low on the list. The artist is not seen as a lens for focusing the world but as a solipsism. We are good at measuring an author's production in terms of his craft. We are not good at analyzing it in terms of his politics,

and by and large we do not do so.

By "politics" I do not mean how you voted in the last election, although 3 that is included. I mean who is entitled to do what to whom, with impunity; who profits by it; and who therefore eats what. Such material enters a writer's work not because the writer is or is not consciously political but because a writer is an observer, a witness, and such observations are the air he breathes. They are the air all of us breathe; the only difference is that the author looks, and then writes down what he sees. What he sees will depend on how closely he looks and at what, but look he must.

In some countries, an author is censored not only for what he says 4 but for how he says it, and an unconventional style is therefore a declaration of artistic freedom. Here we are eclectic; we don't mind experimental styles, in fact we devote learned journals to their analysis; but our critics sneer somewhat at anything they consider "heavy social commentary" or − a worse word − "message." Stylistic heavy guns are dandy, as long as they aren't pointed anywhere in particular. We like the human condition as long as it is seen as personal and individual. Placing politics and poetics in two watertight compartments is a luxury, just as specialization of any kind is a luxury, and it is possible only in a society where luxuries abound. Most countries in the world cannot afford such luxuries, and this North American way of thinking is alien to them. It was even alien in North America, not long ago. We've already forgotten that in the 1950's many artists, both in the United States and here, were persecuted solely on the grounds of their presumed politics. Which leads us to another mistaken Canadian belief: the belief that it can't happen here.

It has happened here, many times. Although our country is one of 5 the most peaceful and prosperous on earth, although we do not shoot artists here, although we do not execute political opponents and although this is one of the few remaining countries in which we can have a gathering like this without expecting to be arrested or blown up, we should not overlook the fact that Canada's record on civil rights issues is less than pristine. Our treatment of our native peoples has been shameful. This is the country in which citizens of Japanese origin were interned during the Second World War and had their property stolen (when a government steals property it is called "confiscation"); it is also the country in which thousands of citizens were arrested, jailed and held without warrant or explanation, during the time of the War Measures Act, a scant eleven years ago. There was no general outcry in either case. Worse things have not happened not because we are genetically exempt but because we lead pampered lives.

6   Our methods of controlling artists are not violent, but they do exist. We control through the marketplace and through critical opinion. We are also controlled by the economics of culture, which in Canada still happen to be those of a colonial branch-plant. In 1960 the number of Canadian books published here was minute, and the numbers sold pathetic. Things have changed very much in twenty years, but Canadian books still account for a mere 25 percent of the overall book trade and paperback books for under 5 percent. Talking about this situation is still considered nationalistic chauvinism. Nevertheless, looked at in the context of the wider picture, I suppose we are lucky to have any percent at all; they haven't yet sent in the Marines and if they do it won't be over books, but over oil.

7   We in this country should use our privileged position not as a shelter from the world's realities but as a platform from which to speak. Many are denied their voices; we are not. A voice is a gift; it should be cherished and used, to utter fully human speech if possible. Powerlessness and silence go together; one of the first efforts made in any totalitarian takeover is to suppress the writers, the singers the journalists, those who are the collective voice. Get rid of the union leaders and pervert the legal system and what you are left with is a reign of terror.

8   As we read the newspapers, we learn we are existing right now in a state of war. The individual wars may not be large and they are being fought far from here, but there is really only one war, that between those who would like the future to be, in the words of George Orwell, a boot grinding forever into a human face, and those who would like it to be a state of something we still dream of as freedom. The battle shifts according to the ground occupied by the enemy. Greek myth tells of a man called Procrustes, who was a great equalizer. He had a system for making all human beings the same size: if they were too small he stretched them, if they were too tall he cut off their feet or their heads. The Procrustes today are international operators, not confined to any one ideology or religion. The world is full of perversions of the notion of equality, just as it is full of perversions of the notion of freedom. True freedom is not being able to do whatever you like to whomever you want to do it to. Freedom that exists as a result of the servitude of others is not true freedom.

9   The most lethal weapon in the world's arsenals is not the neutron bomb or chemical warfare; but the human mind that devises such things and

puts them to use. But it is the human mind also that can summon up the power to resist, that can imagine a better world than the one before it, that can retain memory and courage in the face of unspeakable suffering. Oppression involves a failure of the imagination: the failure to imagine the full humanity of other human beings. If the imagination were a negligible thing and the act of writing a mere frill, as many in this society would like to believe, regimes all over the world would not be at such pains to exterminate them. The ultimate desire of Procrustes is a population of lobotomized zombies. The writer, unless he is a mere word processor, retains three attributes that power-mad regimes cannot tolerate: a human imagination, in the many forms it may take; the power to communicate; and hope. It may seem odd for me to speak of hope in the midst of what many of my fellow Canadians will call a bleak vision, but as the American writer Flannery O'Connor once said, people without hope do not write novels.

(1981)

The Writer's Subject

1. Why is Atwood so critical of the attitudes of Canadians to art and artists?

2. What are the implications of the phrase "a Disneyland of the soul" (para. 2)?

3. What is Atwood's definition of "politics," and how does it bear on her view of the writer's responsibility? (para. 3)

4. Why does Atwood regard the separation of politics and poetics as a "luxury"? (para. 4)

5. After giving examples of Canadian violations of civil rights (para. 5), Atwood concludes that "Worse things have not happened not because we are genetically exempt but because we lead pampered lives." Discuss what Atwood means by this observation.

6. What does Atwood mean by describing the economics of Canadian culture as "those of a colonial branch-plant" (para. 6)?

7. Atwood asserts that "we are existing right now in a state of war" (para. 8). Who are the opponents in this war?

8. What answer does Atwood give to the question she raises in paragraph 1, "what is the writer's responsibility, if any, to the society in which he or she lives? What qualities must the writer possess to fulfil that responsibility?"

The Writer's Style and Strategy

1. Explain the significance of Atwood's use of "amputation" in the opening paragraph.

2. Is there any evidence in style, diction, or tone to indicate that this essay was originally prepared as a spoken address?

3. Why does Atwood first refer to the writer as "she" (para. 2), then shift to a masculine pronoun in subsequent paragraphs?

4. At several points Atwood uses irony as a means of underscoring her point of view. Pick out one or two examples of effective irony.

5. Examine the organization of paragraph 5. What means of development does Atwood employ? Why does she begin the second sentence with four subordinate clauses, each introduced by "although"?

6. Atwood defines "true freedom" negatively rather than positively in paragraph 8. Why does she employ this strategy of definition?

Suggested Topics for Writing and Discussion

1. Atwood provides several examples of the violations of civil rights in Canada. Investigate one of these and explain what climate of opinion or historical events led to the occurrence.

2. Atwood says that our society expects artists "to entertain and divert, nothing more." Is it possible, in your view, for artists to perform the duties which Atwood discusses and, at the same time, entertain and divert? Provide clear examples to support your view.

3. We regard our society as free. We are still subject, however, to various forms of censorship in the arts and in communication. Find and discuss one or two examples of censorship in any medium (books, movies, television, radio, newspapers, exhibitions, advertisements, etc.).

Matata

by Kildare Dobbs

Although his face was not less brown than other faces of his tribe, it **1** had a sort of pallor, as if the blood under the skin were thinner, less warm and confident as it moved in his veins than that of his fellows. Yet you didn't feel any repellent coldness about him. You felt he had been sadly hurt, outraged in some catastrophic way which had caused him to withdraw into himself, to close the damper upon his vital fires. He was now plainly at the nadir of his life, like a tree in the depth of winter from whose twigs and brances the sap has retreated, so that it seems dead beyond all hope of recovery. I saw that he walked with a limp, but that alone did not account for the weariness of his movements. And though there were a few white hairs tangled in his wooly poll, I could see that he was not an old man.

He had come to ask for a job as a clerk; he told me his name was **2** Matata. We talked in English, which he spoke very well — I sensed that it helped his self-esteem to address me in my own language. I asked what experience he had. After a momentary pause he said in a flat tone, 'For fifteen years I was treasury clerk of this district.' I looked up in surprise. The post was one of considerable responsibility involving the management of large sums of money, and I had not seen Matata before. I had prided myself on knowing all the better-educated men in the tribe.

'But where have you been since you left?'   **3**

'In prison,' said Matata.   **4**

It was not hard to find him a job. Men of his ability were too rare **5** in the territory to be discarded merely because of a criminal record, and I was able to give Matata a desk in my own office where he could not have offended even if he had wanted to. The arrangement suited both of us. He had a measure of privacy which he needed and could not otherwise have found. I for my part was able to answer for his good conduct without having to make tedious enquiries. Moreover, I was able to draw on his experience and have the benefit of his advice in many affairs where a knowledge of tribal custom and local history was useful. In time we came to trust one another, and even to be friends. At first his confidences came reluctantly (I never pressed for them), but as the months went by he began to put forth his leaves and be himself again without fear, to tell what he had hoped for from his life, how he had pursued it, and how come to grief. Like most colonial relations, ours was imperfect. I became Matata's patron, and we both knew it. But if he sought my favour (and so, in a sense, was degraded) and sometimes resorted to guile, I myself, for less obvious and even more devious reasons, needed and invited his confidence. The proof of my corruptness is that I am now coldly moralizing upon our relation, whereas true friendship, like true love, is a secret we hug to ourselves and do not speak of aloud, even to hidden listeners.

6   Matata had been convicted of stealing about four hundred shillings from the funds for which he was responsible. His story was that he had borrowed it to meet the needs of some relatives he was bound by custom to support. He had intended to replace the cash and had not falsified his accounts in any way. Unfortunately his books were checked before he had a chance to put the matter straight. The District Commissioner immediately had him arrested and charged, and in due course he was tried in the High Court and sentenced by an impartial judge to three years' imprisonment. 'You have abused a position of public trust,' said the judge. 'It is men like you who hold your country back in its progress towards self-government. There has been too much of this sort of thing recently, and I propose to make an example of you. I take into account your long service and previous good character.' Poor Matata heard all this twice over, once in English and again in his own tongue from the interpreter. He thought over it in prison.

7   Though he had been educated at government schools and so touched with Western knowledge and ideas, his upbringing had been little different from that of his fellow tribesmen. He had been born into a large family. While yet a small child he had learnt to address them all correctly, to distinguish between those with whom he could speak freely and those with whom his relations were governed by tabu. He learnt

to call his father *Dada* and his mother *Yuva*. That was simple enough. But he had to call all his father's brothers *Dada* too, and all his mother's sisters *Yuva*. So he had six fathers and four mothers to start with. But that was not all, for his proper father had two other wives who were also called *Yuva*, and not only they, but their sisters as well. The daughters of all these so-called mothers and fathers were considered his sisters, and their sons his brothers. This army of siblings all had claims on him.

It was not surprising that Matata's first confused thoughts in the early 8 months of his imprisonment were to believe himself completely inno- cent. This is commonly the reaction of a normally law-abiding man who finds himself convicted of a crime. The impersonality of the legal machine which crushes him in its cogs, the remoteness of formal evidence form the inner realities of motive and intention, the brusque efficiency of police and clerks, the patient obtuseness of judges – all these combine to put the whole situation from him as utterly unreal. At the same time the ground of his faith in himself and in other people is sprung like the trap from under the condemned. He has thought of himself as a middling decent person. Now it seems he was mistaken. He is a monster so dangerous that he must be locked away for years.

Matata felt all this and more. For the better part of his adult life he 9 had been working hard at the business of civilizing himself and his people. He believed in civilization. He believed in roads and schools and penicillin and septic tanks. He was not bored, as I was, by the apostles of hygiene, the health officer and his team of sanitary inspec- tors. It is true that he, like the rest of his tribe, always referred to the health officer as Bwana Mavi, or Mister Excrement, but he intended no disrespect. Mr. Excrement was as much a limb of civilization as Matata's gold watch, which he loved very much and at which, in idle moments, he used to stare raptly like a man in a trance. Since Matata loved civilization so well, it went very hard with him to discover that he was not loved equally in return. In his heart, too, he looked at the world as a man of his tribe. Working with the white men in the days of their power was like working with powerful spirits; it conferred wealth and prestige. But these spirits exacted a price. So long as you walked carefully they smiled on you and showed you their secrets. The moment you made a mistake they turned on you without mercy and tore out your heart.

It was the prison superintendent, a severe but good-hearted Afrikaner, 10 who helped Matata recover some of his faith in himself. He gave him a responsible job and cheered him when he felt sorry for himself. Matata was grateful to this rough good man.

11   Though Matata became once more a useful and happy member of his tribe, I could not console myself with any notion that his sufferings had turned out for the best, or that others would profit by his example. Failure teaches a man nothing except compassion for the failure of others. I am still haunted, shall perhaps always be haunted, by the image of Matata as I first saw him, halting towards my desk, his dark eyes full of a pain I did not then understand, but which is now as familiar as a guilty secret.

(1962)

The Writer's Subject

1. Why was Matata a man of rare ability in the territory? (paras. 2-5)

2. What benefits accrued to both Dobbs and Matata through their working together in the same office? (para. 5)

3. Why does Dobbs accuse himself of deviousness and corruptness? (para. 5)

4. How does Matata's theft of money throw light on the clash between his own culture and that of the white man he served?

5. What are Matata's reactions to his arrest and subsequent imprisonment?

6. What did civilization mean to Matata? (para. 9)

7. Why does Dobbs say that he is still haunted by the image of Matata as he first saw him? (para. 11)

The Writer's Style and Strategy

1. Why does Dobbs devote the first paragraph to a physical description of Matata? How does this prepare us for the essay's conclusion?

2. Discuss the use Dobbs makes of the metaphor of the tree in paragraphs 1 and 5.

3. Why does Dobbs give the words of the "impartial" judge in direct speech rather than merely reporting his judgment? (para. 6)

4. What does Dobbs's reference to the health officer and his team as "the apostles of hygiene" convey of his attitude to them? (para. 9)

Suggested Topics for Writing and Discussion

1. Compare this essay with Orwell's "Shooting an Elephant." In what respects did the writers react in similar fashion to their experiences as colonial administrators?

2. To Matata his gold watch is a symbol of civilization. Choose this or some other object or artifact and discuss it as a symbol of civilization (i.e., civilizations in general, or a particular civilization).

3. Describe a person from a culture other than your own and indicate what you have learned about this person's culture and cultural values. What has this contact taught you about your *own* culture and its values?

My True Love Hath My Heart
by Malcolm Muggeridge

1 There is a story going around (it might even be true) of a donor who was lined up for a heart-transplant operation. The recipient, however, at the last moment decided against having a transplant, and died; the putative donor was recently discharged from hospital. This certainly could happen. As everyone now knows, only a living heart can be transplanted, so the donor cannot be dead in the hitherto accepted sense. Thus the fact must be faced that heart transplanting amounts essentially to experimenting with human beings, as has hitherto been done with animals — especially dogs. It is highly significant that the ice should have been broken for such experimentation in South Africa.

2 I raised this question on a television programme with Dr. Christian Barnard himself. Why, I asked him, had the first heart-transplant operation been conducted in his hospital in Cape Town? Was it because the surgeons and equipment there were better than anywhere else? Or, as I believed, because the vile doctrine of apartheid devalued life itself, turning all our bodies into carcasses fit for experiment. The question was ill received. Dr. Barnard evaded it; the twenty or so distinguished doctors on the set with me barracked, and one of them got up to dissociate them all from my ill-chosen observations. Afterwards I was accused of bringing politics into a discussion about medicine and ethics. A number of letters I received in connection with the programme were more understanding — one particularly, which related to a doctor who had worked in South Africa and then decamped because, as he put it, the prevailing attitude to the black African patients was veterinary rather than medical.

It is, indeed, the moral rather than the political implications of apar-   3
theid which make it so hateful. Politically speaking, it amounts to rule
by a white oligarchy, who no doubt will in due course be succeeded
by a black oligarchy, as has happened in all the former African dependen-
cies. The world today is largely governed by entrenched oligarchies,
whether party machine-men, money-men, communist *apparatchiks* etc.,
etc. The replacement of one oligarchy by another can be exciting, and
raise extravagant hopes, especially in the young, but when the dust has
settled and the rhetoric spent itself, there are the same old police, the
same old prisons and the same old cant. When the anarchists marched
with their black flags in a procession in Paris led by party-line communists like Aragon, I remembered how Kropotkin was given a state
funeral in Leningrad when he died there in 1921. The procession passed
the prison where his followers had already been incarcerated. Some
of them were able to get their arms through the bars and salute his coffin,
loaded with flowers, as it passed. It was the last anarchist demonstration ever to be permitted in the USSR.

How sinister that the South African achievement which has won esteem   4
everywhere should be the very one that most exemplifies the true moral
horror of apartheid! How disturbing that drawing attention to this should
so enrage, not so much the upholders of apartheid, as those who ostensibly oppose it on the highest ethical grounds! The really terrible thing
about apartheid is that it reduces the status of human souls, in Christian terms all equally dear to their Creator and made in His Image, to
two categories — the driver and the driven. Seen so, their mortal shape
deserves no particular respect. It can veritably be regarded as a collection of spare parts, to be sliced off and grafted on as required. In South
Africa Dr. Barnard could chance his arm without fear of serious opposition; in California and Texas — where the moral climate comes
nearest to South Africa's — they could follow suit. London came next,
and soon, we may be sure, the knives will be out, and the quest for
donors be on, all over the place. Then factory farming and the broiler
house will loom up as our human lot and way of life, as the dark visions
of the future of an Orwell and an Aldous Huxley have envisaged.

The most ardent advocates of heart transplants are prepared to admit   5
that there will never be enough donors in the foreseeable future for the
operation to be availabe for more than a minute proportion of those
who might benefit from it. This is even taking into account all that the
roads offer on a bright weekend — a fruitful source of spare organs,
as could be gathered from an aside when Dr. Barnard was on the prowl

for a donor. For the moment, it was said, no one suitable had shown up, but over the weekend they might have better luck. Properly organized, the roads should yield quite a harvest of serviceable spare parts, in flesh as well as metal. Nothing wasted on our motorways this weekend! Moreover, the possibility is bound to come under consideration of using the organs of incurables to service productive citizens. After all, imbeciles have hearts and kidneys — often quite good ones. Since they cannot be fitted with new brains, why not put their organs to good use?

6   One wonders on what basis the fortunate recipients are to be chosen. Presumably, in America millionaires would have first call, followed by the luminaries of show business; in Russia, the party hierarchy, followed by spacemen and nuclear physicists. Fitting ex-president Eisenhower with a new heart was, it appears, seriously considered. It was a pity in a way that this need for one did not coincide with Senator Robert Kennedy's assassination. Eisenhower with a Kennedy heart would have been a very powerful ticket. In this country one scarcely knows. Leaving aside the royal family, probably some weird protocol would prevail, with the Archbishop of Canterbury, the Lord Chancellor and the Earl Marshal heading the queue, and Lord Thomson and Mr. Clore able to jump it.

7   Another question I tried, without success, to raise with Dr. Barnard was that of the priorities involved. Can it be seriously maintained that the dedication of such rare skills and resources to protracting the life of a middle-aged Cape Town dentist for a few extra months or years can be justified in a continent where doctors and medical supplies are so woefully lacking? Doctors themselves have spoken out about this. Even in England, as we all know, patients sometimes have to wait an inordinate time for life-and-death operations, and hospital staff and accommodation are desperately short. Surely the resources tied up for heart transplants are out of all proportion to what has been, or may be, achieved in the way of advancing medicine's true aims — to heal the sick and alleviate suffering. So far the chief result of the transplants has been to advertise the transplanters in a highly distasteful and unprofessional manner, and to raise hopes in sufferers from heart complaints which can never be realized.

8   I have in honesty to admit that I feel in myself — as I know others do — a deep, instinctive repugnance for this spare-part surgery which is not capable of a wholly rational explanation. Such feelings, I am well aware, can be, and have been, dismissed as mere obscurantism and

atavism. Yet the feeling of revulsion persists. It is to do with a sense that all creation pre-eminently deserves respect — the animals, the plants and trees and grass, the folds of the hills and the sweep of the plains, the very stones and soil, and especially Man. That our present way of life is carrying us in the opposite direction — towards using creatures and crops and one another without respect; greedily, arrogantly, bull-dozing out whatever stands in our way, breeding weird animal grotes-ques for our meat, subordinating crops, fruits, the forests and the water springs, everything, to our purposes without reference to nature and its exigencies.

Somehow, to me, the heart transplants are part of this process. Man   9
trying to grasp at some kind of crazy renewal of himself — of heart, of kidney, of liver. Toying with the notion, perhaps, deep in his un-conscious, of reanimating his waning fertility. Envisaging, even, a self-induced immortality. Living for ever, like an old vintage car — each part replaceable, even the battery or headpiece — as it wears out. Man achieving everlasting life, not because his soul is immortal and belongs to eternity, but because his body can continue to exist in time till the end of time. What an immortality that would be! It recalls Swift's terrible account of the Struldbrugs, those melancholy creatures of the Kingdom of Laputa, who, unable to die, spend their days envying the dead.

(1968)

The Writer's Subject

1. What connection does Muggeridge draw between the doctrine of apartheid and the fact that the first successful heart transplants were carried out in South Africa? (para. 2)

2. Why is Muggeridge more disturbed by the moral implications of apar-theid than by its political implications? (para. 3)

3. Why does Muggeridge allude to the funeral of the Russian anarchist Kropotkin? (para. 3)

4. What picture of the future does Muggeridge draw at the close of paragraph 4? Why does he invoke the names of George Orwell and Aldous Huxley?

5. What, according to Muggeridge, has been the impact of heart transplants on priorities and practices in medicine? (para. 7)

6. What is the "way of life" or "process" of which, in Muggeridge's view, heart transplants are a part? (paras. 8-9)

7. What is the relevance of the allusion to *Gulliver's Travels* at the end of the essay?

8. What part do Muggeridge's religious views play in the development of his argument?

The Writer's Style and Strategy

1. What is Muggeridge's strategy in opening his essay with the story of a heart transplant that did not take place?

2. Muggeridge makes several references to Dr. Christian Barnard, the South African heart surgeon who pioneered heart-transplant techniques. Show how these references fit the argumentative approach known as "ad hominem" argument.

3. Discuss Muggeridge's use of exclamations, rhetorical questions, and sentence fragments to give force to his argument.

4. What effect is intended by the references to "factory farming and the broiler house" in paragraph 4?

5. Discuss the predominant tone of paragraph 5, and show how it is established, particularly through word choice.

6. Muggeridge admits to strong feelings "not capable of a wholly rational explanation" in paragraph 8. How does he appeal to the *reader's* feelings, in this paragraph and in the essay as a whole?

Suggested Topics for Writing and Discussion

1. Do you agree or disagree with Muggeridge's view that organ transplant surgery is promoting a devaluation of human life?

2. A development in medical research which has aroused much controversy in recent years is *in vitro* fertilization, the creation of "test-tube babies." Write an argument for or against this procedure, in which you attempt to sway your reader by an appeal to the emotions.

3. Muggeridge attacks the use of limited medical resources for the development of expensive surgical techniques which can benefit only a few people. Write an argument for or against the view that society should not support medical research unless it has the potential to bring widespread benefits.

Shooting an Elephant

by George Orwell

1   In Moulmein, in Lower Burma, I was hated by large numbers of people
— the only time I have been important enough for this to happen to
me. I was subdivisional police officer of the town, and in an aimless,
petty kind of way anti-European feeling was very bitter. No one had
the guts to raise a riot, but if a European woman went through the bazaars
alone somebody would probably spit betel juice over her dress. As a
police officer I was an obvious target and was baited whenever it seemed
safe to do so. When a nimble Burman tripped me up on the football
field and the referee (another Burman) looked the other way, the crowd
yelled with hideous laughter. This happened more than once. In the
end the sneering yellow faces of young men that met me everywhere,
the insults hooted after me when I was at a safe distance, got badly
on my nerves. The young Buddhist priests were the worst of all. There
were several thousands of them in the town and none of them seemed
to have anything to do except stand on street corners and jeer at
Europeans.

2   All this was perplexing and upsetting. For at that time I had already
made up my mind that imperialism was an evil thing and the sooner
I chucked up my job and got out of it the better. Theoretically — and
secretly, of course — I was all for the Burmese and all against their
oppressors, the British. As for the job I was doing, I hated it more bitterly
than I can perhaps make clear. In a job like that you see the dirty work
of Empire at close quarters. The wretched prisoners huddling in the
stinking cages of the lock-ups, the grey, cowed faces of the long-term
convicts, the scarred buttocks of the men who had been flogged with

bamboos — all these oppressed me with an intolerable sense of guilt. But I could get nothing into perspective. I was young and ill-educated and I had had to think out my problems in the utter silence that is imposed on every Englishman in the East. I did not even know that the British Empire is dying, still less did I know that it is a great deal better than the younger empires that are going to supplant it. All I knew was that I was stuck between my hatred of the empire I served and my rage against the evil-spirited little beasts who tried to make my job impossible. With one part of my mind I thought of the British Raj as an unbreakable tyranny, as something clamped down, in *saecula saeculorum*,[1] upon the will of prostrate peoples; with another part I thought that the greatest joy in the world would be to drive a bayonet into a Buddhist priest's guts. Feelings like these are the normal by-products of imperialism; ask any Anglo-Indian official, if you can catch him off duty.

One day something happened which in a roundabout way was 3 enlightening. It was a tiny incident in itself, but it gave me a better glimpse than I had had before of the real nature of imperialism — the real motives for which despotic governments act. Early one morning the sub-inspector at a police station the other end of the town rang me up on the 'phone and said that an elephant was ravaging the bazaar. Would I please come and do something about it? I did not know what I could do, but I wanted to see what was happening and I got on to a pony and started out. I took my rifle, an old .44 Winchester and much too small to kill an elephant, but I thought the noise might be useful *in terrorem*. Various Burmans stopped me on the way and told me about the elephant's doings. It was not, of course, a wild elephant, but a tame one which had gone "must". It had been chained up, as tame elephants always are when their attack of "must" is due, but on the previous night it had broken its chain and escaped. Its mahout, the only person who could manage it when it was in that state, had set out in pursuit, but had taken the wrong direction and was now twelve hours' journey away, and in the morning the elephant had suddenly reappeared in the town. The Burmese population had no weapons and were quite helpless against it. It had already destroyed somebody's bamboo hut, killed a cow and raided some fruit-stalls and devoured the stock; also it had met the municipal rubbish van, and, when the driver jumped out and took to his heels, had turned the van over and inflicted violences upon it.

The Burmese sub-inspector and some Indian constables were waiting 4 for me in the quarter where the elephant had been seen. It was a very poor quarter, a labyrinth of squalid bamboo huts, thatched with palm-

1. Forever and ever.

leaf, winding all over a steep hillside. I remember that it was a cloudy, stuffy morning at the beginning of the rains. We began questioning the people as to where the elephant had gone, and, as usual, failed to get any definite information. That is invariably the case in the East; a story always sounds clear enough at a distance, but the nearer you get to the scene of events the vaguer it becomes. Some of the people said that the elephant had gone in one direction, some said that he had gone in another, some professed not even to have heard of any elephant. I had almost made up my mind that the whole story was a pack of lies, when we heard yells a little distance away. There was a loud, scandalized cry of "Go away, child! Go away this instant!" and an old woman with a switch in her hand came round the corner of a hut, violently shooing away a crowd of naked children. Some more women followed, clicking their tongues and exclaiming; evidently there was something that the children ought not to have seen. I rounded the hut and saw a man's dead body sprawling in the mud. He was an Indian, a black Dravidian coolie, almost naked, and he could not have been dead many minutes. The people said that the elephant had come suddenly upon him round the corner of the hut, caught him with its trunk, put its foot on his back and ground him into the earth. This was the rainy season and the ground was soft, and his face had scored a trench a foot deep and a couple of yards long. He was lying on his belly with arms crucified and head sharply twisted to one side. His face was coated with mud, the eyes wide open, the teeth bared and grinning with an expression of unendurable agony. (Never tell me, by the way, that the dead look peaceful. Most of the corpses I have seen looked devilish.) The friction of the great beast's foot had stripped the skin from his back as neatly as one skins a rabbit. As soon as I saw the dead man I sent an orderly to a friend's house nearby to borrow an elephant rifle. I had already sent back the pony, not wanting it to go mad with fright and throw me if it smelt the elephant.

5   The orderly came back in a few minutes with a rifle and five cartridges, and meanwhile some Burmans had arrived and told us that the elephant was in the paddy fields below, only a few hundred yards away. As I started forward practically the whole population of the quarter flocked out of the houses and followed me. They had seen the rifle and were all shouting excitedly that I was going to shoot the elephant. They had not shown much interest in the elephant when he was merely ravaging their homes, but it was different now that he was going to be shot. It was a bit of fun to them, as it would be to an English crowd; besides

they wanted the meat. It made me vaguely uneasy. I had no intention of shooting the elephant — I had merely sent for the rifle to defend myself if necessary — and it is always unnerving to have a crowd following you. I marched down the hill, looking and feeling a fool, with the rifle over my shoulder and an ever-growing army of people jostling at my heels. At the bottom, when you got away from the huts, there was a metalled road and beyond that a miry waste of paddy fields a thousand yards across, not yet ploughed but soggy from the first rains and dotted with coarse grass. The elephant was standing eight yards from the road, his left side towards us. He took not the slightest notice of the crowd's approach. He was tearing up bunches of grass, beating them against his knees to clean them and stuffing them into his mouth.

I had halted on the road. As soon as I saw the elephant I knew with   6
perfect certainty that I ought not to shoot him. It is a serious matter to shoot a working elephant — it is comparable to destroying a huge and costly piece of machinery — and obviously one ought not to do it if it can possibly be avoided. And at that distance, peacefully eating, the elephant looked no more dangerous than a cow. I thought then and I think now that his attack of "must" was already passing off; in which case he would merely wander harmlessly about until the mahout came back and caught him. Moreover, I did not in the least want to shoot him. I decided that I would watch him for a little while to make sure that he did not turn savage again, and then go home.

But at that moment I glanced round at the crowd that had followed   7
me. It was an immense crowd, two thousand at the least and growing every minute. It blocked the road for a long distance on either side. I looked at the sea of yellow faces above the garish clothes — faces all happy and excited over this bit of fun, all certain that the elephant was going to be shot. They were watching me as they would watch a conjurer about to perform a trick. They did not like me, but with the magical rifle in my hands I was momentarily worth watching. And suddenly I realized that I should have to shoot the elephant after all. The people expected it of me and I had got to do it; I could feel their two thousand wills pressing me forward, irresistibly. And it was at this moment, as I stood there with the rifle in my hands, that I first grasped the hollowness, the futility of the white man's dominion in the East. Here was I, the white man with his gun, standing in front of the unarmed native crowd — seemingly the leading actor of the piece; but in reality I was only an absurd puppet pushed to and fro by the will of those yellow faces behind. I perceived in this moment that when the white man turns

tyrant it is his own freedom that he destroys. He becomes a sort of
hollow, posing dummy, the conventionalized figure of a sahib. For it
is the condition of his rule that he shall spend his life in trying to impress the "natives", and so in every crisis he has got to do what the
"natives" expect of him. He wears a mask, and his face grows to fit
it. I had got to shoot the elephant. I had committed myself to doing
it when I sent for the rifle. A sahib has got to act like a sahib; he has
got to appear resolute, to know his own mind and do definite things.
To come all that way, rifle in hand, with two thousand people marching at my heels, and then to trail feebly away, having done nothing —
no, that was impossible. The crowd would laugh at me. And my whole
life, every white man's life in the East, was one long struggle not to
be laughed at.

8   But I did not want to shoot the elephant. I watched him beating his
bunch of grass against his knees, with that preoccupied grandmotherly
air that elephants have. It seemed to me that it would be murder to shoot
him. At that age I was not squeamish about killing animals, but I had
never shot an elephant and never wanted to. (Somehow it always seems
worse to kill a large animal.) Besides, there was the beast's owner to
be considered. Alive, the elephant was worth at least a hundred pounds;
dead, he would only be worth the value of his tusks, five pounds,
possibly. But I had got to act quickly. I turned to some experienced-
looking Burmans who had been there when we arrived, and asked them
how the elephant had been behaving. They all said the same thing: he
took no notice of you if you left him alone, but he might charge if you
went too close to him.

9   It was perfectly clear to me what I ought to do. I ought to walk up
to within, say, twenty-five yards of the elephant and test his behaviour.
If he charged I could shoot, if he took no notice of me it would be safe
to leave him until the mahout came back. But also I knew that I was
going to do no such thing. I was a poor shot with a rifle and the ground
was soft mud into which one would sink at every step. If the elephant
charged and I missed him, I should have about as much chance as a
toad under a steam-roller. But even then I was not thinking particularly
of my own skin, only of the watchful yellow faces behind. For at that
moment, with the crowd watching me, I was not afraid in the ordinary
sense, as I would have been if I had been alone. A white man mustn't
be frightened in front of "natives"; and so, in general, he isn't frightened. The sole thought in my mind was that if anything went wrong
those two thousand Burmans would see me pursued, caught, trampled

on and reduced to a grinning corpse like that Indian up the hill. And if that happened it was quite probable that some of them would laugh. That would never do. There was only one alternative. I shoved the cartridges into the magazine and lay down on the road to get a better aim.

The crowd grew very still, and a deep, low, happy sigh, as of people **10** who see the theatre curtain go up at last, breathed from innumerable throats. They were going to have their bit of fun after all. The rifle was a beautiful German thing with cross-hair sights. I did not then know that in shooting an elephant one would shoot to cut an imaginary bar running from ear-hole to ear-hole. I ought, therefore, as the elephant was sideways on, to have aimed straight at his ear-hole; actually I aimed several inches in front of this, thinking the brain would be further forward.

When I pulled the trigger I did not hear the bang or feel the kick — **11** one never does when a shot goes home — but I heard the devilish roar of glee that went up from the crowd. In that instant, in too short a time, one would have thought, even for the bullet to get there, a mysterious, terrible change had come over the elephant. He neither stirred nor fell, but every line of his body had altered. He looked suddenly stricken, shrunken, immensely old, as though the frightful impact of the bullet had paralysed him without knocking him down. At last, after what seemed a long time — it might have been five seconds, I dare say — he sagged flabbily to his knees. His mouth slobbered. An enormous senility seemed to have settled upon him. One could have imagined him thousands of years old. I fired again into the same spot. At the second shot he did not collapse but climbed with desperate slowness to his feet and stood weakly upright, with legs sagging and head drooping. I fired a third time. That was the shot that did for him. You could see the agony of it jolt his whole body and knock the last remnant of strength from his legs. But in falling he seemed for a moment to rise, for as his hind legs collapsed beneath him he seemed to tower upwards like a huge rock toppling, his trunk reaching skywards like a tree. He trumpeted, for the first and only time. And then down he came, his belly towards me, with a crash that seemed to shake the ground even where I lay.

I got up. The Burmans were already racing past me across the mud. **12** It was obvious that the elephant would never rise again, but he was not dead. He was breathing very rhythmically with long rattling gasps, his great mound of a side painfully rising and falling. His mouth was wide open — I could see far down into caverns of pale pink throat. I waited a long time for him to die, but his breathing did not weaken.

Finally I fired my two remaining shots into the spot where I thought his heart must be. The thick blood welled out of him like red velvet, but still he did not die. His body did not even jerk when the shots hit him, the tortured breathing continued without a pause. He was dying, very slowly and in great agony, but in some world remote from me where not even a bullet could damage him further. I felt that I had got to put an end to that dreadful noise. It seemed dreadful to see the great beast lying there, powerless to move and yet powerless to die, and not even to be able to finish him. I sent back for my small rifle and poured shot after shot into his heart and down his throat. They seemed to make no impression. The tortured gasps continued as steadily as the ticking of a clock.

13   In the end I could not stand it any longer and went away. I heard later that it took him half an hour to die. Burmans were bringing dahs and baskets even before I left, and I was told they had stripped his body almost to the bones by the afternoon.

14   Afterwards, of course, there were endless discussions about the shooting of the elephant. The owner was furious, but he was only an Indian and could do nothing. Besides, legally I had done the right thing, for a mad elephant has to be killed, like a mad dog, if its owner fails to control it. Among the Europeans opinion was divided. The older men said I was right, the younger men said it was a damn shame to shoot an elephant for killing a coolie, because an elephant was worth more than any damn Coringhee coolie. And afterwards I was very glad that the coolie had been killed; it put me legally in the right and it gave me a sufficient pretext for shooting the elephant. I often wondered whether any of the others grasped that I had done it solely to avoid looking a fool.

(1936)

The Writer's Subject

1. What were Orwell's feelings about his role as a representative of British imperialism in Burma? (paras. 1-2)

2. Orwell received his education at Eton, one of the finest schools in England; why, then, does he refer to himself as "ill-educated"? (para. 2)

3. What is Orwell's point in telling us at length about his initial difficulty in finding the elephant? (paras. 3-4)

4. Why did Orwell first take a rifle that he knew was too small to kill an elephant? What does this detail suggest about his state of mind at that point? (para. 3)

5. Why at first did Orwell not want to shoot the elephant? What considerations led him to change his mind? (paras. 6-9)

6. Why was Orwell concerned at the thought that the crowd might laugh if he were trampled to death? (para. 9)

7. Why did Orwell fail to kill the elephant with his first shot? Why did he leave the scene before the elephant finally expired? (paras. 10-13)

8. How does the final paragraph demonstrate Orwell's earlier statement, "I had had to think out my problems in the utter silence that is imposed on every Englishman in the East"? (para. 2)

The Writer's Style and Strategy

1. What is Orwell's purpose in this essay?

2. Why does Orwell choose the form of autobiographical narrative to carry out his purpose?

3. Orwell provides many details of physical setting. Choose some of these and explain their importance in the narrative.

4. Besides setting the scene, how do the details in paragraph 1 prepare the reader for the central events in the narrative?

5. How does Orwell use concrete images to convey his inner conflict in paragraph 2?

6. Why does Orwell provide so many details about the elephant's destructiveness and the appearance of the dead Indian? (paras. 3-4) What relation do these details bear to the essay's conclusion?

7. How does Orwell convey the mood of the Burmans who witness his con-
    duct in dealing with the elephant? Why does he place such emphasis on
    their forming a huge crowd? (paras. 5, 7, 9-10)

8. How does the final paragraph reinforce Orwell's earlier statement,
    "I had had to think out my problems in the utter silence that is imposed
    on every Englishman in the East" (para. 2)?

9. What is Orwell's purpose in providing such a vivid and detailed descrip-
    tion of the elephant's death? (paras. 11-13)

10. How does Orwell's conclusion sum up and re-state the moral issues
    dramatized in the narrative?

Suggested Topics for Writing and Discussion

1. Orwell recounts a personal experience in "Shooting an Elephant." He
    begins his account of the experience by saying, "One day something hap-
    pened which in a roundabout way was enlightening. It was a tiny inci-
    dent in itself, but it gave me a better glimpse that I had had before of
    the real nature of. . . ." Using Orwell's introduction, write a narrative
    in which you discuss an enlightening personal experience and show how
    that experience has given you greater insight.

2. Orwell's essay demonstrates the powerful influence of social pressures
    on the individual. Have you ever found yourself in a situation in which
    you had to go against your own feelings or convictions in order to satisfy
    the rules or expectations of society? Recount this experience.

3. In our daily lives, we encounter many different kinds of authority. Choose
    one example of authority, describe the form it takes, and examine your
    own response to it.

Another Accolade for Charter Arms Corp.
by Mike Royko

I was pleased to see that the stories reporting the death of John Lennon   1
were specific and accurate about the kind of gun that was used to murder
the world-renowned musician.

It was a .38 calibre pistol made by Charter Arms Corp. of Bridgeport,   2
Conn.

You might ask: What difference does it make what kind of gun was   3
used?

It makes a great deal of difference. Especially to Charter Arms Corp.   4

There are guns and then there are guns. Cheap guns, ordinary guns,   5
and finely crafted guns.

And when people become emotional about guns, as many do when   6
somebody famous is killed, they tend to lump all guns together. They
don't show proper respect for an excellent gun, such as the Charter .38.

It happens this is not the first time a famous person has been shot   7
by this make of weapon., When former Alabama Gov. George C.
Wallace was shot and paralyzed for life by another deranged person
in 1974, the bullet that tore into his spine came from a Charter .38.

If I'm not mistaken, that makes the Charter .38 the first gun in modern   8
times to have two famous people to its credit. The weapons used to
blast President Kennedy, the Rev. Dr. Martin Luther King, Jr., and
Sen. Robert F. Kennedy were all of different manufacture.

When Wallace was shot, a CBS reporter made it obvious that he didn't   9
know a fine gun from a cheap gun.

The reporter went on network TV and said that Wallace had been   10
wounded by a "cheap handgun." He obviously had in mind the kind

of Saturday Night Special that is so popular among the criminal riffraff who have no respect for quality and workmanship.

11   When the proud executives of Charter Arms Corp. heard the reporter, they became indignant.

12   They contacted the CBS and demanded an apology. The incident was described in an editorial in the company magazine of the Charter Corp.

13   The editorial, which was headlined "An Apology from CBS," said:

"We are too dedicated to high quality in American-made handguns and have poured too much of ourselves into our products to have one of them even casually referred to as a 'cheap handgun'.

"That was exactly the phrase used in a broadcast description of the handgun used by Arthur Bremer in his assassination attempt on Gov. Wallace, which happened to be one of our Undercover .38 Specials.

"The broadcast emanated from CBS . . . and our public relations people were immediately instructed to bring the error to their attention."

14   The editorial went on to say that an apology was indeed received from CBS network vice-president, who contritely told Charter Arms Corp., "I am sending a copy of your letter to all our TV producers. In the event that we make reference to the Undercover .38 special used by Arthur Bremer, we will certainly avoid characterizing it as a 'Saturday Night Special' or any other term which labels it as a 'cheap weapon'."

15   Presumably that soothed the wounded pride of the gunmakers at Charter Arms Corp., since no further public protests were heard.

16   And you can't blame them for having felt hurt at such a slur on their product. When Wallace was shot, a Charter .38 cost $105. Today, with rising prices, the gun costs about $180 or $190, depending on where you do your gun shopping.

17   That is not a cheap gun, especially when compared to the trashy weapons that some gunmen, to whom quality is unimportant, arm themselves with.

18   Now I don't know if it was mere coincidence that both Bremer, who shot Wallace, and Mark David Chapman, who apparently shot Lennon, used the same weapon. Or if it was that they both recognized quality when they saw it, and were willing to spend money to get the best.

19   But the fact is, both opted for quality and they got what they paid for. There was no misfiring, no jamming, no bullet flying off line, and no gun exploding in their hands — all of which can happen when one uses a cheap gun.

20   True, Wallace wasn't killed. That was the fault of Bremer, not the Charter gun. Bremer shot Wallace in the stomach, which isn't the best

place to shoot a person if you want to kill him.

But even in that case, the gun did its job — blowing a terrible hole 21
in Wallace's gut and putting him into a wheelchair for good.

In the case of Lennon, you couldn't ask for a better performance from 22
a gun. Lennon was shot several times, but according to the doctor who
pronounced him dead, the first bullet hit him in the chest and killed him
on the spot. The other shots weren't even necessary.

You can never be sure of getting those kinds of results from a Saturday 23
Night Special.

Now the Charter Arms Corp. has the unique distinction of having 24
two famous people shot by one of their products, I wonder if they have
considered using it in their advertising. Something simple and tasteful
like: "The .38 that got George Wallace AND John Lennon. See it at
your gun dealer now."

If so, they shouldn't wait. With so many handguns — both cheap and 25
of high quality — easily available to Americans, it could be just a matter of time until another manufacturer moves into the lead in the famous-
person derby. All it would take would be a few pop-pop-pops from say,
a Colt — maybe a politician or two and another rock star or two —
and they would have the lead.

On the other hand, maybe Charter Arms Corp. doesn't want recogni- 26
tion — just the kind of pride one feels in a job of fine craftsmanship.

If so, they have a right to feel proud.   27

Once again, your product really did the job, gents.   28

(1980)

The Writer's Subject

1. What precisely is Royko's target for satire here?

2. What concerns appear to be missing in Royko's references to the various
   victims of assassination? How do these omissions fit his purpose in the
   essay?

3. How does Royko apply the idea of quality and craftsmanship to the subject of guns?

4. Royko first describes the gunmen as "deranged." How does he subsequently
   treat them? How does this treatment fit his satiric purposes?

5. What is Royko's attitude to the Charter Arms Corp.? What does he imply
   about the company's values — and possibly those of business in general?

6. What is Royko's attitude to handguns?

The Writer's Style and Strategy

1. What indications does the essay give that it was originally written for a newspaper audience?

2. What is the tone of Royko's essay? How is it established in the opening paragraph?

3. What persona does Royko create for the speaker of this essay?

4. Why does Royko constantly use "Corp." instead of "corporation" in referring to the gun company?

5. A method frequently employed by satirists is to reverse praise and blame, thus creating an ironic effect. Point out some specific examples of the praise/blame inversion and suggest Royko's real intent.

6. What use does Royko make of the editorial and the "Apology from CBS" published in the Charter Arms Corp. company magazine?

7. Why does Royko say that "Bremer shot Wallace in the stomach" but speak in the next paragraph of "blowing a hole in Wallace's gut"?

8. Discuss the intended effect of the last three sentences.

Suggested Topics for Writing and Discussion

1. Write an argument for or against the view that the individual citizen should have the right to possess a handgun.

2. Find some reports concerning the murder or attempted murder of a well-known public figure. Compare accounts of the incident and show how the attitudes and emphases of the reporters differ in their coverage of two or three particulars.

3. Write an essay in which you attack something you believe is wrong by ironically praising what you wish to criticize.

4. One target in Royko's essay is the marketing of guns. Choose another product with potential for harm (such as cigarettes, diet pills, instant formula for babies), and discuss the ways in which the product's manufacturer attempts to persuade consumers to buy it, despite its dangers.

Sport and Nationalism
by Alan Sillitoe

Sometime during February 1969 a certain person wrote to me from 1
Munich — I forget his name, because I destroyed the letter — asking
for my views on sport. His request was short, and put in rather general
terms, yet my mind immediately understood it in a particular way, as
it was meant to do, perhaps. For some reason I copied the body of my
reply into my notebook at the time, and this is what I told him:

'I have never practised any kind of sport. It has always seemed to 2
me that sport only serves to enslave the mind and to enslave the body.
It is the main "civilising" weapon of the western world ethos, a way
of enforcing collective discipline which no self-respecting savage like
myself could ever take to . Society was built on "competition", and "sport"
is a preliminary to this society and an accompaniment to it. It is a sort
of training ground for entering into the war of life. The Olympic torch
is a flame of enslavement — run from it as fast as you can , and that
in itself will give you plenty of exercise.'

In olden days sport was the king's pastime. Now, it can be everybody's. 3
By sport I mean competitive sport, when one man or woman matches
himself or herself against another, either for so-called glory, or for cash
gain.

Even as late as the end of the nineteenth century a particularly vicious 4
sport existed in a certain area of south-east England. Its name was
'kickshins' — which is as good a description of it as any. Two men would
stand facing, arms on each other's shoulders, and take it in turns to give
a kick at each other's shins. Matches were arranged between the kickshin
champions of various villages, and the local squires would bet on their
favourites.

5   Just as universal literacy was necessary to get people into the modern age, so mass competitve sport was used as further cement to enslave them. Like every such distraction offered to the people, the people reached out to it with alacrity.

6   Why was this?

7   First of all, sport of big business and big propaganda was allied to nationalism. If England lost a football match against Germany the people were made to feel as if the Battle of the Somme had just been refought (and that maybe it would have been a better result if they'd played cricket). If England won the game of football the Union Jack was in blatant evidence, as a symbol of a national victory. It is no accident that the English say (a false claim in any case), that 'the Battle of Waterloo was won on the playing fields of Eton.'

8   One might easily think that sport has taken the place of war. Not at all. Sport is a means of keeping the national spirit alive during a time of so-called peace. It prepares the national spirit for the eventuality of war.

9   The ceremony of the Olympic Games is initiated by shields and flags, artillery salutes and fanfares of trumpets. The honour of each nation is invoked and put at stake immediately the runner sets out with his flaming torch.

10   It is almost as if sport is diplomacy carried on by other means. Sport is encouraged in schools so that young boys won't masturbate. It is encouraged among the grown-ups, as participants or spectators, to take their minds off urgent social problems, and the need to rebel when they are not resolved quickly enough.

11   If England wins an international football match, or clears twenty gold-plated tin medals at some games or other, then production goes up in England's factories. Likewise when England lost at football in Mexico in 1970, Mr. Harold Wilson, the Labour Party Prime Minister of the day, lost the following general election to his Conservative opponent Mr. Edward Heath.

12   Perhaps Mr. Heath is even looking for victories at the present Olympic Games to increase his chances at the next election! Woe betide him if England loses against Poland, or Brazil!

13   You might almost think that England's sporting prowess was linked to the floating of the pound. One lost goal, and a few more cents are chipped off it in the world's financial arenas. A few centimetres off the high jump, and a left wing demonstration gets too close to the American Embassy in Grosvenor Square.

If England loses, faces are long for a week. Or they might be, if radio 14
and television had its way, for those media too pander to the lowest
common denominator of nationalism when it comes to sport. They ex-
ult in what is known as victory, but hide as best they can so-called defeat.

True sport — I'm not sure that there is such a thing — but true sport, 15
as I see it, is not to set people competing against each other both in
deed and thought, but to work together as a team perhaps, against some
arduous enterprise or obstacle. If a dozen people set out on foot to cross
South America gathering scientific information on the way — that is
good. But if two such groups set out in order to see who can do it
quickest, or who can get to know most — that is demoralising.

If one man can jump sixteen feet, and another tries to jump seven- 16
teen in order to get a piece of gold with his name stamped on it — in
smaller letters though than the name of his country — and so that he
will become a national hero for a few weeks as well, that is both ludicrous
and sinister.

He is surrounded by flags and partisan spectators while he performs 17
his act, his national ritual, and all those people are getting some semi-
sexual power-drive from the fact that his jump would be their jump
if only they had trained for it, and hadn't eaten such big meals during
their recent lives.

His power is their power. They see him or her, for a moment, as 18
them, and them as him. And if at that moment a government minister
or national general came into the stands and ordered them to jump to
their feet, and then to jump sixteen feet the same as he — or she —
they would no doubt all stand up fully confident that they could do it
— or something close.

If some mechanism were fitted into every television set which, im- 19
mediately after the big jump, put out a voice which said to all the wat-
chers: 'Now *YOU* jump — for the good of your country, because those
in every other country are doing the same to compete with you, and
the honour of your country is at stake' — the nation would jump as one
person. The nation in armchairs would become the nation in arms.

The Olympic Games cannot, therefore, be considered as anything other 20
than a mass rally. Under the guise of international friendly competition the same old nationalist values and rivalries are fostered. It is not
the thing to engender real friendship between countries, or between the
people of these countries.

As soon as a man participates, either in body or spirit, either at the 21
actual place or vicariously through the medium of the television set,

or the radio, or the newspapers, he loses his individuality, and becomes part of his nation — with unreasonable yearning in his heart.

22   We all know that in the totalitarian state sport is used to drill and make the individual subservient to the totalitarian system. In a so-called democratic state, competitive sport is used for the same ends, in the same way, but so that the participants appear to be competing primarily for themselves and not their country. But as soon as they enter that stadium or arena they are just as much representatives of their country as are those who belong to a totalitarian system. The media sees to that and so do the people who take up the message of the media.

23   When that Olympic torch is lit we must see it for what it is. It is a symbol of the oppression of the free human spirit. That flame is a burning torch being carried along the highway, and all sensible people would get out ot its way, flee from it and take to the hills. When it gets to the stadium and the crowd roars, you know that that is the place to keep away from.

24   Gladitorial combats in Ancient Rome, chariot races in Constantinople, bull-fights in modern Spain, and the Olympic Games in whatever place they are held — it means that the true and human spirit of man is being killed there, the body wrecked and abused, and the heart broken.

25   Just as all war supposes human weakness, and is directed against that weakness, so all sport is a human way of arranging the survival of the fittest. Thus the arena is a sort of jungle concocted by so-called civilisation, wherein the fittest people are made to be the human measurement of nationalist aspirations.

26   It is a thing that the truly civilised must instinctively abominate, and then with reason protest against. We must somehow make our sane voices heard — even while the crowd roars.

27   The voice of civilisation is not measured by the loudness of the roaring. And civilisation itself must not be jeopardised by the contests in the arena. The Olympic torch lights up the hollow eyes of the dictator, and turns all eyes toward the national flag.

28   After the death of the Israelis the voices of commentators from the Olympic Games in Munich have taken on tones of vile obscenity — real obscenity, the deepest obscenity of the spirit which henceforth will be represented by the Olympic Games.

29   The resumption of these so-called games in such indecent haste only emphasised their true spirit — that of a host country unwilling to give up its pride, its financial investments; and of athletes who are in the grip of their physical investment at the expense of all human feeling.

That the 'games' should go on after the black-hearted murder of eleven   30
participants shows that true sporting spirit is so dead that one must doubt
whether it ever existed. The continuation of the games is a victory for
the Arab terrorists, for it is the quickest and most effective way of drawing a curtain on this atrocity.

(1972)

The Writer's Subject

1. Why does Sillitoe refer to himself in paragraph 2 as a "savage"?

2. What parallel does Sillitoe draw between the rise of literacy and the growth
    of competitive sport? (para. 5)

3. What is the connection, in Sillitoe's view, between sport and the spirit
    of nationalism? (paras. 7-9)

4. According to Sillitoe, what impact does sport have on the social or political
    climate of a nation? (paras. 10-14)

5. What contrast does Sillitoe draw between competitive sport and what he
    calls "true sport"? (para. 15)

6. How, in Sillitoe's opinion, are both athletes and spectators affected by com-
    petitive sport? What sinister influence does he imagine might be exerted
    over a television audience? (paras. 16-19)

7. On what grounds does Sillitoe maintain that the Olympic torch is "a sym-
    bol of the oppression of the free human spirit" (para. 23)? What parallels
    does he draw between the Olympics and totalitarianism?

8. This essay was written after the murder of eleven Israeli athletes at the
    Munich Olympics in 1972. Why is Sillitoe so outraged that the Games
    should have been resumed after this event? (paras. 28-30) How does that
    resumption seem to him a confirmation of his views on competitive sport?

The Writer's Style and Strategy

1. What is Sillitoe's strategy in beginning an essay written in 1972 with a brief anecdote and an excerpt from a notebook, both dating from 1969?

2. Sillitoe offers an argument against competitive sport based on assertion and appeals to emotion rather than on factual evidence and logical reasoning. Pick out passages in which you feel that the appeal to emotion is particularly evident.

3. Note the use of "loaded" language (e.g., "so-called glory," "gold-plated tin medals," "his national ritual"). Choose some examples of such language, and discuss the intended effect.

4. What is the purpose of the description in paragraph 4 of the game called "kickshins"? Does it add anything to Sillitoe's thesis?

5. On what does Sillitoe base his argument that there is a correlation between victory or defeat in sport and events on the English political scene? (paras. 11-13) How convincing is this argument?

6. Discuss how Sillitoe's paragraph structures, sentence lengths, and word choice suit his purpose. How do they serve it convey his tone?

7. How would you characterize the tone of this essay? Does the tone change as the essay progresses?

Suggested Topics for Writing and Discussion

1. At several points, Sillitoe attacks the media for helping to foster the spirit of nationalism in competitive sport. Argue for or against Sillitoe's position, bringing supporting evidence from radio, T.V., or the print media.

2. Sillitoe maintains that the Olympic Games promote an unhealthy, warlike nationalism among competitors. Do you agree? What elements of the Games, if any, do you think should be changed?

3. Like Ken Dryden, in his essay "The Game," Sillitoe sees sport as a function of "big business." To what extent, in your view, has commercialism helped or hindered the development of sport?

4. Sillitoe concludes his essay by asserting that "true sporting spirit" is dead. Write an essay in which you explain what you mean by "true sporting spirit," and indicate whether you agree with Sillitoe.

5. Does competition build a strong character? Explain your view.

A Modest Proposal

For Preventing The Children of Poor People in Ireland, From Being a Burden to Their Parents or Country; and for Making Them Beneficial to the Public

by Jonathan Swift

It is a melancholy object to those who walk through this great town   1
or travel in the country, when they see the streets, the roads and cabin
doors crowded with beggars of the female sex, followed by three, four,
or six children, all in rags and importuning every passenger for an alms.
These mothers, instead of being able to work for their honest livelihood,
are forced to employ all their time in strolling to beg sustenance for
their helpless infants; who as they grow up either turn thieves for want
of work, or leave their dear native country to fight for the Pretender
in Spain, or sell themselves to the Barbadoes.

I think it is agreed by all parties that this prodigious number of children   2
in the arms, or on the backs, or at the heels of their mothers, and frequently of their fathers, is in the present deplorable state of the kingdom
a very great additional grievance; and, therefore, whoever could find
out a fair, cheap, and easy method of making these children sound and
useful members of the Commonwealth, would deserve so well of the
public as to have his statue set up for a preserver of the nation.

But my intention is very far from being confined to provide only for   3
the children of professed beggars; it is of a much greater extent, and
shall take in the whole number of infants at a certain age who are born
of parents in effect as little able to support them as those who demand
our charity in the streets.

As to my own part, having turned my thoughts for many years upon   4
this important subject, and maturely weighed the several schemes of
other projectors, I have always found them grossly mistaken in their
computation. It is true a child, just dropped from its dam, may be sup-

ported by her milk for a solar year, with little other nourishment; at most not above the value of two shillings, which the mother may certainly get, or the value in scraps, by her lawful occupation of begging; and it is exactly at one year old that I propose to provide for them in such a manner as instead of being a charge upon their parents or the parish, or wanting food and raiment for the rest of their lives, they shall on the contrary contribute to the feeding, and partly to the clothing, of many thousands.

5   There is likewise another great advantage in my scheme, that it will prevent those voluntary abortions, and that horrid practice of women murdering their bastard children, alas! too frequent among us, sacrificing the poor innocent babes, I doubt, more to avoid the expense than the shame, which would move tears and pity in the most savage and inhuman breast.

6   The number of souls in Ireland being usually reckoned one million and a half, of these I calculate there may be about two hundred thousand couples whose wives are breeders; from which number I subtract thirty thousand couples who are able to maintain their own children (although I apprehend there cannot be so many, under the present distresses of the kingdom); but this being granted, there will remain an hundred and seventy thousand breeders. I again subtract fifty thousand for those women who miscarry, or whose children die by accident or disease within the year. There only remain an hundred and twenty thousand children of poor parents annually born. The question therefore is, how this number shall be reared and provided for? which, as I have already said, under the present situation of affairs, is utterly impossible by all the methods hitherto proposed. For we can neither employ them in handicraft or agriculture; we neither build houses (I mean in the country) nor cultivate land; they can very seldom pick up a livelihood by stealing, till they arrive at six years old, except where they are of towardly parts; although I confess they learn the rudiments much earlier; during which time they can, however, be properly looked upon only as probationers; as I have been informed by a principal gentleman in the county of Cavan, who protested to me that he never knew above one or two instances under the age of six, even in a part of the kingdom so renowned for the quickest proficiency in that art.

7   I am assured by our merchants, that a boy or a girl before twelve years old is no saleable commodity; and even when they come to this age they will not yield above three pounds or three pounds and half a crown at most on the Exchange; which cannot turn to account either

to the parents or the kingdom, the charge of nutriment and rags having been at least four times that value.

I shall now therefore humbly propose my own thoughts, which I hope 8 will not be liable to the least objection.

I have been assured by a very knowing American of my acquain- 9 tance in London, that a young healthy child well nursed is, at year old, a most delicious, nourishing, and wholesome food, whether stewed, roasted, baked, or boiled; and I make no doubt that it will equally serve in a fricassee or a ragout.

I do therefore humbly offer it to public consideration that of the hun- 10 dred and twenty thousand children already computed, twenty thousand may be reserved for breed, whereof only one-fourth part to be males; which is more than we allow to sheep, black cattle, or swine; and my reason is, that these children are seldom the fruits of marriage, a circumstance not much regarded by our savages; therefore one male will be sufficient to serve four females. That the remaining hundred thousand may, at a year old, be offered in sale to the persons of quality and fortune through the kingdom; always advising the mother to let them suck plentifully in the last month, so as to render them plump and fat for a good table. A child will make two dishes at an entertainment for friends; and when the family dines alone, the fore or hind quarter will make a reasonable dish, and seasoned with a little pepper or salt will be very good boiled on the fourth day, especially in winter.

I have reckoned upon a medium that a child just born will weigh twelve 11 pounds, and in a solar year, if tolerably nursed, will increase to twenty-eight pounds.

I grant this food will be somewhat dear, and therefore very proper 12 for landlords, who, as they have already devoured most of the parents, seem to have the best title to the children.

Infant's flesh will be in season throughout the year, but more plenti- 13 ful in March, and a little before and after: for we are told by a grave author, an eminent French physician, that fish being a prolific diet, there are more children born in Roman Catholic countries about nine months after Lent than at any other season; therefore reckoning a year after Lent, the markets will be more glutted than usual, because the number of popish infants is at least three to one in this kingdom: and therefore it will have one other collateral advantage, by lessening the number of Papists among us.

I have already computed the charge of nursing a beggar's child (in 14 which list I reckon all cottagers, laborers, and four-fifths of the farmers) to be about two shillings per annum, rags included; and I believe no gentleman would repine to give ten shillings for the carcass of a good fat child, which, as I have said, will make four dishes of excellent nutritive meat, when he has only some particular friend or his own family to dine with him. Thus the squire will learn to be a good landlord, and grow popular among his tenants; the mother will have eight shillings net profit, and be fit for work till she produces another child.

15   Those who are more thrifty (as I must confess the times require) may flay the carcass; the skin of which artifically dressed will make admirable gloves for ladies, and summer boots for fine gentlemen.

16   As to our city of Dublin, shambles may be appointed for this purpose in the most convenient parts of it, and butchers we may be assured will not be wanting: although I rather recommend buying the children alive, and dressing them hot from the knife as we do roasting pigs.

17   A very worthy person, a true lover of his country, and whose virtues I highly esteem, was lately pleased in discoursing on this matter to offer a refinement upon my scheme. He said that many gentlemen of this kingdom, having of late destroyed their deer, he conceived that the want of venison might be well supplied by the bodies of young lads and maidens, not exceeding fourteen years of age nor under twelve; so great a number of both sexes in every county being now ready to starve for want of work and service; and these to be disposed of by their parents, if alive, or otherwise by their nearest relations. But with due deference to so excellent a friend and so deserving a patriot, I cannot be altogether in his sentiments. For as to the males, my American acquaintance assured me from frequent experience that their flesh was generally tough and lean, like that of our schoolboys by continual exercise, and their taste disagreeable; and to fatten them would not answer the charge. Then as to the females, it would, I think, with humble submission be a loss to the public, because they soon would become breeders themselves: and besides, it is not improbable that some scrupulous people might be apt to censure such a practice (although indeed very unjustly) as a little bordering upon cruelty; which, I confess, has always been with me the strongest objection against any project, how well soever intended.

18   But in order to justify my friend, he confessed that this expedient was put into his head by the famous Salmanaazor, a native of the island Formosa, who·came from thence to London above twenty years ago: and in conversation told my friend, that in his country when any young person happened to be put to death, the executioner sold the carcass to persons of quality as a prime dainty; and that in his time the body

of a plump girl of fifteen, who was crucified for an attempt to poison the emperor, was sold to his imperial majesty's prime minister of state, and other great mandarins of the court, in joints from the gibbet, at four hundred crowns. Neither indeed can I deny, that if the same use were made of several plump young girls in this town, who without one single groat to their fortunes cannot stir abroad without a chair, and appear at the playhouse and assemblies in foreign fineries which they never will pay for, the kingdom would not be the worse.

Some persons of a desponding spirit are in great concern about that **19** vast number of poor people, who are aged, diseased, or maimed, and I have been desired to employ my thoughts what cause may be taken to ease the nation of so grievous an encumbrance. But I am not in the least pain upon that matter, because it is very well known that they are every day dying and rotting by cold and famine, and filth and vermin, as fast as can be reasonably expected. And as to the young, labourers, they are now in as hopeful a condition: they cannot get work, and consequently pine away for want of nourishment, to a degree that if at any time they are accidentally hired to common labour, they have not strength to perform it; and thus the country and themselves are in a fair way of being soon delivered from the evils to come.

I have too long digressed, and therefore shall return to my subject. **20** I think the advantages by the proposal which I have made are obvious and many, as well as of the highest importance.

For first, as I have already observed, it would greatly lessen the **21** number of Papists, with whom we are yearly overrun, being the principal breeders of the nation as well as our most dangerous enemies; and who stay at home on purpose with a design to deliver the kingdom to the Pretender, hoping to take their advantage by the absence of so many good Protestants, who have chosen rather to leave their country than stay at home and pay tithes against their conscience to an idolatrous Episcopal curate.

Secondly, the poor tenants will have something valuable of their own, **22** which by law may be made liable to distress and help to pay their landlord's rent, their corn and cattle being already seized, and money a thing unknown.

Thirdly, whereas the maintenance of an hundred thousand children **23** from two years old and upwards, cannot be computed at less than ten shillings apiece per annum, the nation's stock will be thereby increased fifty thousand pounds per annum, beside the profit of a new dish introduced to the tables of all gentlemen of fortune in the kingdom who have any refinement in taste. And the money will circulate among ourselves, the goods being entirely of our own growth and manufacture.

24   Fourthly, the constant breeders besides the gain of eight shillings sterling per annum by the sale of their children, will be rid of the charge of maintaining them after the first year.

25   Fifthly, this food would likewise bring great custom to taverns, where the vintners will certainly be so prudent as to procure the best receipts for dressing it to perfection, and consequently have their houses frequented by all the fine gentlemen, who justly value themselves upon their knowledge in good eating; and a skilful cook who understands how to oblige his guests, will contrive to make it as expensive as they please.

26   Sixthly, this would be a great inducement to marriage, which all wise nations have either encouraged by rewards or enforced by laws and penalties. It would increase the care and tenderness of mothers towards their children, when they were sure of a settlement for life to the poor babes, provided in some sort by the public, to their annual profit instead of expense. We should soon see an honest emulation among the married women, which of them could bring the fattest child to the market. Men would become as fond of their wives during the time of their pregnancy as they are now of their mares in foal, their cows in calf, their sows when they are ready to farrow; nor offer to beat or kick them (as is too frequent a practice) for fear of a miscarriage.

27   Many other advantages might be enumerated. For instance, the addition of some thousand carcasses in our exportation of barreled beef, the propagation of swine's flesh, and improvement in the art of making good bacon, so much wanted among us by the great destruction of pigs, too frequent at our tables, and which are no way comparable in taste or magnificence to a well-grown, fat, yearling child, which roasted whole will make a considerable figure at a Lord Mayor's feast or any other public entertainment. But this and many others I omit, being studious of brevity.

28   Supposing that one thousand families in this city would be constant customers for infant's flesh, besides others who might have it at merry meetings, particularly weddings and christenings, I compute that Dublin would take off annually about twenty thousand carcasses; and the rest of the kingdom (where probably they will be sold somewhat cheaper) the remaining eighty thousand.

29   I can think of no one objection that will possibly be raised against this proposal, unless it should be urged that the number of people will

be thereby much lessened in the kingdom. This I freely own, and it was indeed one principal design in offering it to the world. I desire the reader will observe, that I calculate my remedy for this one individual kingdom of Ireland and for no other that ever was, is, or I think ever can be upon earth. Therefore let no man talk to me of other expedients: of taxing our absentees at five shillings a pound: of using neither clothes nor household furniture except what is of our own growth and manufacture: of utterly rejecting the materials and instruments that promote foreign luxury: of curing the expensiveness of pride, vanity, idleness, and gaming in our women: of introducing a vein of parsimony, prudence, and temperance: of learning to love our country, wherein we differ even from Laplanders and the inhabitants of Topinamboo: of quitting our animosities and factions, nor act any longer like the Jews, who were murdering one another at the very moment their city was taken: of being a little cautious not to sell our country and conscience for nothing: of teaching landlords to have at least one degree of mercy towards their tenants. Lastly, of putting a spirit of honesty, industry, and skill into our shopkeepers; who, if a resolution could now be taken to buy only our native goods, would immediately unite to cheat and exact upon us in the price, the measure, and the goodness, nor could ever yet be brought to make one fair proposal of just dealing, though often and earnestly invited to it.

Therefore, I repeat, let no man talk to me of these and the like expe-   30
dients, till he has at least a glimpse of hope that there will ever be some hearty and sincere attempt to put them in practice.

But as to myself, having been wearied out for many years with of-   31
fering vain, idle, visionary thoughts, and at length utterly despairing of success, I fortunately fell upon this proposal; which, as it is wholly new, so it has something solid and real, of no expense and little trouble, full in our own power, and whereby we can incur no danger in disobliging England. For this kind of commodity will not bear exportation, the flesh being of too tender a consistence to admit a long continuance in salt, although perhaps I could name a country which would be glad to eat up our whole nation without it.

After all, I am not so violently bent upon my own opinion as to re-   32
ject any offer proposed by wise men, which shall be found equally innocent, cheap, easy, and effectual. But before something of that kind shall be advanced in contradiction to my scheme, and offering a better, I desire the author or authors will be pleased maturely to consider two points. First, as things now stand, how they will be able to find food

and raiment for a hundred thousand useless mouths and backs? And secondly, there being a round million of creatures in human figure throughout this kingdom, whose whole subsistence put into a common stock would leave them in debt two millions of pounds sterling, adding those who are beggars by profession to the bulk of farmers, cottagers, and labourers, with the wives and children who are beggars in effect; I desire those politicians who dislike my overture, and may perhaps be so bold to attempt an answer, that they will first ask the parents of these mortals, whether they would not at this day think it a great happiness to have been sold for food at a year old in the manner I prescribe, and thereby have avoided such a perpetual scene of misfortunes as they have since gone through by the oppression of landlords, the impossibility of paying rent without money or trade, the want of common sustenance, with neither house nor clothes to cover them from the inclemencies of weather, and the most inevitable prospect of entailing the like or greater miseries upon their breed for ever.

33   I profess, in the sincerity of my heart, that I have not the least personal interest in endeavouring to promote this necessary work, having no other motive than the public good of my country, by advancing our trade, providing for infants, relieving the poor, and giving some pleasure to the rich. I have no children by which I can propose to get a single penny; the youngest being nine years old, and my wife past child-bearing.

(1729)

The Writer's Subject

1. How does the speaker demonstrate that the problems of poverty in Ireland have reached crisis proportions? (paras. 1-6)

2. What image of himself does the speaker project in the first six paragraphs of his Proposal? What clues are contained in the early paragraphs that might contradict that image?

3. What are the real values of the speaker, as revealed in paragraphs 7-9?

4. Why does the speaker propose to preserve only one male child to every four female children? (para. 10). How does this fit in with the speaker's general attitude to the poor of Ireland?

5. Who might be the speaker's "very knowing American acquaintance" in paragraph 9, and where is his identity made clearer?

6. At what points is the speaker's inhumanity most extreme?

7. What religious, economic, and social advantages does the speaker maintain would accrue to Ireland if his Proposal were to be implemented? (paras. 21-26)

8. What are the realities of life in Ireland, as these emerge from the Proposal? How are conditions in Ireland determined by its relation to England?

9. What is the function of the concluding paragraph? How does the final sentence undercut the speaker's intention?

The Writer's Style and Strategy

1. Why does Swift create a persona as the author of this Proposal? Would his intentions have been better served by a more direct attack on English policies in Ireland?

2. To what audience does the speaker address his Proposal, and what are its supposed values?

3. What effect is gained by delaying the revelation of the Proposal, with its details, until paragraph 10?

4. Discuss the speaker's use of statistics and his reference to authorities as ways of supporting his argument.

5. At what points in the essay does Swift's own voice seem to emerge from behind the mask? Why does Swift allow this to happen?

6. Irony consists in the reader's perception of a discrepancy between the appearance of things and their reality. Discuss the operation of irony in paragraph 17. What makes the speaker's references to his friend in that paragraph ironic?

7. How does Swift make the reader recognize that the inhumanity of the supposed writer is not so far removed from the real attitudes of the English rulers of Ireland?

8. Discuss the speaker's tone in this essay. Does the tone remain the same throughout, or does it change? Account for any shifts in tone.

Suggested Topics for Writing and Discussion

1. Choose an issue about which there has been some controversy (e.g. apartheid, the treatment of native Indians in North America, abortion, pornography) and offer a "Modest Proposal" to solve the problem.

2. Swift would have been horrified to see that the attitudes he burlesques
    through the speaker of "A Modest Proposal" have found grim expression
    in the twentieth century (e.g., Hitler's "final solution," Stalin's "purges,"
    South Africa's apartheid policy). Describe to Swift one or more of the
    horrors of modern history and the attitudes which gave rise to them.

3. Find one or two examples of writing that uses satire and/or humour in
    dealing with serious subjects. Do you think that humour is an appropriate
    means of dealing with topics of an horrific or disturbing nature? Are there
    any topics which you would consider a taboo subject, too sensitive to be
    treated in a humorous way?

Society and the Individual

The Game

by Ken Dryden

Once I used to wait in line like everyone else. Then one day a bank   1
teller motioned me out of the line, and I haven't been back in one since.
I feel no small guilt each time; nonetheless I continue to accept such
favours. For the tellers and me, it has become normal and routine. They
treat me the way they think people like me expect to be treated. And
I accept.

It is the kind of special treatment professional athletes have grown   2
accustomed to, and enjoy. It began with hockey, with teenage names
and faces in local papers, with hockey jackets that only the best players
on the best teams wore, with parents who competed not so quietly on
the side; and it will end with hockey. In between, the longer and better
we play the more all-encompassing the treatment becomes. People give,
easily and naturally. And we accept. Slippers, sweaters, plant holders,
mitts, baby blankets, baby clothes sent in the mail. Paintings, carv-
ings, etchings, sculptures in clay, metal, papier-mâché. Shirts, slacks,
coats, suits, ties, underwear; cars, carpets, sofas, chairs, refrigerators,
beds, washers, dryers, stoves, TVs, stereos, at cost or no cost at all.
After all, a special person deserves a special price. A hundred letters
a week, more than 3,000 a year − "You're the best," all but a few of
them say. On the street, in restaurants and theatres, we're pointed at,
talked about like the weather. "There he is, the famous hockey player,"
your own kids announce to their friends. In other homes, your picture
is on a boy's bedroom wall. Magazines, newspapers, radio, TV; hockey
cards, posters, T-shirts, and curios, anywhere, everywhere, name, face,
thousands of times.

3   And we love it. We say we don't, but we do. We hate the nuisance
and inconvenience, the bother of untimely, unending autographs, hand-
shakes, and smiles, living out an image of ourselves that isn't quite real,
abused if we fail to, feeling encircled and trapped, never able to get
away. But we also feel special — head-turning, chin-dropping, forget-
your-name special. What others buy Rolls-Royces and votes and hockey
teams for, what others take off their clothes for, what others kill for,
we have. All we have to do is play.

4   If exposure is the vehicle of celebrity, attention is what separates one
celebrity from another. Guy Lafleur and Yvon Lambert are both
celebrities, yet on the same ice, the same screen, Lafleur is noticed,
Lambert is not. Lambert, methodical and unspectacular, has nothing
readily distinctive about him. His image is passed over, his name
unheard. Lafleur *is* distinctive. The way he skates, the sound of the
crowd he carries with him, the goals he scores.

5   And so, too, others, for other reasons. Mario Tremblay, for his fiery,
untamed spirit; Bob Gainey, for his relentless, almost palpable will;
Tiger Williams, Eddie Shack, Ron Duguay, each colourful and exciting;
and Dave Schultz, once king of the mountain. As sports coverage pro-
liferates beyond games, as it becomes entertainment and moves to prime
time, as we look for the story behind the story, off-ice performance
becomes important. And so personas are born, and sometimes made,
and cameras and microphones are there as it happens. The crazies, the
clowns, the "sports intellectuals," the anti-jock rebels (Jim Bouton, Bill
"Spaceman" Lee), the playboys (Joe Namath, Derek Sanderson), each
a distinctive personality, each a bigger celebrity because of what he
does away from the game.

6   TV has given us a new minimum off-ice standard. The modern player
must be articulate (or engagingly inarticulate, especially southern style).
It's not enough to score a goal and have it picked apart by the all-seeing
eyes of replay cameras. A player must be able to put it in his own eloquent words. How did you do it? How did you feel? Live, on-camera
words that cannot be edited for the morning paper.

7   Celebrity is a full, integrated life, earned on-ice, performed, sustained,
strengthened, re-earned off-ice. As Roger Angell once put it, we want
our athletes to be "good at life." Role models for children, people we
want to believe earned what they have, every bit as good at things off
the ice as on. If they're inarticulate, harsh and pejorative, they're suddenly just jocks. Merely lucky, less likable, less good at life, less
celebrated; finally, they even seem less good *on* the ice.

At its extreme, the process creates the category of professional cele- **8**
brity, people "famous for being famous," so accomplished at being
celebrities that their original source of deity is forgotten. At the least,
it encourages all celebrities to learn the *skills* of the public person. How
to look good, how to sound modest and intelligent, funny and self-
deprecatory, anything you want. It's a celebrity's short-cut to the real
thing, but it works. Walter Cronkite *looks* trustworthy, Ronald Reagan
seems like a nice guy, Denis Potvin *sounds* intelligent; or is he only
articulate? Good enough at something to be a public person, or simply
a good public person? You'll never get close enough long enough to
know.

All around us are people anxious to help us look better. Not just flacks **9**
and PR types but a whole industry of journalists, commentators,
biographers, award-givers. Ghost-writers who put well-paid words under
our names, then disappear; charity organizers, volunteers who give time
and effort so that "honorary presidents," and "honorary directors" may
look even better. Children in hospitals, old folks in old folks' homes
— we autograph their casts, shake their hands, make them props to our
generosity and compassion. And never far away, photographers and
cameramen record the event. It is the bandwagon momentum of
celebrityhood.

In the end, for us, is an image. After thousands of confused messages, **10**
we cut through what is complex and render it simple. One image, concrete and disembodied. What agents call "Ken Dryden."

Recently, I asked an executive at an advertising agency to pretend **11**
he was trying to persuade a client to use me as a commercial spokesman
for his company. We'd met two or three times, several years before,
so he knew me mostly as others do. He wrote the following memo to
his client: "Historically I know you have had some concerns about using
an athlete . . . either because of potential problems developing out of
their careers and public life, or due to simply their lack of availability.
I think Ken is quite different from the rest. He is known as a thoughtful,
articulate and concerned individual. I think it would go without saying
he would not participate in any endorsation unless he was fully committed to and satisfied with the product. (His Ralph Nader exposures
would assure that.) He is serious, respected and appears to be very much
his own man. I don't think we could ever consider using him in humorous
or light approaches (like Eddie Shack) unless it would be by juxtaposi-
tion with another . . . actor or player. He has good media presence. . . .

His physical presence is also commanding. He is quite tall and impressive. . . . Other encouraging things would be his intelligence and
educational background. He would be more in tune with our target
audience with his credentials as a college graduate (Cornell) and a
fledgling professional person (law). Also, during production, I think
this intelligence and coolness would help in case of commercial production as well as helping to keep costs under control due to mental
errors. . . ."

12   So that's my image. Is it accurate? It doesn't matter. It's what people
think, it presupposes how they'll react to me. And for the ad man and
his client, how people will react is what matters.

13   If I don't like my image, I can do something about it. I can do things
that are "good for my image." I can stop doing things that are "bad for
my image." As actors remind us casually and often, I can do things
to change my image. Is it too serious? If I run around the dressing room
throwing water at the right moment, someone is bound to notice. A
journalist with a deadline to meet and space to fill, a new angle, news
– "Dryden misunderstood."

14   Want to be known as an antique collector? Collect an antique. A
theatre-goer? Go. Once is enough. Tell a journalist, sound enthusiastic,
and, above all, play well. Then stand back and watch what happens.
Clipped and filed, the news spreads like a chain letter, to other journalists who don't have time to check it out. Presto, it's part of your standard bio. And your image.

15   If you substitute the word "reputation" for "image," as you might have
done a few years ago, you'd have something quite different. A reputation is nothing so trifling or cynical. Like an old barge, it takes time
to get going. It's slow and relentless, difficult to manoeuvre, even harder
to stop. An image is nothing so solemn. It is merely a commercial asset,
a package of all the rights and good-will associated with "Ken Dryden"
– something I can sell to whomever I want.

16   But it's a sticky matter. For the image I'm selling is *your* image of
me. The good-will, though it relates to me, is your good-will. Whatever
commercial value there is in my name, my image, it's you who puts
it there. You like me or trust me, and any prospective buyer of my image,
anxious to put my name alongside his product, knows that and counts
on it to make you buy his product. And you might, even though it may
not be in your best interest. So by selling my name, I have perhaps
taken your trust and turned it against you.

17   I did a commercial once, six years ago. I'd decided I never would,

but this one was different enough to start a web of rationalizations until I forgot the point and accepted. A fast-food chain was looking for a winter promotion; Hockey Canada, the advisory and promotional body, wanted a fundraiser and a way to deliver the message to kids and their parents that minor hockey can be approached and played differently. The idea was a mini-book done by Hockey Canada, then sold through the restaurant chain. I was to be a collaborator on the book, and its public spokesman. But after doing the TV and radio ads (for the book, but with a corporate jingle at the end), and seeing the point-of-purchase cardboard likenesses of me in the restaurant, I realized my mistake.

Since then, I have turned down endorsements for, among other things, **18** a candy bar ("The way I see it, a full body shot of you in the net, mask up, talking, then we draw in tight on your catching glove, you open it, the bar's inside. . . ."), a credit card company ("You may not know me without my mask, but. . . ."), and a roll-on deodorant that would also be promoted by several other people whose names begin with the sound "dry."

It's a game — an ad game, an image game, a celebrity game — that **19** no one really loses. Everyone needs someone to talk about — why not about us? Everyone needs heroes and villains. We earn a little money, get some exposure. The commercials are going to be done anyway. Besides, it doesn't last long. A few years and images change, celebrity cools, it's over. It all evens out.

But it doesn't. We all lose, at least a little. We lose because you think **20** I'm better than I am. Brighter than I am, kinder, more compassionate, capable of more things, as good at life as I am at the game. I'm not. Off the ice I struggle as you do, but off the ice you never see me, even when you think you do. I appear good at other things because I'm good at being a goalie; because I'm a celebrity; because there's always some- one around to say I'm good. Because in the cozy glow of success, of good news, you want me to be good. It's my angle, and so long as I play well the angle won't change. I appear bright and articulate because I'm an athlete, and many athletes are not bright and articulate. "Like a dog's walking on his hind legs," as Dr. Johnson once put it, "it is not done well; but you are surprised to find it done at all."

But you don't believe that, just as I don't believe it about celebrities **21** I don't know. They're taller, more talented, more compassionate. They glitter into cameras and microphones, give each other awards for talent and compassion, "great human beings" every one. Wet-eyed I applaud, and believe. And all of us lose. You, because you feel less worthy than

you are. Me, because once, when I was twenty-three years old and trying to learn about myself, I wanted to believe I was, or soon would
be, everything others said I was. Instead, having learned much and grown
older, I feel co-conspirator to a fraud.

22   Professional athletes do exciting, sometimes courageous, sometimes
ennobling things, as heroes do, but no more than you do. Blown up
on a TV screen or a page, hyped by distance and imagination, we seem
more heroic, but we're not. Our achievement seems grander, but it isn't.
Our cause, our commitment, is no different from yours. We are no more
than examples, metaphors, because we enter every home; we're models
for the young because their world is small and we do what they do.

23   A few years ago, Joe McGinniss, author of *The Selling of the President, 1968*, wrote a book called *Heroes*. It sketches McGinniss's own
tormented trail from being *the youngest*, to *the highly acclaimed*, to
the former — all before he was thirty. At the same time, he ostensibly
searches for the vanished American hero. He talks to George McGovern
and Teddy Kennedy, General William Westmoreland, John Glenn,
Eugene McCarthy, author William Styron, playwright Arthur Miller
— some of them heroes of his, all of them heroes to many.

24   But it's like chasing a rainbow. He finds that, as he gets closer, his
heroes disappear. In homes and bars, on campaign trails, they're distinctly, disappointingly normal. Not wonderfully, triumphantly, down-to-
earth normal, but up-close, drinking-too-much, sweating, stinking,
unheroically normal. And for heroes, normal isn't enough. We are
allowed one image; everything must fit.

25   The Greeks gave their gods human imperfections. In the modern hero,
however, every flaw is a fatal flaw. It has only to be found, and it *will*
be. Moving from celebrity to hero is like moving from a city to a small
town. In a city, the camera's eye, though always present, is distant.
In a small town, there isn't that distance. There's no place to hide.

26   "Whom the gods would destroy," Wilfrid Sheed wrote in *Transatlantic
Blues*, "they first oversell." Superficially created, superficially destroyed
— for the hero, for the celebrity, it all evens out. Except a heavy price
is paid along the way. We all lose again. You, because, saddened and
hurt by heroes who turn out not to be heroes at all, you become cynical
and stop believing. Me, because I'm in a box. What is my responsibility? Is it, as I'm often told, to be the hero that children think I am?
Or is it to live what is real, to be something else.

27   Recently, a friend asked me to speak to his college seminar. Near
the end of two hours, we began to talk about many of these questions.

A girl raised her hand. She said that a year or two earlier, on the Academy Awards, she had seen Charlton Heston receive an award for his "humanitarian" work. Heston had made the point, the girl said, that thousands of volunteers had done far more than he, that they deserved the award.

I asked the class what that story told them about Charlton Heston. 28 That he's even modest, they decided. A few of the students laughed; then, one by one, several others joined in.

(1983)

The Writer's Subject

1. In the opening paragraph Dryden describes the guilt he feels in accepting favours. What is the source of this feeling, and where is it most explicitly discussed in this essay?

2. Why, according to Dryden, is an athlete's "off-ice performance" so important if he achieves celebrity status? (paras. 5-7)

3. Dryden argues that "celebrity" is really an image, "one image, concrete and disembodied." Who or what creates this image, and for what reasons? Is the presumed reader involved in this process in any way? (paras. 8-10)

4. According to Dryden, how difficult is it for celebrities to change their images? (paras. 13-15)

5. Why, after making one commercial, did Dryden decline to be further involved in the advertising of products? (paras. 17-18)

6. What loss is involved in accepting the "image" of the celebrity at face value? (paras. 20-26)

7. What does Dryden mean when he says "In the modern hero . . . every flaw is a fatal flaw" (para. 25)?

8. What is the dilemma of the professional athlete who attains celebrity? (para. 26)

9. What point is Dryden making with his concluding anecdote about Charlton Heston?

The Writer's Style and Strategy

1. How does Dryden's opening sentence prepare the reader for what is to follow?

2. What method of development does Dryden employ in paragraph 2 to demonstrate his assertion that professional athletes have grown accustomed to special treatment?

3. What effect does Dryden achieve by italicising "looks," "seems," and "sounds" in paragraph 8? By putting his own name, "Ken Dryden," in quotation marks in paragraph 10?

4. Why does Dryden provide actual excerpts from the advertising agency's description of him? (para. 11)

5. Why does Dryden use so many short sentences and fragments in paragraph 14? How does this particular paragraph contribute to the overall tone of the essay?

6. What figure of speech does Dryden use to illustrate the difference between "reputation" and "image"? (para. 15)

7. Why does Dryden repeat "game" so many times in the opening sentence of paragraph 19?

8. How would you characterize Dryden's attitude to his own celebrity? How is this attitude revealed throughout the essay?

Suggested Topics for Writing and Discussion

1. Discuss the distinctions Dryden perceives between "jocks," sports celebrities, and professional celebrities, providing your own examples. Can you think of any professional athlete who might fit into all of these categories?

2. Examine Dryden's discussion of the modern hero (note especially paragraphs 23-26). He says, ". . . for heroes, normal isn't enough"; do you agree with this view? What is the role of the hero in our society? Is heroism possible in modern times?

3. Choose an advertisement in print or on television that makes use of a celebrity from the worlds of sport or entertainment. What is the image of the celebrity that the advertisement conveys? How is that image intended to influence our view of the product? Indicate whether, in your opinion, the advertisement affirms Dryden's views about "the ad game."

My Wood
by E.M. Forster

A few years ago I wrote a book which dealt in part with the difficulties 1
of the English in India. Feeling that they would have had no difficulties
in India themselves, the Americans read the book freely. The more they
read it the better it made them feel, and a cheque to the author was
the result. I bought a wood with the cheque. It is not a large wood —
it contains scarcely any trees, and it is intersected, blast it, by a public
footpath. Still, it is the first property that I have owned, so it is right
that other people should participate in my shame, and should ask
themselves, in accents that will vary in horror, this very important question: What is the effect of property upon the character? Don't let's touch
economics; the effect of private ownership upon the community as a
whole is another question — a more important question, perhaps, but
another one. Let's keep to psychology. If you own things, what's their
effect on you? What's the effect on me of my wood?

In the first place, it makes me feel heavy. Property does have this 2
effect. Property produces men of weight, and it was a man of weight
who failed to get into the Kingdom of Heaven. He was not wicked,
that unfortunate millionaire in the parable, he was only stout; he stuck
out in front, not to mention behind, and as he wedged himself this way
and that in the crystalline entrance and bruised his well-fed flanks, he
saw beneath him a comparatively slim camel passing through the eye
of a needle and being woven into the robe of God. The Gospels all
through couple stoutness and slowness. They point out what is perfectly obvious, yet seldom realized: that if you have a lot of things you
cannot move about a lot, that furniture requires dusting, dusters require

servants, servants require insurance stamps, and the whole tangle of
them makes you think twice before you accept an invitation to dinner
or go for a bathe in the Jordan. Sometimes the Gospels proceed further
and say with Tolstoy that property is sinful; they approach the difficult
ground of asceticism here, where I cannot follow them. But as to the
immediate effects of property on people, they just show straightforward
logic. It produces men of weight. Men of weight cannot, by definition,
move like the lightning from the East unto the West, and the ascent
of a fourteen-stone bishop into a pulpit is thus the exact antithesis of
the coming of the Son of Man. My wood makes me feel heavy.

3   In the second place, it makes me feel it ought to be larger.

4   The other day I heard a twig snap in it. I was annoyed at first, for
I thought that someone was blackberrying, and depreciating the value
of the undergrowth. On coming nearer, I saw it was not a man who
had trodden on the twig and snapped it, but a bird, and I felt pleased.
My bird. The bird was not equally pleased. Ignoring the relation between us, it took fright as soon as it saw the shape of my face, and
flew straight over the boundary hedge into a field, the property of Mrs.
Henessy, where it sat down with a loud squawk. It had become Mrs.
Henessy's bird. Something seemed grossly amiss here, something that
would not have occurred had the wood been larger. I could not afford
to buy Mrs. Henessy out, I dared not murder her, and limitations of
this sort beset me on every side. Ahab did not want that vineyard —
he only needed it to round off his property, preparatory to plotting a
new curve — and all the land around my wood has become necessary
to me in order to round off the wood. A boundary protects. But — poor
little thing — the boundary ought in its turn to be protected. Noises
on the edge of it. Children throw stones. A little more, and then a little
more, until we reach the sea. Happy Canute! Happier Alexander! And
after all, why should even the world be the limit of possession? A rocket
containing a Union Jack, will, it is hoped, be shortly fired at the moon.
Mars. Sirius. Beyond which. . . . But these immensities ended by sad-
dening me. I could not suppose that my wood was the destined nucleus
of universal dominion — it is so very small and contains no mineral
wealth beyond the blackberries. Nor was I comforted when Mrs.
Henessy's bird took alarm for the second time and flew clean away from
us all, under the belief that it belonged to itself.

5   In the third place, property makes its owner feel that he ought to do
something to it. Yet he isn't sure what. A restlessness comes over him,

a vague sense that he has a personality to express — the same sense which, without any vagueness, leads the artist to an act of creation. Sometimes I think I will cut down such trees as remain in the wood, at other times I want to fill up the gaps between them with new trees. Both impulses are pretentious and empty. They are not honest movements towards money-making or beauty. They spring from a foolish desire to express myself and from an inability to enjoy what I have got. Creation, property, enjoyment form a sinister trinity in the human mind. Creation and enjoyment are both very very good, yet they are often unattainable without a material basis, and at such moments property pushes itself in as a substitute, saying, 'Accept me instead — I'm good enough for all three.' It is not enough. It is, as Shakespeare said of lust, 'The expense of spirit in a waste of shame': it is 'Before a joy proposed; behind, a dream.' Yet we don't know how to shun it. It is forced on us by our economic system as the alternative to starvation. It is also forced on us by an internal defect in the soul, by the feeling that in property may lie the germs of self-development and of exquisite or heroic deeds. Our life on earth is, and ought to be, material and carnal. But we have not yet learned to manage our materialism and carnality properly; they are still entangled with the desire for ownership, where (in the words of Dante) 'Possession is one with loss'.

And this brings us to our fourth and final point: the blackberries. 6

Blackberries are not plentiful in this meagre grove, but they are easily 7 seen from the public footpath which traverses it, and all too easily gathered. Foxgloves, too — people will pull up the foxgloves, and ladies of an educational tendency even grub for toadstools to show them on the Monday in class. Other ladies, less educated, roll down the bracken in the arms of their gentlemen friends. There is paper, there are tins. Pray, does my wood belong to me or doesn't it? And, if it does, should I not own it best by allowing no one else to walk there? There is a wood near Lyme Regis, also cursed by a public footpath, where the owner has not hesitated on this point. He has built high stone walls each side of the path, and has spanned it by bridges, so that the public circulate like termites while he gorges on the blackberries unseen. He really does own his wood, this able chap. Dives in Hell did pretty well, but the gulf dividing him from Lazarus could be traversed by vision, and nothing traverses it here. And perhaps I shall come to this in time. I shall wall in and fence out until I really taste the sweets of property. Enormously stout, endlessly avaricious, pseudo-creative, intensely selfish, I shall

weave upon my forehead the quadruple crown of possession until those
nasty Bolshies come and take it off again and thrust me aside into the
outer darkness.

(1926)

The Writer's Subject

1. Why does Forster begin his essay with an oblique reference to his novel
   Passage to India?

2. What does Forster mean by the phrase "men of weight" (para. 2)?

3. Summarize the four points which Forster makes about the effect of property. Are these points all of the same kind?

4. How does Forster demonstrate the absurdity of the property owner's attempt to lay claim to property, and of his desire for expansion? (para. 4)

5. Why, according to Forster, are the desires to chop down or to plant trees
   "not honest movements towards money-making or beauty" (para. 5)?

6. Explain what Forster means by saying "creation, property, enjoyment form
   a sinister trinity in the human mind" (para. 5).

7. Why does Forster give such prominence to the public footpath in Lyme
   Regis? (para. 7)

8. Who are the "nasty Bolshies" that Forster refers to in his closing sentence?
   Why does he say that they will throw him "into the outer darkness"?

9. While Forster restricts his discussion to his wood, he may be comment-
   ing on broader issues. What might these be?

The Writer's Style and Strategy

1. What is Forster's tone in the opening paragraph, and how does he establish
   it? Is it maintained throughout the essay? Discuss the appropriateness of
   Forster's tone to his topic.

2. How does Forster narrow his discussion of the very large topic of property?

3. Forster uses many allusions in this brief essay. What use does he make
   of the allusions to the Gospels (to the Rich Man in *Matthew* 19:24; to the
   story of Dives and Lazarus in *Luke* 16:19-31)? To the story of Ahab (in
   I Kings 21:17-29)? To Canute and Alexander? To Tolstoy and Dante?

4. Trace Forster's references to the blackberries. What purpose do these references serve? Comment on his use of a single-sentence paragraph to introduce the subject of the blackberries.

5. Comment on Forster's final sentence, its meaning, structure and tone.

Suggested Topics for Writing and Discussion

1. What is the effect of ownership on you?

2. Forster says that he may one day "wall in and fence out." Discuss one or two examples of walls that are used to bound international "properties" and discuss what the makers of the walls were or are hoping to wall in and fence out. You may wish to discuss real walls (e.g., the Great Wall of China, Hadrian's Wall, the Berlin Wall) or symbolic walls (e.g., the closed borders of Albania).

3. Forster uses very specific, concrete, and personal details to write on a highly abstract subject. Using Forster's method, write an essay on an abstraction which interests you (e.g., identity, loyalty, education, community, faith).

Thoughts on a Shirtless Cyclist, Robin Hood and One or Two Other Things

by Russell Hoban

1   The other day when I was going to my office in the morning I saw a man without a shirt riding a bicycle in circles at a traffic light and shouting unintelligibly. It was a chilly morning, so he must have been uncomfortable without a shirt on, and he wasn't a hippy. He looked like a workman, and he didn't look drunk. So it seemed to me that he must be having a mental breakdown of some sort.

2   I thought about it for a while, and then it occurred to me that maybe the man's mind wasn't breaking down. Maybe what had broken down was the system of restraints and conventions inside him that ordinarily made him keep his shirt on and not shout. That system, I think, is part of what could be called an inner society. The inner society has its ballrooms and bedrooms and kitchens, its shops and offices, its narrow alleys and its open places, its figures of authority and rebellion, of usage and surprise, love and hate, should and should not, is and isn't. As in the outer society, some things are done and some are not.

3   When I had thought that far, my next thought was that on that particular day man's inner society was rioting. The windows of the shops were being smashed, the offices were being deserted, and he was doing what he was doing.

4   My next thought was that the previous thought had been wrong: he was doing what he was doing because there were no rioters and no provision for riot in his inner society, and so there was no one for the job but him. His trouble, perhaps, was that his inner society was not suffi-

ciently different from the outer one: too many of the same things were done and not done. And having no interior colleague to whom he could assign the task or delegate the responsibility, he himself had to take off his shirt and ride in circles at a traffic light and shout. And it must have taken something out of him to do it.

Now my inner society, on the other hand, has always had that shirtless 5 shouting cyclist in it. I know him of old as I know myself, even though I hadn't given him much thought until I actually saw him in the outer world. So it isn't likely that I shall ever have to go out into the street and do that myself; he's always there to take care of it for me. There may, of course, come a day when I shall riotously put on a bowler hat and a neat black suit, buy a tightly furled umbrella, and mingle in wild silence with brokers in the city. One never knows what will come up.

Which brings me, by cobweb bridges perhaps invisible to the naked 6 eye, to a book I threw into an incinerator.

The book was *Robin Hood*. My edition, an American one, was bound 7 in what I think was Lincoln Green. I don't remember who it was that wrote that particular version of the story, but it had large black type and was illustrated by an artist named Edwin John Prittie with line drawings and paintings in full colour. I used to read that book up in an old wild-cherry tree, and it was the cosiest reading I can remember.

But there came a time when I got to be eighteen years old, and there 8 was a war, and I was going off to be a soldier, and it seemed to me that I had better stop being a child and be a man altogether. So I took *Robin Hood* and pitched it into the incinerator. It's a crime that I am driven to confess from time to time, as I do now.

When I came home from the war and found myself, surprisingly, 9 alive and having to go on with the business of growing up, I looked for that same edition that I had thrown away. Years later I found a copy. I haven't it with me now; it is gone again, lost in a removal. But I remember how it was when I held it in my hands again. There were all the pictures looking just as good as ever, and that whole dappled word-world of sun and shade with nothing lost whatever — Little John and Robin fighting on the plank bridge with their quarterstaves; the hateful Sheriff of Nottingham in his arrogance and his scarlet cloak; the beautiful Maid Marian and all the merry men in Lincoln Green; Robin in the *capul hide*, standing over the corpse of Guy of Gisborne. I've always liked the sound of the words *capul hide*: the skin of a horse, with the eyes of a man looking out through the eyeholes in the head — the skin of a dead beast hiding a live man, magical and murderous.

10   Obviously Robin Hood is a part of my inner society and has never stopped being in my thoughts, but it's only recently that I've become fully aware of how much he is to me, of how far the theme of that child's book has gone beyond childhood. Now as I think about him Robin Hood grows deeper and darker and stronger. Constantly he takes on new shadowy identities, and in his *capul hide* he sometimes evokes the dancing *Shaman* in the drawing on the cave wall at Les Trois Frères, sometimes Frazer's *Rex Nemorensis*, doomed King of the Wood, the killer waiting for his killer who will be next king.

11   In the absence of my found-and-lost-again edition I bought Roger Lancelyn Green's Puffin *Robin Hood*. On the title page was a stanza from the Alfred Noyes poem, *Sherwood*, and it gave me gooseflesh when I read it:

Robin Hood is here again: all his merry thieves
Hear a ghostly bugle-note shivering through the leaves. . .
The dead are coming back again, the years are rolled away
In Sherwood, in Sherwood, about the break of day.

12   I wanted it to be Sherwood again, about the break of day. I turned the pages, reading with impatience. But it wasn't the same. This book started with Robin Hood's birth, and I didn't want that, I wanted the opening that had been in the cherry-tree book of childhood, and it wasn't there and I couldn't remember it.

13   Then, on page 19 I found it − the incident in which the Sheriff of Nottingham and his men capture a serf who had killed a royal deer. The beginning of my book came back to me then, just like Proust's Combray − all at once and clear and vivid. 'Saxon hind' was what my book called the serf, and I could see the scene again as it first came to me through the passing leaves, the prisoner trussed up on the sledge like meat, helpless, rolling his eyes in terror as the Sheriff's foresters drag him to his death. Robert Fitzooth, not yet Robin Hood the outlaw, encounters the group and questions the Sheriff's men. The Chief Forester taunts him about the power of the bow he carries, doubts that such a stripling can wield such a weapon. Fitzooth shows his strength and skill with a long shot that brings down one of the King's deer. And with that he has fallen into the forester's trap − like the prisoner, he has forfeited his life with that shot. The Sheriff's men attempt to take him, but he kills some of them and frees the 'Saxon hind.' They escape into the greenwood, and the outlaw life of Robin Hood begins.

14   The light and the air of that first encounter have never left my mind,

and the sounds of the forest, the hissing of the sledge runners over the grass, the rattle of weapons, the shouts, the whizzing arrows. It is the metaphorical value of that action that has made it so memorable for me: the free and active wild self of the forest, armed and strong, freed the bound and helpless captive self and so became the outlaw self I recognized within me — the self indwelling always, sometimes kept faith with, sometimes betrayed.

Free and savage, the Robin Hood who has always walked the pathways   15
of my inner society has been exemplary — a standard and a reminder to the unfree and unsavage boy that I was, who lusted for that green-wood world: excellence was the price of Robin Hood's freedom, his untamedness, and his power. He was able to be what he was only because of his matchless skill; he was the archer who could shoot farther and truer than any other; he was a hero and a winner who had a thing that he could do better than anybody else.

Heroes who can do something well are still considered necessary for   16
children. And if many of today's books for grownups offer us a selec-tion of the infirm and the awkward, the losers who lap up defeat like chicken soup ladled out by a Jewish-mother kind of fate, we need those too: the composite hero of the collective, cumulative, juvenile-adult im-agination has got to have some antiheroism about him in order to be complete. Certainly anything that closes the gap between the real and the ideal makes the hero more useful for everyday reference — and here I can't help thinking about the god Krishna, who disported himself with fifty or sixty cowgirls at a wonderful party out on the meadow that lasted many nights, during which he made all the cowgirls think he was making love with each of them. But despite his divine powers — or because of them — he did it all with his mind, which I think is charming. A hero no better than the reader, however, will scarcely last a lifetime. And I think that heroes who excel and win all kinds of good things are the best kind. Myself, I can't use a mythology in which there is nothing to win and consequently nothing to lose. I have to have something to try for, and the more excellence I can manage the better I feel. In that respect Robin Hood has been a great help to me all my life.

Reading the Roger Lancelyn Green version, I realize that there was   17
a great deal more to the story and the archetypes than I had thought before. In my edition Marian was simply called Maid Marian, and nothing more was said about it. Once or twice as I grew older and more cynical I may have questioned the validity of her title. She was, after all,

presumably sleeping rough like everyone else in the outlaw band, and Robin being her lover, what could have been more natural than for them to sleep together? But Green spells it out and no mistake: Marian *was* a maid; she kept her virginity the whole time that she and Robin lived together in the forest. Although she had pledged herself to him the marriage was not to be consummated until the return of Richard the Lion-Hearted, the true and lawful king.

18   Robin Hood has no other woman that I ever heard of in any of the stories. So I have to think of him as celibate, as putting off the assumption of a full male role, as being less than a complete, grown-up man. He is asexual and pure, mercurial, airy almost, Ariel -like — a natural innocent, murderous but sweet-natured, light and quick. And he shares with Marian that mystical virtue that chastity confers, so useful for catching unicorns. The male and the female elements, the *yang* and the *yin* of this legend, are allied but not conjoined at the peak of their vigour, and when later a legitimate union is formed, they decline.

19   Robin Hood is more often with Little John than with Maid Marian. He and his giant companion are like a clean-cut, somewhat prim ego and id. They continually test and prove themselves, tempting fate, daring all comers, looking for trouble, never content with safety and boredom. They fight with quarterstaves at their first meeting; they quarrel from time to time; they rescue each other from capture; they compete with each other against the terrible strong beggar with potent quarterstaff and the bag meal that blinds the usually cunning Robin. And so they stay young and jolly until King Richard, the lawful ruler, the inevitable mature authority, returns.

20   And with that return Robin Hood is absorbed into grownupness and legitimacy. He is pardoned, and no more an outlaw; he is married, and no more a child-man. His best men are called into the service of King Richard. Robin Hood's power is drained off into the lawful self; the puissant youth becomes the waning man.

21   I'm no scholar, and I have no idea of the origin of the legend that is Robin Hood. What is inescapable is that the stone of the legend is worn into shape by the sea of human perception and need that continually washes over it. Legends, myth and fantasy both ask and tell us how life is, and there seems to be a strong need in us to think about the theme that is in *Robin Hood*: the absorption into law and order of that mysterious, chthonic, demiurgic power that we vitally need but cannot socially tolerate. We regret the loss of it and we rationalize the necessity

of that loss. We say to it, 'Yes, be there. But lose yourself in us at the proper time. Grow up.' But I wonder what the proper time is, and I wonder if the loss is necessary. And I wonder what growing up is. And I wonder whether young people now are not validly reconsidering and reshaping that theme, reclassifying it as well, so that the values assigned are no longer the same as those agreed upon until now. Maybe what we've always called growing up is sometimes growing down. It bears thinking about.

Robin Hood is only one development of that theme; there must be 22 many others. In *Great Expectations*, for instance, Magwitch, the outlaw self, is content to subsidize anonymously Pip, the lawful self. And it is Magwitch the outlaw who refines what is base and shallow in the respectable youth. Pip thinks that Miss Havisham is financing him, but the money that makes it possible for him to cut a dash as a young gentleman does not come from her decaying beauty, wealth and gentility, but from the starveling and tenacious humanity of what in us is violent, inchoate, unshapen and fit only to be put in prison.

Again, in Conrad's *Secret Sharer*, a young captain, a young lawful 23 authority in his first command, is appealed to by a young man who closely resembles him, a fugitive fleeing trial for killing a mate on another vessel. With characteristic genius Conrad opens his story with the unfledged captain taking the anchor watch alone at night on his ship that is still unfamiliar to him. He looks over the side and sees looking up at him from the water a face like his own, the face of a desperate swimmer. The captain shelters his criminal *doppelganger* aboard his ship during a period of self doubt before putting to sea. But when the barque leaves port the fugitive must be put ashore to take his chances alone. A wide-brimmed hat, given him by the captain as protection against the sun, falls into the water and becomes a sea mark by which the young master gauges the current while negotiating a difficult offing under sail in light and baffling airs.

The fugitive's hat gets the lawful master safely out to sea, but the 24 fugitive cannot go with the ship. Magwitch gives Pip what he can and dies. Robin Hood is killed by the establishment that has no use for him. The predatory church that he has always fought will take him in, ailing and ageing, will bleed him to death at the end by the hand of the treacherous Prioress of Kirkleys Nunnery. Robin Hood, supported by Little John, will loose his last arrow from his deathbed and be buried where it falls. Marian, first magical maid and then magicless woman, will become a nun and Prioress in her turn. Robin in the earth and she in the nunnery will both regain their innocence and power.

25   After the first reading of the book, the death and the last arrow were always there waiting for Robin Hood and me; he carried that death with him, carried that last arrow in his quiver always. He seems such a year-king! He seems, in his green and lightsome strength, always to hasten toward his sacrificial death that will bring forth from the winter earth another spring. And like a year-king, he must be given up, cannot be kept.

26   But I cannot give him up entirely. I think that we need our outlaw strength alive and brother to our lawful vigour. The one is not healthy without the other. I keep calling the elements outlaw self and lawful self, but that is unfair, really, to the essence of the thing. Society defines the terms of lawful and unlawful, because society makes the laws. And society is a retarded child with a loaded gun in its hands; I don't completely accept society's terms. Something in us makes us retell that myth; some drive there is in us to find and name the demon in us that is more real than laws and conventions that tell us what is right and what is wrong. And that demon is, I think, the radical spirit of life: it is the dark and unseen root system of our human tree whose visible branches are so carefully labelled and scientifically pruned by us. Maybe we think we don't need to know more about that nameless creative chaos, but we do, because in it we must find all real order. Polite gentlemen wearing suits and ties and with neat haircuts sit around tables with the death of the world in their briefcases, and they do not hesitate to tell us what is order. But to me it seems disorder. Other polite gentlemen some years ago sent up human smoke signals from the chimneys of crematoria, and they too defined order with great clarity. I think that fewer definitive definitions and many more tentative ones are needed now.

27   The fantasy of our legends, myths and stories helps with those definitions. It is as close as we can get to noumena through phenomena, as close as we can get to the thingness of things through the appearances of things. Fantasy isn't separate from reality; it is a vital approach to the essence of it. As to its importance, it is simply a matter of life and death. If we don't find out more about the truly essential thingness of things, then some future generation, if not this one, won't have anything left to find out about. So we must have fantasy constructed as scaffolding from which to work on actualities. And to work with fantasy is a risky business for the writer: it can change his whole world of actualities.

28   Which brings me back to the man on the bicycle, shirtless and

shouting. I was sorry for that man. I know how he felt. I wish he had been able to do something better with the baffled demon in him. I think he might have found something better to do if he had had more workable material in his mind, more useful people in his inner society. Robin Hood would have helped him, perhaps Captain Ahab too, and Lord Jim and Raskolnikov and goodness knows who else, functioning as surrogate actors-out of extreme and exaggerated degrees of the human condition. They might have taken on for him certain time-consuming and self-defeating tasks. They might have shown him other ways to be, might have freed him to do something more effective than what he was doing, might have helped him to find an identity in that wild surge of random creation that vanished into silence on the indulgent and indifferent air.

Well, you may say, perhaps that man wasn't a reader, and whatever 29 is in books won't help him. But books permeate both the outer and inner societies, moving through readers to non-readers with definitions and provision for societal roles, expectations and probabilities. Always more figures are needed to people our inner societies — personifications of all the subtly different modes of being, *avatars* of the sequential and often warring selves within us. Books in nameless categories are needed — books for children and adults together, books that can stand in an existential nowhere and find a centre that will hold.

(1971)

The Writer's Subject

1. What is the relevance of the opening anecdote of the shirtless cyclist to the essay as a whole?

2. Hoban gives prominence to the story of Robin Hood and his outlaws. What personal significance does he derive from the story? What meanings does he attach to it?

3. What connection is there between the outcome of the Robin Hood story and the growth of a child to adulthood? (paras. 19-21)

4. Why, according to Hoban, do we need a "composite hero" with anti-heroic as well as heroic qualities? (para. 16)

5. Why does Hoban think that "we need our outlaw strength alive and brother to our lawful vigour" (para. 26)?

6. Why does Hoban believe that fantasy is so important? (paras. 27-28)

7. Why does Hoban think that the shirtless cyclist might have done "something better with the baffled demon in him" if he had more experience of books? What importance does Hoban attach to books for the well-being of children and adults generally? (paras. 28-29)

The Writer's Style and Strategy

1. How does Hoban's title reflect the pattern of development of the essay?

2. Comment on Hoban's use of "riotously" in his statement, "There may, of course, come a day when I shall riotously put on a bowler hat and a neat black suit, buy a tightly furled umbrella, and mingle in wild silence with brokers in the City" (para. 5).

3. How does Hoban signal the shift from the introductory material to the main body of his essay?

4. Hoban alludes to a number of examples from literature in addition to *Robin Hood*. How does he use these to advance his thesis?

5. What figure of speech is Hoban employing when he says, "Maybe we think we don't need to know more about that nameless creative chaos, but we do, because in it we must find all real order" (para. 26)?

6. What is the dominant tone of this essay and how does Hoban create it? Identify places where the tone seems to shift, and account for the shifts.

Suggested Topics for Writing and Discussion

1. Discuss a book that was important to you in your childhood.

2. Hoban says that Robin Hood, as a symbol of excellence, has been a great help to him all his life. Choose another literary hero or heroine. Identify and discuss those qualities that you think make the character a helpful model.

3. Hoban says, "we must have fantasy constructed as scaffolding from which to work on actualities." Choose a work of fantasy in any genre (film, drama, literature, painting) and discuss the ways in which the work helps us to a better understanding of reality. Make clear your definition of fantasy at the outset.

4. "Maybe what we've always called growing up is sometimes growing down" (para. 21). Apply Hoban's comment to your own experience; do you think that your growth into adulthood has involved losses as well as gains? (You may wish to read Wordsworth's poem "Ode: Intimations of Immortality" for another view of this subject.)

The Shadow of Captain Bligh

by Hugh MacLennan

1 Not long ago, in the same evening, I listened to my gramophone recording of Haydn's *Mass for St. Cecilia* and then went upstairs and began
rereading the account of the mutiny on H.M.S. *Bounty* as written by
Nordhoff and Hall. The grand cadences of the Mass kept sounding
through my mind, and every now and then I stopped reading to let them
swell and subside. I was rereading the book for a purpose and I didn't
feel I could put it down. But the counterpoint made me realize with
a sensation of shock that Joseph Haydn and Captain Bligh were contemporaries, that the society that had produced and honoured the one
was the same society that had employed and respected the other.

2   Haydn's *Mass for St. Cecilia,* which was partially lost until Dr. Brand
recovered it little more than a decade ago, and which hardly anyone
had heard performed until it appeared recently in a recording of the
Haydn Society, is certainly one of the most sublime works the human
spirit has ever created. It seems to me worth all the music composed
since the death of Beethoven. Beethoven himself was never able to sustain
the power that is manifest here, for his struggle with himself and his
medium was too great. Haydn's Mass, like the greatest work of
Shakespeare, is at once majestic and intimate. Above all it seems ef-
fortless, and its joy and triumph are so breath-taking that no one who
is moved by music can easily listen to it without reflecting that our
modern world has produced no creative genius with his originality, his
joyousness, or his power.

3   Yet Haydn was not unique in his time. His career overlapped those
of Bach, Handel, Mozart, and Beethoven. Though his age acclaimed

him a master, it occurred to nobody in the eighteenth century to think
it miraculous that he was able to compose those immensely complex
works, some of great length, in so short a time. The best of his contemporaries were equally prolific and worked with equal speed. Handel
composed *The Messiah* in a few weeks and Mozart wrote one of his
most famous symphonies in a few days. Compared to these eighteenth-
century masters, a modern creative artist moves at a snail's pace. Our
most famous poets will die leaving behind only a slim body of published verse. The average modern novelist takes from two to three years
to write a single good novel. Our musicians — men like Sibelius, Stravinsky, and Vaughan Williams — have together, in their long lives, equalled
only a fraction of Haydn's output.

How lucky Haydn was to have lived before the radio and the telephone, 4
before civic societies which would have made exorbitant and unavoidable
demands on his time and energy, before publicity and interviewers and
income tax and traffic horns and metropolitan dailies — to have lived,
in short, before the age of distraction.

But *Mutiny on the Bounty* reminded me of the other side of the eigh- 5
teenth century. The very fact of Captain Bligh implies that the forces
which have made ours an age of distraction are far subtler and less
avoidable than technical innovations like the telephone and the radio.
Mutiny on the Bounty should be required reading for anyone who is
apt, like myself, to be romantic about past ages and to decry his own.
For Captain Bligh was just as typical of the eighteenth century as Haydn
was. When I bow before Haydn I must remember that Haydn accepted
without question and apparently without remorse the fact that he lived
in a world that contained Captain Bligh.

Nothing Mickey Spillane has ever written can be compared in horror 6
to some of the factual scenes in *Mutiny on the Bounty*. Few passages
in literature describe more revolting episodes than those of the *Bounty*
sailors being seized in the gangway and flogged until the flesh hung
in strips from their backs. With our modern knowledge of neurology,
we know that the agonies of these poor creatures did not end when the
boatswain's mate ceased swinging the cat. Such beating damaged the
nerve roots along the spine and condemned the victims to permanent
suffering. What makes those scenes of torture so unbearable to think
about is the added realization that they were not sporadic, were not the
offshoots of a psychopathic movement like Nazism, but were standard
practice in one of the most stable and reflective societies that ever existed.
Captain Bligh's cruelty had the weight and approval of his entire soci-

ety behind it. When the mutineers were later court-martialled, the court had no interest in determining whether Bligh had been cruel or not. It was interested solely in whether the accused had obeyed to the letter the harsh laws of the British Navy.

7   Haydn, Bach, Handel, and Mozart, sublime spirits full of mercy, with sensibilities exquisitely delicate, knew that men like Bligh were the mainstays of the societies they inhabited. Yet this knowledge, which to us would be a shame, felt personally, seldom if ever troubled their dreams or ruffled their serenity. The humanitarianism that disturbed Beethoven a generation later had not dawned when Haydn wrote the *Mass for St. Cecilia.*

8   Haydn reached his prime in the last moments when it was possible for a creative artist to mind his own business in the sense that his conscience could remain untroubled by the suffering of the unfortunate. If sailors were flogged to death and peasants had no rights, if a neighbouring country was ruined by famine or pestilence, if laws were unjust or princes cruel, none of it was Haydn's affair. He was compelled to no empathy in the suffering of others as modern artists are.

9   It is this awareness of personal responsibility for the welfare of strangers that makes uneasy all men of imagination today, that troubles their work and makes much of it seem tortured, that frustrates it, too, for seldom can a modern man of creative imagination do anything concrete to change the world he lives in.

10   Responsible only to himself, to his family, and to his God, Haydn enjoyed a freedom few artists have known since. The result was as glorious as it is inimitable. It is on most of his successors that the shadow of Captain Bligh has fallen and remained.

11   As Haydn represents the spiritual grandeur of the eighteenth-century imagination, Bligh represents its irresponsibility. In Bligh's own words, it was only through fear and cruelty that the stupid, the weak, the incompetent, the ignorant, and the unfortunate could be ruled and compelled to do what their masters considered to be their duty. Unless they were so compelled, the supporters of the system argued, there could be no fineness, no spiritual grandeur, no great literature or beautiful buildings, no masses for St. Cecilia. Civilization, as men of Haydn's day conceived it, could not exist if it yielded to the prompting of a social conscience.

12   When we realize this it becomes easier to reconcile ourselves to the fact that the world we live in is producing no more Haydns or Mozarts. In the nineteenth century men of imagination turned their attention to

the miseries of the world they saw about them, accepted responsibility for it, and forever lost the peace and concentration of spirit which enabled the Haydns and Mozarts to devote the full force of their genius to the realization of the gifts God had given them.

Could a modern artist witness a public flogging and then go home 13 and compose exquisite music? Could he even live quietly under a régime that permitted such atrocities and retain his own respect and that of others?

Merely to ask such questions is to answer them. Musicians who took 14 no more active part in the Hitler régime than perform for a Nazi audience have had to spend years as outcasts before western society would accept them again. The social conscience of today demands the service of every artist alive, and does not forgive him if he refuses it.

On the other hand western society did not make outcasts of the 15 physicists, chemists, and engineers who served Hitler. Until very recently science reserved for itself the same mental freedom that art enjoyed in Haydn's day. If politicians or monsters used the work of science for evil purposes, the scientists felt no personal responsibility. Enjoying such peace of mind, physicists and chemists have been able to devote the full force of their intellects to their work, and so their work has been more impressive than that of the artists who were their contemporaries. No wonder our age, when it looks for a genius to match Bach or Haydn, does not even stop to search among the ranks of the artists. It picks Einstein.

But when the atomic bomb fell on Hiroshima any number of scien- 16 tists succumbed to a social conscience as the artists had done long ago. Einstein, Oppenheimer, and hundreds of others were overcome with a Hamlet-like self-questioning. If our world lasts long enough it will be interesting to see whether science in the next generation will be as original and productive as it has been in the last three. For a conscience, as Shakespeare knew when he created Hamlet, inhibits action and beclouds genius. Our collective conscience may not have made the modern artist a coward, but it has certainly made him a prisoner.

Consider in contrast to Haydn the life of Albert Schweitzer. Schweitzer 17 began as a musician, and had he lived in the eighteenth century there is no knowing what masterpieces he might have composed. But his conscience would not permit him to devote his entire life to music, so he studied theology and became a minister of the Gospel. Then his conscience told him that preaching was not enough, so he studied medicine and became a doctor. His conscience then informed him that it was self-indulgent to practise medicine in a comfortable European city while there were millions in the world without medical care of any kind. So Schweitzer took his gifts to one of the most primitive parts of Africa. There he has lived and worked ever since, among men so elemental that they can know nothing of Bach or Haydn and cannot even guess at the greatness of the strange healer who came to help them.

18   Albert Schweitzer will die leaving behind him no tangible or audible monument, no record of objective achievement beyond a few books which are mere by-products of his life and interests. His enormous powers have been spread so widely in the service of others that neither as a musician, nor as a theologian, nor as a doctor-scientist, has his work, in itself, been such as to ensure his immortality. An earlier age would have said that Schweitzer had squandered his gifts on savages. But our age, rightly or wrongly, acclaims him as one of its noblest representatives because his life has translated into action, as hardly any other life has done, the highest aspirations of our social conscience.

19   No other modern artist I know of has made the total sacrifice of his talents that Schweitzer made; yet no modern artist (musician or poet or even the great individualist, Picasso) has been undisturbed by the social conscience of our day.

20   Critics who argue that the subject-matter of modern art is proof of the decadence of modern society don't really understand what they are talking about. Art has always been a reflection of the aspirations and obsessions of its time and the art of today is no exception. If it is haunted and distracted, if it is often ugly and even horrifying, it does not mean that the artists themselves are worse men than Haydn was. It means only that they have not refused, as Haydn did, to accept responsibility for Captain Bligh. For all its horrors, the twentieth century is better than the eighteenth; no politician or dictator who has tried to defy its conscience has been able, in the end, to succeed.

21   Some time in the future art may reflect the tranquillity that Haydn knew. If it does so, it will not be because those artists of the future are likely to be abler men than artists of today. It will happen because, after this age of transition, the shadow of Captain Bligh has been removed from the whole world.

                                                                          (1953)

The Writer's Subject

1. Why did MacLennan feel shock at the realization that the same society had produced both Haydn and Captain Bligh? (paras. 1-7)

2. What contrast does MacLennan draw between the productivity of eighteenth-century artists and that of modern artists? (para. 3)

3. What does MacLennan find most disturbing about the treatment of the sailors on the *Bounty*? (para. 6)

4. Why, in MacLennan's view, were artists such as Haydn not disturbed by the savagery of the world around them? What does MacLennan mean when he says that the shadow of Captain Bligh has fallen not on Haydn but on his successors? (para. 7-11)

5. Why does MacLennan think it is no longer possible for the world to produce any more Haydns or Mozarts? (paras. 12-14)

6. What contrast does MacLennan draw between the achievements of modern artists and those of modern scientists? (para. 15)

7. MacLennan says that today scientists, like artists, have become prisoners of conscience. How does he demonstrate this point? (para. 16)

8. What is MacLennan's attitude to Haydn?

The Writer's Style and Strategy

1. Explain the meaning of "counterpoint" as MacLennan uses it in the first paragraph.

2. How does MacLennan establish the contrast between the two sides of eighteenth-century life? How does MacLennan signal the shift in his discussion from the one to the other?

3. MacLennan's essay works, in part, on the principle of cause and effect. That is, because Haydn was not distracted by his society he could produce great works. What other instances of cause and effect are evident in this essay?

4. Despite the extensive use of detail and supporting examples, this essay relies heavily upon assertions or generalizations to convey a very personal impression of the relationship between art and life. Find one or two examples of such assertions or generalizations; examine the assumptions that underlie them; and comment on their persuasiveness, or lack of it.

Suggested Topics for Writing and Discussion

1. MacLennan suggests that modern artists can seldom do anything concrete to change the world they live in. Do you agree?

2. MacLennan chooses Haydn as representative of the great artists of the eighteenth century. Choose another artist (e.g., painter, writer, architect, composer) either from a past age or from our own time, and show why, in your view, this artist represents his or her age.

3. Do you agree with MacLennan's view that the development of a social conscience in modern times has made the production of great art an impossibility?

4. "Art has always been a reflection of the aspirations and obsessions of its time and the art of today is no exception." Choose a well-known work of twentieth-century art in any medium and explain how the work reflects the concerns of its time.

5. MacLennan uses Captain Bligh as a symbol of evil in the eighteenth century. Write an essay about the dark side of the twentieth century and focus on one individual as a symbol of the evil of the age.

Confessions of a Wood-Chopping Man
by Hugh MacLennan

Pleasure, profit, and beauty from a single afternoon's exercise – what 1
more could a puritan ask, especially when the profit will not be reaped
till next year, and the beauty harvested for years to come. As for the
pleasure, merely to be alive on an Indian-summer afternoon in my part
of the country is as close to heaven as my imagination extends.

After the first frost has turned ferns to brown dust and the birds have 2
flocked south, the woods around my house in the country are filled with
the living presence of silence. My feet crunch outrageously in the dry
undergrowth as I make my way to the heart of the grove. My jeans
are stiff with ancient sweat and my jersey is out at the elbows, the red
paint has long ago been rubbed off the bow of my Swedish saw and
my axe blade, several ounces lighter than when I bought it nine years
ago, is honed sharp enough to sever a hair on my forearm. Looking
up to the sky through the leaf-patterns I shame my environment by the
academic thought that this scene is the equal of Sainte-Chapelle, but
the comparison lasts only a few seconds. A hardwood copse in the
Eastern Townships of Quebec in Indian summer can be compared to
nothing else on this earth, being itself an absolute. By some recurring
good fortune I am here; I am here with the axe, the saw, the wedge,
and the determination to alter the landscape a little. It is a moment that
involves every aspect of the slow change in my whole view of life over
the past decade and a half.

I was born and raised in a part of Canada where nobody is able to 3
change the landscape. Along the Atlantic coast of Nova Scotia you grow
up with the conviction that everything in nature here is as it is forever,
and that man, living with the shifting immutability of the ocean and

the unshifting immutability of granite rocks, can never dominate his fate, never play artist with nature, but must take life and the world as he finds them. The glacier that set the mould of the Nova Scotia coast (and the coast set the mould of the Nova Scotian character) so denuded the rocks of topsoil that for evermore only a spruce will thrive there. From childhood I accepted the belief that summer, spring, and fall are much the same. One is grateful for a spruce if it is the only tree one really knows, but since any spruce is much the same as any other, and since no spruce ever changes its colours, the trees of my childhood helped the granite and the ocean to confirm me in the belief that nature can neither be altered nor improved.

4   It took me a good many years to respond to the soft luxuriance of the Eastern Townships, where the eye, the ear, and the sense of smell are played upon gently and with subtle variations. It took me no time at all, however, to learn that here the landscape can and must be altered from time to time because it is continually altering itself to your disadvantage. A house in the country for summer living must be tied to the earth by close planting of shrubs and trees, to give protection from the winds and to take away its aspect of being a brash intruder. But a maple sapling grows eight feet a year in this rich, rainy land, and a small fir that looks like an incipient Christmas tree when you transplant it soon becomes a dense screen breeding swarms of blackflies. Where there was one butternut there is soon a grove, and within a decade the pasture in which your house was built has been taken over by a stand of maples, oaks, poplars, wild cherries, honey locusts, old apple trees, hornbeams, birches, beeches, and even some stray pines. Their roots are now under your cottage, their branches are joined over your roof, and they have made your home as dark as an animal's den.

5   The year I bought my house, I cut away every cedar, pine, and spruce that crowded it. This was an act with a double meaning for me. I intended to let the sun filter down through the branches of the great hardwoods farther back, and I also needed a symbol of emancipation from the stern acceptance of my youth, I suppose.

6   "You'll feel naked without some kind of protection, won't you?" said a neighbour. "Now there's only the garden and the lawn between you and the road."

7   He meant that he would; I felt as though cobwebs had been swept from a dirty window. What good to keep other people from looking in, if at the same time I was prevented from looking out? Anyway, I live high on a hill away from the village, on a dirt road that leads to

nowhere, and the passers-by are few and friendly. Since my land slopes at a twenty-five-degree angle and the road is below the house, I can overlook any activity on the road and let my eye take in a view that extends for ten miles over a deep lake indented with bays that lap the feet of thrusting hills. I can look across wind-blown farms and red-pine headlands and the shining roofs of new cattle barns.

I began to cut in order to get sun and air into the house and I con- **8** tinued to cut in order to get sun and air into the surrounding woods. The second year I was mildly surprised to discover that the wood I cut had saved me many dollars. Then I bought a lot across the road and down the hill to protect our view. But the view gradually disappeared behind a wall of rapidly growing trees. They were a fine mixture of greens in summer and an unbelievable blend of colours in the fall, but living with them in front of me was like living behind a seventy-foot hedge.

So, over the years, those rapidly growing trees have given a pattern **9** to my life in much the same way that his rotating wheatfields pattern the life of the farmer. Come the fall and I must get to work on them.

I have a neighbour who thinks it a crime to cut any oak, but what **10** do you do if you have two oaks within six feet of one another? I run my hand over the smooth, olive-green trunk and feel the hard muscles inside the bark. An oak, especially a young one, feels human when your hand strokes it. But more than any tree in the forest, the oak needs room to grow. Its roots spread wide and lie close to the surface of the earth. I look up at this pair and see that they have grown like basketball players, tall, thin, and not much good for anything else but growing tall and thin. Their lowest branches are at least twenty-five feet above the ground, since it was always dark in here before I got busy cutting out the saplings, and the trees had to thrust high in order to reach the life-giving sun. I feel the trunks of both and decide that the spindlier one must go, to give the other a chance to fulfil the destiny of an oak.

So I go down on both knees, set the saw at the trunk of the victim, **11** and get to work. In such a close-grained tree the opening made by the slim saw-blade is almost invisible once the saw has buried itself in the trunk. White dust spurts out, to become brown as the blade reaches the darker heart of the tree. Then comes the crack — hard, solid, vibrating up the entire length of the trunk and echoing through the silent copse. There is a shiver, a twitch in the pinky-brown plumage, a moment of hesitation. As I stand up and watch, one hand on the trunk, the tree nods in the direction I had intended it to fall, then goes down in a swooshing, stately plunge. There is a flash of scarlet as a maple is brushed on the way down. Inevitably the oak comes to rest at an angle, its cascading upper branches caught by the interlocking branches of neighbouring trees.

12   In the new silence I consider my next move. A fallen tree, even one as modest as this, creates a sizable wreckage. I think of Mr. Gladstone, who used to slay giant oaks, Royal Navy oaks, to relieve his emotions. When Disraeli was extraordinarily witty or the Queen ordinarily rude, another oak on the estate of the Grand Old Man was doomed to fall. And then there was the labour of cleaning up the mess, a job that I know from experience must have taken days. So far as I can discover from my reading, the Prime Minister gave little thought to this aspect of forestry. He was able to sate his aggressions and stalk off, sweaty under the armpits but with his Victorian waistcoat still in place, while humbler men took over the long task of trimming the oak, sawing its trunk into logs, splitting them and trundling them into the woodshed. Humbler men without the need to sublimate a libido must have stacked and burned Mr. Gladstone's slash.

13   Perhaps the psychiatrist who lives below me on his own tree-enclosed acreage, hearing the crash of my falling oak, thinks I am ridding myself of aggressions, too. He may even think I am slaying a father-image. But no matter what he thinks, my oak has merely been severed at the base, it has not been transformed into cordwood.

14   It was cold last night. It was colder still at six this morning when I peered out at the thermometer and saw that the mercury stood at twenty-seven degrees. When I got out of bed at eight and built a fire there was still rime on the lawn. The day was fine and clear, but it was so cold my fireplace consumed ten logs before one o'clock. This year a short cord sells at seven dollars, a long cord at anything from fifteen to twenty, depending on what kind of wood it contains. No matter what my wood-pile represents to a psychologist, it gives me an intense pleasure to use it for warmth, even though (as the country-woman remarked yesterday when she came in to clean the house) it takes a lot of sweat to build a woodpile.

15   I think, sometimes, that Mr. Gladstone missed the best part of tree-cutting. Each fallen tree presents its own problems, and the man who walks off and leaves them is as bad a tree-butcher as the one who murders a copse with a power saw. This oak of mine is entangled with two other trees and of course the simplest thing to do is cut them both down so that all three are prone. But the tree supporting the oak on the left is

a rowan, a fugitive from an old garden, probably, and under no circumstances, under absolutely none, will I cut a rowan tree in my own woods. The other is a rock maple, a tree which still fills me with wonder and joy because it was scarce in Nova Scotia, and in England almost non-existent. I always have a twinge of conscience when I cut down a maple. But here the maples grow like weeds and this particular one is so close to the rowan it will rob it of nutriment as both try to grow. So the maple goes, and the crack of its fall echoes over the hill.

Still the oak is suspended; when the maple went, its weight was taken   **16** by more stuff beyond. There is nothing for it but to cut the oak down to size in the only way left. I start sawing the trunk in eight-foot lengths, each cut about four and a half feet above the ground, which is as high as I can drive the saw. With the entire tree exerting hundreds of pounds of pressure on the saw blade, I must use the wedge. And this means that for the rest of the afternoon these two trees, the oak and the maple, are going to keep me busy.

Toward sunset the logs are piled and split and fragrant, the slash   **17** dragged off into a great angular pile to dry and await my pleasure on a future moist day. I come out of the copse and look to see what effect my work has made on the landscape. A little, and the beginning of a lot, because a splendid butternut has now been uncovered and must be given its chance. With that poplar out of the way the sun will slant deeply into the copse and I will have the beginnings of a woodland nave. A forest without sun is like a church without God; I reflect that the thought is corny, but I don't care. Disposing of the poplar will put no burden on my conscience. Along with a ragged spruce, it exists to be destroyed, for if the axe doesn't get to it the insects will, and after the insects will come the flickers and the pileated woodpeckers. Tomorrow afternoon's work is now planned, and it, in turn, will lead to the work of the day after and the day after that. Carving out the raw material of a forest to create a civilized wood is like making a picture or writing a book. One vista suggests another and there is no absolute end to it in a country like ours. But when the season's cutting is over after Thanksgiving, and I go muscle-bound back to the city, I feel as Melville did when he finished *Moby Dick*, as pure as the lamb.

(1956)

The Writer's Subject

1. Why does MacLennan draw attention to himself as a "puritan"? What does this tell us about his attitudes to work and pleasure?

2. What led MacLennan in his youth to believe that landscape could not be changed? What made him change his mind?

3. Why did MacLennan feel the need to cut away the trees crowding his house?

4. What is the relevance of MacLennan's reference to the tree-cutting activities of Mr. Gladstone? Why does he think that Gladstone "missed the best part of tree-cutting" (para. 15)?

5. Why would a psychiatrist possibly interpret MacLennan's tree-cutting as "slaying a father image"?

6. What do you understand by MacLennan's statement that "a forest without sun is like a church without God"?

The Writer's Style and Strategy

1. At the beginning of the essay MacLennan draws a comparison between the beauty of the wooded landscape and of Sainte-Chapelle, a gothic church in Paris which is famous for its stained glass windows and light-filled interior. How does MacLennan develop the church-like qualities of the forest elsewhere in the essay?

2. How does MacLennan convey the differences between the landscape of Nova Scotia and that of Quebec's Eastern Townships?

3. Why does MacLennan mention his neighbour? (para. 6 and 10)

4. What details in paragraph 10 tell the reader about MacLennan's attitude to trees?

5. How does MacLennan convey his indignation towards those who do not share his feelings about the forest landscape? (para. 15)

6. This personal essay deals with highly individual views and experiences. How does MacLennan succeed in giving this essay broader interest and significance?

Suggestions for Writing and Discussion

1. In paragraph 11, MacLennan describes the activity of felling a tree. Describe a similar, commonplace activity (e.g., rigging a sail, preparing skis for the season, cleaning out your refrigerator, washing and polishing your car) and show what it reveals about your own attitudes.

2. Write an essay about an unusual interest you may have — a hobby, a pastime, an academic pursuit, or a sports activity. Aim to share your enthusiasm with your reader.

3. Describe a particular landscape in detail and make clear what personal significance this landscape (or features of the landscape) holds for you.

Specifications for a Hero
by Wallace Stegner

1   In our town, as in most towns, everybody had two names — the one his parents had given him and the one the community chose to call him by. Our nicknames were an expression of the folk culture, and they were more descriptive than honorific. If you were underweight, you were called Skinny or Slim or Sliver; if overweight, Fat or Chubby; if left-handed, Lefty; if spectacled, Four Eyes. If your father was the minister, your name was Preacher Kid, and according to the condition and color of your hair you were Whitey, Blacky, Red, Rusty, Baldy, Fuzzy, or Pinky. If you had a habit of walking girls in the brush after dusk, you were known as Town Bull or T.B. If you were small for your age, as I was, your name was Runt or Peewee. The revelation of your shape at the town swimming hole by the footbridge could tag you for life with the label Birdlegs. The man who for a while ran one of our two grocery stores was universally known as Jew Meyer.

2   Like the lingo we spoke, our nicknames were at odds with the traditional and educational formalisms; along with them went a set of standard frontier attitudes. What was appropriate for Jimmy Craig in his home or in church or in school would have been shameful to Preacher Kid Craig down at the bare-naked hole. When we were digging a cave in the cutbank back of my house, and someone for a joke climbed up on top and jumped up and down, and the roof caved in on P.K. and he had to be dug out and revived by artificial respiration, even P.K. thought the hullabaloo excessive. He did not blame us, and he did not tattle on anyone. His notions of fortitude and propriety — which were at the other end of the scale from those of his parents — would not have let him.

When we first arrived in Whitemud the Lazy-S was still a working 3
ranch, with corrals, and calves, and a bunkhouse inhabited by heroes
named Big Horn, Little Horn, Slivers, Rusty, and Slippers. There was
a Chinese cook named Mah Li, who had been abused in imaginative
ways ever since he had arrived back at the turn of the century. In the
first district poll for a territorial election, in 1902, someone had taken
Mah Li to the polls and enfranchised him on the ground that, having
been born in Hong Kong, he could swear that he was a British subject
and was not an Indian, and was hence eligible to vote. When I knew
him, he was a jabbering, good-natured soul with a pigtail and a loose
blue blouse, and I don't suppose a single day of his life went by that
he was not victimized somehow. He couldn't pass anybody, indoors
or out, without having his pigtail yanked or his shirt tails set on fire.
Once I saw the cowboys talk him into licking a frosty doorknob when
the temperature was fifteen or twenty below, and I saw the tears in his
eyes, too, after he tore himself loose. Another time a couple of Scandinavians tried to get him onto a pair of skis on the North Bench hill.
They demonstrated how easy it was, climbed up and came zipping by,
and then offered to help his toes into the straps. But Mah Li was too
many for them that time. "Sssssssssss!" he said in scorn. "Walkee half
a mile back!" When I was ten or eleven Mah Li was a friend of mine.
I gave him suckers I caught in the river, and once he made me a present of a magpie he had taught to talk. The only thing it could say was
our laundry mark, the number O Five, but it was more than any other
magpie in town could say, and I had a special feeling for Mah Li because
of it. Nevertheless I would have been ashamed not to take part in the
teasing, baiting, and candy-stealing that made his life miserable after
the Lazy-S closed up and Mah Li opened a restaurant. I helped tip over
his backhouse on Hallowe'en; I was part of a war party that sneaked
to the crest of a knoll and with .22 rifles potted two of his white ducks
as they rode a mud puddle near his shack in the east bend.

The folk culture sponsored every sort of crude practical joke, as it 4
permitted the cruelest and ugliest prejudices and persecutions. Any visible
difference was enough to get an individual picked on. Impartially and
systematically we persecuted Mah Li and his brother Mah Jim, Jew
Meyer and his family, any Indians who came down into the valley in
their wobble-wheeled buckboards, anyone with a pronounced English
accent or fancy clothes or affected manners, any crybaby, any woman
who kept a poodle dog and put on airs, any child with glasses, anyone
afflicted with crossed eyes, St. Vitus's dance, feeble-mindedness, or

a game leg. Systematically the strong bullied the weak, and the weak did their best to persuade their persecutors, by feats of courage or endurance or by picking on someone still weaker, that they were tough and strong.

5   Immune, because they conformed to what the folk culture valued, were people with Texas or Montana or merely Canadian accents, people who wore overalls and worked with their hands, people who snickered at Englishmen or joined the bedevilment of Chinamen, women who let their children grow up wild and unwashed. Indignation swept the school one fall day when the Carpenter kids were sent home by the new teacher from Ontario. She sent a note along with them saying they had pediculosis and should not return to school until they were cured. Their mother in bewildered alarm brought them in to the doctor, and when she discovered that pediculosis meant only the condition of being lousy, she had to be restrained from going over and pulling the smart-alec teacher's hair out. We sympathized completely. That teacher never did get our confidence, for she had convicted herself of being both overcleanly and pompous.

6   Honored and imitated among us were those with special skills, so long as the skills were not too civilized. We admired good shots, good riders, tough fighters, dirty talkers, stoical endurers of pain. My mother won the whole town because once, riding our flighty mare Daisy up Main Street, she got piled hard in front of Christenson's pool hall with half a dozen men watching, and before they could recover from laughing and go to help her, had caught the mare and remounted and ridden off, tightly smiling. The fact that her hair was red did not hurt: among us, red hair was the sign of a sassy temper.

7   She was one of the immune, and so was my father, for both had been brought up on midwestern farms, had lived on the Dakota frontier, and accepted without question — though my mother would have supplemented it — the code of the stiff upper lip. She had sympathy for anyone's weakness except her own; he went strictly by the code.

8   I remember one Victoria Day when there was a baseball game between our town and Shaunavon. Alfie Carpenter, from a riverbottom ranch just west of town, was catching for the Whitemud team. He was a boy who had abused me and my kind for years, shoving us off the footbridge, tripping us unexpectedly, giving us the hip, breaking up our hideouts in the brush, stampeding the town herd that was in our charge, and generally making himself lovable. This day I looked up from something just in time to see the batter swing and a foul tip catch

Alfie full in the face. For a second he stayed bent over with a hand over his mouth; I saw the blood start in a quick stream through his fingers. My feelings were very badly mixed, for I had dreamed often enough of doing just that to Alfie Carpenter's face, but I was somewhat squeamish about human pain and I couldn't enjoy seeing the dream come true. Moreover I knew with a cold certainty that the ball had hit Alfie at least four times as hard as I had ever imagined hitting him, and there he stood, still on his feet and obviously conscious. A couple of players came up and took his arms and he shook them off, straightened up, spat out a splatter of blood and teeth and picked up his mitt as if to go on with the game. Of course they would not let him — but what a gesture! said my envious and appalled soul. There was a two-tooth hole when Alfie said something; he freed his elbows and swaggered to the side of the field. Watching him, my father broke out in a short, incredulous laugh. "Tough kid!" he said to the man next, and the tone of his voice goose-pimpled me like a breeze on a sweaty skin, for in all my life he had never spoken either to or of me in that voice of approval. Alfie Carpenter, with his broken nose and bloody mouth, was a boy I hated and feared, but most of all I envied his competence to be what his masculine and semi-barbarous world said a man should be.

As for me, I was a crybaby. My circulation was poor and my hands 9 always got blue and white in the cold. I always had a runny nose. I was skinny and small, so that my mother anxiously doctored me with Scott's Emulsion, sulphur and molasses, calomel, and other doses. To compound my frail health, I was always getting hurt. Once I lost both big-toe nails in the same week, and from characteristically incompatible causes. The first one turned black and came off because I had accidentally shot myself through the big toe with a .22 short; the second because, sickly thing that I was, I had dropped a ten-pound bottle of Scott's Emulsion on it.

I grew up hating my weakness and despising my cowardice and try- 10 ing to pretend that neither existed. The usual result of that kind of condition is bragging. I bragged, and sometimes I got called. Once in Sunday School I said that I was not afraid to jump off the high diving board that the editor of the Leader had projected out over the highest cut-bank. The editor, who had been a soldier and a hero, was the only person in town who dared use it. It did not matter that the boys who called my bluff would not have dared to jump off it themselves. I was the one who had bragged, and so after Sunday School I found myself out on that thing, a mile above the water, with the wind very cold around my knees. The tea-brown whirlpools went spinning slowly around the deep water of the bend, looking as impossible to jump into as if they had been whorls in cement. A half dozen times I sucked in my breath and grabbed my courage with both hands and inched out to the burlap pad on the end of the board. Every time, the vibrations of the board started such sympathetic vibrations in my knees that I had to creep back for fear of falling off. The crowd on the bank got scornful, and then ribald, and then insulting; I could not rouse even the courage to answer back, but went on creeping out, quaking back, creeping out again, until they finally all got tired and left for their Sunday dinners. Then at once I walked out to the end and jumped.

11   I think I must have come down through thirty or forty feet of air, bent over toward the water, with my eyes out on stems like a lobster's, and I hit the water just so, with my face and chest, a tremendous belly-flopper that drove my eyes out through the back of my head and flattened me out on the water to the thickness of an oil film. The air was full of colored lights; I came to enough to realize I was strangling on weed-tasting river water, and moved my arms and legs feebly toward shore. About four hours and twenty deaths later, I grounded on the mud and lay there gasping and retching, sick for the hero I was not, for the humiliation I had endured, for the mess I had made of the jump when I finally made it — even for the fact that no one had been around to see me, and that I would never be able to convince any of them that I really had, at the risk of drowning, done what I had bragged I would do.

12   Contempt is a hard thing to bear, especially one's own. Because I was what I was, and because the town went by the code it went by, I was never quite out of sight of self-contempt or the contempt of my father or Alfie Carpenter or some other whose right to contempt I had to grant. School, and success therein, never fully compensated for the lacks I felt in myself. I found early that I could shine in class, and I always had a piece to speak in school entertainments, and teachers found me reliable at cleaning blackboards, but teachers were women, and school was a woman's world, the booby prize for those not capable of being men. The worst of it was that I liked school, and liked a good many things about the womanish world, but I wouldn't have dared admit it, and I could not respect the praise of my teachers any more than I could that of my music teacher or my mother.

13   "He has the arteestic tempera*ment*," said Madame Dujardin while collecting her pay for my piano lessons. "He's *sensitive*," my mother would tell her friends, afternoons when they sat around drinking coffee and

eating Norwegian coffee cake, and I hung around inside, partly for the sake of coffee cake and partly to hear them talk about me. The moment they did talk about me, I was enraged. *Women* speaking up for me, noticing my "sensitivity," observing me with that appraising female stare and remarking that I seemed to like songs such as "Sweet and Low" better than "Men of Harlech," which was *their* sons' favorite – my mother interpolating half with pride and half with worry that sometimes she had to drive me out to play, I'd rather stay in and read Ridpath's *History of the World*. Women giving me the praise I would have liked to get from my father or Slivers or the Assiniboine halfbreed down at the Lazy-S. I wanted to be made of whang leather.

Little as I want to acknowledge them, the effects of those years re- **14** main in me like the beach terraces of a dead lake. Having been weak, and having hated my weakness, I am as impatient with the weakness of others as my father ever was. Pity embarrasses me for the person I am pitying, for I know how it feels to be pitied. Incompetence exasperates me, a big show of pain or grief or any other feeling makes me uneasy, affectations still inspire in me a mirth I have grown too mannerly to show. I cannot sympathize with the self-pitiers, for I have been there, or with the braggarts, for I have been there too. I even at times find myself reacting against conversation, that highest test of the civilized man, because where I came from it was unfashionable to be "mouthy."

An inhumane and limited code, the value system of a life more limited **15** and cruder than in fact ours was. We got most of it by inheritance from the harsher frontiers that had preceded ours-got it, I suppose, mainly from our contacts with what was left of the cattle industry.

So far as the Cypress Hills were concerned, that industry began with **16** the Mounted Police beef herd at Fort Walsh, and was later amplified by herds brought in to feed treaty Indians during the starving winters after 1879. In practice, the Indians ate a good deal of beef that hadn't been intended for them; it took a while to teach them that the white man's spotted buffalo were not fair game when a man was hungry. The raiding of cattle and horse herds was never controlled until the Canadian Indians were moved to reservations far north of the Line after 1882. Nevertheless it was the Indians who first stimulated the raising of cattle on that range, and the departure of the Indians which left the Whitemud River country open to become the last great cattle country.

In some ways, the overlapping of the cattle and homesteading phases **17** of the plains frontier was similar to the overlapping of the horse and gun cultures earlier, and in each case the overlapping occurred latest around the Cypress Hills. Cattle came in from the south, homesteaders from the east and southeast. Among the homesteaders — Ontario men, Scandinavians and Americans working up from the Dakotas, and Englishmen, Scots, and Ukrainians straight off the immigrant boats — there was a heavy percentage of greenhorns and city men. Even the experienced dryland farmers from the States were a prosaic and law-abiding lot by comparison with the cowboys they displaced. As it turned out, the homesteaders, by appropriating and fencing and plowing the range, squeezed out a way of life that was better adapted to the country than their own, and came close to ruining both the cattlemen and themselves in the process, but that is a later story. What succeeded the meeting and overlapping of the two cultures was a long and difficult period of adaptation in which each would modify the other until a sort of amalgamation could result. But while the adaptations were taking place, during the years of uneasy meeting and mixture, it was the cowboy tradition, the horseback culture, that impressed itself as image, as romance, and as ethical system upon boys like me. There were both good and bad reasons why that should have been true.

18   Read the history of the northern cattle ranges in such an anti-American historian as John Peter Turner and you hear that the "Texas men" who brought the cattle industry to Canada were all bravos, rustlers, murderers, gamblers, thugs, and highwaymen; that their life was divided among monte, poker, six-guns, and dancehall girls; and that their law was the gun-law that they made for themselves and enforced by hand. Allow sixty or seventy per cent of error for patriotic fervor, and Mr. Turner's generalizations may be accepted. But it is likewise true that American cow outfits left their gun-law cheerfully behind them when they found the country north of the Line well policed, that they cheer-fully cooperated with the Mounted Police, took out Canadian brands, paid for grazing leases, and generally conformed to the customs of the country. They were indistinguishable from Canadian ranchers, to whom they taught the whole business. Many Canadian ranches, among them the 76, the Matador, the Turkey Track, and the T-Down-Bar, were simp-ly Canadian extensions of cattle empires below the border.

19   So was the culture, in the anthropological sense, that accompanied the cattle. It was an adaptation to the arid Plains that had begun along the Rio Grande and had spread north, like gas expanding to fill a vacuum, as the buffalo and Indians were destroyed or driven out in the years following the Civil War. Like the patterns of hunting and war that had

been adopted by every plains tribe as soon as it acquired the horse, the cowboy culture made itself at home all the way from the Rio Grande to the North Saskatchewan. The outfit, the costume, the practices, the terminology, the state of mind, came into Canada ready-made, and nothing they encountered on the northern Plains enforced any real modifications. The Texas men made it certain that nobody would ever be thrown from a horse in Saskatchewan; he would be piled. They made it sure that no Canadian steer would ever be angry or stubborn; he would be o'nery or ringy or on the prod. Bull Durham was as native to the Whitemud range as to the Pecos, and it was used for the same purposes: smoking, eating, and spitting in the eye of a ringy steer. The Stetson was as useful north as south, could be used to fan the fire or dip up a drink from a stream, could shade a man's eyes or be clapped over the eyes of a bronc to gentle him down. Boots, bandanna, stock saddle, rope, the ways of busting broncs, the institution of the spring and fall roundup, the bowlegs in batwing or goatskin chaps — they all came north intact. About the only thing that changed was the name for the cowboy's favorite diversion, which down south they would have called a rodeo but which we called a stampede.

It was a nearly womanless culture, nomadic, harsh, dangerous, essentially romantic. It had the same contempt for the dirtgrubbers that Scythian and Cossack had, and Canadian tillers of the soil tended to look upon it with the same suspicion and fear and envy that tillers of the soil have always expressed toward the herdsmen. As we knew it, it had a lot of Confederate prejudices left in it, and it had the callousness and recklessness that a masculine life full of activity and adventure is sure to produce. I got it in my eyes like stardust almost as soon as we arrived in Whitemud, when the town staged its first stampede down in the western bend. Reno Dodds, known as Slivers, won the saddle bronc competition and set me up a model for my life. I would grow up to be about five feet six and weigh about a hundred and thirty pounds. I would be bowlegged and taciturn, with deep creases in my cheeks and a hide like stained saddle leather. I would be the quietest and most dangerous man around, best rider, best shot, the one who couldn't be buffaloed. Men twice my size, beginning some brag or other, would catch my cold eye and begin to wilt, and when I had stared them into impotence I would turn my back contemptuous, hook onto my pony in one bowlegged arc, and ride off. I thought it tremendous that anyone as small and skinny as Slivers could be a top hand and a champion rider. I don't think I could have survived without his example, and he was

still on my mind years later when, sixteen years old and six feet tall
and weighing a hundred and twenty-five pounds, I went every afternoon to the university gym and worked out on the weights for an hour
and ran wind sprints around the track. If I couldn't be big I could be *hard*.

21   We hung around the Lazy-S corrals a good deal that first year or two,
and the cowpunchers, when they had no one else to pester, would egg
us into what they called shit-fights, with green cow manure for snowballs;
or they would put a surcingle around a calf and set us aboard. After
my try I concluded that I would not do any more of it just at that time,
and I limped to the fence and sat on the top rail nursing my sprains
and bruises and smiling to keep from bawling out loud. From there I
watched Spot Orullian, a Syrian boy a couple of years older than I,
ride a wildly pitching whiteface calf clear around the corral and halfway
around again, and get piled hard, and come up wiping the cow dung
off himself, swearing like a pirate. They cheered him, he was a favorite
at once, perhaps all the more because he had a big brown birthmark
on his nose and so could be kidded. And I sat on the corral rail hunch-
ing my winglike shoulder-blades, smiling and smiling and smiling to
conceal the black envy that I knew was just under the skin of my face.
It was always boys like Spot Orullian who managed to be and do what
I wanted to do and be.

22   Many things that those cowboys represented I would have done well
to get over quickly, or never catch: the prejudice, the callousness, the
destructive practical joking, the tendency to judge everyone by the same
raw standard. Nevertheless, what they themselves most respected, and
what as a boy I most yearned to grow up to, was as noble as it was
limited. They honored courage, competence, self-reliance, and they
honored them tacitly. They took them for granted. It was their absence,
not their presence, that was cause for remark. Practising comradeship
in a rough and dangerous job, they lived a life calculated to make a
man careless of everything except the few things he really valued.

23   In the fall of 1906 it must have seemed that the cowboy life was certain to last a good while, for the Canadian range still lay wide open,
and stockmen from the western states had prospected it and laid large
plans for moving bigger herds across the Line to escape the nesters and
sheepmen who had already broken up the Montana ranges. Probably
the entire country from Wood Mountain to the Alberta line would have
been leased for grazing, at the favorable Canadian rate of a few cents
an acre, if the winter of 1906-07 had not happened.

24   That winter has remained ever since, in the minds of all who went

through it, as the true measure of catastrophe. Some might cite the winter of 1886-87, the year of the Big Die-Up on the American range, but that winter did not affect the Whitemud country, where cattle came in numbers only after 1887. Some who had punched cows in Alberta in the early days might cast a vote for the fatal Cochran drive of 1881, when 8,000 out of 12,000 cattle died over by Lethbridge; and some would certainly, just as weather, mention the April blizzard of 1892, or the winter that followed it, or the big May blizzard of 1903. But after 1907 no one would seriously value those earlier disasters. The winter of 1906-07 was the real one, the year of the blue snow. After it, the leases that might have been taken up were allowed to lapse, the herds that might have been augmented were sold for what they would bring — fifteen to twenty dollars a head with suckling calves thrown in. Old cattlemen who had ridden every range from Texas north took a good long look around in the spring and decided to retire.

The ranches that survived were primarily the hill ranches with shelter 25 plus an access to bench or prairie hay land where winter feed could be cut. The net effect of the winter of 1906-07 was to make stock farmers out of ranchers. Almost as suddenly as the disappearance of the buffalo, it changed the way of life of the region. A great event, it had the force in the history of the Cypress Hills country that a defeat in war has upon a nation. When it was over, the protected Hills might harbor a few cowboys, and one or two of the big ranches such as the 76 might go on, but most of the prairie would be laid open to homesteading and another sort of frontier.

That new frontier, of which my family was a part, very soon squeezed 26 out the Lazy-S. The hay lands in the bottoms were broken up into town lots, my father was growing potatoes where whitefaces had used to graze, the punchers were drifting off to Alberta. But while we had them around, we made the most of them, imitating their talk and their walk and their songs and their rough-handed jokes; admiring them for the way they tormented Mah Li; hanging around in the shade of the bunkhouse listening to Rusty, who was supposed to be the second son of an earl, play the mouth organ; watching the halfbreed Assiniboine braid leather or horsehair into halter ropes and hackamores. I heard some stories about the winter of 1906-07, but I never heard enough. Long afterward, digging in the middens where historians customarily dig, I found and read some more, some of them the reminiscences of men I knew. What they record is an ordeal by weather. The manner of recording is laconic, deceptively matter of fact. It does not give much idea of how it feels to ride sixty or eighty miles on a freezing and exhausted pony, or how cold thirty below is when a fifty-mile wind is driving it into your face, or how demoralizing it is to be lost in a freezing fog where north, south, east, west, even up and down, swim and shift before the slitted and frost-stuck eyes.

27   They do not tell their stories in Technicolor; they would not want to seem to adorn a tale or brag themselves up. The calluses of a life of hardship blunt their sensibilities to their own experience. If we want to know what it was like on the Whitemud River range during that winter when the hopes of a cattle empire died, we had better see it through the eyes of some tenderfoot, perhaps someone fresh from the old country, a boy without the wonder rubbed off him and with something to prove about himself. If in inventing this individual I put into him a little of Corky Jones, and some of the boy Rusty whose mouth organ used to sweeten the dusty summer shade of the Lazy-S bunkhouse, let it be admitted that I have also put into him something of myself, the me who sat on a corral bar wetting with spit my smarting skinned places, and wishing I was as tough as Spot Orullian.

(1955)

The Writer's Subject

1. On what principle were nicknames bestowed on the inhabitants of Stegner's town? (para. 1)

2. What does Stegner mean by "the standard frontier attitudes" shown by his companions? (para. 2)

3. Stegner says that the Chinese cook Mah Li was a friend of his, yet he still took part in the "persecution" of Mah Li; why did he do so? (paras. 3 and 4) Which of Stegner's townsfolk were immune from such persecution, and why? (paras. 5-7)

4. What is meant by "the code of the stiff upper lip"? (para. 7) How is this code related to the stories of Alfie Carpenter's accident (para. 8) and Spot Orullian's calf riding? (para. 21) Account for Stegner's feelings of envy.

5. What is the importance of Stegner's anecdote of his dive from the high diving board into the river? (paras. 10-11)

6. Why did the young Stegner find no satisfaction in his success at school, or in the praise of his mother's friends? (paras. 12-13)

7. What were the values of the "horseback culture" that impressed themselves so strongly on Stegner and boys like him? Which of these values does Stegner see as having been potentially damaging? (paras. 17-22)

8. What were the particularly romantic elements of the cattle culture? (para. 20)

9. Why did Stegner see Reno Dodds ("Slivers") as a model? (para. 20)

10. What was the impact of the winter of 1906-07 on the Cypress Hills country and the cattle culture? (paras. 23-26)

The Writer's Style and Strategy

1. Stegner's account forms a chapter of his book *Wolf Willow: A History, a Story and a Memory of the Last Plains Frontier*. What elements of this chapter reflect the book's subtitle?

2. Stegner is writing as an adult recalling his childhood. Choose one or two paragraphs which focus on Stegner's childhood experiences (e.g., paras. 10-11, or 21), and show how he manages to convey a sense of how he felt as a child.

3. How would you characterize the adult Stegner's attitude to the code of the frontier that he admired so much as a child? Where, and how, is that attitude revealed?

4. What function is performed by paragraph 14? How is it related to the preceding paragraphs?

5. What function is performed by paragraph 15?

6. What differences in diction are apparent in paragraphs 21 and 22? How does the style of each paragraph reflect its substance and purpose?

7. Stegner provides portraits of a number of characters, including Mah Li, Alfie Carpenter, Reno Dodds, and Spot Orullian. Choose one of these characters and explain how Stegner's description throws light on Stegner's childhood and the society he grew up in.

Suggested Topics for Writing and Discussion

1. Stegner describes a major change in the region of his childhood, from cattle-ranching and the cowboy culture to "homesteading and another sort of frontier." Find out what you can about the significant changes that have taken place in the neighbourhood or region in which you grew up. What gains or losses have the changes brought, in your view?

2. Stegner specifies the qualities that were demonstrated by the heroes of his childhood. Write an essay in which you use anecdote to describe the childhood heroes of your neighbourhood or region. In what ways are your "specifications" similar to or different from Stegner's?

3. Stegner describes at length his mortifying experience on the diving board. Re-create an event in your own childhood which caused you extreme embarrassment, fear, or humiliation. What feelings about the event do you have now as you look back on it?

4. What, in your view, are the qualities that constitute true heroism? What model would you offer for the admiration of children today?

Marilyn Monroe: The Woman
Who Died Too Soon

by Gloria Steinem

Saturday afternoon movies — no matter how poorly made or incred- 1
ible the plot, they were a refuge from my neighborhood and all my
teenage miseries. Serials that never ended, Doris Day, who never
capitulated, cheap travelogues, sci-fi features with zippers in the monster
suits: I loved them all, believed them all, and never dreamed of leaving until the screen went sickeningly blank.

But I walked out on Marilyn Monroe. I remember her on the screen, 2
huge as a colossus doll, mincing and whispering and simply hoping her
way into total vulnerability. Watching her, I felt angry, even humiliated,
but I didn't understand why.

After all, Jane Russell was in the movie, too (a very bad-taste ver- 3
sion of *Gentlemen Prefer Blondes*), so it wasn't just the vulnerability
that all big-breasted women seem to share. (If women viewers prefer
actresses who are smaller, neater — the Audrey Hepburns of the world
— it is not because we're jealous of the *zoftig* ones as men suppose. It's
just that we would rather identify with a woman we don't have to worry
about, someone who doesn't seem in constant danger.) Compared to
Marilyn, Jane Russell seemed in control of her body and even of the
absurd situations in this movie.

Perhaps it was the uncertainty in the eyes of this big, blond child- 4
woman; the terrible desire for approval that made her different from
Jane Russell. How dare she express the neediness that so many women
feel, but try so hard to hide? How dare she, a movie star, be just as
unconfident as I was?

So I disliked her and avoided her movies, as we avoid that which 5
reflects our fears about ourselves. If there were jokes made on her name

and image when I was around, I joined in. I contributed to the laughing, the ridicule, the put-downs, thus proving that I was nothing like her. Nothing at all.

6   I, too, got out of my neighborhood in later years, just as she had escaped from a much worse life of lovelessness, child abuse, and foster homes. I didn't do it, as she did, through nude calendar photographs and starlet bits. (Even had there been such opportunities for mildly pretty girls in Toledo, Ohio, I would never have had the courage to make myself so vulnerable.) Yes, I was American enough to have show-business dreams. The boys in my neighborhood hoped to get out of a lifetime in the factories through sports; the girls, if we imagined anything other than marrying a few steps up in the world, always dreamed of show-business careers. But after high-school years as a dancer on the Toledo show-business circuit, or what passed for show business there, it seemed hopeless even to me. In the end, it was luck and an encouraging mother and a facility with words that got me out; a facility that helped me fake my way through the college entrance exams for which I was totally unprepared.

7   But there's not much more confidence in girls who scrape past college boards than there is in those who, like Marilyn, parade past beauty-contest judges. By the time I saw her again, I was a respectful student watching the celebrated members of the Actors Studio do scenes from what seemed to me very impressive and highbrow plays (Arthur Miller and Eugene O'Neill were to be served up that day). She was a student, too, a pupil of Lee Strasberg, leader of the Actors Studio and American guru of the Stanislavski method, but her status as a movie star and sex symbol seemed to keep her from being taken seriously even there. She was allowed to observe, but not to do scenes with her colleagues.

8   So the two of us sat there, mutually awed, I think, in the presence of such theater people as Ben Gazzara and Rip Torn, mutually insecure in the masculine world of High Culture, mutually trying to fade into the woodwork.

9   I remember thinking that Strasberg and his actors seemed to take positive pleasure in their power to ignore this great and powerful movie star who had come to learn. Their greetings to her were a little too studiously casual, their whispers to each other about her being there a little too self-conscious and condescending. Though she stayed in the back of the room, her blond head swathed in a black scarf and her body hidden in a shapeless black sweater and slacks, she gradually became a presence, if only because the group was trying so hard *not* to look,

to remain oblivious and cool.

As we filed slowly out of the shabby room after the session was over, **10**
Marilyn listened eagerly to the professional postmortem being carried
on by Ben Gazzara and others who walked ahead of us, her fingers
nervously tracing a face that was luminous and without makeup, as if
she were trying to hide herself, to apologize for being there. I was suddenly glad she hadn't participated and hadn't been subjected to the
criticisms of this rather vulturous group. (Perhaps it was an unschooled
reaction, but I hadn't enjoyed watching Strasberg encourage an initimate
love scene between an actor and actress, and then pick them apart with
humiliating authority.) Summoning my nerve, I did ask the shy, blond
woman in front of me if she could imagine playing a scene for this group.

"Oh, no," Marilyn said, her voice childish, but much less whispery **11**
than on the screen, "I admire all these people so much. I'm just not
good enough." Then, after a few beats of silence: "Lee Strasberg is a
genius, you know. I plan to do what he says."

Her marriage to Arthur Miller seemed quite understandable to me **12**
and to other women, even those who were threatened by Miller's casting
off of a middle-aged wife to take a younger, far more glamorous one.
If you can't be taken seriously in your work, if you have an emotional
and intellectual insecurity complex, then marry a man who has the
seriousness you've been denied. It's a traditional female option — far
more acceptable than trying to achieve that identity on one's own.

Of course, Marilyn's image didn't really gain seriousness and intellec- **13**
tuality. Women don't gain serious status by sexual association any more
easily than they do by hard work. (At least, not unless the serious man
dies and we confine ourselves to being keepers of the flame. As Margaret
Mead has pointed out, widows are almost the only women this country
honors in authority.) Even Marilyn's brave refusal to be intimidated
by threats that she would never work in films again if she married Miller,
who was then a "subversive" called to testify before the House Un-
American Activities Committee, was considered less brave than Miller's
refusal to testify. Indeed, it was barely reported at all.

Perhaps she didn't take her own bravery seriously either. She might **14**
be giving up her livelihood, the work that meant so much to her, but
she was about to give that up for marriage anyway. As Mrs. Arthur
Miller, she retired to a Connecticut farm and tried to limit her life to
his solitary work habits, his friends, and his two children. Only when
they badly needed money did she come out of retirement again, and
that was to act in *The Misfits*, a film written by her husband.

15   On the other hand, the public interpretation was very different. She was an egocentric actress forcing one of America's most important playwrights to tailor a screenplay to her inferior talents: that was the gossip-column story here and in Europe. But her own pattern argues the case for her. In two previous marriages, to an aircraft factory worker at the age of sixteen and later to Joe Di Maggio, she had cut herself off from the world and put all her energies into being a housewife. When it didn't work out, she blamed herself, not the role, and added one more failure to her list of insecurities. "I have too many fantasies to be a housewife," she told a woman friend sadly. And finally, to an interviewer: "I guess I *am* a fantasy."

16   *The Misfits* seemed to convey some facets of the real Marilyn: honesty, an innocence and belief that survived all experience to the contrary, kindness toward other women, a respect for the life of plants and animals. Because for the first time she wasn't only a sex object and victim, I also was unembarrassed enough to notice her acting ability. I began to see her earlier movies — those in which, unlike *Gentlemen Prefer Blondes*, she wasn't called upon to act the female impersonator.

17   For me as for so many people, she was a presence in the world, a life force.

18   Over the years, I heard other clues to her character. When Ella Fitzgerald, a black artist and perhaps the greatest singer of popular songs, hadn't been able to get a booking at an important Los Angeles nightclub in the fifties, it was Marilyn who called the owner and promised to sit at a front table every night while she sang. The owner hired Ella, Marilyn was faithful to her promise each night, the press went wild, and, as Ella remembers with gratitude, "After that, I never had to play a small jazz club again."

19   Even more movingly, there was her last interview. She pleaded with the reporter to end with "What I really want to say: That what the world really needs is a real feeling of kinship. Everybody: stars, laborers, Negroes, Jews, Arabs. We are all brothers. . . . Please don't make me a joke. End the interview with what I believe."

20   And then she was gone. I remember being told, in the middle of a chaotic student meeting in Europe, that she was dead. I remember that precise moment on August 5, 1962 — the people around me, what the room looked like — and I've discovered that many other people remember that moment of hearing the news, too. It's a phenomenon usually reserved for the death of family and presidents.

21   She was an actress, a person on whom no one's fate depended, and

yet her energy and terrible openness to life had made a connection to strangers. Within days after her body was discovered, eight young and beautiful women took their lives in individual incidents clearly patterned after Marilyn Monroe's death. Some of them left notes to make that connection clear.

Two years later, Arthur Miller's autobiographical play, *After the Fall*,   22
brought Marilyn back to life in the character of Maggie. But somehow that Maggie didn't seem the same. She had Marilyn's pathetic insecurity, the same need to use her sexual self as her only way of getting recognition and feeling alive. But, perhaps naturally, the play was about Miller's suffering, not Marilyn's. He seemed honestly to include some of his own destructive acts. (He had kept a writer's diary of his movie-star wife, for instance, and Marilyn's discovery of it was an emotional blow, the beginning of the end for that marriage. It made her wonder: Was her husband exploiting her, as most men had done, but in a more intellectual way?) Nonetheless, the message of the play was mostly Miller's view of his attempts to shore up a creature of almost endless insecurities; someone doomed beyond his helping by a mysterious lack of confidence.

To women, that lack was less mysterious. Writer Diana Trilling, who   23
had never met Marilyn, wrote an essay just after her death that some of Marilyn's friends praised as a more accurate portrayal than Miller's. She described the public's "mockery of [Marilyn's] wish to be educated"; the sexual awareness that came only from outside, from men's reactions, "leaving a great emptiness where a true sexuality would have supplied her with a sense of herself as a person with connection and content." She questioned whether Marilyn had really wanted to die, or only to be asleep, not to be conscious through the loneliness of that particular Saturday night.

Trilling also recorded that feeling of connection to Marilyn's loneliness   24
felt by so many strangers ("especially women to whose protectiveness her extreme vulnerability spoke so directly"), so much so that we fantasized our ability to save her, if only we had been there. "But we were the friends," as Trilling wrote sadly, "of whom she knew nothing."

"She was an unusual woman — a little ahead of her times," said Ella   25
Fitzgerald. "And she didn't know it."

Now that women's self-vision is changing, we are thinking again about   26
the life of Marilyn Monroe. Might our new confidence in women's existence with or without the approval of men have helped a thirty-six-year-old woman of talent to stand on her own? To resist the insecurity

and ridicule? To stop depending on sexual attractiveness as the only proof that she was alive - and therefore to face aging with confidence? Because the ability to bear a child was denied to her, could these new ideas have helped her to know that being a woman included much more? Could she have challenged the Freudian analysts to whom she turned in her suffering?

27   Most of all, we wonder if the support and friendship of other women could have helped. Her early experiences of men were not good. She was the illegitimate daughter of a man who would not even contribute for her baby clothes; her mother's earliest memory of her own father, Marilyn's grandfather, was his smashing a pet kitten against the fireplace in a fit of anger; Marilyn herself said she was sexually attacked by a foster father while still a child; and she was married off at sixteen because another foster family could not take care of her. Yet she was forced always to depend for her security on the goodwill and recognition of men; even to be interpreted by them in writing because she feared that sexual competition made women dislike her. Even if they had wanted to, the women in her life did not have the power to protect her. In films, photographs, and books, even after her death as well as before, she has been mainly seen through men's eyes.

28   We are too late. We cannot know whether we could have helped Norma Jean Baker or the Marilyn Monroe she became. But we are not too late to do as she asked. At last, we can take her seriously.

(1972)

The Writer's Subject

1. Why was Steinem's first response to Marilyn Monroe one of anger and humiliation? (paras. 2-5)

2. In what ways was Steinem's early life like Monroe's? (para. 6)

3. How was Monroe treated by members of the Actors Studio? How did this episode affect Steinem's view of Monroe? (paras. 7-10)

4. Why, according to Steinem, did Monroe marry the celebrated American playwright, Arthur Miller? (para. 12)

5. What qualities in Monroe's character does Steinem find admirable? How are those qualities illustrated?

6. What is the importance of Marilyn's last interview described in paragraph 19?

7. Why, according to Steinem, did the news of Monroe's death have an impact on so many people? (paras. 20-21, 24)

8. Steinem suggests that Miller may have exploited his marriage to Monroe. How? (para. 22)

9. What, according to Steinem's account, was missing in Monroe's life?

10. Why, in Steinem's view, was Marilyn Monroe "the woman who died too soon"? (paras. 25-28)

The Writer's Style and Strategy

1. Steinem's essay presents an initially hostile view which is re-evaluated and then altered. Analyze the stages of the essay to show how Steinem presents this shift in view.

2. What use does Steinem make of her own experiences in her attempt to explain the mysterious appeal of Marilyn Monroe?

3. What tone does Steinem create by means of the transition from paragraph 5 into paragraph 6?

4. What is Steinem's purpose in repeating "mutually" in paragraph 8?

5. What use does Steinem make of the Actors Studio anecdote to illustrate Monroe's character? Why does she quote directly Monroe's comments about Lee Strasberg? (para. 11)

6. This essay was originally published in *Ms.* magazine. What features of Steinem's style or approach suggest that she was writing specifically for a feminist audience?

Suggested Topics for Writing and Discussion

1. Marilyn Monroe achieved considerable fame as the sex symbol for a generation, but her particular beauty and sexiness are no longer in style. Who, in your view, is today's sex symbol? Explain the appeal of this person for the present generation.

2. Steinem alludes to the American dreams of escape from an ordinary life to fame and fortune, chiefly through sports for the boys and show business for the girls. Are these, in your view, still the stuff of escape dreams for American — and Canadian — youth?

3. Steinem says that a traditional option for a woman has been to marry a man in order to gain an identity rather than achieve that identity on her own. Do you think that is still the case?

The World of Science

The Body in the Bog
by Geoffrey Bibby

The business of the archaeologist is the digging up of the past, the   1
reconstruction of remote history. He does his best to find out what our
remote ancestors did and thought and felt from the material remains
they left in the ground. A distinguished archaeologist has unflattering-
ly described himself and his colleagues as surgeons probing into the
workings of the human brain with picks, shovels, and builders' trowels.
"Fortunately," he adds "our patients are already dead."

This comparison must not be taken too literally. When Sir Mortimer   2
Wheeler describes the archaeologist as investigating people who are
dead, he means, I am afraid, that we are trying to find out about these
dead-and-gone people by studying the things they left behind them, their
implements and weapons and coins and pots and pans. The nearest we
normally get to the people themselves is their skeletons, and there is
a limit to what can be deduced from dry bones.

I wish to tell an archaeological detective story that is different — a   3
detective story that begins with a body and no artifacts.

My part in the story began on Monday, April 28, 1952, when I ar-   4
rived at the Prehistoric Museum of Aarhus, in mid- Denmark, to find
a dead body on the floor of my office. On an iron sheet stood a large
block of peat, and at one end of it the head and right arm of a man
protruded, while one leg and foot stuck out from the other end. His
skin was dark brown, almost chocolate colored, and his hair was a
brownish red.

He had been found on Saturday afternoon by workers cutting peat   5
in a little bog near Grauballe, about twenty miles away. He lay a yard

below the surface, but peat had been dug for generations there so that the "surface" had lain much higher, even within living memory. The finders had informed the local doctor of their discovery, not so much because he was a doctor but because he was known to be an antiquary of repute. And he had informed Professor Peter Glob, who was the director of our museum.

6   This was not Professor Glob's first "bog body"; he knew what to expect and made preparations accordingly. The next day he drove out to the bog, cut a section through the peat exposing the lie of the body, drew and photographed that section, took samples of the peat surrounding the body, and then cut out the whole block in which the body lay and brought it in to the museum in a truck.

7   That Monday we carefully dug away the peat covering the body, taking samples every two inches. The body lay face down, with one leg drawn up and the arms twisted somewhat behind it. It was completely naked. When we removed the peat from below the body (after turning it over in a plaster cast to preserve its original position), we still found nothing, no trace of clothing, no artifacts — nothing except the naked body.

8   At this point we turned for help to the professor of forensic medicine at Aarhus University, who carried out a thorough autopsy and presented us with a lengthy and detailed report:

9   "This most unusually well-preserved body has, as a result of the particular composition of the earth in which it has lain, undergone a process of conservation which appears to resemble most closely a tanning. This has made the skin firm and resistant, and has to a high degree counteracted the various processes of decay which normally commence soon after death . . . the subject is an adult male, and the condition of the teeth suggests that he was of somewhat advanced age. . . . On the front of the throat was found a large wound stretching from ear to ear. . . . This wound may with certainty be interpreted as an incised lesion, probably caused by several cuts inflicted by a second person. The direction of the wound and its general appearance make it unlikely that it could be self-inflicted or accidentally inflicted after death. . . . The investigation of the hair suggests that the subject was dark-haired. The reddish coloration is presumably accounted for by the body having lain in peat."

10   So the man from Grauballe had had his throat cut, and we had a murder mystery on our hands.

11   The investigation went on. The police expert reported: "There is nothing unusual about the fingerprints obtained. I myself possess the

same type of pattern on the right thumb and middle finger — without 12
therefore claiming any direct descent from Grauballe Man. Among the
present-day Danish population the two patterns occur with a frequency
of, respectively, 11.2 and 68.3 per cent."

More important were the results we got from the peat samples and 13
from a portion of the liver region that we had excised and sent to the
radioactive-carbon laboratory.

It happens that the botanists of Scandinavia have worked out in great 14
detail the changing composition of the vegetation of the region since
the last ice age ended more than ten thousand years ago. They do this
by means of the thousands of infinitesimal grains of pollen to be found
in any cubic centimeter of peat. The time within this sequence when
any particular specimen of peat was formed is shown by the proportion
of certain types of pollen grains, particularly of tree pollen. And the
pollen analysts could tell us that the peat immediately below Grauballe
Man had been formed early in the period the Danes call the Roman
Iron Age, a period extending from the beginning of the Christian Era
to about A.D. 300.

But they could tell us more. The peat *above* the body was of *earlier* 15
date than that directly below and around the body, and the peat at a
little distance to either side of the body was earlier still. The body had
clearly been buried in a hole cut in the peat — but not in a hole cut
to receive it. The only explanation to fit the facts was that a hole had
been cut, probably to obtain peat for fuel, had stood open for some
years (long enough for new peat to form in the water at the bottom of
the hole), and then Grauballe Man had been thrown into this new peat
and the hole had been filled in with peat from the surface layers.

The radio-carbon laboratory — which determines the age of organic 16
substances by measuring the residual carbon-14 in the specimen — could
tell us that this had occurred and that Grauballe Man had died in A.D.
310, with a possible error of a hundred years in either direction. This
did not surprise us; for, though local newspapers and gossip had made
much of a certain "Red Christian," a drunkard farmhand who was said
to have disappeared one night some sixty years before, not far from
the Grauballe peat bog, we should have been very surprised indeed if
the pollen laboratory and the radio-carbon laboratory had *not* given us
a date in the region of 100 B.C.-A.D. 300.

For Grauballe Man was far from being an isolated example. Bodies 17
have always been turning up in the peat bogs of Denmark — and not
only in Denmark. They are frequently found in northwest Germany and

even as far south as Holland. In that area there are records of something like two hundred bog bodies. Since the earlier records are not very detailed, sometimes merely an entry in a parish registry of the "body of a poor man drowned in such and such a bog," the statistics are far from exact. The earliest doubtful record of this nature is from 1450, at Bonstorf in Germany. And the first detailed report is from 1773, when a completely preserved body of a man was found three feet deep in the peat at Ravnholt on the Danish island of Fünen. The body lay on its back with its arms crossed behind it − "as though they had been bound," says the parish clerk. Apart from a sheepskin around the head, it was naked. When the sheepskin was removed, it could be seen that the man had had his throat cut.

18   In 1797, in southwest Jutland, another well-preserved male body was found, naked save for one oxhide moccasin but covered with two calfskin cloaks. The cause of death is not recorded, and the body was hurriedly buried in a nearby churchyard when it began to dry out and decompose.

And so it went. Every few years a body would be found, would be a nine-day wonder in its immediate locality because of its surprising state of preservation, and would be buried again when it began to smell.

19   A few of the bodies achieved more than local fame. In 1853, about fifty miles south of Copenhagen a body was found, probably that of a woman, though there was little left besides the skeleton and the long, fair hair. The body was noteworthy because it was accompanied by a bronze brooch and seven glass beads, which even then could be dated to the Iron Age and which we can now date to about A.D. 300.

20   Eight years earlier a much more complete female body had been found at Haraldskaer, in south Jutland, not far from the burial mounds of Gorm, the last heathen king of Denmark and his queen, nor from the site of the first Christian church in Denmark, built about A.D. 950 by Gorm's son, Harald Bluetooth. The body lay in the peat with its hands and feet held down by forked sticks, and it achieved some notoriety in Denmark because some learned antiquaries claimed that it was Queen Gunhild of Norway, who, according to legend, had been enticed to Denmark by Harald Bluetooth and drowned by him in a morass. Even at the time of discovery, though, the evidence for this identification was regarded as too slender.

21   The first photograph of a peat-bog body dates from 1873 and is of a body found near Kiel. It was a man's body with a triangular hole in the forehead. He was naked except for a piece of leather bound around the left shin, but his head was covered with a large square woollen blanket

and a sewn skin cape. An attempt was made to preserve him for exhibition by smoking, and several photographs were taken, some extravagantly posed. The first photograph of a body *in situ* was taken in 1892. The body was found not many miles away from the place where Grauballe Man was discovered sixty years later, and very close indeed to another recent find, the Tollund Man.

The list could be continued almost indefinitely. But it is only within 22
recent years that pollen analysis has been developed to a stage where the bodies can be accurately dated. And all the bodies found since have proved to date to the same restricted period of Danish prehistory, the first three centuries of the Christian Era. This fact makes it possible-indeed essential — to regard them as a single "case."

Apart from Grauballe Man, four bodies have been found in the peat 23
bogs of Denmark since World War II, and all have been subjected to the same thorough analysis that we gave Grauballe Man. Three came from the same bog, the large peat area of Borremose in north Jutland. The first was a man, naked like so many of the others but with two cloaks of skin beside him. Around his neck was a rope noose, which may have been the cause of death, although the body was too badly preserved to be certain. There were odd features about the noose; it had been knotted at the neck, and both of the fairly short ends had been bent over and lashed with leather thongs to prevent them from unraveling, surely an unduly elaborate treatment for an ordinary hangman's noose.

The second body was that of a woman, again poorly preserved. The 24
upper part of the body appeared to have been naked, while the lower part was covered with a blanket, a shawl, and other bits of clothing. There was a leather cord around the neck, but the cause of death was apparently a crushing blow on the skull.

The third body was also a woman's, a rather stout lady who lay face 25
downward in the peat with only a blanket wrapped around her middle and held in place by a leather strap. She was no sight for squeamish archaeologists — she had been scalped and her face battered to pieces, though perhaps after death.

It is with quite unjustified relief that one turns from the rather macabre 26
Borremose bodies to the well-known Tollund Man whose portrait has been in the press of the world and who has had the honor of appearing on British television. Tollund Man was discovered in 1950, two years before Grauballe Man and under the same circumstances, by farmers cutting peat. The discovery was reported to the police, and they called

in Professor Glob, who described what he saw:

27   "In the peat cut, nearly seven feet down, lay a human figure in a crouched position, still half-buried. A foot and a shoulder protruded, perfectly preserved but dark-brown in color like the surrounding peat which had dyed the skin. Carefully we removed more peat, and a bowed head came into view.

28   "As dusk fell, we saw in the fading light a man take shape before us. He was curled up, with legs drawn under him and arms bent, resting on his side as if asleep. His eyes were peacefully shut; his brows were furrowed, and his mouth showed a slightly irritated quirk as if he were not overpleased by this unexpected disturbance. . . ."

Tollund Man was found to be naked except for a leather belt around his waist and a leather cap upon his head, a cap made of eight triangular gussets of leather sewn togeter. There was one other item. Around his neck was the elaborately braided leather rope with which they had hanged him.

29   It is clear, I think, that we have a case of mass murder. There are too many points of similarity between the killings for it to be possible to consider each independently of the others. I should point out, though, that their generally fantastic state of preservation is not one of these points of similarity. It is merely our good fortune. The preservation is due the fact that the peat bogs contain sufficient humic acid and tannic acid to halt the processes of decay and start a tanning process that can preserve the body. (This process, incidentally, we have carried to its logical conclusion with Grauballe Man. Eighteen months in an oak vat in a concentrated solution based on oak shavings has completed the tanning process that nature commenced some eighteen hundred years ago. Grauballe Man, on exhibition at the Prehistoric Museum in Aarhus, needs only a little linseed oil now and then in order to last indefinitely.)

30   There is one condition for preservation, however, for otherwise the peat bogs would be full of the bodies of every animal that falls into them. The body must be *buried* in the peat, deep enough down to be below the oxygen-containing surface levels. And this — the fact that all these bodies were disposed of in old cuttings in the peat — *is* one of the common factors that cause us to regard all the killings as a single phenomenon.

31   Another is the fact that all the bodies are naked. Though it is the rule rather than the exception for articles of clothing to be found with the bodies, and sometimes wrapped around the bodies, they are never regularly clothed in the garments. But the most obvious similarity is

that all have died violent deaths and that all are found in bogs.

And that leads to the next step in the inquiry: the question of motive.   32
Why are these bodies there at all?

These are not ordinary burials. Archaeologists are very well acquainted   33
with the burials of this period of Danish prehistory. They were elaborate,
clearly showing evidence of belief in an afterlife in which the dead would
have need of material things. The graves are large and edged with stones.
The body lies carefully arranged on its side, together with a whole set
of pottery vessels, or in the case of the wealthy, with glass and silver
ware imported from the Roman Empire. The vessels must have held
provisions for the journey to the afterworld, for there is often a leg of
pork or of mutton with the rest of the provisions, and even a knife to
carve the joint.

It is clear that whatever it was that resulted in the deaths of the bodies   34
in the bogs also deprived them of regular, ritual burial.

We must dismiss the most obvious explanation — that the bodies were   35
victims of robbery with violence. All are dated to the comparatively
short period of three hundred years at the beginning of our era. It may
have been a lawless time — though farther south it is the period of the
Pax Romana — but certainly it was no more lawless than many other
periods: the period before, of the great Celtic and Germanic wander-
ings; or the period after, when the Roman Empire was breaking up and
all the vultures flocked to the kill; or the Viking period; or much of
the Middle Ages. We should expect a much greater spread in date if
the bodies are to be explained as the victims of robber bands.

We must widen our scope and look not so much at the bodies as at   36
the bogs. What do we find there?

Any Danish archaeologist can answer that question at length. And   37
he can illustrate his answer at the Danish National Museum in
Copenhagen, where room after room is full of things found in bogs.
More than half of the best treasures of Danish prehistory have been
found in bogs, and the archaeologist will tell you that these treasures
were offerings to the gods.

Now, archaeologists have often been accused of calling in hypothetical   38
gods and cult practices whenever they find anything they cannot explain by obvious mundane means. A theory of offerings in the peat bogs
must not be accepted uncritically. But how else is one to explain why
a Stone Age farmer, some four thousand years ago, very carefully laid
seven large, new, unused stone axes side by side in a row in a peat
bog? How is one to explain why several pairs of the big bronze trumpets

known as lurs, the finest known products of the Danish Bronze Age, have been found in the bogs in good working order?

39   It begins to look as though anything of prehistoric date found in the bogs of Denmark is a priori likely to be an offering to the gods. If we move forward to the actual period of the bog bodies, we find the offerings in the bogs getting more numerous and more varied and richer. In the early 1950's I spent three years a few miles south of our museum, helping to dig out an immense offering of weapons — several thousand iron swords and spearheads and arrowheads and shield bosses — all of them burned, bent, hacked to pieces, and then deposited in a lake in the middle of a peat bog. They had been deposited at various times — it was a regular place of offering — but all during the period A.D. 150-300. Among the weapons lay the skeletons of two horses — and here perhaps we approach quite close in spirit to the bog bodies, for the horses had been beheaded before they were offered, and marks on the bones showed quite clearly where spears had been stuck into the carcasses, before or after death.

40   We are entering a dark region. Our probings into the minds of our distant ancestors are lifting a corner of a veil that seems to cover an area of deep superstition, a time when the peat bogs were the abodes of gods and spirits, who demanded sacrifice. When we look now at the bodies in the bogs it seems by no means impossible that they, too, were offerings; that the sacrifices to the gods also included human sacrifices.

41   We must ask ourselves what we know about the gods and goddesses of this period.

42   At the northern end of that very bog at Borremose in which three of the bodies were found, there was discovered in 1897 a large caldron of solid silver. In itself the Gundestrup caldron is far and away the most intrinsically valuable of all the bog offerings. But it is more than that; it is a picture book of European religion around the beginning of the Christian Era. Its sides are decorated, inside and out, with a series of panels bearing pictures, in relief, of gods and goddesses, of mythical animals, and of ritual scenes. Admittedly the caldron is believed to have been manufactured in southeast Europe and to have been brought to Denmark as booty, but the deities portrayed are like the native Danish gods of the period.

43   It is particularly noteworthy that each one of these deities, although otherwise naked, bears a torque, or broad necklet, at the throat, which appears to have been a symbol of kingship and of divinity. It has even

been suggested — perhaps not entirely fancifully — that the oddly elaborate nooses around the necks of Tollund and Borremose Man in some way set them apart as consecrated to the gods. We know from the sagas, not many hundreds of years later, that in Viking times hanged men were sacred to Odin, the chief god of the Viking pantheon.

One of the interior caldron panels shows clearly that the idea of human 44 sacrifice was not alien to the religion of the time. It is admittedly a different ceremony of sacrifice, with the victim dropped headfirst into, or perhaps slaughtered above, a caldron, perhaps the Gundestrup caldron itself. The cutting of the throats of animal victims and the draining of their blood into a caldron was not unknown even among the civilized Greeks and Romans — and Grauballe Man, like many of the victims in the Danish bogs, had had his throat cut.

Speculation concerning details of ritual, though fascinating, can hardly 45 be justified by the slender evidence at our disposal. But the general picture cannot be questioned: the Danes of the early Christian centuries worshipped torque-bearing gods and goddesses; they were not averse to human sacrifice; and the holy places of the divinities were the peat bogs.

There is one source of information that we have not yet tapped. The 46 historians and geographers of the Roman Empire wrote books, some of which describe the manners and customs of peoples beyond the imperial frontiers. The books must be used with caution; few of the authors had visited the regions they describe, and their accounts may well be as full of misunderstandings and fanciful explanations as anything the modern archaeologist can invent to explain what he finds.

But there is a passage in Tacitus's *Germania,* an account of the peoples 47 beyond the Rhine written in A.D. 98, that bears on our study of the Danish bog bodies. Tacitus names seven tribes to the north of Germany, including the Angles, who are known to have lived in south Jutland before they invaded England in the fifth century together with the Saxons and Jutes. And he says: "these people . . . are distinguished by a common worship of Nerthus, or Mother Earth. They believe that she interests herself in human affairs and rides through their peoples. In an island of Ocean stands a sacred grove, and in the grove stands a car draped with a cloth which none but the priest may touch. The priest can feel the presence of the goddess in this holy of holies, and attends her, in deepest reverence, as her car is drawn by oxen. Then follow days of rejoicing and merrymaking in every place that she honors with her advent and stay. No-one goes to war, no-one takes up arms; every object of iron is locked away; then, and only then, are peace and quiet known and prized, until the goddess is again restored to her temple by the priest, when she has had her fill of the society of men. After that, the car, the cloth and, believe it if you will, the goddess herself are washed clean in a secluded lake. This service is performed by slaves who are immediately afterwards drowned in the lake. Thus mystery begets terror and a pious reluctance to ask what that sight can be which is allowed only to dying eyes. "

48   Here we may be getting close to an answer. Nerthus — Mother Earth — is clearly a goddess of fertility; she may be the "goddess with the torque." And the time of peace and rejoicing when the goddess is driven around the countryside in her draped carriage wiil be the time of sowing, the vernal equinox. Pagan survivals of this spring festival still exist in many parts of Europe, in mummers' plays and Maypole dancing and Queens of the May. And in the National Museum in Copenhagen may be seen one of the ox-drawn carriages that almost certainly was used to carry the image of the fertility goddess around the fields. It was found — inevitably — in a peat bog, Dejbjerg in east Jutland, in the 1880's. Richly carved and decorated with ornaments of bronze, it is far too fine a wagon to have been used for mundane purposes. Upon it stands a palanquin, a carrying chair with a canopy, within which the image of the goddess must have rested.

49   A final point brings the evidence full circle to the bodies in the bogs. Microscopic examination of the stomach contents of the men from Borremose, Tollund, and Grauballe shows that their food for several days before death had been vegetarian. It seems to have consisted of some sort of porridge or mash composed of various kinds of corn, or sorrel and heart's ease (both cultivated during the Iron Age), and of the seeds of such weeds as were accidentally harvested along with the corn. It has been suggested that this was a ritual diet, part of the ceremony needed to make the corn grow. Be that as it may, it is significant that there was no trace of any of the edible plants or fruits of summer in the stomach contents. So whatever our uncertainty about the precise year of death, we can say with confidence that the season of the year was winter or early spring.

50   Further we cannot go. We have been probing, with our picks and shovels and builders' trowels, not merely into the brains but perhaps also into the souls of men, and we must be content if our diagnosis is imprecise and inconclusive. But it does take us a little way beyond the conventional archaeological picture of the material lives of the simple

peasants of barbarian Europe. Behind the material life, interleaved with it and perhaps dominating it, was the world of taboos and magic and superstition, the spirits of the earth and of the heavens, who had to be bribed or placated or bought off. One of the occupational risks of Iron Age Europe, right up to the end of the Viking period scarcely a thousand years ago, was that of being chosen as victim, as the price to be paid for prosperity in the next harvest or victory in the next war. It was only with the coming of Christianity that human sacrifice ceased in Europe; looking on the bodies from the Danish bogs we should do well to realize that there, but for the grace of God, lie we.

(1968)

The Writer's Subject

1. How did Bibby and his colleagues first come to realize that they had a murder mystery on their hands?

2. What part did the Scandinavian botanists play in the investigation? (paras. 12-15)

3. Bibby describes the characteristics of a number of bog bodies. What features did these have in common that led him to conclude that these bodies represented "a case of mass murder" (para. 29)?

4. Why did the archaeologists dismiss "the most obvious explanation — that the bodies were victims of robbery with violence" (para. 35)?

5. What led Bibby and his colleagues to conclude that these bodies were ritual offerings?

6. What was the significance of the Gundestrup cauldron in the unravelling of the mystery of the bog bodies? (paras. 42-44)

7. How does Tacitus's account of the goddess Nerthus throw light on the circumstances of the ritual murders? (paras. 47-48)

8. How does Bibby's conclusion demonstrate that the archaeologist's interests are not restricted to a study of material remains?

The Writer's Style and Strategy

1. Bibby speaks of his intention to tell "an archaeological detective story." In what ways does the essay follow the pattern implied by such a description?

2. Is this essay intended for a specialist or a generalist audience? Pick out details of content, style, or diction that support your opinion.

3. Was the reasoning employed in Bibby's investigation primarily deductive or inductive?

4. Discuss the uses that Bibby makes of paragraphs of one or two sentences.

5. What features of Bibby's approach lead the reader to have confidence in the plausibility of his conclusions?

Suggestions for Writing and Discussion

1. Find out what you can about archaeological excavations in your region or community. What conclusions have been reached about the history of your region through such investigations? (A good place to begin your study is your local museum.)

2. Bibby speaks of the part played by scientific experts in his investigation (e.g., pollen analysis, carbon dating). With the help of a librarian, locate an account of a fairly recent archaeological "dig" or underwater expedition (e.g., in the Mediterranean, in China). Show what part science and technology have played in helping the archaeologists understand their finds.

3. Bibby points to the importance of ritual in pre-Christian Danish society. Though we no longer subscribe to rituals of the kind Bibby describes, we do practise other kinds of rituals. Discuss one or two rituals still practised in your community in connection with such occasions as births, deaths, marriages, harvest, etc.

The Real Responsibilities of the Scientist

by Jacob Bronowski

We live in times of very difficult decisions for scientists, for statesmen, 1
and for the lay public. Many of these decisions are forced on us by
new scientific discoveries, and the difficulties in making them are created
by the distance between the scientist and the public. (Indeed, there is
a frightening distance even between scientists in one field and those
in another.) This sense of distance is, I think, a grave threat to the survival of the kind of society in which science can flourish at all.

People hate scientists. There is no use in beating about the bush here. 2
The scientist is in danger of becoming the scapegoat for the helplessness
which the public feels. And if an immense revulsion of public feeling
does lead to the destruction of the scientific tradition, then the world may
again enter a dark age as it did after the Goths destroyed Rome. It is
not impossible that the whole mechanical and intellectual society which
we know could be abolished by a great wave of fanaticism.

That is the danger which faces us, because people hate scientists. But 3
even if this danger does not materialize, something as terrible can happen — and is happening. This is that the scientist is forced, by the hatred
of public opinion, to side with established authority and government.
He becomes a prisoner of the hatred of the lay public, and by that
becomes the tool of authority.

My purpose is not to underline these obvious dangers, which we may 4
hide from ourselves but which in our hearts we all know to exist. My purpose is to try to give a picture, as I see it, of the real responsibilities
of scientists, government, and public, in order that, beginning from this
diagnosis, we may begin to cure the great and threatening division
between them.

The Abuse of Science

5   What the lay public does when it hates the scientist is what it does
also when it hates policemen and ministers of state and all symbols of
authority. It tries to shift the responsibility for decisions from its own
shoulders to the shoulders of other people. "They have done this," it
says. And "They" is always the law, the government — or in this case,
the scientist.

6   You must allow me here to make a digression which is not strictly
part of my theme, but which I think needs saying. It is this: that we
must not forget that scientists do bear a heavy responsibility. I am of
course about to explain that really the public and governments bear the
main responsibility. But this does not shift from us, the scientists, the
grave onus of having acquiesced in the abuse of science. We have contrived weapons and policies with our public conscience, which each
of us individually would never have undertaken with his private conscience. Men are only murderers in large groups. They do not individually go out and strangle their neighbor. And scientists are only murderers
in large groups — collectively. For scientists are very ordinary human
beings. Any collection of people in any laboratory contains good and
bad, people with consciences and without, and what we have allowed
to happen is the conquest of science by the minority without conscience
which exists in every group.

7   It is sad that scientists have been exceptionally corruptible. Look into your own experience. Most of us have come from poor parents. We
have worked our own way up. The practice of science has enabled us
to earn salaries which would be unthinkable to us if we had stayed peddling whatever our fathers peddled. Quite suddenly, the possession of
a special skill has opened to us a blue door in the antechambers of prime
ministers. We sit at conference tables, we have become important people,
because we happen to be able to be murderers. And therefore scientists
have been bought with large salaries and fellowships and rewards quite
inappropriate to their merits, because a policy was furthered by their
techniques. The scientist has proved to be the easiest of all men to blind
with the attractions of public life.

8   Having said this I now propose to stop abusing the scientist. I think
it is right that we should all make this confession of guilt — I have been
as guilty as anyone else — but this is all spilt milk, this is all water
over the dam. We must now look toward what we can do to remedy
what has happened. And it cannot be remedied by a gigantic strike of

scientists, who will suddenly refuse to have anything to do with commercial or war research, because the society of scientists contains too many fallible human beings to make this practicable.

When the public dreams of such a strike, when it says: "scientists **9** ought not to have invented this or disclosed that secret," it is already demanding something of the individual scientist which lies beyond his personal responsibility.

The voters of Great Britain elect for the purpose of making their policy **10** six hundred and thirty members of Parliament. They do not elect the people who go to Harwell or the people who go to my own research laboratory. That is: we have already deputed to those whom we elect the responsibility for framing policy in peace and war, and it is quite wrong to ask a body of professional experts like the scientists to take this responsibility from the men whom our society has named.

The individual scientist is not the keeper of the public conscience, **11** because that is not what he was chosen for. The population at large, through its deputed ministers, has chosen scientists to execute certain public orders which are thought to represent the public will. And you cannot ask the scientist to be executioner of this will, and judge as well. If you have given a body of scientists this particular hangman's task, you cannot ask them also to form a collective opposition to it. The collective responsibility belongs to the lay public and through that, to those who were elected by that public to carry it out.

Thus when Einstein on August 2, 1939, wrote a letter to President **12** Roosevelt in order to draw his attention to the possibility of an atomic bomb, he was acting with exemplary correctness. He was disclosing to the elected head of government a matter of public importance on which the decision was not his, the writer's, but was the President's to make.

We must explain to people that they are asking of scientists quite the **13** wrong collective decision when they say, "you should not have invented this," or "you should not have disclosed that." This is asking us all to betray the public in the same way as Dr. Klaus Fuchs did, by asking scientists to make decisions which are for the nation to make. The only man who ever, on his own responsibility, was willing to shoulder public responsibility in this way, was Dr. Fuchs. But so far from being hailed as the only sane scientist, he was treated as quite the opposite — as of course he was, since scientists have no right to betray the will of the nation. Yet Fuchs did just what the public asks of every scientist — he decided what to do with a scientific invention.

The Private Conscience

14   Very well. We will agree that the scientist is not the keeper of the nation's policy. Then what is he the keeper of? He is the keeper of his own private conscience. His responsibility is not to be seduced as a person. He has the right to act individually as a conscientious objector. Indeed, I believe he has the duty to act as a conscientious objector. I would like to repeat this point. It is in this country an offense to betray the armed forces or to seduce their members from their allegiance. It is not an offense to refuse to be a soldier. And I believe that this is exactly like the position of the scientist. He has no business to act as if he commands the army, but he has a business to settle with his own conscience: the serious business whether he personally will engage in forms of research of which he does not morally approve.

15   My claim then is that the individual scientist should exercise his own personal conscience. This is his duty. What is the duty of governments in this respect? It is to make it possible for him to exercise his conscience. The responsibility of governments in this is to create the conditions in which a scientist can say: No! to projects in which he does not want to take part. He must even be able to give advice which is distasteful to those in authority, and still must not be hounded out of public life or prevented from making a living.

16   In all countries the serious threat to scientists who have once touched the fringes of secret subjects is that they are then caught in something from which they can never escape again. They do not get a passport, in case somebody captures them. They cannot get a job because, if they do not want to do this, then they are too dangerous or awkward to be trusted with anything else. This is what we must prevent governments from doing, and this can only be prevented by the opinion of quite ordinary citizens. This is the duty which citizens owe to scientists, to insist that governments shall make it possible for scientists to be conscientious objectors if they wish.

17   I have explored this subject in general terms, and I would now like to be specific. I would like to tell you precisely what I think is the responsibility of the public, of the scientists, and of governments.

18   The responsibility of the public is to make the decisions of policy on which their future depends, and to make them themselves. And in a democracy the apparatus for this is to elect those people in whose judgment you have confidence — and to elect them on the issues which in fact face the world. Now you can only elect such people, you can

only put pressure on them about public issues, if you are well informed. The greatest lack of public opinion today is lack of information about what is possible and not possible in science. This sets my teeth on edge every time I read a scientific newsflash. I will quote one of many instances which I find distasteful: the use of the phrase "cobalt bomb." This is a technical term for a piece of medical equipment, but has suddenly become transformed into something to describe how a hydrogen bomb might be clothed. As a result, of the fifty million people in this country, forty-nine million and nine hundred odd thousand have heard the words "cobalt bomb," but are helplessly confused between radioactive treatment and something that you blow people up with. The public must be well informed; and the public gets not only the government it deserves, but the newspapers it deserves.

If this is once granted, the next step I think is simple. If it is once 19 granted that we believe in democratic election, and that in our generation this can only be carried out by a public informed on the scientific issues on which the fate of nations hangs, then the duty of the scientist is clear. The duty of the scientist is to create the public opinion for right policies, and this he can only create if the public shares his knowledge.

My generation has a heavy task here, because it ought to spend the 20 bulk of its time — alas — not in laboratories at all, but in explaining to the voting public what is going on in the laboratories. What are the choices which face us? What could be done with antibiotics, with new materials, with coal (if you like), and with alternative forms of energy? These are urgent questions and yet, however many times we raise them, the layman still does not understand the scale of the changes which our work is making, and on which the answers must hang.

There is a slightly irreverent story about this. At the time the Smyth 21 Report was published in America there was published in this country a White Paper on the British contribution to atomic energy. One of the documents in it is the directive which Mr. Winston Churchill, as he then was, gave about the setting up of an atomic energy project. This directive begins with the words, "Though personally satisfied with the power of existing explosives. . . ." This bland phrase is a monument to a nonscientific education. For it could only have been written by a man, an intelligent man, who simply does not understand how big a million is. The difference between atomic explosives and ordinary explosives is the difference between the length of a nuclear bond and a molecular bond; and this is a factor of more than a million. To suppose somehow that in multiplying the energy of an explosive by a million, you are doing nothing very different from multiplying it by two, or five, or ten — this is simply not to grasp the scale of the world.

22   And the public does not grasp it. To say "ten to the sixth" to anybody, however educated, is still to invite the reproof today that one is stressing mere numerical details. One of our tasks, as scientists, must be to educate people in the scale of things.

23   While I am telling improper stories — improper only in the amusing sense — I will tell you that everybody who works in industrial research has this trouble all the time, when he discusses the economics of new processes. We put forward the result of research, or we simply estimate what would happen if a piece of research proved successful. And at once we get back a balance sheet from the finance department which says: The current process makes a profit of 2/2d a ton, and what you have in mind might make a loss of 8d a ton; it is therefore not worth pursuing. This, if you please, is the comment on a piece of research which, if it works on the full scale, might cut costs by a factor of five. But no accountant understands a factor of five; he budgets in shillings and pence, and what is liable to loss is to him as good as lost. One cannot explain a factor of five, or a factor of a million, to people who have not been brought up in a scientific tradition. This is what I mean when I say that the scientist has a duty to become a teacher to the public in understanding the pace, the nature, the scale of the changes which are possible in our lifetime.

Government and Opportunity

24   I have detailed the duties of the public and of the scientist. What are the duties of government? The duties of government are to give its public the opportunity to learn, and therefore to give scientists the opportunity to teach. And I have already suggested that these duties are twofold. One is to give scientists freedom to live their own lives if they do not want to go on with research projects which seem to them without conscience. The other is the duty to allow scientists to speak freely on subjects of world importance.

25   As for the second, everyone who has ever been connected with the atomic energy projects knows how it is met today. We spend our time waiting for some American journalist to publish some piece of information which we know to be accurate, so that we may then quote it as being the opinion of the *New York Times*. I am being frank about this: I do it all the time. I read what the greatest indiscreet senator said to the small indiscreet reporters, and I know that nine statements are

nonsense and one statement is accurate. Then I quote the one that is accurate — but not as my opinion.

Of course it is natural that governments resist the explosive opinions 26 of scientists. All governments, all societies are resistant to change. Rather over two thousand years ago, Plato was anxious to exile poets from his society; and in our lifetime, for the same reason, governments are, in effect, anxious to exile or at least silence scientists. They are anxious to exile all dissidents, because dissidents are the people who will change society.

There is a simple difference between governments and scientists. 27 Governments believe that society ought to stay the way it is for good — and particularly, that there ought to be no more elections. Scientists believe that society ought to be stable, but this does not mean the same thing to them as being static. We scientists want to see an *evolving* society, because when the physical world is evolving (and we are helping to evolve it) the forms of society and government cannot be kept the same.

The Moral Contract

Having described the duties of the public, of scientists, and of govern- 28 ments, let me now underline what I have said by describing what happens in all three cases if these duties are not kept. If governments do not allow scientists freedom of conscience, to work at what they like and to refuse to work at what they do not like, and to speak freely about why they do so, then you get the gravest of all disasters — the disaster of state intolerance. This is a disaster because it saps both sides of the moral contract. For there is a moral contract between society and its individuals which allows the individual to be a dissident; and if the state breaks this moral contract, then it leaves the individual no alternative but to become a terrorist. I do not know whether the great state trials in Russia were just or were false. But I know that if they were just, if men like Radek and Trotsky and Zinoviev really committed those enormities, then this in itself condemns the system of government which does not allow any other form of protest than such a form. The grave danger to our society too is that this becomes the only choice which is left open to scientists, if state intolerance imprisons them and tries to turn them into a secret Egyptian priestcraft.

The great sin of the public is acquiescence in this secrecy. I am hor- 29 rified by the feeling that I get, from such trifling things as American advertisements, that people really enjoy the sense that they are not to be trusted. There is an advertisement running in the *New Yorker* at the moment (I think for a clothing firm) which shows a man who has just got out of an airplane. He has a face like a prizefighter, he is well-dressed and wears what in New York is called a sharp hat, and he carries a bag in one hand which is chained to his wrist. He is carrying secret documents. This is the holy of holies. This is what we are to admire — the man with his mouth shut tight who is not trusting you and me, because of course you and I are not to be trusted. When people come to believe this, when they themselves believe that it is better for them not to know, then totalitarianism is on the doorstep. Then you are ready for Hitler to get up and say: "I am the man who will take your communal responsibilities. I will make your decisions for you."

30   And the third in our scheme, the scientist, must preserve the tradition of quarrelling, of questioning, and of dissent on which science (and I believe all post-Renaissance civilization) has been built. He must do this for two reasons. First, there is the mundane reason which is obvious in the failure of German research after Hitler took power. It is this: that you do not get good science as soon as you have reduced the scientists to yes-men. It is the nature of scientists to be thoroughly contrary people — let us own up to that. It is the nature of science as an activity to doubt your word and mine. As soon as you get a science, such as atomic energy research in totalitarian Germany, in which the young men are no longer allowed to question what the great men have said, then that science is dead. You can find in the files of the German Atomic Energy Commission that several young men made what I suppose must be called very good suggestions, but they were not followed because (such is the influence of totalitarianism) Heisenberg already knew the answers already.

31   This does not happen in English laboratories yet. Mr. Churchill begins by saying that he is satisfied with existing explosives, but after the comma he does give scientists the opportunity to be dissatisfied. This tradition, this independence and tolerance, is I believe the base of all our values; and this is what we as scientists must preserve.

The Duty of Heresy

32   I have given you the simple practical grounds for allowing scientists to be awkward, but I believe also that imaginatively and intellectually this is equally important. The sense of intellectual heresy is the lifeblood of our civilization. And the heresy of scientists cannot be confined to their science. Newton was thoroughly and rightly contrary in science,

and he was also a thorough heretic in religious matters. For the same reason, people like Oppenheimer and Einstein are found to associate with such unreliable characters. You cannot say to scientists: "When you get into the laboratory at nine in the morning you are going to become a dissenter; and when you go out at five-thirty you are going to become a citizen who touches his cap and who is politically sound. The intellect is not divided into these simple categories.

I have said that the duty of the scientist is today publicly to become 33 a teacher. Let me end by saying something of what he is to teach. There is, of course, the scientific method. There are things about the scale and order of size, of which I have spoken. There are the possibilities which are open to us in controlling nature and ourselves. Above all, he can teach men to ask whether the distance between promise and achievement in our age need be quite so large; whether there must be such a gap between what society is capable of doing and what it does. All this, every scientist can teach.

But every scientist can also teach something deeper. He can teach 34 men to resist all forms of acquiescence, of indifference, and all imposition of secrecy and denial. We must resist the attitude of officials, that there ought to be a good reason why something should be published before you allow it. We must teach even officials that there will have to be a very good reason indeed before anyone is silenced by secrecy.

Mr. Gordon Dean, former chairman of the American Atomic Energy 35 Commission, has just been complaining against secrecy on practical grounds. He says that the commercial reactors which are being built in America are still on the secret list and that this is handicapping American business in its competition with English business for world reactor markets. God works in a mysterious way and it may be that by this anxiety to sell atomic power, science will be liberated. At any rate, let us not look askance at any ally in the drive against silence. My message, in this and in all else, has been the scientist's duty to speak. There is one thing above all others that the scientist has a duty to teach to the public and to governments: it is the duty of heresy.

(1956)

The Writer's Subject

1. What is the chief responsibility of the scientist, as Bronowski sees it?

2. Why, according to Bronowski, do people regard scientists in the same way that they regard other symbols of authority? (para. 5)

3. How, in Bronowski's view, have scientists contributed to the abuse of science? (para. 7)

4. How does Bronowski answer those who think that scientists should oppose government policy on such matters as war research? (paras. 8-13)

5. How does Bronowski illustrate the danger of allowing a scientist rather than a government to make the decision about what to do with a scientific invention? (para. 13)

6. Why does Bronowski say the scientist "has the duty to act as a conscientious objector"? (para. 14)

7. Why is it so important for the public to be well informed, and what are the responsibilities of the scientist in this regard? (paras. 18-22)

8. What are the consequences of governments' not allowing scientists freedom of conscience? (para. 28)

The Writer's Style and Strategy

1. How does Bronowski make clear that his audience is made up of scientists?

2. What evidence in the style of this essay indicates that it was also intended to reach a wider audience?

3. "The Real Responsibilities of the Scientist" is a good example of a public address. Bronowski skilfully identifies himself with his audience and employs direct appeals to his listeners, anecdotes, clear transitions between the stages of his argument, and restatements of central ideas for clarity. Find examples of these and other techniques which demonstrate Bronowski's command as a public speaker.

4. What use does Bronowski make of anecdote and historical example?

Suggested Topics for Writing and Discussion

1. Bronowski is opposed to "all imposition of secrecy and denial." Do you think there are ever circumstances in which a scientist should observe total secrecy in connection with his or her research?

2. Bronowski speaks of the importance of educating the public on matters of science. What does an educated citizen need to know about science in order to perform his or her duties as a responsible member of a democratic society?

3. In recent times several fields of science have led to controversy (e.g., *in vitro* fertilization, organ transplants, genetic engineering, irradiation of food, nuclear energy). Focusing on one area of scientific research, discuss the extent to which you think governmental controls should be exercised.

4. Bronowski speaks of the anxiety of the English and the Americans to sell atomic power, a business in which Canada is also involved. Do you think Canada should limit or halt its sale of CANDU reactors?

Posture Maketh the Man

by Stephen Jay Gould

1   No event did more to establish the fame and prestige of The American Museum of Natural History than the Gobi Desert expeditions of the 1920s. The discoveries, including the first dinosaur eggs, were exciting and abundant, and the sheer romance fit Hollywood's most heroic mold. It is still hard to find a better adventure story than Roy Chapman Andrews's book (with its chauvinistic title): *The New Conquest of Central Asia*. Nonetheless, the expeditions utterly failed to achieve their stated purpose: to find in Central Asia the ancestors of man. And they failed for the most elementary of reasons — we evolved in Africa, as Darwin had surmised fifty years earlier.

2   Our African ancestors (or at least our nearest cousins) were discovered in cave deposits during the 1920s. But these australopithecines failed to fit preconceived notions of what a "missing link" should look like, and many scientists refused to accept them as bona fide members of our lineage. Most anthropologists had imagined a fairly harmonious transformation from ape to human, propelled by increasing intelligence. A missing link should be intermediate in both body and brain — Alley Oop or the old (and false) representations of stoopshouldered Neanderthals. But the australopithecines refused to conform. To be sure, their brains were bigger than those of any ape with comparable body size, but not much bigger. Most of our evolutionary increase in brain size occurred after we reached the australopithecine level. Yet these small-brained australopithecines walked as erect as you or I. How could this be? If our evolution was propelled by an enlarging brain, how could upright posture — another "hallmark of hominization," not just an in-

cidental feature — originate first? In a 1963 essay, George Gaylord Simpson used this dilemma to illustrate

> the sometimes spectacular failure to predict discoveries even when there is a sound basis for such prediction. An evolutionary example is the failure to predict discovery of a "missing link," now known [*Australopithecus*], that was upright and tool-making but had the physiognomy and cranial capacity of an ape.

We must ascribe this "spectacular failure" primarily to a subtle prejudice that led to the following, invalid extrapolation: We dominate other animals by brain power (and little else); therefore, an increasing brain must have propelled our own evolution at all stages. The tradition for subordinating upright posture to an enlarging brain can be traced throughout the history of anthropology. Karl Ernst von Baer, the greatest embryologist of the nineteenth century (and second only to Darwin in my personal pantheon of scientific heroes) wrote in 1828: "Upright posture is only the consequence of the higher development of the brain . . . all differences between men and other animals depend upon construction of the brain." One hundred years later, the English anthropologist G. E. Smith wrote: "It was not the adoption of the erect attitude or the invention of articulate language that made man from an ape, but the gradual perfecting of a brain and the slow building of the mental structure, of which erectness of carriage and speech are some of the incidental manifestations." 3

Against this chorus of emphasis upon the brain, a very few scientists upheld the primacy of upright posture. Sigmund Freud based much of his highly idiosyncratic theory for the origin of civilization upon it. Beginning in his letters to Wilhelm Fliess in the 1890s and culminating in his 1930 essay on *Civilization and Its Discontents,* Freud argued that our assumption of upright posture had reoriented our primary sensation from smell to vision. This devaluation of olfaction shifted the object of sexual stimulation in males from cyclic odors of estrus to the continual visibility of female genitalia. Continual desire of males led to the evolution of continual receptivity in females. Most mammals copulate only around periods of ovulation; humans are sexually active at all times (a favorite theme of writers on sexuality). Continual sexuality has cemented the human family and made civilization possible; animals with strongly cyclic copulation have no strong impetus for stable family structure." The fateful process of civilization," Freud concludes, "would thus have set in with man's adoption of an erect posture." 4

5   Although Freud's ideas gained no following among anthropologists, another minor tradition did arise to stress the primacy of upright posture. (It is, by the way, the argument we tend to accept today in explaining the morphology of australopithecines and the path of human evolution.) The brain cannot begin to increase in a vacuum. A primary impetus must be provided by an altered mode of life that would place a strong, selective premium upon intelligence. Upright posture frees the hands from locomotion and for manipulation (literally, from *manus* = "hand"). For the first time, tools and weapons can be fashioned and used with ease. Increased intelligence is largely a response to the enormous potential inherent in free hands for manufacture — again, literally. (Needless to say, no anthropologist has ever been so naive as to argue that brain and posture are completely independent in evolution, that one reached its fully human status before the other began to change at all. We are dealing with interaction and mutual reinforcement. Nevertheless, our early evolution did involve a more rapid change in posture than in brain size; complete freeing of our hands for using tools preceded most of the evolutionary enlargement of our brain.)

6   In another proof that sobriety does not make right, von Baer's mystical and oracular colleague Lorenz Oken hit upon the "correct" argument in 1809, while von Baer was led astray a few years later. "Man by the upright walk obtains his character," writes Oken, "the hands become free and can achieve all other offices. . . . With the freedom of the body has been granted also the freedom of the mind." But the champion of upright posture during the nineteenth century was Darwin's German bulldog Ernst Haeckel. Without a scrap of direct evidence, Haeckel reconstructed our ancestor and even gave it a scientific name, *Pithecanthropus alalus,* the upright, speechless, small-brained ape-man. (*Pithecanthropus,* by the way, is probably the only scientific name ever given to an animal before it was discovered. When Du Bois discovered Java Man in the 1890s, he adopted Haeckel's generic name but he gave it the new specific designation *Pithecanthropus erectus.* We now usually include this creature in our own genus as *Homo erectus.*)

7   But why, despite Oken and Haeckel's demurral, did the idea of cerebral primacy become so strongly entrenched? One thing is sure; it had nothing to do with direct evidence — for there was none for any position. With the exception of Neanderthal (a geographic variant of our own species according to most anthropologists), no fossil humans were discovered until the closing years of the nineteenth century, long after the dogma of cerebral primacy was established. But debates based on no evidence

are among the most revealing in the history of science, for in the absence of factual constraints, the cultural biases that affect all thought (and which scientists try so assiduously to deny) lie nakedly exposed.

Indeed, the nineteenth century produced a brilliant exposé from a **8** source that will no doubt surprise most readers — Friedrich Engels. (A bit of reflection should diminish surprise. Engels had a keen interest in the natural sciences and sought to base his general philosophy of dialectical materialism upon a "positive" foundation. He did not live to complete his "dialectics of nature," but he included long commentaries on science in such treatises as the *Anti-Dühring*.) In 1876, Engels wrote an essay entitled, *The Part Played by Labor in the Transition from Ape to Man*. It was published posthumously in 1896 and, unfortunately, had no visible impact upon Western science.

Engels considers three essential features of human evolution: speech, **9** a large brain, and upright posture. He argues that the first step must have been a descent from the trees with subsequent evolution to upright posture by our ground-dwelling ancestors. "These apes when moving on level ground began to drop the habit of using their hands and to adopt a more and more erect gait. This was the decisive step in the transition from ape to man." Upright posture freed the hand for using tools (labor, in Engels's terminology); increased intelligence and speech came later.

Thus the hand is not only the organ of labor, it is also the product of labor. Only by labor, by adaptation to ever new operations . . . by the ever-renewed employment of these inherited improvements in new, more and more complicated operations, has the human hand attained the high degree of perfection that has enabled it to conjure into being the pictures of Raphael, the statues of Thorwaldsen, the music of Paganini.

Engels presents his conclusions as though they followed deductively **10** from the premises of his materialist philosophy, but I am confident that he cribbed them from Haeckel. The two formulations are almost identical, and Engels cites the relevant pages of Haeckel's work for other purposes in an earlier essay written in 1874. But no matter. The importance of Engels's essay lies, not in its substantive conclusions, but in its trenchant political analysis of why Western science was so hung up on the a priori assertion of cerebral primacy.

As humans learned to master their material surroundings, Engels **11** argues, other skills were added to primitive hunting — agriculture, spinning, pottery, navigation, arts and sciences, law and politics, and finally,

"the fantastic reflection of human things in the human mind: religion."
As wealth accumulated, small groups of men seized power and forced
others to work for them. Labor, the source of all wealth and the primary
impetus for human evolution, assumed the same low status of those who
labored for the rulers. Since rulers governed by their will (that is, by
feats of mind), actions of the brain appeared to have a motive power
of their own. The profession of philosophy followed no unsullied ideal
of truth. Philosophers relied on state or religious patronage. Even if
Plato did not consciously conspire to bolster the privileges of rulers
with a supposedly abstract philosophy, his own class position encouraged
an emphasis on thought as primary, dominating, and altogether more
noble and important than the labor it supervised. This idealistic tradition dominated philosophy right through to Darwin's day. Its influence
was so subtle and pervasive that even scientific, but apolitical, materialists
like Darwin fell under its sway. A bias must be recognized before it
can be challenged. Cerebral primacy seemed so obvious and natural
that it was accepted as given, rather than recognized as a deep-seated
social prejudice related to the class position of professional thinkers and
their patrons. Engels writes:

> All merit for the swift advance of civilization was ascribed to the
> mind, to the development and activity of the brain. Men became
> accustomed to explain their actions from their thoughts, instead of
> from their needs. . . . And so there arose in the course of time
> that idealistic outlook on the world which, especially since the
> downfall of the ancient world, has dominated men's minds. It still
> rules them to such a degree that even the most materialistic natural
> scientists of the Darwinian school are still unable to form any clear
> idea of the origin of man, because under that ideological influence
> they do not recognize the part that has been played therein by labor.

12   The importance of Engels's essay does not lie in the happy result that
Australopithecus confirmed a specific theory proposed by him — via
Haeckel — but rather in his perceptive analysis of the political role of
science and of the social biases that must affect all thought.

13   Indeed, Engels's theme of the separation of head and hand has done
much to set and limit the course of science throughout history. Academic
science, in particular, has been constrained by an ideal of "pure" research,
which in former days barred a scientist from extensive experimentation and empirical testing. Ancient Greek science labored under the
restriction that patrician thinkers could not perform the manual work

of plebeian artisans. Medieval barber-surgeons who had to deal with battlefield casualties did more to advance the practice of medicine than academic physicians who rarely examined patients and who based their treatment on a knowledge of Galen and other learned texts. Even today, "pure" researchers tend to disparage the practical, and terms such as "aggie school" and "cow college" are heard with distressing frequency in academic circles. If we took Engels's message to heart and recognized our belief in the inherent superiority of pure research for what it is — namely social prejudice — then we might forge among scientists the union between theory and practice that a world teetering dangerously near the brink so desperately needs.

(1973)

The Writer's Subject

1. Why did anthropologists formerly believe that growth of the brain must have preceded upright posture in the evolution of man? (para. 3)

2. What effect did the discovery of australopithecine man have upon older theories of the brain in the evolution of man?

3. What is the modern view regarding the relationship between brain size and posture as summarized by Gould in paragraph 5?

4. Why does Gould give so much prominence to the essay on evolution by the nineteenth-century political philosopher Engels, when, as Gould himself says, the scientific aspects of the essay were probably derived from the work of Ernst Haeckel? (paras. 8-13)

5. What is the particular class bias which Gould cites as operative in western society (i.e., from Plato's time onward)? How has this bias affected attitudes towards scientific research? (para. 11)

6. What is Gould's concluding plea concerning attitudes towards scientific research? (para. 13)

The Writer's Style and Strategy

1. What is the function of the opening paragraph of the essay?

2. Much of Gould's argument is conducted by reference to nineteenth and twentieth century authorities. How does Gould use these authorities to develop his thesis?

3. What use does Gould make of asides and parenthetical comments?

4. Why does Gould put the word "pure" in quotations in paragraph 13?

5. Gould is a scientist writing for non-scientists. What features of his style reflect his awareness of his intended audience? Where might he be addressing his arguments to his fellow scientists, too?

6. Comment on Gould's title. What phrase is it meant to echo?

Suggested Topics for Writing and Discussion

1. Gould says, "Debates based on no evidence are among the most revealing in the history of science, for in the absence of factual constraints, the cultural biases that affect all thought . . . lie nakedly exposed." Consider one controversial topic (e.g., creationism vs. Darwinism, whether life exists on other planets, whether God exists, at what moment human life begins), and discuss the "cultural biases" that seem to underlie one side or other of the debate.

2. Gould is critical of what he calls "pure" research and implies an irresponsibility on the part of the scientific community. What do you think are the primary considerations that should govern scientific research? (Compare Gould's comments about the scientist's relationship to the society to those made by Bronowski in "The Real Responsibilities of the Scientist.")

3. Gould speaks of the class attitude, which he says prevailed until Darwin's day, that thought was "more noble and important than the labour it supervised." What attitudes does our own society have toward labour today?

Some Enemies of Science
by J.B.S. Haldane

Last week my wife successfully poisoned a number of rats. They were   1
eating the food of our chickens, and would have eaten the smaller of
the birds if they had got the chance. Owing to the failure of a more
humane poison she found herself compelled to use phosphorous; which
is a slow and, to judge from the experience of the human beings who
commit suicide by eating matches, often rather painful means of death.

During the same period I killed two rats in the course of experimen-   2
tal work intended to advance medical science. One of them, if we can
judge from human experience (and we have no more direct means of
evaluating the consciousness of animals), died after a period of rather
pleasant delirium like that of alcoholic intoxication. The other had con-
vulsions, and may have been in pain for three or four minutes. I should
be very thankful if I knew that I should suffer no more than it did before
my death. It therefore seems to me somewhat ridiculous that, whereas
my wife is encouraged by the Government and the Press, I should be
compelled to apply to the President of the Royal Society and another
eminent man of science for signatures to an application to the already
overworked Home Secretary, before I can even kill a mouse in a slightly
novel manner.

It is probably right that some control should be kept over experiments   3
likely to involve severe and prolonged pain to animals; but it is monstrous
that with regard to wholly or nearly painless procedures the scientific
man should be worse treated than any other member of the community.

Under the present law, or, at any rate, under the law as at present   4
interpreted, a license is required for a large number of absolutely painless

experiments, and, what is more serious, they can only be performed in a limited number of laboratories. In consequence, the isolated amateur worker, who has played so great a part in the development of British science, is debarred from wide fields of physiology. The sportsman may go out and shoot as many rabbits as he pleases; and if some of them are wounded and escape to die a lingering death in their holes, no blame attaches to him. But if he anaesthetizes one of his own rabbits at home, and opens its abdomen to observe the effect of a drug on its intestines, killing it before it recovers consciousness, he will be lucky if he escapes with a fine.

5   Nor may the doctor, after his day's shooting of unanaesthetized partridges, acquire surgical skill by an operation on an anaesthetized animal, even in a licensed laboratory. He has to practise on human patients. There are, of course, a few operations of human surgery for which animals would furnish relatively little guidance. In the majority of cases, however, they would be of very real value, and have been proved to be so in America. Not only is medical science already greatly hampered by the law, but a constant fight has to be kept up to preserve what possibilities are left it. It is worth while enquiring into the reasons which have led to this state of affairs.

6   There are a few honest anti-vivisectionists. They are, of course, vegetarians; for the painless killing of animals for physiology is no more reprehensible than their killing for meat. They wear canvas shoes, cotton or woollen gloves, and artificial pearls if any. They refuse to sit on leather-covered chairs, or to wear horn-rimmed spectacles. They do not spray their roses, or employ Keating's powder even under the gravest provocation. I have not met any of them, but I am quite prepared to believe that they exist. No one who does not come up to this rather exacting standard can logically demand the total abolition of vivisection. But logic is not the strongest point of the enemies of science.

7   All others who demand the prohibition of experiments on anaesthetized animals are quite definitely hypocrites, engaged in the familiar pursuit of

'Compounding sins they are inclined to
By damning those they have no mind to.'

There are few more disgusting spectacles in our public life than that of the two or three sporting peers who habitually introduce or support Bills to prohibit such experiments. Each of them has caused more pain to animals in a single day's sport than the average physiologist inflicts in a lifetime, and usually for no end except his personal pleasure. For it seems to me that from the ethical point of view a fairly sharp distinction can be drawn between the killing of animals bred for this purpose at considerable expense, which would produce far more food if applied to agriculture; and that of rabbits, hares, and pigeons which must be kept down in the interest of crops and livestock. Personally, since I have realized from my own experience with shell splinters that it is no fun to carry bits of metal about one's person, I would no more shoot a rabbit than kill my bacon for breakfast. But I certainly do not condemn those who do so.

We must next consider the relatively small number of anti-vivisection- 8 ists who would merely prohibit all painful or possibly painful experiments. Now, the world is so constituted that we cannot avoid inflicting pain on others. I cannot dig in my garden without bisecting a number of earthworms, or drive a car for any time without running over a few of the various animals whose flattened corpses decorate our country roads. But it is our duty, as far as possible, to diminish the amount of pain in the world. The question therefore is whether medical research does this or not.

Now, anti-vivisectionist literature distorts both sides of the account. 9 It states that a great deal of severe suffering is inflicted on animals in the name of science, and that there is little or no return for this in the diminution of human and animal suffering. With regard to the first of these assertions I can speak with a certain degree of experience. I have seen numerous experiments on animals, but I have never seen an animal undergoing pain which I would not have been willing to undergo myself for the same object. Why, then, it may be asked, should not all painful experiments be done on human volunteers?

There are several reasons why not. One is the very simple fact that 10 many of these experiments possibly or necessarily involve the death of the animal. For example, rats are frequently inoculated under the skin of their sides with transplantable cancers. These are not painful, for the rat does not wince or squeak when the lump is pressed. If it were allowed to die of cancer it would often suffer; for the original tumour or its metastases elsewhere would press on nerves, and one of them would probably start to ulcerate. But before either of these events occurs, all such rats in the laboratory in which I work are killed, and the tumours used for chemical study of inoculation. A man, even if he could legally be used for such a purpose and chloroformed before pain began, would presumably suffer from the anticipation of an early death.

Just the same applies to deformity. A rickety child suffers mainly 11 because it cannot take part in the activities of its comrades and is made to realize that it is deformed. A rickety rat has none of these disadvantages, not only because it is probably not self-conscious, but because under laboratory conditions all its acquaintances are rickety too. Finally, there is the question of expense. Human beings cost a lot in board and lodging, and must be compensated for loss of time. If, as in experiments on the effects of small changes in the diet, hundreds of individuals and years of time are needed, this consideration is generally final.

12   However, if we are to believe anti-vivisectionists, animals constantly undergo tortures which no human being would voluntarily endure. I recently received an illustrated pamphlet, which I should think is fairly typical, describing the sufferings of laboratory animals. There was a picture of an oven in which dogs were slowly heated till they died, while a physiologist watched their agonies through a window. The thought of such cruelty would have made my blood boil, if it had not already been partially boiled in such a chamber on several occasions. Under such circumstances one becomes dizzy long before there is any definite pain, and death, if it occurs, is from heat stroke, not from burning. Personally, I prefer being overheated in a bath. Immersion of all but the head in water kept hot enough just not to be painful, causes loss of consciousness, after a good deal of panting, in about twenty minutes. Hence there is reason to think that a lobster, if put into cold water and heated fairly slowly, feels no pain, which it must certainly do if dropped into boiling water. Probably, however, it would suffer still less if about 2½ per cent of salt were added to the cold water.

13   Then came a picture of a dog's mouth held open by a somewhat brutal-looking contrivance. This was said to be taken from a scientific periodical called the 'Transactions of the Physiological Society.' There is, unfortunately, no such journal, nor could I find the picture in the Proceedings of that body for the date given. Perhaps, therefore, it was the anti-visectionist's idea of what an instrument of scientific torture ought to look like. But if I had been a maiden lady with a pet dog and no knowledge either of the facts or the literature of physiology, I might have sent a cheque to one of the ladies and gentlemen who make a living by compiling documents of this kind.

14   In some cases experiments are supposed to be painful out of ignorance rather than malice. A group of experiments by Sir John Bradford, in which parts of the kidneys of dogs were removed under an anaesthetic, are constantly described in parliament as torture. Some of these dogs

recovered completely, others died with the symptoms of chronic kidney disease, which in human beings seldom causes any pain worse than a headache. Stone in the kidney can, of course, be very painful, but the dogs were not so treated as to cause them pain of this type, nor did they show any signs of suffering it. As a matter of fact, too, dogs can stand a good deal of wounding without much suffering, so far as one can judge. I know this, not from laboratory experience, but because I have owned a dog whose courage and love affairs constantly led him into fights with larger dogs.

A large part of the unhappiness of dogs in English laboratories is direct- **15** ly due to the anti-vivisectionists. In the laboratory where I work there are a number of dogs, each of which, for two or three months in the year, eats certain organic compounds which it transforms in its body. The newly formed compounds are excreted in the urine. To facilitate the collection of urine an operation has been performed on them analogous to circumcision, and not nearly so severe as tail-docking. Of course, an anaesthetic was used. But because the operation has been performed in the cause of science rather than fashion, these dogs are forbidden by law to leave the laboratory. They are exercised in the grounds twice daily, but may not go into the street, and must lead a rather dull life. This regulation is typical of the present law, which is designed quite as much to hamper research as to protect animals.

While the large majority of experiments performed annually are nearly **16** painless, a few dozen, which attempt to reproduce a painful human disease, and thus to discover its cause or cure, are as painful as the disease which they imitate, except that when the animal's condition is clearly hopeless it can be killed.

I do not think it will be necessary to convince any reader of this book **17** of the value of medical research. It has been the principal cause which renders the worst slum of to-day healthier than the palace of a century ago. If that result had been reached by the infliction of appalling tor- ture on millions of animals the ethical justification of this torture would certainly be a matter for discussion. Actually the fate of experimental rats, for example, is no worse than that of pet rats, which generally die from deficient diet or epidemic disease.

It remains to consider the psychology of anti-vivisectionists. I think **18** that their most important motive is a hatred of science, which they at- tack at its weakest point. They hate science partly because they do not understand it, and will not take the trouble to; partly because it is ethically neutral. Many of them feel that disease must be a punishment for sin, and that it could be avoided if we lived according to their own particular prejudices. This view has been taken by most religions, though, of course, Jesus did not share it (John, chap. 9,v.3). Almost all believe that there is some short cut to health. So a great many simple-lifers, vegetarians, faith-healers, Christian scientists, and so forth, are opposed to medical research, and say that its results are worthless.

19   In some cases anti-vivisection goes with pacifism. The fallacy involved in this association is rather interesting. Non-resistance of human evil is sometimes effective. A certain percentage of human smiters are seriously disconcerted if one turns the other cheek to them. But this kind of method does not work on bacteria, which have no finer feelings. We cannot find out how they behave, and thus acquire power over them, except by experiments on men or animals. This is a very unfortunate fact, but then the universe differs in a great many ways from what we should wish it to be. Medicine continued on non-experimental lines (with a very few exceptions) from the dawn of history till the seventeenth century. And in consequence it remained stationary during thousands of years. If its enemies get their way it will begin to stagnate again.

20   But there is a less respectable side to the anti-vivisectionist mind. During the recent agitation aginst experiments on dogs I made an offer of £100 (published in the *Daily Mail*) to the National Canine Defence League, if they would produce any evidence for certain libels on the medical profession which they were circulating in order to obtain signatures for a petition. I got no answer from the League, but a number of abusive and most instructive letters.

21   One of them, from E. Hough of Hammersmith, objected to experiments 'on the dear, faithful doggies for the benefit of worthless human beings.' 'I like to think,' she wrote (for I picture the writer as an elderly and soured spinster) 'that God will torture physiologists in a future life. I would not lift a finger to save one of them if he were writhing in agony.' There is, then, a group of anti-vivisectionists who like to think about torture. As they can no longer attend the burning of atheists and witches, they gloat over imaginary stories of animal torture till their blood boils; and then cool it with the thought of physiologists in hell fire. Thanks largely to the psychological mutilation to which our society subjects adults, and more particularly children, the world is over-full of

'Ceux dont le rêve obscur salit tout ce qu'il touche,'[1]

and I suspect that a fair number of them become anti-vivisectionists.

---

1. "Those whose dark dream dirties all that it touches."

Those who have benefited by the results of medical research and wish 22
it to continue might do worse than support the Research Defence Society,
which carries on a lonely fight against a vast flood of lies. And they
should urge the following alterations in the law, none of which would
increase animal suffering in the faintest degree. Stray dogs impounded
by the police should be used for experiment. This would abolish dog
stealing for laboratories, and save the lives of some thousand dogs per
year. No licence should be required for experiments on fully anaesthetized animals which are killed under the anaesthetic. Surgeons should
be allowed to practise their art under the same conditions. Animals should
not be condemned to imprisonment for life because an experiment has
been done on them. And in the interests of national economy the number
of officials and of Government forms used in the supervision of research
should be cut down.

At present biological and medical research workers are enormously 23
handicapped by the law and by public opinion. Several hospitals, out
of deference to subscribers, do not allow animal experiments. They thus
render the rapid diagnosis of various diseases impossible, and kill a
certain number of patients annually. And medical teaching is seriously
handicapped in the same way. These are some of the reasons why
England is less healthy than a number of other European countries. Anti-
vivisectionists are responsible for far more deaths per year in England
than motor vehicles, smallpox, or typhoid fever.

(1928)

The Writer's Subject

1. What is Haldane's point in contrasting his wife's use of rat poison and
    his own experiments? (paras. 1-2)

2. What, in Haldane's view, distinguishes the "honest anti-vivisectionists" from
    those he calls hypocrites? (paras. 6-7)

3. What are Haldane's reasons for rejecting the idea that all painful ex-
    periments should be carried out on human volunteers? (paras. 9-11)

4. On what grounds does Haldane blame the anti-vivisectionists for "a large
    part of the unhappiness of dogs in English laboratories" (para. 15)?

5. What motives does Haldane attribute to the anti-vivisectionists? (paras.
    18-19)

6. What does he fear may happen to medical research if the anti-vivisectionists get their way? (para. 19)

7. Why, according to Haldane, is England "less healthy than a number of European countries" (para. 23)?

The Writer's Style and Strategy

1. How does Haldane seek to convince his reader that animals used in experiments suffer little or no pain? (paras. 10, 12, 14)

2. What picture does Haldane draw of his opponents, the anti-vivisectionists? What tone does he generally adopt in his description of them? Does he make use of any loaded terms in his references to them? (See, for example, paras. 6, 7 and 18.)

3. For what reason does Haldane allude to his own experience with shell splinters? (para. 7)

4. How does Haldane deal with the charges in the anti-vivisectionists' pamphlet described in paragraphs 12 and 13? What does he imply about its authors at the end of paragraph 13?

5. How does Haldane make use of irony to answer his opponents in paragraph 19?

6. Why does Haldane give prominence to the letter from E. Hough in paragraph 21? Why does he picture the writer as "an elderly and soured spinster"?

7. Explain the function of paragraph 22.

Suggested Topics for Writing and Discussion

1. Haldane argues against the restrictions placed on scientists who wish to use animals for medical research. What is your view of this issue? Do you believe that scientists should be free to experiment with animals in the interests of reducing human suffering? Are there any restrictions which you think should be imposed?

2. Haldane complains that a hunter, unlike the scientist, may kill or maim animals without penalty. Write an argument for or against recreational hunting, addressing your argument to an audience opposed to your own views.

3. Choose one area of modern medical research (e.g., artificial organs or limbs, drug therapy, disease control, plastic surgery) and show the con-

tribution it has made to the quality of life, either of the individual or of the society at large.

4. Haldane's essay originally appeared in 1928, but the issue which he addresses is still widely discussed. The present-day spokesman for those opposing the use of animals in experiments is Peter Singer, the author of *Animal Liberation*. Consult Singer's work and shape a response to Haldane's arguments.

The Discus Thrower
by Richard Selzer

"Do not go gentle"

I spy on my patients. Ought not a doctor to observe his patients by any means and from any stance, that he might the more fully assemble evidence? So I stand in the doorways of hospital rooms and gaze. Oh, it is not all that furtive an act. Those in bed need only look up to discover me. But they never do.

From the doorway of Room 542 the man in the bed seems deeply tanned. Blue eyes and close-cropped white hair give him the appearance of vigor and good health. But I know that his skin is not brown from the sun. It is rusted, rather, in the last stage of containing the vile repose within. And the blue eyes are frosted, looking inward like the windows of a snowbound cottage. This man is blind. This man is also legless — the right leg missing from midthigh down, the left from just below the knee. It gives him the look of a bonsai, roots and branches pruned into the dwarfed facsimile of a great tree.

Propped on pillows, he cups his right thigh in both hands. Now and then he shakes his head as though acknowledging the intensity of his suffering. In all of this he makes no sound. Is he mute as well as blind?

The room in which he dwells is empty of all possessions — no get-well cards, small, private caches of food, day-old flowers, slippers, all the usual kickshaws of a sickroom. There is only the bed, a chair, a nightstand, and a tray on wheels that can be swung across his lap for meals.

"What time is it?" he asks.

"Three o'clock."

"Morning or afternoon?"

"Afternoon."

He is silent. There is nothing else he wants to know.

"How are you?" I say.

"Who is it?" he asks.

"It's the doctor. How do you feel?"

He does not answer right away.

"Feel?" he says.

"I hope you feel better," I say.

I press the button at the side of the bed.

"Down you go," I say.

"Yes, down," he says.

He falls back upon the bed awkwardly. His stumps, unweighted by legs and feet, rise in the air, presenting themselves. I unwrap the bandages from the stumps, and begin to cut away the black scabs and the dead, glazed fat with scissors and forceps. A shard of white bone comes loose. I pick it away. I wash the wounds with disinfectant and redress the stumps. All this while, he does not speak. What is he thinking behind those lids that do not blink? Is he remembering a time when he was whole? Does he dream of feet? Of when his body was not a rotting log?

He lies solid and inert. In spite of everything, he remains impressive, as though he were a sailor standing athwart a slanting deck.

"Anything more I can do for you?" I ask.

For a long moment he is silent.

"Yes," he says at last and without the least irony. "You can bring me a pair of shoes."

In the corridor, the head nurse is waiting for me.

"We have to do something about him," she says. "Every morning he orders scrambled eggs for breakfast and, instead of eating them, he picks up the plate and throws it against the wall."

"Throws his plate?"

"Nasty. That's what he is. No wonder his family doesn't come to visit. They probably can't stand him any more than we can."

She is waiting for me to do something.

"Well?"

"We'll see," I say.

The next morning I am waiting in the corridor when the kitchen delivers his breakfast. I watch the aide place the tray on the stand and swing it across his lap. She presses the button to raise the head of the bed. Then she leaves.

In time the man reaches to find the rim of the tray, then on to find

the dome of the covered dish. He lifts off the cover and places it on
the stand. He fingers across the plate until he probes the eggs. He lifts
the plate in both hands, sets it on the palm of his right hand, centers
it, balances it. He hefts it up and down slightly, getting the feel of it.
Abruptly, he draws back his right arm as far as he can.

There is the crack of the plate breaking against the wall at the foot
of his bed and the small wet sound of the scrambled eggs dropping to
the floor.

And then he laughs. It is a sound you have never heard. It is something
new under the sun. It could cure cancer.

Out in the corridor, the eyes of the head nurse narrow.

"Laughed, did he?"

She writes something down on her clipboard.

A second aide arrives, brings a second breakfast tray, puts it on the
nightstand, out of his reach. She looks over at me shaking her head
and making her mouth go. I see that we are to be accomplices.

"I've got to feed you," she says to the man.

"Oh, no you don't" the man says.

"Oh, yes I do," the aide says, "after the way you just did. Nurse says
so."

"Get me my shoes," the man says.

"Here's oatmeal," the aide says. "Open." And she touches the spoon
to his lower lip.

"I ordered scrambled eggs," says the man.

"That's right," the aide says.

I step forward.

"Is there anything I can do?" I say.

"Who are you?" the man asks.

In the evening I go once more to that ward to make my rounds. The
head nurse reports to me that Room 542 is deceased. She has discovered
this quite by accident, she says. No, there has been no sound. Nothing.
It's a blessing, she says.

I go into his room, a spy looking for secrets. He is still there in his
bed. His face is relaxed, grave, dignified. After a while, I turn to leave.
My gaze sweeps the wall at the foot of the bed, and I see the place
where it has been repeatedly washed, where the wall looks very clean
and very white.

(1977)

The Writer's Subject

1. This essay takes the form of narration, with the usual elements of a story: character, plot, setting. The focus is on the central action, and there is no "thesis" in the sense of an explicit statement of meaning or intention. What, then, is the point of the essay? What meaning, or meanings, may be derived from the story Selzer tells?

2. Why does the doctor compare himself to a spy in the first and last paragraphs?

3. What is suggested about the doctor's patients by the last two sentences of the first paragraph?

4. What details reveal the doctor's feelings about the patient in Room 542? In what ways are the nurses' feelings different from the doctor's?

5. Suggest why the patient laughs as he breaks the plate of eggs. Why does it seem to the doctor that this laugh is "something new under the sun. It could cure cancer"?

6. Why does the patient ask for his shoes? What is Selzer's point in noting that the patient does so "without the least irony"?

The Writer's Style and Strategy

1. Discuss the purpose and the effectiveness of the comparisons of the patient to a snowbound cottage and a bonsai.

2. What is the effect of the phrase "vile repose" ?

3. Discuss Selzer's use of dialogue as a means of revealing elements of character in the patient, the doctor, and the two nurses.

4. Why does Selzer choose not to give names to any of the people in his narrative?

5. How does Selzer use details of setting to enhance the mood of his narrative?

6. What is the effect of the phrase "Room 542 is deceased" in the conclusion?

7. How has the reader been prepared for the ending? How is it related to the essay's opening?

8. What are the connotations of the phrase, "The Discus Thrower"? Why is this title so effective (as compared with "The Plate Thrower," "A Difficult Patient," "The Dying Man," or some such title)?

Suggested Topics for Writing and Discussion

1. Offer an argument for or against the view that the terminally ill should be cared for, and allowed to die, at home rather than in a hospital.

2. Write a narrative describing an experience in which you have found yourself an involved observer (e.g., visiting a hospital patient, witnessing an accident).

3. Read Dylan Thomas's poem "Do not go gentle into that good night," and discuss Selzer's reasons for alluding to that poem in the epigraph to his essay. How does your reading of the poem enrich your understanding of Selzer's essay?

Humanities and Science

by Lewis Thomas

Lord Kelvin was one of the great British physicists of the late nine- **1**
teenth century, an extraordinarily influential figure in his time, and in
some ways a paradigm of conventional, established scientific leadership. He did a lot of good and useful things, but once or twice he, like
Homer, nodded. The instances are worth recalling today, for we have
nodders among our scientific eminences still, from time to time, needing
to have their elbows shaken.

On one occasion, Kelvin made a speech on the overarching impor- **2**
tance of numbers. He maintained that no observation of nature was worth
paying serious attention to unless it could be stated in precisely quantitative terms. The numbers were the final and only test, not only of
truth but about meaning as well. He said, "When you can measure what
you are speaking about, and express it in numbers, you know something
about it. But when you cannot — your knowledge is of a meagre and
unsatisfactory kind."

But, as at least one subsequent event showed, Kelvin may have had **3**
things exactly the wrong way round. The task of converting observations into numbers is the hardest of all, the last task rather than the first
thing to be done, and it can be done only when you have learned,
beforehand, a great deal about the observations themselves. You can,
to be sure, achieve a very deep understanding of nature by quantitative
measurement, but you must know what you are talking about before
you can begin applying the numbers for making predictions. In Kelvin's
case, the problem at hand was the age of the earth and solar system.
Using what was then known about the sources of energy and the loss

of energy from the physics of that day, he calculated that neither the earth nor the sun were older than several hundred million years. This caused a considerable stir in biological and geological circles, especially among the evolutionists. Darwin himself was distressed by the numbers; the time was much too short for the theory of evolution. Kelvin's figures were described by Darwin as one of his "sorest troubles."

4   T.H. Huxley had long been aware of the risks involved in premature extrapolations from mathematical treatment of biological problems. He said, in an 1869 speech to the Geological Society concerning numbers, "This seems to be one of the many cases in which the admitted accuracy of mathematical processes is allowed to throw a wholly inadmissible appearance of authority over the results obtained by them. . . . As the grandest mill in the world will not extract wheat flour from peascods, so pages of formulas will not get a definite result out of loose data."

5   The trouble was that the world of physics had not moved fast enough to allow for Kelvin's assumptions. Nuclear fusion and fission had not yet been dreamed of, and the true age of the earth could not even be guessed from the data in hand. It was not yet the time for mathematics in this subject.

6   There have been other examples, since those days, of the folly of using numbers and calculations uncritically. Kelvin's own strong conviction that science could not be genuine science without measuring things was catching. People in other fields of endeavor, hankering to turn their disciplines into exact sciences, beset by what has since been called "physics envy," set about converting whatever they knew into numbers and thence into equations with predictive pretensions. We have it with us still, in economics, sociology, psychology, history, even, I fear, in English-literature criticism and linguistics, and it frequently works, when it works at all, with indifferent success. The risks of untoward social consequences in work of this kind are considerable. It is as important — and as hard — to learn when to use mathematics as how to use it, and this matter should remain high on the agenda of consideration for education in the social and behavioral sciences.

7   Of course, Kelvin's difficulty with the age of the earth was an exceptional, almost isolated instance of failure in quantitative measurement in nineteenth-century physics. The instruments devised for approaching nature by way of physics became increasingly precise and powerful, carrying the field through electromagnetic theory, triumph after triumph, and setting the stage for the great revolution of twentieth-century physics. There is no doubt about it: measurement works when the instruments

work, and when you have a fairly clear idea of what it is that is being measured, and when you know what to do with the numbers when they tumble out. The system for gaining information and comprehension about nature works so well, indeed, that it carries another hazard: the risk of convincing yourself that you know everything.

Kelvin himself fell into this trap toward the end of the century. (I **8** don't mean to keep picking on Kelvin, who was a very great scientist; it is just that he happened to say a couple of things I find useful for this discussion.) He stated, in a summary of the achievements of nineteenth-century physics, that it was an almost completed science; virtually everything that needed knowing about the material universe had been learned; there were still a few anomalies and inconsistencies in electromagnetic theory, a few loose ends to be tidied up, but this would be done within the next several years. Physics, in these terms, was not a field any longer likely to attract, as it previously had, the brightest and most imaginative young brains. The most interesting part of the work had already been done. Then, within the next decade, came radiation, Planck, the quantum, Einstein, Rutherford, Bohr, and all the rest — quantum mechanics — and the whole field turned over and became a brand new sort of human endeavor, still now, in the view of many physicists, almost a full century later, a field only at its beginnings.

But even today, despite the amazements that are turning up in physics **9** each year, despite the jumps taken from the smallest parts of nature — particle physics — to the largest of all — the cosmos itself — the impression of science that the public gains is rather like the impression left in the nineteenth-century public mind by Kelvin. Science, in this view, is first of all a matter of simply getting all the numbers together. The numbers are sitting out there in nature, waiting to be found, sorted and totted up. If only they had enough robots and enough computers, the scientists could go off to the beach and wait for their papers to be written for them. Second of all, what we know about nature today is pretty much the whole story: we are very nearly home and dry. From here on, it is largely a problem of tying up loose ends, tidying nature up, getting the files in order. The only real surprises for the future — and it is about those that the public is becoming more concerned and apprehensive — are the technological applications that the scientists may be cooking up from today's knowledge.

I suggest that the scientific community is to blame. If there are **10** disagreements between the world of the humanities and the scientific enterprise as to the place and importance of science in a liberal-arts

education, and the role of science in twentieth-century culture, I believe
that the scientists are themselves responsible for a general misunderstanding of what they are really up to.

11   Over the past half century, we have been teaching the sciences as
though they were the same academic collection of cut-and-dried subjects as always, and — here is what has really gone wrong — as though
they would always be the same. The teaching of today's biology, for
example, is pretty much the same kind of exercise as the teaching of
Latin was when I was in high school long ago. First of all, the fundamentals, the underlying laws, the essential grammar, and then the
reading of texts. Once mastered, that is that: Latin is Latin and forever
after will be Latin. And biology is precisely biology, a vast array of
hard facts to be learned as fundamentals, followed by a reading of the
texts.

12   Moreover, we have been teaching science as though its facts were
somehow superior to the facts in all other scholarly disciplines, more
fundamental, more solid, less subject to subjectivism, immutable. English
literature is not just one way of thinking, it is all sorts of ways. Poetry
is a moving target. The facts that underlie art, architecture, and music
are not really hard facts, and you can change them any way you like
by arguing about them, but science is treated as an altogether different
kind of learning: an unambiguous, unalterable, and endlessly useful
display of data needing only to be packaged and installed somewhere
in one's temporal lobe in order to achieve a full understanding of the
natural world.

13   And it is, of course, not like this at all. In real life, every field of
science that I can think of is incomplete, and most of them — whatever
the record of accomplishment over the past two hundred years — are
still in the earliest stage of their starting point. In the fields I know best,
among the life sciences, it is required that the most expert and
sophisticated minds be capable of changing those minds, often with a
great lurch, every few years. In some branches of biology the mind-
changing is occurring with accelerating velocities. The next week's issue
of any scientific journal can turn a whole field upside down, shaking
out any number of immutable ideas and installing new bodies of dogma,
and this is happening all the time. It is an almost everyday event in
physics, in chemistry, in materials research, in neurobiology, in genetics,
in immunology. The hard facts tend to soften overnight, melt away,
and vanish under the pressure of new hard facts, and the interpretations of what appear to be the most solid aspects of nature are subject

to change, now more than at any other time in history. The conclusions reached in science are always, when looked at closely, far more provisional and tentative than are most of the assumptions arrived at by our colleagues in the humanities.

The running battle now in progress between the sociobiologists and the antisociobiologists is a marvel for students to behold, close up. To observe, in open-mouthed astonishment, the polarized extremes, one group of highly intelligent, beautifully trained, knowledgeable, and imaginative scientists maintaining that all sorts of behavior, animal and human, are governed exclusively by genes, and another group of equally talented scientists saying precisely the opposite and asserting that all behavior is set and determined by the environment, or by culture, and both sides brawling in the pages of periodicals such as *The New York Review of Books*, is an educational experience that no college student should be allowed to miss. The essential lesson to be learned has nothing to do with the relative validity of the facts underlying the argument, it is the argument itself that is the education: we do not yet know enough to settle such questions. **14**

It is true that at any given moment there is the appearance of satisfaction, even self-satisfaction, within every scientific discipline. On any Tuesday morning, if asked, a good working scientist will gladly tell you that the affairs of the field are nicely in order, that things are finally looking clear and making sense, and all is well. But come back again, on another Tuesday, and he may let you know that the roof has just fallen in on his life's work, that all the old ideas — last week's ideas in some cases — are no longer good ideas, that something strange has happened. **15**

It is the very strangeness of nature that makes science engrossing. That ought to be at the center of science teaching. There are more than seven-times-seven types of ambiguity in science, awaiting analysis. The poetry of Wallace Stevens is crystal-clear alongside the genetic code. **16**

I prefer to turn things around in order to make precisely the opposite case. Science, especially twentieth-century science, has provided us with a glimpse of something we never really knew before, the revelation of human ignorance. We have been used to the belief, down one century after another, that we more or less comprehend everything bar one or two mysteries like the mental processes of our gods. Every age, not just the eighteenth century, regarded itself as the Age of Reason, and we have never lacked for explanations of the world and its ways. Now, we are being brought up short, and this has been the work of science. **17**

We have a wilderness of mystery to make our way through in the centuries ahead, and we will need science for this but not science alone. Science will, in its own time, produce the data and some of the meaning in the data, but never the full meaning. For getting a full grasp, for perceiving real significance when significance is at hand, we shall need minds at work from all sorts of brains outside the fields of science, most of all the brains of poets, of course, but also those of artists, musicians, philosophers, historians, writers in general.

18   It is primarily because of this need that I would press for changes in the way science is taught. There is a need to teach the young people who will be doing the science themselves, but this will always be a small minority among us. There is a deeper need to teach science to those who will be needed for thinking about it, and this means pretty nearly everyone else, in hopes that a few of these people — a much smaller minority than the scientific community and probably a lot harder to find — will, in the thinking, be able to imagine new levels of meaning that are likely to be lost on the rest of us.

19   In addition, it is time to develop a new group of professional thinkers, perhaps a somewhat larger group than the working scientists, who can create a discipline of scientific criticism. We have had good luck so far in the emergence of a few people ranking as philosophers of science and historians and journalists of science, and I hope more of these will be coming along, but we have not yet seen a Ruskin or a Leavis or an Edmund Wilson. Science needs critics of this sort, but the public at large needs them more urgently.

20   I suggest that the introductory courses in science, at all levels from grade school through college, be radically revised. Leave the fundamentals, the so-called basics, aside for a while, and concentrate the attention of all students on the things that are *not* known. You cannot possibly teach quantum mechanics without mathematics, to be sure, but you can describe the strangeness of the world opened up by quantum theory. Let it be known, early on, that there are deep mysteries, and profound paradoxes, revealed in their distant outlines, by the quantum. Let it be known that these can be approached more closely, and puzzled over, once the language of mathematics has been sufficiently mastered.

21   Teach at the outset, before any of the fundamentals, the still imponderable puzzles of cosmology. Let it be known, as clearly as possible, by the youngest minds, that there are some things going on in the universe that lie beyond comprehension, and make it plain how little is known.

Do not teach that biology is a useful and perhaps profitable science; 22
that can come later. Teach instead that there are structures squirming
inside all our cells, providing all the energy for living, that are essentially foreign creatures, brought in for symbiotic living a billion or so
years ago, the lineal descendants of bacteria. Teach that we do not have
the ghost of an idea how they got there, where they came from, or how
they evolved to their present structure and function. The details of ox-
idative phosphorylation and photosynthesis can come later.

Teach ecology early on. Let it be understood that the earth's life is 23
a system of interliving, interdependent creatures, and that we do not
understand at all how it works. The earth's environment, from the range
of atmospheric gases to the chemical constituents of the sea, has been
held in an almost unbelievably improbable state of regulated balance
since life began, and the regulation of stability and balance is accomplished solely by the life itself, like the internal environment of an immense organism, and we do not know how that one works, even less
what it means. Teach that.

Go easy, I suggest, on the promises sometimes freely offered by 24
science. Technology relies and depends on science these days, more
than ever before, but technology is nothing like the first justification
for doing research, nor is it necessarily an essential product to be expected from science. Public decisions about what to have in the way
of technology are totally different problems from decisions about science,
and the two enterprises should not be tangled together. The central task
of science is to arrive, stage by stage, at a clearer comprehension of
nature, but this does not mean, as it is sometimes claimed to mean,
a search for mastery over nature. Science may provide us, one day,
with a better understanding of ourselves, but never, I hope, with a set
of technologies for doing something or other to improve ourselves. I
am made nervous by assertions that human consciousness will some-
day be unraveled by research, laid out for close scrutiny like the workings of a computer, and then, *and then!* I hope with some fervor that
we can learn a lot more than we now know about the human mind,
and I see no reason why this strange puzzle should remain forever and
entirely beyond us. But I would be deeply disturbed by any prospect
that we might use the new knowledge in order to begin doing something
about it, to improve it, say. This is a different matter from searching
for information to use against schizophrenia or dementia, where we are
badly in need of technologies, indeed likely one day to be sunk without
them. But the ordinary, everyday, more or less normal human mind

is too marvelous an instrument ever to be tampered with by anyone, science or no science.

25   The education of humanists cannot be regarded as complete, or even adequate, without exposure in some depth to where things stand in the various branches of science, and particularly, as I have said, in the areas of our ignorance. This does not mean that I know how to go about doing it, nor am I unaware of the difficulties involved. Physics professors, most of them, look with revulsion on assignments to teach their subject to poets. Biologists, caught up by the enchantment of their new power, armed with flawless instruments to tell the nucleotide sequences of the entire human genome, nearly matching the physicists in the precision of their measurements of living processes, will resist the prospect of broad survey courses; each biology professor will demand that any student in his path must master every fine detail within that professor's research program. The liberal-arts faculties, for their part, will continue to view the scientists with suspicion and apprehension. "What do the scientists want?" asked a Cambridge professor in Francis Cornford's wonderful *Microcosmographia Academica*. "Everything that's going," was the quick answer. That was back in 1912, and universities haven't much changed.

26   The worst thing that has happened to science education is that the great fun has gone out of it. A very large number of good students look at it as slogging work to be got through on the way to medical school. Others look closely at the premedical students themselves, embattled and bleeding for grades and class standing, and are turned off. Very few see science as the high adventure it really is, the wildest of all explorations ever undertaken by human beings, the chance to catch close views of things never seen before, the shrewdest maneuver for discovering how the world works. Instead, they become baffled early on, and they are misled into thinking that bafflement is simply the result of not that everyone else — from the professor in his endowed chair down to the platoons of post doctoral students in the laboratory all night — is baffled as well. Every important scientific advance that has come in looking like an answer has turned, sooner or later — usually sooner — into a question. And the game is just beginning.

27   An appreciation of what is happening in science today, and of how great a distance lies ahead for exploring, ought to be one of the rewards of a liberal-arts education. It ought to be a good in itself, not something to be acquired on the way to a professional career but part of the cast of thought needed for getting into the kind of century that is now just

down the road. Part of the intellectual equipment of an educated person, however his or her time is to be spent, ought to be a feel for the queernesses of nature, the inexplicable things.

And maybe, just maybe, a new set of courses dealing systematically 28 with ignorance in science might take hold. The scientists might discover in it a new and subversive technique for catching the attention of students driven by curiosity, delighted and surprised to learn that science is exactly as Bush described it: an "endless frontier." The humanists, for their part, might take considerable satisfaction watching their scientific colleagues confess openly to not knowing everything about everything. And the poets, on whose shoulders the future rests, might, late nights, thinking things over, begin to see some meanings that elude the rest of us. It is worth a try.

(1983)

The Writer's Subject

1. What, according to Thomas, was the nineteenth-century view of the importance of numbers and quantitative measurement? What showed the limitations of this view? (paras. 1-5)

2. How does the uncritical use of numbers and calculations persist into our own day? (para. 6)

3. What "trap" did Lord Kelvin fall into? (paras. 7-8)

4. According to Thomas, what is the impression of science held by the general public? Who does he maintain is primarily responsible for creating this impression? (paras. 9-10)

5. What point is Thomas making when he compares the current teaching of science with the teaching of Latin? (para. 11)

6. How does Thomas counter the view that scientific facts are "more solid, less subject to subjectivism" than facts in other disciplines? (paras. 12-13)

7. What "essential lesson" is to be learned from following the public con-
    troversy between sociobiologists and their opponents? (para. 14)

8. What does Thomas mean by his assertion that "The poetry of Wallace
    Stevens is crystal-clear alongside the genetic code"? (para. 16)

9. Why does Thomas attach importance to the scientific education of non-
    scientists? What role does he foresee for poets, historians, and
    philosophers? (paras. 17-19)

10. What changes does Thomas suggest in the teaching of science? What does
    he think such teaching should emphasize? (paras. 20-24)

11. What are Thomas's objections to specialization in education? (para. 25)

The Writer's Style and Strategy

1. What is Thomas's purpose?

2. What kind of audience does Thomas have in mind for this essay? Support
    your view with specific references.

3. What are the general characteristics of Thomas's diction and sentence
    style? How appropriate are they to his purpose and audience?

4. Why does Thomas begin his essay by recounting the errors of the famous
    nineteenth-century English scientist, Lord Kelvin?

5. At what point does Thomas shift from an attack on erroneous ways of
    thinking about science to proposals for change? How is this shift signalled?

6. What patterns of diction and sentence structure does Thomas employ to
    add force to his arguments in paragraphs 20-23?

Suggested Topics for Writing and Discussion

1. Thomas argues that a knowledge of science should be "part of the in-
    tellectual equipment of an educated person, however his or her time is
    spent." What aspects of modern science do you think an educated person
    should know something about? Provide examples to support your view.

2. Thomas believes that it is vital for humanists to acquire some understand-
    ing of science. Discuss the corollary of this view: that courses in the
    humanities should be included in the education of scientists.

3. In the course of his essay, Thomas rejects the view that the task of science is to seek "mastery over nature," and expresses concern at the possibility that technology may be misapplied to achieve such a goal. Is there any evidence that Thomas's fears may be justified? What developments in modern science or medicine do you think should be regarded with concern?

4. Thomas says, "The worst thing that has happened to science education is that the great fun has gone out of it." Do you agree? To support your view, use examples from a particular area of science education (e.g., a programme in college or university, the curriculum for children in a particular stage of school).

5. Lewis Thomas, Rachel Carson, and David Suzuki all point to the dangers and problems of living in, as Carson says, "an era of specialists, each of whom sees his own problem and is unaware of the larger frame into which it fits." Argue for or against the training of specialists in our society.

Unexpected Vistas

by James Trefil

1   One of the great rewards of hiking or backpacking is to follow a trail and, suddenly and without warning, top a hill or come to a break in the trees and see the panorama of the coutryside laid out before you. The view of the distant waterfall or rolling hills is often remembered as the high point of the entire excursion.

2   Such experiences occur in intellectual life, too. The moment of the "Aha!" — which cartoonists usually render by showing a light bulb coming on above someone's head — is an analogous happening. So too is the unexpected discovery that two things seemingly unconnected with each other are in fact intimately related. But while every hiker on a given trail will see the same view, the intellectual vista has the property that each person who comes to it can see something entirely different.

3   For example, imagine a line of motorists at a traffic light. Each of them is looking at the same thing, a rectangular yellow box with three colored lights in it. But it is possible, even likely, that each of them *sees* something very different from the others. Suppose that the first person in line is an electrical engineer. To him, the traffic light is just one appendage of a large computer-operated grid that regulates the movement of vehicles throughout the downtown area. If you pressed him to go on — to describe the far reaches of his view — he might start musing about the light as one example of control systems and eventually wind up talking about the best-designed control system of them all, the human brain.

4   The driver of the second car in line is the representative of a large

manufacturing firm. He sees the traffic light as an item that is built in a factory and sold to the city. After thinking for a while, he might go on to talk about the vast interconnecting web of economic activity, from mining to maintenance work, that has to be in place before something like a traffic signal is possible. He might even end with some general speculations about human beings as tool-making animals.

In the third car is an attorney. To him the traffic light might symbolize the set of laws human beings have developed. The mechanical or economic aspect of the device would be much less important than the rules of conduct it symbolizes. After all, at any given moment there are thousands of cars being driven in a city, and almost every driver obeys the traffic signals. Behind this display of mass obedience, our attorney may see the vast structure of the modern legal system, from legislators to courts to police officers. If pressed, he might go on to speculate about those aspects of the human character that require such a system to allow large groups of people to live together in relative harmony. 5

Each of our motorists sees the traffic light as part of a large interconnected network. The simple apparatus is seen to be just one aspect of an important system that governs some aspect of our lives. In a sense, the traffic light is like an object in the foreground of some marvelous medieval landscape painting, a device the artist uses to induce us to look further and see the rich tapestry of nature and civilization that lies behind it. I will call each driver's view of the traffic light a vista, a term that carries with it the connotation of wide-ranging view. 6

So the traffic light teaches us several important lessons. It tells us that the breadth and scope of the vista really have very little to do with the object that starts us looking. Whether the traffic light is seen as just a self-contained mechanical device or as part of a much larger system is primarily a function of the individual looking at it, and, more importantly, of that individual's training and habits of thought. 7

The traffic light also teaches us that two individuals looking at the same thing need not see the same vista. It's almost as if two hikers reach the same point in a trail, from which one sees a waterfall while the other sees a shady forest. We can often get an entirely different view of the world just by talking to people whose backgrounds lead them to see vistas different from our own. 8

Like other professionals, scientists have their unique vistas. It would be a mistake, however, to assume that all scientists share a common view of things. I was frequently surprised during the several years I 9 spent as part of an interdisciplinary team in cancer research by just how much the training of the other team members affected the way they looked at our work. To a biologist a cell is part of an evolving, growing, living system; to a physicist it is a "black box" that processes energy and produces an ordered system; to a statistician it is one more bit of data to put into a computer program. Clearly, there is no such thing as a single, monolithic "scientific" vista.

(1983)

The Writer's Subject

1. How does Trefil's use of the word "vista" unite the ideas in paragraphs 1 and 2?

2. Trefil says in paragraph 2 that "every hiker on a given trail will see the same view," but he goes on to say in paragraph 8 that "two individuals looking at the same thing need not see the same vista." Is this simply a contradiction?

3. What principle is Trefil demonstrating by his example of the motorists and the traffic light?

4. Why does Trefil state that "there is no such thing as a single, monolithic 'scientific' vista" (para. 9)?

The Writer's Style and Strategy

1. In discussing the nature of perception and the "intellectual vista," Trefil is dealing with abstract, intangible ideas. How does he help the reader to grasp these ideas?

2. What is Trefil's general pattern of reasoning: inductive or deductive?

3. Examine the concluding paragraph. How does its development reflect the pattern of discussion that precedes it?

Suggested Topics for Writing and Discussion

1. Trefil makes the point that "two individuals looking at the same thing need not see the same vista." With this in mind, put yourself into the place of two different persons and write brief descriptions on one of the topics below. Or, choose two "vistas" of another subject which interests you.
   (a) A prison, from the viewpoint of an inmate and of a guard.
   (b) A college or university from the viewpoint of a student and of a worker in the campus cafeteria.
   (c) An alpine meadow from the point of view of a hiker and of a real estate developer.
   (d) A funeral from the point of view of a child and of an adult.

2. Choose a process or concept which you have recently been introduced to in one of the subjects which you are studying. Put yourself in the position of a tutor and use an extended analogy to explain the matter in everyday, simple, or familiar terms.

3. Write a well-developed paragraph using an analogy. You may wish to use one of the topics which follow.
   (a) A university or college education as a savings account.
   (b) A selling technique as a method for catching fish.
   (c) A freshman at registration as a mouse in a maze.
   (d) The university or college curriculum as a smorgasbord.

4. Using one of the following topics as a starting point, develop an essay of explanation by means of an analogy.
   (a) Falling in love.
   (b) Writing an essay.
   (c) Stopping trade in drugs.
   (d) Listening to music.

Biographical Notes

ADDISON, Joseph (1672-1719)
English playwright, essayist, and critic; celebrated for his style, particularly in his contributions to the periodicals *The Spectator, Tatler,* and *The Guardian.*

ALLEN, Woody (b. 1935)
Pseudonym of Heywood Allen Konigsberg; American film director, writer, actor, and comedian; widely acclaimed for such films as *Annie Hall* (1977; Academy Award) and *Hannah and Her Sisters* (1986); author of *Getting Even* (1971), *Without Feathers* (1975), and *Side Effects* (1981).

ARKIN, William M.
Director of the Arms Race and Nuclear Weapons Research Project at the Institute for Policy Studies in Washington, D.C., and a contributing editor of the *Bulletin of the Atomic Scientists.*

ATWOOD, Margaret (b. 1939)
Canadian poet, critic, novelist; winner of Governor General's awards for poetry (*The Circle Game,* 1966), and for fiction (*The Handmaid's Tale,* 1985).

AVIS, Walter (b. 1919)
Lexicographer and historian of language; editor of *A Dictionary of Canadianisms on Historical Principles* (1967).

BACON, Francis (1561-1626)
English statesman and philosopher; writer on learning and scientific method (*The Advancement of Learning,* 1605; *Novum Organum,* 1620).

BAKER, Russell (b. 1925)
American journalist and humourist; columnist for the *New York Times* since 1962; winner of two Pulitzer Prizes.

BETTELHEIM, Bruno (b. 1903)

Austrian-born American professor of educational psychology, author of studies on emotionally-disturbed children and child rearing, including *The Empty Fortress* (1967), *The Children of the Dream* (1969), and *The Uses of Enchantment: The Meaning and Importance of Fairy Tales* (1976).

BIBBY, Geoffrey (b. 1917)

British archaeologist, author of *Testimony of the Spade* (1956) and *Four Thousand Years Ago: A World Panorama of Life in the Second Millenium B.C.* (1961).

BRODY, Hugh (b. 1943)

British anthropologist; participant in research on Inuit and Indian language and customs in Canada, and author of a number of studies, including *The People's Land* (1975) and *Maps and Dreams: Indians and the British Columbia Frontier* (1981).

BRONOWSKI, Jacob (1903-1974)

Polish-born English scientist, critic, essayist; concerned for much of his life with the relationship between art, science, and human values, examined in such books as *The Common Sense of Science* (1951), *Science and Human Values* (1956), *The Ascent of Man* (1973).

CARSON, Rachel (1907-1964)

Biologist for U.S. Fish and Wildlife Service from 1936-1952; author of *The Sea Around Us* (1951), *The Edge of the Sea* (1955), *Silent Spring* (1962).

COWLEY, Malcolm (b. 1898)

Literary historian and critic; long-time literary advisor to Viking Press; author of *Exile's Return* (1934), a celebrated accountof literary life in the 1920's.

DAVIES, Robertson (b. 1913)

Canadian playwright, critic, journalist, academic; won international acclaim for the "Deptford Trilogy" of novels (*Fifth Business,* 1970; *The Manticore,* 1972; *World of Wonders,* 1975) and most recently for *What's Bred in the Bone* (1985).

DOBBS, Kildare (b. 1923)

Canadian journalist; born in India, served in British colonial service in Tanganyika 1948-52; author of *Running to Paradise* (1962; Governor General's Award).

DRYDEN, Ken (b. 1947)

Canadian lawyer, formerly star goaltender for the Montreal Canadiens; author of *The Game* (1984), a study of professional hockey.

EISELEY, Loren (1907-1977)

Anthropologist, historian, and philosopher of science, author of many books and articles explaining science to the lay reader (*Darwin's Century,* 1958; *Firmament of Time,* 1960; *The Star Thrower,* 1978).

FLANNER, Janet (1892-1978)
Regular contributor to the *New Yorker* from 1925-75, with her "Letter from Paris," under the pseudonym "Genet."

FORSTER, E.M. (1879-1970)
Novelist, essayist, writer of short stories; best known for *A Room with a View* (1908), *Howards End* (1910), and *A Passage to India* (1924).

FOX, Terry Curtis (b. 1948)
Playwright, screenwriter, drama critic for the New York *Village Voice* (1975-81).

FRYE, Northrop (b. 1912)
Critic, editor, professor of English at University of Toronto; one of the most influential literary theorists of his time; author of many books, including *Anatomy of Criticism* (1957); *The Bush Garden: Essays on the Canadian Imagination* (1971); *The Great Code: The Bible and Literature* (1982).

FULFORD, Robert (b. 1932)
Canadian journalist, film reviewer, contributor to CBC Radio and Television; since 1968, editor of *Saturday Night* magazine.

GOULD, Glenn (1932-1982)
Renowned Canadian pianist and musical prodigy; retired from concert performance in 1964 to devote himself to recording; writer and editor of documentaries for CBC Radio, of notes for his own recordings, and of articles for music magazines.

GOULD, Stephen J. (b. 1941)
Harvard paleontologist and geology professor, author of award-winning books on evolution and biological determinism, including *Ever Since Darwin* (1977), *The Mismeasure of Man* (1981) and *The Flamingo's Smile: Reflections in Natural History* (1985).

HALDANE, J.B.S. (1892-1964)
Controversial English geneticist and biochemist, known for his eccentric scientific methods, and for his work on heredity; author of many books and essays on science and society.

HOBAN, Russell (b. 1925)
American author of books for children, including *The Mouse and His Child* (1967) and for adults, including *Turtle Diary* (1975) and *Riddley Walker* (1980).

HOGGART, Richard (b. 1918)
British academic, critic, and educator. Contributor to many collections of critical essays; author of the influential study *The Uses of Literacy* (1957) and numerous other books, including *Only Connect* (The Reith Lectures, 1972) and *The Future of Broadcasting* (1982).

JOHNSON, Samuel (1709-1784)
English essayist, poet, critic, editor, and lexicographer (*A Dictionary of the English Language*, 1755).

KENNEDY, X.J. (b. 1929)
Pseudonym of Joseph Charles Kennedy, poet, professor of English, editor of literary anthologies.

LAURENCE, Margaret W. (1926-1987)
Canadian writer best known for her novels of prairie life, including *A Jest of God* (1966) and *The Diviners* (1974), both of which received a Governor General's Award.

LEACOCK, Stephen (1869-1944)
Economics professor at McGill, and a prolific writer of humorous books, including *Literary Lapses* (1910), *Sunshine Sketches of a Little Town* (1912), and *Arcadian Adventures with the Idle Rich* (1914).

LURIE, Alison (b. 1926)
Cornell English professor and novelist; Pulitzer Prize in fiction for *Foreign Affairs* (1984).

MacLENNAN, Hugh (b. 1907)
Canadian novelist, essayist, and former English professor at McGill University; winner of five Governor General's Awards; his novels include *Two Solitudes* (1945), *The Watch That Ends the Night* (1959), and *Voices in Time* (1980).

MOWAT, Farley (b. 1921)
Born in Ontario; a fierce and controversial defender of life in the Canadian Arctic (*People of the Deer*, 1952) and of animals threatened by man (*Never Cry Wolf*, 1963, and *A Whale for the Killing*, 1972).

MUGGERIDGE, Malcolm (b. 1903)
British journalist, broadcaster, and satirist, editor of the humorous magazine *Punch* from 1953-1957.

O'CONNOR, (Mary) Flannery (1925-1964)
American author of short stories and novels, including *Wise Blood* (1952), and *Everything That Rises Must Converge* (stories, 1965).

ORWELL, George (1903-1950)
Pseudonym of English political journalist and satirist Eric Blair; served with the Indian Imperial Police in Burma, 1922-27; fought with the Republicans in Spain, describing the experience in *Homage to Catalonia* (1938); author of *Animal Farm* (1945) and *Nineteen Eighty-Four* (1949).

PLUMB, John Harold (b. 1911)
Cambridge historian, broadcaster, contributor to journals; author of many books on cultural and political history, and of a work on the nature of history, *The Death of the Past* (1969).

RICHLER, Mordecai (b. 1931)
Canadian satirist, author of essays and novels, including The *Apprenticeship of Duddy Kravitz* (1959) and *St. Urbain's Horseman* (1971; Governor General's Award).

ROSENBAUM, Jonathan
Film critic and historian. Author of *Moving Places: A Life at The Movies* (1980), *Midnight Movies* (with J. Hoberman, 1983), and *Film: The Front Line* (1983).

ROYKO, Mike (b. 1932)
Reporter and columnist for Chicago newspapers since 1959, winner of Pulitzer Prize in 1972.

RYBCZYNSKI, Witold Marian (b. 1943)
Scottish-born architect and planner, professor at McGill University in Montreal. Author of *Taming the Tiger: The Struggle to Control Technology* (1983) and *Home: A Short History of an Idea* (1986).

SELZER, Richard (b. 1928)
Surgeon, essayist, writer of short stories. Collections of his essays include *Confessions of a Knife* (1979).

SILLITOE, Alan (b. 1928)
Self-educated English novelist and short-story writer, author of such anti-establishment works as *Saturday Night and Sunday Morning* (1958) and *The Loneliness of the Long-Distance Runner* (1959).

STEGNER, Wallace (b. 1909)
Formerly professor of English at Stanford; writer about the American and Canadian West; author of short stories and novels, winning a Pulitzer Prize for *Angle of Repose* (1971).

STEINEM, Gloria (b. 1934)
Journalist; a leading figure in the American feminist movement; founded *Ms* magazine in 1972. Author of *Marilyn* (1986), a book on Marilyn Monroe.

SUZUKI, David (b. 1936)
Canadian scientist, academic, and broadcaster, renowned for his work in genetics; the host of the CBC television programme *The Nature of Things*.

SWIFT, Jonathan (1667-1745)
Irish satirist and pamphleteer; dean of St. Patrick's in Dublin; critic of English policy in Ireland; author of *Gulliver's Travels* (1726).

THOMAS, Lewis (b. 1913)
Formerly professor of pathology; head of Sloan-Kettering Cancer Center; contributor of many articles to medical and scientific journals, some collected in the National Book Award-winning *Lives of a Cell: Notes of a Biology Watcher* (1974) and in *Late Night Thoughts on Listening to Mahler's Ninth Symphony* (1983).

THURBER, James (1894-1961)
> Journalist and humorist, long-time contributor to the *New Yorker*; collaborated with E.B. White on *Is Sex Necessary?* (1929). Collections of his essays and drawings include *The Thurber Carnival* (1945).

TREFIL, James (b. 1938)
> Professor of physics at University of Virginia; author of works explaining developments in science to the general public (*From Atoms to Quarks*, 1980; *The Unexpected Vista*, 1983).

TUCHMAN, Barbara (b. 1912)
> Journalist, historian, winner of Pulitzer Prizes for *The Guns of August* (1962) and *Stillwell and the American Experience in China, 1911-1945* (1971).

TWAIN, Mark (1835-1910)
> Pseudonym of Samuel Langhorne Clemens, steamboat pilot, prospector, journalist; celebrated as a lecturer and humorist; author of *The Adventures of Tom Sawyer* (1876), *Life on the Mississippi* (1883), *The Adventures of Huckleberry Finn* (1884).

VANDERHAEGHE, Guy (b. 1951)
> Canadian novelist and short story writer; author of collection *Man Descending* (1982; Governor General's Award).

WHITE, E.B. (1899-1985)
> Journalist, essayist, contributor to the *New Yorker* for over half a century; author of renowned children's books *Stuart Little* (1945) and *Charlotte's Web* (1952).

WOODCOCK, George (b. 1912)
> Canadian critic; friend and biographer of George Orwell (*The Crystal Spirit*, 1966); prolific writer of travel books, critical studies, literary and social histories. In 1959 founded *Canadian Literature*, which he edited until 1977.

WOOLF, Virginia (1882-1941)
> Innovative and influential English novelist (*To the Lighthouse*, 1927; *The Waves*, 1931), a literary critic, and an early advocate of feminism (*A Room of One's Own*, 1929).

Glossary

Abstract This is used in two ways: first, to mean general as opposed to specific or particular; second, to mean general as distinguished from **concrete,** a physical embodiment (e.g., *home* is abstract; a *wooden-frame house* is concrete). While writers may rely upon abstractions to some extent, they usually introduce **concrete** or specific details to give the abstraction matter, body, and meaning.

Allusion A fleeting or casual reference to a well known person, place, thing, event, or phrase. These may be real or fictional. Allusions are generally drawn from history, literature, mythology, the *Bible,* or other such sources. Examples: Cleopatra, the shot heard around the world (the assassination of the Archduke Ferdinand), Tom Sawyer, Athena, Eve. Allusions are an economical way for writers to enlarge upon a statement.

Analogy A comparison of some length; analogy is usually employed to explain something new in terms of something familiar, something unknown in terms of the known. (See Trefil's "Unexpected Vistas.") Analogy is frequently employed in argument, usually to dramatize the writer's position, but it is often open to question because the two things compared, though they may be alike in many points, may not be alike in all essential points.

Analysis A method of exposition which employs logical division. The writer uses analysis to break the topic into component parts as a means of organizing the discussion.

Argument A prose form which, in presenting a particular view, assumes that there are two sides to the issue under discussion; the writer of argument aims to influence readers to see the matter from the writer's point of view, to change their beliefs and opinions. The writer usually employs one or more of the other prose forms — exposition, narration, description — to present an argument. In trying to prove a point, the argumentative writer employs **logic** by appealing to reason with various kinds of proofs. The writer of argument usually defines terms and explains facts and ideas. Logical argument usually proceeds by **inductive reasoning** (from specific examples to a general conclusion) or **deductive reasoning** (from premises to a logical conclusion).

Another element of argument which has some importance is the demonstration of the speaker's good character in the establishing of the line of argument. Look, for example, at the closing paragraphs of Swift's "Modest Proposal" to see how the speaker seeks to demonstrate his disinterestedness in the cause he advances.

A distinction is usually made between **argument** and **persuasion.** The argumentative writer employs *logic* to appeal to the reader's intellect with the aim to change the reader's mind whereas the persuasive writer employs various devices of *pathos* to appeal to the reader's feelings or emotions with the aim to instigate action. While the proof in argument rests upon the presentation of objective evidence, that in persuasion derives in large part from the writer's use of controlled language, particularly **diction** with powerful connotations. Whatever the technique used, the writer aims to convince readers to share the writer's own values and opinions (and, in the case of persuasion, possibly to take action to change a situation). Whether an author chooses to emphasize logic or pathos depends on the subject and the audience.

Assumption   That part of an argument which is not stated because the writer takes for granted the clarity of the position or the sympathy of the audience. (A good example is the belief of the Proposer in Swift's "A Modest Proposal" that his audience will share his view that any solution proposed for Ireland's problems will be acceptable.)

Burlesque   A form of comedy in which people, actions, or literary works are made ridiculous by incongruous imitation and by exaggeration. The sublime may be made ridiculous, a serious subject approached with considerable silliness, or a frivolous subject treated with high seriousness. Style is important (e.g., a style which is usually reserved for serious matters is used to treat trivial matters, or the reverse). **Parody** and **caricature** are species of burlesque. Generally, burlesque makes fun of a literary *form*, whereas **parody** makes fun of a particular *work*. (See Woody Allen's "Slang Origins.")

Caricature   A type of portrait which makes its subject ridiculous by exaggerating or distorting prominent features without losing the general likeness. In visual art, the cartoon — especially the political cartoon — is the commonest form.

Classification   A strategy of expository writing used to break a subject into categories or classes. Once the subject is placed in classes, the writer discusses the characteristics which distinguish the members of the class one from another.

Cliché   An over-used expression that has lost its original power. Clichés are entirely predictable (e.g., "as old as the hills," "as innocent as a new-born babe," "as fresh as a daisy").

Coherence Logical connection or congruity of thought within writing. When the various parts of an essay fit together and the flow of thought from section to section is clear and easy to follow, the essay has coherence. This quality is also achieved when the essay develops a single, central idea, since it is difficult to separate coherence from **unity.**

Colloquialism A word used chiefly in conversation. Appropriate to informal writing, but not to formal writing.

Comparison and Contrast A strategy of expository writing used to explore similarities and differences between two subjects. In strict terms, **comparison** is used to present a subject by means of showing similarities between two or more things. To be comparable, the components of the comparison should be members of the same class. In common practice, however, comparison often includes differences or elements of **contrast** as well, for the writer may be striving to emphasize only general similarities rather than point-by-point similarities (as, for example, the strict comparisons required for effective **analogy**).

Conclusion The closing of an essay, that part which gives the reader a sense of resolution of ideas, and a sense of an ending. The conclusion may be brief — a line or two — or it may be a section of the essay on its own. There are many strategies for conclusions, from the signals of transitional phrases such as "finally" and "in conclusion" to a reiteration of the opening stance with a variation. Writers may conclude with such techniques as an answer to an opening question, with echoes of the instruction, with a plea for action, with an allusion, a quotation, an ironic statement, or an illustrative anecdote.

Concrete Definite, particular, capable of being seen and understood directly; the opposite of **abstract.** *Rain* and *Tokyo* are concrete, *weather* and *city* are abstract.

Connotation The associative meanings of a word; implications and overtones that may be added to the dictionary meaning of a word. While the denotation of "mother" is "a female who has borne offspring," its connotation is emotionally charged with associations of love, security, nurture, protection, warmth, etc. Connotations of "mother" are so powerful, for example, that we speak of issues which are not readily open to attack as "motherhood" issues.

Contrast The presentation of a subject by means of showing differences between two or more things. To be contrasted, the subjects discussed should be members of the same class. See **comparison.**

Deductive Reasoning The process of reasoning from premises to a logical conclusion. Deduction is often presented in the form of a logical syllogism. The classic example is: "All men are mortal; Socrates is a man; therefore, Socrates is mortal" (inference or conclusion). If the syllogism is correctly constructed, then the inference is *logically* valid. Logical *fallacies* occur when the conclusion does not follow from the premises (e.g., "Some students are radical; John is a student; therefore, John is a radical"). Even if the logic is sound, however, the conclusion will not be true if one of the premises is false (e.g., "All students are radicals; John is a student; therefore, John is a radical").

Definition   The act of stating what a word, term, phrase or set of terms signifies, usually by means of placing it in a class and demonstrating how it differs from other members of the class. The essay of definition generally extends a definition by means of details, anecdotes, examples, and metaphorical language (e.g., Forster employs definition in part to answer the central question of his essay, "My Wood"; Allen parodies the essay of definition in "Slang Origins").

Denotation   The dictionary meaning of a word. "Mother," for example, denotes "a female who has borne offspring; a female parent." (See also **connotation**.)

Description   A type of writing which uses details or images appealing to the five senses to create a mental picture. A descriptive essay or passage of description in an essay employs specific details and concrete diction to explain a person, place, scene, thing, or sensory experience.

Diction   Choice of words. Diction will depend upon the writer's intended audience, purpose, and the stylistic effect aimed at. The writer may choose many different levels of diction: simple or colloquial rather than Latinate diction in order to address a school-aged audience; words with strong connotations rather than words relatively free of associations in order to persuade; archaic or foreign words and phrases in order to impress, or to give a false seriousness to the topic. A writer may draw from formal or standard language, informal or colloquial language, slang, or dialect (e.g., old man, old coot, eighty-year-old, octogenarian).

Emphasis   The arrangement of the components of a composition to ensure that the important points are prominent (in an essay as a whole, in an argument, in a paragraph, in a sentence). Emphasis may be achieved through order of increasing importance, proportion of evidence, repetition of elements, transitional markers (e.g., "the single most important factor is. . . ."), metaphorical language, rhetorical questions, and mechanical devices such as underlinings, exclamation marks, or the highlighting of material in obvious ways (headings, indentations).

Epigraph   A quotation or motto which prefaces a work. Epigraphs are often in foreign languages. (See Addison's "On Party-lying," Selzer's "The Discus Thrower.")

Euphemism   The substitution of a mild or roundabout expression for another felt to be distasteful, blunt, or painful (e.g., "pass away" for "die").

Exposition   A prose form which explains or informs. Definition, classification, illustration and example, analysis, and comparison and contrast are some of the common means of developing an expository piece.

Figures of Speech   A form of expression in which the usual, literal meanings of words are extended. Figures of speech are based upon comparisons of unlike things which have some point of similarity. See this glossary for some of the common figures of speech: **metaphor, simile, personification, allusion, analogy, irony, paradox.**

Inductive Reasoning The process of reasoning from specific examples or illustrations to a general principle. Inductive reasoning, the method of the scientist, is generally more common in argumentation than deductive reasoning. A writer may, in practice, state the conclusion first and then proceed to show the specifics which lead to the general principle. An inductive argument is only as valid as its supporting evidence; this evidence must be relevant, representative, accurate, and complete; the writer who employs induction must be certain that the evidence will bear close scrutiny.

Introduction The opening of an essay. Introductions are remarkably variable, but they do have some functions in common: they establish the **tone** of the essay; and they often show the plan of the essay as a whole. A writer may try to "grab" readers by means of rhetorical questions, surprising statements or statistics, engaging anecdotes, allusions, paradoxes, quotations, or a particular claim about the importance of the subject.

Irony A reality that differs significantly from appearance. In its broadest terms, *verbal irony* is a sarcastic or humorous means of discourse in which what is expressed literally means the opposite, as for example, when "I had an absolutely great day" means "I had a terrible day." *Irony of situation* presents a discrepancy between what is expected to happen and what actually does happen (e.g., see Thurber's "Courtship Through the Ages"). To sustain irony, authors often employ a naive narrator or expositor; the well-intentioned but simplistic Proposer in Swift's "A Modest Proposal" is a striking example (see also **Persona**).

Jargon A specialized vocabulary used by a particular group; the language of "insiders" intended for a particular audience within a profession or special-interest group (pilots, psychoanalysts, skiers, motorcycle gangs). (See Cowley's "Sociological Habit Patterns in Linguistic Transmogrification.")

Metaphor A figure of speech which compares two unlike things without using "like" or "as," and which asserts the identity of the two terms of comparison: e.g., "The road was a ribbon of light." (See also **simile.**) A metaphor's effectiveness is dependent upon its power of association. Dead metaphors are those in such frequent use that their metaphorical nature is hardly ever thought of (e.g., "a head of state" or "the hands of a clock" no longer recall the parts of the body they refer to). See Orwell's "Politics and the English Language" for a discussion of dying metaphors.

Narration The telling of a story which may be real or fictional. When a story is told for the sake of the story itself, it may be said to be "pure" narration. Narration is, however, commonly employed to support an argument or to illustrate an exposition.

Objective The detached way in which a writer sees the material, characterized by an impersonal, fact-based and unbiased approach. In contrast,

subjective writing is characterized by an individual, opinion-based, and judgmental approach (e.g., "The douglas fir is a conifer" is a fact; "the douglas fir is the noblest of the conifers" is an opinion.) Totally objectivity is not possible, of course, since the writer is an individual with individual perceptions and a unique consciousness. (See also **Point of view**.)

Paradox   A statement that seems self-contradictory or absurd but which actually contains some truth in it. This rhetorical device is used to attract attention. An example taken from Wordsworth: "The child is father of the man."

Parallel Structures or Constructions   Elements with similar rhetorical importance (e.g., words, phrases, clauses) used in similar patterns. A writer will use two or more words from the same grammatical category, and relate them in the same way in order to achieve a particular effect. Virginia Woolf's "How Should One Read a Book?" has many examples: "It may be one letter — but what a vision it gives! It may be a few sentences — but what vistas they suggest!" See also Samuel Johnson, an author celebrated for his use of parallel structures.

Parody   A composition which mimicks the language and style of another work. Parody is generally intended to ridicule an author or a particular work — one which is usually serious. The parody has been used as a powerful means of satire by authors from ancient Greece to modern times. (See also **Burlesque**.)

Persona   The Latin word for the mask worn by actors in classical drama. A persona is a character, "second self," or voice created by an author for a specific audience. An author might, for various reasons, be able to speak more freely through a persona than in his own voice. Often, a persona is used for satiric purposes as, for example, in Swift's "A Modest Proposal" and Royko's "Another Accolade for Charter Arms Corp."

Personification   A figure of speech which endows an inanimate object or abstraction with human qualities (e.g., "the heavens wept").

Persuasion   A writing approach used to convince an audience to do something or to share the writer's beliefs. The writer employs various devices of *pathos* to move the reader to action. An important part of persuasive writing is the establishment of the author's credibility or *ethos* — the writer's ethical stance, fairness, knowledge, honesty. (See **Argument**.)

Point of View   Literally, the point from which something is seen, the angle from which a writer tells a story. Writers use the first-person point of view (characterized by "I") to establish a familiar tone and to emphasize personal involvement; the third-person point of view (characterized by "he," "she," and "it") to maintain distance; and the second-person point of view (characterized by "you") to establish an immediate one-to-one relationship with the reader. Writers often shift point of view for a particular purpose. (See Thurber's "Courtship Through the Ages" and Gloria Steinem's "Marilyn Monroe: The Woman Who Died Too Soon.") In a loose way, point of view may refer to the writer's closeness to or distance from the subject. (See also **objective/subjective**.)

Pun A humorous play on the meaning of words, or on their sound (e.g., "How big is this bookstore?" "Oh — about two stories"). An author may also pun upon a well known phrase (e.g., Lewis Thomas's "physics envy," a pun on "penis envy").

Refutation A technique in argument in which the writer recognizes and then counters the arguments or objections of those opposed him; sometimes called rebuttal. (See Gould's "Let's Ban Applause!")

Rhetorical Question Often used to suggest only questions which do not require an answer. In practice, a rhetorical question may also be the starting point for a discussion which does, in fact, provide the answer (e.g., Virginia Woolf's "How Should One Read a Book?")

Rhythm Patterned emphasis in language through the use of light and heavy stresses, long or short syllables, or repetitions of phrase or clause. Rhythm is a characteristic feature of good prose, but it does not have the regularity of rhythm in poetry.

Sarcasm The blatant and caustic use of apparent praise for actual disapproval or criticism. It is the commonest form of irony.

Satire The literary art of diminishing a subject by making it ridiculous and creating in the reader attitudes of amusement, contempt, or scorn. The laughter arising from satire is not laughter for the fun of laughter; rather, the laughter is a weapon, usually directed against a particular target (e.g., a particular individual, a character type, an institution, a class, a nation, or perhaps mankind itself). Satire is usually employed with the aim of correcting human vice and folly.

Simile A figure of speech which, using "like" or "as," compares two distinctly different things or actions (e.g., Orwell's "The friction of the great beast's foot had stripped the skin from his back as neatly as one skins a rabbit").

Slang A level of language associated with conversation and informal writing. It is characterized by liveliness of expression employed for effect, and it is considered to be at the "low" end of colloquial expression. Slang tends to date quickly (e.g., "tin lizzie" for automobile). In general, it should be avoided, but an isolated example or two may create a special effect.

Style The appropriate use of language or, in the words of Swift, "proper words in proper places." But style is more than the fitting of language with context, for it is highly individualistic — as the old adage "the style is the man" suggests; style is *how* the writer says what he says. Writers establish a personal style and create a sense of life in written work by many different means. Among these are choice of diction, figures of speech, sentence structure (length and variety), particular rhetorical patterns, tonal variations, and rhythm.

Subjective   An attitude of personal involvement with the topic discussed. The writer clearly reveals personal feelings and opinions about the topic discussed. (See **Objective**.)

Syllogism   An argument which takes two premises and joins them to produce a logical conclusion. See **deductive reasoning.**

Symbol   A person, place, or thing that exists in itself but which also stands for something else, something abstract or intangible (e.g., a flag, a tangible piece of cloth, may symbolize a nation or a political movement; an object such as a cross or a menorah may symbolize a particular religion).

Thesis or thesis statement   That part of the essay which states most clearly the writer's position or attitude. It is what the writer has to say — the chief idea or proposition advanced — about the subject. In brief essays the thesis is usually, though not always, expressed in a single sentence, and placed in the opening paragraph or paragraphs.

Tone   A writer's attitude toward the subject. A writer's involvement with the subject and attitude towards the audience determines tone. In speech, a speaker's attitude may be conveyed through tone of voice; in writing, tone is expressed chiefly through style, especially diction and sentence structure. The tone may be **objective,** appealing chiefly to the reader's intellect; or it may be **subjective,** appealing chiefly to the reader's emotions. Tone has many shades (cool, amused, mocking, cynical, bitter, joyful).

Topic sentence   The sentence in the paragraph that carries the main idea. While the thesis statement directs the development of an essay, the topic sentence directs the development of a paragraph.

Transition   The linking of parts of an essay. Depending upon the length of the essay, the transition may be a word, phrase, sentence or paragraph (e.g., "consequently," "another factor to consider," "And this brings us to our fourth and final point: the blackberries"). Transitions contribute to the smooth flow of ideas within a paragraph and between paragraphs. (See also **coherence**.)

Understatement   A form of **irony** which creates its effect by deliberately representing something as much less than it is in fact. In general, the speaker's emotional response is less than the response normally expected as, for example, when a speaker describes a movie star thought to be outstandingly beautiful or handsome as "not bad looking."

Unity   Oneness, the relevance of all the materials contained in an essay to its **thesis** or central idea. Within the paragraph, unity is achieved when all the materials relate to the **topic sentence** of the paragraph. (See also **coherence**.)

Index of Authors and Titles